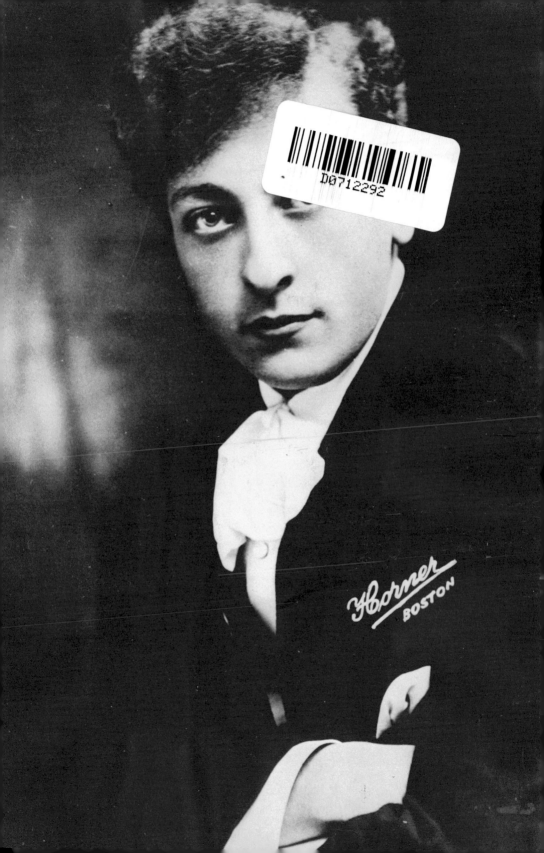

Horner
BOSTON

HEIFETZ

Jascha Heifetz, circa 1907.

Edited by Dr. Herbert R. Axelrod with contributions by Henry Roth, John A. Maltese, Constance Hope and quotations from interviews with Heifetz himself.

Published by PAGANINIANA PUBLICATIONS, INC.
211 West Sylvania Avenue, Neptune City, N.J. 07753

Printed in the U.S.A.

ISBN 0-87666-600-4

Contents

Acknowledgements and Confessions

Having been collecting material on Heifetz for so many years, I am uncertain about the source of much of it. Many of the publicity photographs were obtainable from several sources, and a great deal of the editorial material was copied without the courtesy of credit simply because I didn't know to whom the credit should be given.

I certainly can recall receiving substantial help from Professor John Maltese and his son John Anthony Maltese, Jacksonville State University, Jacksonville, Alabama. Not only did they write the discography, but they loaned me rare and valuable autographs and prints of Heifetz. Professor George Zazofsky, University of Miami, Coral Gables, Florida gave me the unique films made during the Heifetz-Munch recording sessions of 1959. Mr. and Mrs. Paul Paradise were invaluable for their help in doing intensive research, date and fact checking, and picture searching. Their huge knowledge of music came in handy.

Many agencies sell photos of Heifetz, but I am especially indebted to Wide World, Time-Life Picture Agency, Los Angeles Times Newspaper, New York Times Newspaper, RCA Records, and the Bobbs-Merrill Company for allowing me to use the material "Dr. Jekyll and Mr. Heifetz" which appeared in the book *Publicity is Broccoli* by Constance Hope, copyright 1941 (renewed 1969).

I am solely responsible for selecting the photographs and for writing the captions. The spelling throughout the book, especially of Slavic names of artists and composers, may vary since reviewers, recording companies and the artists themselves changed the spelling at different times in their careers.

These are the last lines I am writing for the book HEIFETZ. It has been a very difficult task and I'll steal one of Heifetz's replies: *For those of you who liked it, thanks; for those who didn't, perhaps you'll like the next Heifetz volume better.*

For Benno Rabinoff.
He started this book.
I wish he could have
lived long enough to
finish it. He loved
Heifetz as much as
I loved Benno.

Heifetz, as a teacher, enjoying a relaxed outdoor practice session with one of his students. He always hoped "to be good enough to teach." With Heifetz, music is a religion, a philosophy and a way of life. A piece of music is a holy writing and he has always treated it as such. Capable, dedicated musicians and composers are the high priests and Heifetz has spent a good part of his life elevating them to the stature he felt they deserved. He has tried to imbue this same elegance and style into his students. Circa 1970.

6

Introduction

by Dr. Herbert R. Axelrod

Someone once wrote that it was an impertinence to criticize Heifetz. Of course they meant in terms of his music. There might have been violinists with more technique, or violinists with more musicianship, or artists with a greater visual appeal and stage presence, but there never was ONE person who had more of each of these important characteristics than Heifetz.

There is no authority on Heifetz. Not even Heifetz knows Heifetz. He was born with a rare talent, fortified with an honest dignity and a sincere desire to play music as best he could. He strictly disciplined himself most of the time, both professionally and personally, both on the stage and off. When he tried, in his earlier years, to explain how HE thought he was able to play so well, he couldn't put it into words. People could not believe it was only a matter of being born with skills which disciplined, excellent training developed into a most rare performer of great music.

It is easy to prove that Heifetz was the greatest violinist to have appeared on the musical scene in all recorded history. "Greatest" in the sense that more people wanted to hear him . . . and were willing to pay to do so; "greatest" in the sense that he made more money playing the violin than anyone else; "greatest" in the sense that he had more stature (and thus more "pull") than any other violinist and was able to impress management with his, at that time, seemingly outlandish requests.

I have spent many years working on this Heifetz book. It has been difficult, as anyone who is familiar with Heifetz must appreciate. I am presenting a documented record of his career as a performer. It lasted about 70 years, perhaps longer than any other known musician of any instrument. (Rubenstein started at age forty! Heifetz at age 6!) The reviews are almost all taken from New York newspapers from the day of his debut until his last concert in Dorothy Chandler Pavilion

LAW OFFICES

GRAYSON & GROSS, INC.

10880 WILSHIRE BOULEVARD, SUITE 2121

LOS ANGELES, CALIFORNIA 90024

AREA CODE 213

475-0808 · 879-9200 · 272-9786

SAUL GRAYSON
MARVIN GROSS
BARRY A. FRIEDMAN
JERRY S. PHILLIPS
HOWARD L. RASCH
PHILIP J. DICHTER

July 13, 1976

Mr. Herbert R. Axelrod
T.F. H. Publications, Inc.
211 West Sylvania Avenue
Neptune, New Jersey 07753

Re: Mr. Jascha Heifetz

Dear Mr. Axelrod:

Please be advised that I represent Mr. Jascha
Heifetz, who has forwarded to me various letters
of yours in connection with your proposed biography.

At the outset, let me make it clear that Mr. Heifetz
has in no way consented to nor condoned your book
nor any of its contents. We would be willing to
consider assisting you in the preparation of this
work only on condition that appropriate terms can
be agreed upon:

1. An adequate royalty to be paid to Mr. Heifetz.

2. Mr. Heifetz is to have the right of approval of
    the contents of said book before it is released.
    Such approval shall not be unreasonably withheld.

3. The contents of the book shall be consistent with
    the stature of Mr. Heifetz, and shall in no way
    demean or lessen the image he has created over
    the years, either as a musician or an individual.

If you will submit a proposed contract to me, incorporating
the above terms and conditions, I will be glad to review
it and submit the same to Mr. Heifetz with my suggestions,
if any.

Very truly yours,

MARVIN GROSS

MG:cmr

cc: Mr. Jascha Heifetz

August 30, 1976

Dr. Herbert R. Axelrod
T.F.H. Publications, Inc.
211 West Sylvania Avenue
Neptune, New Jersey 07753

Re: Mr. Jascha Heifetz

Dear Dr. Axelrod:

I have reviewed the matter with Mr. Heifetz and for several reasons he absolutely refuses to cooperate with you on the production of your book.

We want it clearly understood that he in no way consents to, condones, nor agrees that your book involving his life may be published, or that the facts stated therein are in any way accurate or correct.

In fact, Mr. Heifetz strongly objects to the publication of this material, and if necessary, will do all that is required to see that it is not distributed to the public.

Very truly yours,

MARVIN GROSS

MG:cmr

cc: Mr. Jascha Heifetz

After the author accepted the terms of the July 13, 1976 offer, the letter dated August 30, 1976 was received.

9

in Los Angeles. I wasn't able to hear his first recital, though my father told me all about it (he also studied with Auer), but I did hear his last concert in Los Angeles on October 23, 1972. Sitting with me at the concert were his son, Jay, and Benno and Sylvia Rabinoff. We were invited to dine with Heifetz after the concert. When Jay, Benno and I went to his dressing room after his sole encore piece, Heifetz would not let us in! He didn't keep the date for dinner, either. Heifetz has never been predictable.

My negotiations with him for this book resulted in a complete lack of cooperation, as evidenced by the letter from his attorney. Yet, with all his shortcomings in terms of normal human behavior, *I cannot fairly judge him.* No one can impeach him. He is simply the greatest violinist who ever lived and he can only be judged by his peers. . . *and there aren't any!*

My proof that Heifetz was the highest paid violinist comes from the facts that he played more concerts during his lifetime and for higher fees than any other classical musician. The schedule of fees paid by the New York Philharmonic Society to its artists speaks for itself.

FEES PAID BY NEW YORK PHILHARMONIC SOCIETY
TO ASSISTING ARTISTS

Date	Soloist	Fee
Dec. 2, 3, 1904	Anton Hekking	$200
Dec. 6, 7, 1905	Fritz Kreisler	$400
March 2, 3, 1906	Henri Marteau	$550
Nov. 20, 21, 1919	Fritz Kreisler	$2000
Dec. 6, 1919	Toscha Seidel	$1000
Dec. 11, 12, 1919	Jascha Heifetz	$2250
Jan. 2, 1920	Rosita Renard	$200
Feb. 26, 27, 1920	Sergei Rachmaninoff	$1500
March 3, 4, 1920	Albert Spalding	$700
Aug. 19, 1945	Isaac Stern	$500
Sept. 9, 1945	Nathan Milstein	$1600
Oct. 27, 1945	Joseph Fuchs	$200
Dec. 6, 7 & 9, 1945	Yehudi Menuhin	$5000
Jan. 12, 13, 1946	Patricia Travers	$300

Date	Soloist	Fee
March 23, 1946	Angel Reyes	$200
March 28, 1946	Zino Francescatti	$1750
April 7, 1946	Camilla Wicks	$200
Oct. 10, 11, 13, 1946	Maryla Jonas	$750
Oct. 17, 18, 20, 1946	Yehudi Menuhin	$5000
Oct. 26, 1946	Henryk Szeryng	$200
Nov, 14, 15, 17, 1946	Mischa Elman	$1500
Dec. 7, 8, 1946	Joseph Fuchs	$500
Jan. 2, 3, 5, 1947	Jack Adams	$1500
Oct. 21, 22, 24, 1948	Joseph Szigeti	$1600
Oct. 28, 29, 31, 1948	Rudolf Serkin	$2200
Oct. 30, 1948	Dorotha Powers	$250
Nov. 6, 7, 1948	Isaac Stern	$800
Nov. 11, 12, 14, 1948	Francis Poulenc	$1250
Nov. 18, 19, 21, 1948	Benedetto Michelangeli	$1500
Nov. 25, 26, 28, 1948	Zino Francescatti	$1800
Dec. 2, 3, 5, 1948	Nadine Conner	$1000
Dec. 2, 3, 5, 1948	Jean Watson	$1000
Dec. 4, 1948	Szymon Goldberg	$250
Dec. 11, 1948	Hilde Somer	$250
Dec. 22, 24, 26, 1948	Nathan Milstein	$2000
Dec. 30, 31 & Jan. 2, 1949	Ginette Neveu	$1100
Jan. 9, 1949	Seymour Lipkin	$600
Jan. 20, 21, 1949	Rudolf Firkusny	$600
Feb. 3, 4, 6, 1949	Myra Hess	$4000
Feb. 26, 1949	Lubka Kolessa	$200
March 3, 4, 6, 1949	Clifford Curzon	$1000
March 10, 11, 13, 1949	Erica Morini	$1500
April 14, 15, 17, 1949	Nan Merriman	$600
April 14, 15, 17, 1949	Eleanor Steber	$1600
April 14, 15, 17, 1949	Raoul Jobin	$1250
April 14, 15, 17, 1949	Mack Harrell	$1000
Oct. 27, 1949	Martha Lipton	$600
Oct. 29, 1949	Eugene Istomin	$300
Nov. 3, 4, 6, 1949	Pierre Fournier	$2250
Nov. 10, 11, 13, 1949	William Kapell	$2700
Nov. 17, 18, 20, 1949	Wanda Landowska	$2650
Nov. 17, 18, 1949	Women's Chorus	$350

Fees Paid by N.Y. Philharmonic Society to Assisting Artists

Date	Soloist	Fee
Nov. 17, 18, 1949	Ginette Martenot	$200
Nov. 24, 25, 27, 1949	Jacques Abram	$2150
Dec. 1, 2, 4, 1949	Isaac Stern	$2800
Dec. 15, 16, 18, 1949	Joseph Szigeti	$2800
Dec. 22, 23, 25, 1949	Elinor Warren (singer)	$150
Dec. 22, 23, 25, 1949	Astrid Varnay	$1200
Dec. 22, 23, 25, 1949	Frederick Jagel	$1000
Dec. 22, 23, 25, 1949	Herbert Janssen	$1000
Dec. 22, 23, 25, 1949	Irene Jessner	$950
Dec. 22, 23, 25, 1949	Elena Nikolaidi	$1200
Dec. 22, 23, 25, 1949	Michael Rhodes	$350
Dec. 29, 30, 1949	Oscar Levant	$3500
Jan. 5, 6, 7, 8, 1950	Rudolf Serkin	$4100
Jan. 14, 15, 1950	Szymon Goldberg	$1350
Jan. 19, 20, 22, 1950	Zino Francescatti	$3600
Jan. 21, 1950	Leonard Pennario	$300
Jan. 26, 27, 29, 1950	Casadesus	$4150
Feb. 2, 3, 5, 1950	Myra Hess	$7000
Feb. 5, 1950	Rudolf Firkusny	$350
Feb. 11, 1950	Nikita Magaloff	$300
Feb. 16, 17, 19, 1950	**Jascha Heifetz**	**$9500**
Feb. 23, 24, 26, 1950	Lukas Foss	$550
March 16, 17, 19, 1950	Nathan Milstein	$3800
March 18, 1950	Miriam Solovieff	$250
March 23, 24, 26, 1950	Artur Rubinstein	$8000
March 25, 1950	Moura Lympany	$300
April 1, 1950	Joseph Battista	$250
April 6, 7, 9, 1950	Camilla Williams	$500
April 6, 7, 9, 1950	Carlos Alexander	$450
April 6, 7, 9, 1950	Uta Graf	$500
April 6, 7, 9, 1950	Frances Yeend	$700
April 6, 7, 9, 1950	George London	$500
April 6, 7, 9, 1950	Louise Bernhardt	$400
April 6, 7, 9, 1950	Martha Lipton	$600
April 6, 7, 9, 1950	Eugene Conley	$700
April 13, 1950	Adolph Anderson	$100
April 22, 1950	Leonid Hambro	$200

One of the little known facts of Heifetz's success story was the part played by the Bohemians (New York Musicians' Club). This club was. . . and still is. . . composed of the most sophisticated membership of musicians in the world. When Heifetz made his debut in October 1917 almost the entire membership of the Bohemians was present, and they were so impressed they immediately arranged to have a dinner in Heifetz's honor. The dinner took place on Saturday, December 29th, 1917 at the Biltmore Hotel in New York. Everybody who was anybody was there including Kreisler, Zimbalist, Franz Kneisel, Rubin Goldmark, Sigmund Herzog, Josef Stransky, Walter Damrosch, etc. Opera and music accompanied every course of food! It was a magnificent affair. . . but the real impact was that made upon the critics. How could the critics be critical of a violinist who was praised to the stars

Heifetz played for Fritz Kreisler's birthday party on December 22, 1940 at the Bohemian's dinner in Kreisler's honor. The gentlemen, left to right: Albert Spalding, Fritz Kreisler, and Jascha Heifetz.

The dinner menu of the Bohemians' tribute to Heifetz.
Courtesy of Brent Williams.

Administration of 1917=1918

Officers

Franz Kneisel, President
August Fraemcke, Vice-President
Rubin Goldmark, Vice-President
Sigmund Herzog, Vice-President
Ludwig Marum, Secretary
Hugo Grunwald, Treasurer

Board of Governors

Ernest T. Carter	Victor Harris
Carl Deis	Alexander Lambert
Albert von Doenhoff	Abraham W. Lilienthal
Edwin F. Goldman	Josef Stransky

14

Dinner to
Jascha Heifetz

The Bohemians
(New York Musicians' Club)

Saturday, December 29th, 1917
at the Hotel Biltmore

Le Mariage Aux Lanternes

(The Treasure Trove)

Operetta in One Act

By

Jacques Offenbach

English Version by

Virginia and Lawton Mackall

The Cast

Peter, A Peasant	Mr. Albert Reiss
Flora, A Young Cousin	Miss Sue Harvard
Annette } Two Young Widows	Miss Amparito Farrar
Cathrina }	Miss Blanche da Costa

Scene: A "Village" Somewhere in France

Mr. Walter Damrosch, Conductor

Stage Director Mr. Jacques Coini

Menu

March • • • • *Victor Herbert*	ROBBINS ISLAND OYSTERS
The World's Progress	———
The Orchestra	
	CREAM OF TOMATOES, METTERNICH
	———
	CELERY SALTED ALMONDS OLIVES
	———
	BROOK TROUT SAUTE, MEUNIERE
	POTATOES PERSILLADE
	———
Humorous Overture on Wagner, Strauss, Debussy	BREAST OF CHICKEN, "IDEAL"
By	NEW PEAS IN BUTTER
Albert Chiaffarelli	
Dedicated to "The Bohemians"	———
Conducted by	
Edwin F. Goldman	EMERALD PUNCH
	———
———	
Serenade • • • *Joseph Haydn*	RACK OF SPRING LAMB A LA BROCHE
Re-instrumented with modern improvements	RUSSIAN SALAD
By	
George Barrere	———
Conducted by the Composer	
	FANCY ICE CREAM
———	CAKES
1. *March Melodies by The Army Quartet*	———
2. *"We Never Let Our Old Flag Fall"*	
Sung by	
Vernon Styles	DEMI-TASSE

by his peers!!! Heifetz made it because of Heifetz. The Bohemians helped make it happen and Heifetz has remained a member to this day. He reciprocated by playing a concert at the Bohemians in honor of Kreisler's birthday many years later.

I have also included some random memorandums which are part of my file on Heifetz. It fixes the time of his dropping the "Jascha" in favor of just HEIFETZ; it cites a few examples of his cantankerous nature.

MEMORANDUM   **DATE: May 16, 1949**

THE PHILHARMONIC-SYMPHONY SOCIETY OF NEW YORK
113 WEST 57th STREET, NEW YORK 19. N.Y.
PHONE: CIrcle 7-4733

To: BILL JUDD
From: BRUNO ZIRATO

In discussing the program with Bernstein, he was not very keen about Walton but he said that if Heifetz insists, he will do it Thursday and Friday. We would not be very happy to do it on Sunday for many reasons, especially as Carnegie Hall is not well-subscribed on Sunday and we would like to play some classic concerto. His suggestion of Beethoven on Sunday is perfectly all right. But I understand that Heifetz will play on Sunday only in case we have the commercial broadcast. Otherwise he will not do the Sunday concert. Am I correct?

z/v

MEMORANDUM   **DATE: February 17, 1950**

THE PHILHARMONIC-SYMPHONY SOCIETY OF NEW YORK
113 WEST 57th STREET, NEW YORK 19. N.Y.
PHONE: CIrcle 7-4733

To: MR. JUDSON
From: DORLE JARMEL

Heifetz with the Philharmonic—
1940-41. . . covered by Olin Downes, Jan. 3, 1941.
1941-42. . . covered by Olin Downes, Feb. 13, 1942.
1942-43. . . did not play with the orchestra.
1943-44. . . did not play with the orchestra.

18

NOVO-ALEXANDRIA
(POULAVY.)

Ruvin Heifetz, the infant, with his mother and
grandmother. Ruvin (or Rubin in English) was

1944-45. . . covered by Olin Downes, Jan. 12, 1945.
1945-46. . . covered by Olin Downes, April 4, 1946.
1946-47. . . covered by Olin Downes, March 28, 1947.
1947-48. . . did not play with the orchestra.
1948-49. . . did not play with the orchestra, but Downes covered recital.

OFFICE MEMORANDUM   **DATE: November 24, 1952**

COLUMBIA ARTISTS MANAGEMENT Inc.

To: BRUNO ZIRATO
From: ADA COOPER

You have asked for information about HEIFETZ' availability, fee, etc. for the Philharmonic season 1953-54.

Mr. Heifetz has paid me his annual booking visit and given me the information you desire.

He will be very glad indeed to accept an invitation to play with the Philharmonic that season. The terms and conditions for Thursday, Friday and Sunday would be the same as written in the contract for Mr. Heifetz' last appearances with you, i.e., $3500 for the pair and $2500 for the Sunday if sustaining broadcast or, $3500 for the pair and $6000 for the Sunday if the broadcast is commercially sponsored.

This time, however, Mr. Heifetz does not desire to make any private arrangements for a return check to the orchestra.

MEMORANDUM   **DATE: November 25, 1952**

THE PHILHARMONIC-SYMPHONY SOCIETY OF NEW YORK
113 WEST 57th STREET, NEW YORK 19. N.Y.
PHONE: COlumbus 5-4480

To: MRS. COOPER
From: MR. ZIRATO

Thank you for the information about Heifetz. I am really upset to hear that Heifetz does not desire to make any private arrangement for a return check to the Orchestra, because I see that the Orchestra cannot really afford to pay $6,000 for 3 performances, in the event that the Society decides to engage him for the pair of Thursday, Friday and Sunday. It is most essential that Heifetz play on Sunday on account of the smaller subscription on Sunday and for the broadcast. Of course the fee of $6,000 for commercial sponsorship depends upon the acceptance by the sponsor. However, I don't anticipate any difficulty in putting this over.

Thank you for your cooperation.

20

Original memorandum.

Office Memorandum   COLUMBIA ARTISTS MANAGEMENT Inc.

To   BRUNO ZIRATO

From   ADA COOPER

DATE November 24, 1952

You have asked for information about HEIFETZ' availability, fee, etc. for the Philharmonic season 1953-54.

Mr. Heifetz has paid me his annual booking visit and given me the information you desire.

He will be very glad indeed to accept an invitation to play with the Philharmonic that season. The terms and conditions for Thursday, Friday and Sunday would be the same as written in the contract for Mr. Heifetz' last appearances with you, i.e. $3500 for the pair and $2500 for the Sunday if sustaining broadcast or, $3500 for the pair and $6000 for the Sunday if the broadcast is commercially sponsored.

This time, however, Mr. Heifetz does not desire to make any private arrangements for a return check to the orchestra.

21

WESTERN UNION CABLEGRAM   **DATE: April 2, 1953**

PHILHARMONIC-SYMPHONY SOCIETY, 113 WEST 57 ST.

HEIFETZ
CARE PALPHILORCH
TELAVIV (Israel)

PLEASE CABLE ANSWER REPERTOIRE MATTER PHILHAR-
MONIC DISCUSSED WITH JUDSON   GREETINGS

ZIRATO PHILHARMON

WESTERN UNION CABLEGRAM   **DATE: April 5, 1953**

ZIRATO C/ THE PHILHARMONIC SYMPHONY SOCIETY OF NY
113 W 57th ST

LT ZIRATO PHILHARMON NEWYORK

ELGAR FOR THURSDAY AND MENDELSSOHN UNDER PROTEST
FOR SUNDAY   GREETINGS

HEIFETZ

AMERICAN CABLE & RADIO SYSTEM   **DATE: April 6th, 1953**
NIGHT LETTER

SENDER'S NAME: PHILHARMONIC-SYMPHONY SOCIETY
113 WEST 57th St.

VIA: Mackay Cable

HEIFETZ PALPHILORCH
TELAVIV

CANTELLI ASKS THAT YOU PLAY MENDELSSOHN THURSDAY
FRIDAY AND SUNDAY TO FIT HIS PROGRAMS. HOPE YOU WILL
ACCEDE HIS REQUEST.   GREETINGS.

JUDSON PHILHARMON

WESTERN UNION CABLEGRAM   **DATE: April 12, 1953**

JUDSON C/O COLUMBIA CONCERTS INC. 113 WEST 57 St N.Y.

LT JUDSON COLCONCERT

SURPRISED YOUR CABLE AS ELGAR AGREED BEFORE LEAVING.
THEREFORE REPEAT ELGAR THURSDAY FRIDAY AND MEN-
DELSSOHN SUNDAY ONLY. IF ABOVE NOT FITTING WITH ANY-
ONES PROGRAMS SUGGEST ANOTHER SOLOIST.   GREETINGS.

HEIFETZ

22

AMERICAN CABLE & RADIO SYSTEM   DATE: April 13th, 1953
NIGHT LETTER

SENDER'S NAME: PHILHARMONIC-SYMPHONY SOCIETY
                    113 WEST 57TH ST.

VIA: Mackay Cable

HEIFETZ PALPHILORCH
TELAVIV

CANTELLI HAS SO MANY COMMITMENTS SYMPHONIC REPER-
TOIRE THAT HE HAS NO TIME TO PREPARE ELGAR AS IT
SHOULD BE PREPARED ON HIS PART. YOU WILL GREATLY
OBLIGE PHILHARMONIC AND HIM IF YOU CAN HELP US OUT IN
THIS EMERGENCY.   REGARDS.

JUDSON

WESTERN UNION   DATE: April 20th, 1953

COLUMBIA ARTISTS MANAGEMENT, INC.

HEIFETZ
HOTEL VESUVIO
NAPLES (ITALY)

TRYING ADJUST YOUR PHILHARMONIC DATES SO YOU CAN
PLAY ELGAR THURSDAY FRIDAY MENDELSSOHN SUNDAY.
MITROPOULOS WILL CHANGE HIS PLANS SO THAT THIS CAN
BE DONE ON OCTOBER 22 23 and 25 PROVIDING YOU CAN MAKE
IT. PLEASE CABLE REPLY. CONGRATULATIONS SAFE ARRIVAL
ITALY.

JUDSON

WESTERN UNION   DATE: April 26, 1953

JUDSON COLCONCERT (COLUMBIA CONCERTS INC
     NEW YORK NY (113 WEST 57TH ST)

THANKS. GOOD WISHES. SORRY OCTOBER IMPOSSIBLE.
REGARDS

HEIFETZ

23

VIA: W.U. CABLES

HEIFETZ
DANDELOSTAD
PARIS

THANKS FOR YOUR FINE GESTURE TO HELP US WITH OUR PRO-
GRAMS. HOWEVER EVERYTHING MORE COMPLICATED THAN
EVER NOW. TCHAIKOVSKY BEING PLAYED TWO WEEKS LATER
SAME SERIES. ONLY SOLUTION SEEMS TO BE TO TAKE TCHAI-
KOVSKY AWAY FROM OTHER ARTIST AND ASK HIM PLAY LALO
ON SUNDAY THEN GIVE YOU TCHAIKOVSKY SUNDAY WITH
REQUEST YOU PLAY MENDELSSOHN THURSDAY AND FRIDAY.
ONLY OTHER COMPLICATIONS ARE TO GET CONSENT OF
OTHER ARTIST AND TO ASK MITROPOULOS TO CHANGE AND
ASSUME CANTELLI AGREEABLE. FOR GOD'S SAKE HELP US!
KINDEST WISHES TO FRANCES AND YOU.

JUDSON

WESTERN UNION   DATE: June 16, 1953

PHILHARMONIC-SYMPHONY SOCIETY

NLT ZIRATO
VESUVIO
NAPLES

HEIFETZ ACCEPTED BACH MENDELSSOHN PAIR MENDELS-
SOHN ALONE SUNDAY BON VOYAGE

JUDSON

June 30th, 1953

MR. JASCHA HEIFETZ
1520 Gilcrest Drive
Beverly Hills, California

Dear Jascha:

This is to confirm the arrangements for your appearances with the
Philharmonic-Symphony Society with Guido Cantelli conducting. I do
not need to mention the dates or financial conditions because they are included in the contract itself.

It is understood that you will play on Thursday and Friday the Bach A Minor Concerto and the Mendelssohn Concerto. The Bach is to conclude the first half of the program and the Mendelssohn Concerto the last half. It is understood that the compositions preceding the Bach will be chosen with reference to their musical fitness.

On the Sunday program, you will play the Mendelssohn to end the broadcast.

Best wishes!

Sincerely,
Judson

August 17, 1953

1520 Gilcrest Drive
Beverly Hills, California

Dear Miss Hanenfeldt:

Your note and list of orchestral repertoire received.

Dallas is arranged with Bach "A Minor" and Sibelius at the end.

Would not need another rehearsal in Wichita if I have ample time during the first one.

For the New York Philharmonic, would not want more than one rehearsal on the 11th, since I am playing that night. Provision should be made for any available time on the 10th. Mrs. Cooper is right in saying that there will be difficulty in getting there on the 9th—besides it is not necessary for me to be in New York two days before the first rehearsal. Please see that Mr. Judson is contacted—and have things straightened out.

Hope you had a nice vacation and can face the cruel world again. With cordial greetings.

Jascha Heifetz

OFFICE MEMORANDUM   **DATE: August 20, 1953**

To: MISS HANNENFELDT
From: MR. ZIRATO

I am returning the letter of Heifetz as per your request. In accordance with my memorandum to Mrs. Cooper there is no possibility of rehearsing on March 10th because on that day we have a recording session and the orchestra does not rehearse on a recording day. That is why I suggested the 9th, but if Mr. Heifetz will be satisfied with one rehearsal on the morning of the 10th, that will be all right.

On the 11th, anyhow, there will be only one rehearsal so Heifetz should not be worried about scheduling two rehearsals because the contract with the Union forbids us to hold two rehearsals on the day of the concert.

z/k

September 3, 1953

MR. JASCHA HEIFETZ
1520 Gilcrest Drive
Beverly Hills, Calif.

Dear Jascha:

Maestro Mitropoulos is just back from Italy and he informed me that he had a conference with Cantelli regarding the programs with the Philharmonic. Both Mitropoulos and Cantelli find it very difficult to frame the concerts in which you are going to be the eminent soloist, with Bach in the first part and Mendelssohn in the second part (I am speaking of course, only of Thursday and Friday because on Sunday there will be no complication). Mitropoulos suggested to Cantelli to do the first part of orchestral numbers and have the second part dedicated completely to you with Bach and Mendelssohn. In this way there will not be the complication of mixing Bach with other numbers and you will have the entire second part of the program of Thursday and Friday yourself. Mitropoulos and I think it is an excellent solution and I would like to have your reaction which I think will be a good one.

I hope that you are enjoying cool weather. Just for your information, if you don't read the papers, we are sweltering here with heat at 97 degrees.

My best to you always.

Sincerely,
Bruno Zirato

WESTERN UNION   **DATE: September 17, 1953**

PHILHARMONIC-SYMPHONY SOCIETY OF NY

MR. JASCHA HEIFETZ
1520 GILCREST DRIVE
BEVERLY HILLS   CALIF.

YOU WOULD OBLIGE ME GREATLY IF YOU WOULD ANSWER MY LETTER OF SEPTEMBER THIRD   THANK YOU SO VERY MUCH   GREETINGS

ZIRATO

OFFICE MEMORANDUM   **DATE: September 23, 1953**

COLUMBIA ARTISTS MANAGEMENT INC.

To: MISS O'NEILL
From: Z. HANENFELDT

Dear Miss O'Neill:

The enclosed letter from HEIFETZ was sent to Mr. Zirato who replied that on March 10th the orchestra records so there is no possibility of rehearsing Heifetz that day; and that on the 11th there will be ONE rehearsal as contract with the Union forbids two rehearsals the day of the concert.

Since Heifetz particularly said to see Mr. Judson about this, I wonder if you will talk to him and perhaps Mr. Judson will write Heifetz?

With thanks,
Z

September 29, 1953

MR. JASCHA HEIFETZ
1520 Gilcrest Drive
Beverly Hills, Calif.

Dear Jascha:

Miss Hanenfeldt spoke to me about the rehearsals with the Philharmonic. In that week we have long-standing commitments for Wednesday which cannot be changed, and therefore the Orchestra is not available for rehearsal on that day. There will be one rehearsal on Monday, the 8th, two on Tuesday, the 9th and one rehearsal on Thursday, the 11th. You are welcome to rehearse at any two of the four above-mentioned, if you think that you need two rehearsals. But if you cannot get here in time for Tuesday, then I think you can rehearse both works on Thursday morning. The rehearsal on Thursday will start at 10:00 a.m. and finish at 12:30.

Please let me know your wishes.

Very sincerely,
Judson

AJ/f

P.S. The rehearsal on Monday, the 8th is from 9:30 to 12:00; and the two rehearsals on Tuesday are scheduled from 10:00 to 12:30 and 2:00 to 4:30.

October 8th, 1953

MR. JASCHA HEIFETZ
1520 Gilcrest Drive
Beverly Hills, California

Dear Heifetz:

I have consulted with Zirato and he tells me that we may give you as much time as you want on Thursday. I trust that this will solve your problem. When complications arise around any date, it seems they do a good job of it!

Regards.

Yours Sincerely,
Judson

November 10, 1953

MR. JASCHA HEIFETZ
1520 Gilcrest Drive
Beverly Hills, Calif.

Dear Jascha:

I have been trying for the last month or so to re-arrange the schedule of recording and rehearsals for the week of March 8th, and I think I will succeed in having the recording session take place on Monday, March 8th. Therefore we can hold the rehearsal at Carnegie Hall on Wednesday from 1:30 to 4:00. If you wish to rehearse on Wednesday, I can schedule this for you. Of course, we have also the rehearsal on Thursday morning, and in the event that you would like to come back on Thursday morning, that will be agreeable to all of us.

Please let me know. Best wishes.

Sincerely yours,
Zirato

OFFICE MEMORANDUM   **DATE: November 11, 1953**

COLUMBIA ARTISTS MANAGEMENT INC.

To: LOUISE FRY
From: Z. HANENFELDT

Dear Louise:

I still have HEIFETZ down for the Mendelssohn. Is that correct?

Z

OFFICE MEMORANDUM   **DATE:** November 12, 1953

THE PHILHARMONIC-SYMPHONY SOCIETY

To: MISS HANENFELDT
From: L. FRY

Yes, Heifetz plays the Mendelssohn on all three dates; also the Bach A minor on Thursday and Friday.

MEMORANDUM   **DATE:** February 9, 1953

To: MISS BETTY RANDOLPH BEAN
    MR. KRIM

From: GEORGE E. JUDD, JR.

Please note that in Heifetz contract there is no addendum which reads "Artist to be billed as HEIFETZ not as Jascha Heifetz."

GEJ, Jr.:ah

OFFICE MEMORANDUM   **DATE:** March 15, 1954

THE PHILHARMONIC-SYMPHONY SOCIETY

To: MISS O'NEILL
From: MR. ZIRATO

Yesterday Schuyler Chapin was quite surprised that I did not give him the check for the artistic services of Heifetz. I told him that the procedure of the Philharmonic is to send the check to CAMI because if we make it directly to him, we have to deduct the tax.

Here is the check.

z/f

OFFICE MEMORANDUM   **DATE:** January 19, 1955

COLUMBIA ARTISTS MANAGEMENT INC.

To: LOUISE FRY
From: Z. HANENFELDT

Dear Louise:
    Mrs. Serkin tells me that RS has been in correspondence with the Maestro about the February program but she doesn't know what they decided. Do you?

29

Have they also been discussing next season?

I saw Mitropoulos talking to Jean Casadesus so maybe that is taken care of.

HEIFETZ who offered the Beethoven for next year, as you know, would like to receive a confirmation on the road. How soon can you give me this?

Many thanks

cc: Mr. Judson
cc: Mr. Zirato
cc: Mr. Chapin

March 8, 1955

MR. JASCHA HEIFETZ
1520 Gilcrest Drive
Beverly Hills, California

Dear Jascha:

Thanks for returning my letter of February 25 about Carnegie Hall with your penciled notations.

I have shown the letter, together with your comments, to both A.J. and Bruno, and this morning I have a memo from Bruno, "I am giving instructions to Carnegie Hall to give you the date of November 22nd for His Excellency, Jascha. You may assure him there is no string attached."

We are therefore proceeding with the lease for this date.

With all good wishes,

Sincerely,
William M. Judd

WMJ:nh

OFFICE MEMORANDUM   **DATE: March 8, 1955**

THE PHILHARMONIC-SYMPHONY SOCIETY

To: BILL JUDD
From: BRUNO ZIRATO

I am giving instructions to Carnegie Hall to give you the date of November 22nd for His Excellency, Jascha. You may assure him there is no string attached, except his moral obligation to do something for us season 1957-57. Is that too much?

z/f

30

OFFICE MEMORANDUM DATE: March 8, 1955

COLUMBIA ARTISTS MANAGEMENT, INC.

To: MR. ZIRATO
From: WILLIAM M. JUDD

Dear Bruno:
Many, many thanks indeed for having cleared the November 22 date for the HEIFETZ recital. I very greatly appreciate all your help in this.

Sincerely

WMJ:nh

March 12, 1955

1520 Gilcrest Drive
Beverly Hills, California

Dear Bruno:
Understand that November 22nd has been cleared for me by his Eminence, Honorable Zirato—with no strings attached, which might make it somewhat embarrassing for a violin recital by a certain Mr. Heifetz at Carnegie Hall.
Joking aside—thank you kindly, and cordial good wishes.

Yours,
Jascha

The selections I have made from thousands of reviews, photos and articles, fairly represent Heifetz as an artist. There are good reviews and bad reviews, but through it all Heifetz comes out on top; the reviewers are the ones who may have suffered for their shortsightedness. While there is enough material on Heifetz to fill a dozen books of this size, almost everything that should be said, has been said. Additional photographs and reviews would merely be variations on the same theme.

Hopefully, when you have finished reading this book, you'll arrive at the same conclusion I came to. . . and which was so beautifully phrased by the writer-violinist Henry Roth:

31

March 12, 1955

Dear Bruno:

Understand that November 22d has been
cleared for me by his Eminence, Honorable Zirato--
with no strings attached, which might make it
somewhat embarrassing for a violin recital by a
certain Mr. Heifetz at Carnegie Hall.

Joking aside -- thank you kindly, and
cordial good wishes.

Yours,

Original Heifetz letter.

32

*The Heifetz family in St. Petersburg, circa 1911. Jascha
at the left with his mother standing. Sister Pauline is at
her mother's left with sister Elza in front of her. Father
Ruvin (or Rubin in English) is at the extreme right.*

"Had Heifetz never lived, violin playing might never
have attained the pinnacle of perfection on the instrumental
level that it enjoys today—a fact freely admitted by his colleagues everywhere. His influence upon two generations (or is
it three, including his own) has been staggering, and that does
not except such modern Soviet artists as Kogan, Bezrodny and
many others.

"A host of brilliant violinists were relegated to the second
and third rank with the emergence of Heifetz—most of whom
were far superior in polish, technique and tone to the leading
players of the latter 19th century.

*This has had the effect of immeasurably raising the
calibre of symphonic and commercial violinists the world
over.*"

Heifetz, circa 1909. His appearance on the musical scene established a completely new set of standards for violin playing.

HEIFETZ — A CRITICAL APPRECIATION
by Henry Roth*

PART 1
"THE INSTRUMENTALIST"

During the intermission of Jascha Heifetz's New York debut recital in 1917, Mischa Elman reportedly complained, *"It's a warm night."* When pianist Leopold Godowsky retorted, *"Not for pianists!"* the quip was not only witty—it was prophetic. For violinists everywhere, the warm night turned into a warm half-century. But the event was more than merely significant—it was historic—since an in-depth assessment of his accomplishments will reveal that the sheer instrumental criteria established by Heifetz constitute a revolution in violin playing fully as profound as that of Paganini in the 19th century. To better understand the nature and impact of the Heifetz phenomenon, it is helpful to **briefly** survey the status of violin art as it existed in the several decades before he appeared on the scene.

After the momentous technical contributions of Nicolo Paganini (1782-1840), which heralded the conquest of the fingerboard from bottom to top, violin playing gradually channeled into two main streams. One, through the influence of Paganini himself, favored brilliance of execution and flamboyant musicality. Its most gifted executants were Heinrich Ernst (1814-1865), Henri Vieuxtemps (1820-1880), Henry Wieniawski (1835-1880) and Pablo de Sarasate (1844-1908). Their general violinistic approach is vested in their bravura-oriented compositions. The best examples are well

---

Henry Roth, an internationally known music critic and musicologist, is a frequent contributor to "The Strad" magazine. He is also a very successful concert and recording violinist in Los Angeles.

*In the studio of Luthier Jacques Francais in New York
City, where the walls are decorated with significant
photographs of great string instrumentalists, this rare*

constructed, ardently romantic, thematically inventive and calculated to dazzle and enchant lay audiences— though in no way are they musically or intellectually profound. Vieuxtemps was the leading artisan of the French-Belgian school which rose to dominance in the post-Paganini 19th century, and Wieniawski ultimately introduced its principles into Russia. Sarasate, though handicapped by small hands, brought the bravura traditions of Paganini to an advanced level of intonation, euphony of sound and general polish of execution, tinctured with the flavor of his native Spain.

The counter-force to this flowering of violinistic romanticism was given impetus by Ludwig Spohr (1784-1859), the German competitor of Paganini, a model of conservative sobriety, a scrupulously conscientious violinist and somewhat academic composer. He disdained anything that smacked of triviality or vulgar display. Ferdinand David (1810-1873), his pupil, continued along similar lines, but the giant of violin scholasticism was the great purifier, Joseph Joachim (1831-1907), à Hungarian who eventually came to head the so-called "German school." Though a confirmed romantic in spirit, who saw fit to transcribe the entire body of Brahms' *Hungarian Dances* for the violin and popularize them in the concert hall, Joachim was responsible for greatly elevating the standards of violin programming. He re-introduced the Bach solo sonatas, the Beethoven concerto and sonatas, and championed a long list of classical masterworks which such contemporaries as Sarasate either ignored or rattled off in superficial fashion. He also was a bastion against the sea of musical banality that continued to clutter up programs in violin recital halls. (Even such an immortal as Vieuxtemps featured his own blustery set of *Variations on Yankee Doodle* on his American tour.)

picture may be viewed in the original. It shows, from left to right, Joachim, Ernst and Wieniawski, circa 1862.

These two historic trends are still major influences in our time. Yet, for all their transcendental glory, all of these violinistic greats would sound quite *un*satisfactory to ears inured to the lustre of modern violin art. Bowing was rough and scratchy; intonation, inexact; violin tone, limited, as were intellectual discipline and musical fidelity as we now know them.

Prof. Leopold Auer poses with his class in St. Petersburg, Russia, circa 1913. Seated second from the left is Heifetz.

Around 1880 a new violinistic mechanical device began to emerge—the conscious development and deliberate usage of that oscillation of the left hand fingertip known as the **vibrato**—a revolutionary happening that ultimately altered all previous concepts of violin tone production. The new gospel spread like wildfire, yet it met with stubborn opposition which required many years to overcome. Traditionally, the use of any sort of finger oscillation had been despised and forbidden by every respectable violin school. It was considered gross evidence of poor musical taste, though a few individual players may have applied some semblance of a vibrato to long, sustained tones, strictly as a subconscious kinetic emotional reflex. The sensational contribution of the vibrato was to enable violinists to play with a new, enriched beauty of sound, to add new dimensions of emotional communication, to play with "feeling." With the advantage of a well-developed, wisely-used vibrato, it became possible for a violinist of moderate, or even limited emotional and visceral force, to sound much superior to a player with a poor vibrato who possessed powerful, deeply-felt sentiments.

Along with the vibrato, a new arsenal of stylistic nuances were developed. Subtleties of portamentos, decorative finger slides, glissandos and position changes, added new elements of allure and elegance to violin art. Of course, some of these digital fripperies were all-too-often grossly exaggerated, resulting in countless instances of bad taste and emoting that would sound comical to our ears. But for all that, violin playing had progressed far beyond the extremely limited world of Paganini who scarcely played anything in public other than his own musically simplistic compositions. Those idolaters of legend who still persist in acclaiming Paganini as "the greatest violinist of all time," should ask themselves how he would sound in a Bach, Mozart, Beethoven or Brahms sonata, or a Beethoven, Mozart, Brahms, Sibelius, Tchaikovsky or Prokofiev concerto, or for that matter, the Schubert-Wilhelmj *Ave Maria*. After all, the invention of the steam engine was a miraculous event in its time, but scarcely comparable to atomic power.

Unlike today, when great virtuosi play nearly everything, the old-timers believed in doing their own thing. Sarasate, for example, avoided such concertos as

Joseph Joachim, 1903.

Brahms and Tchaikovsky, though they appeared during the prime of his career; Joachim never attempted Lalo, Tchaikovsky, Saint-Saens or many other popular romantic favorites, composed in his era. . . and violinistic careers were generally shorter than those of today. Antiquated training methods helped to induce serious technical adversity at the first sign of muscular decline.

The chief beneficiaries of the newly developed violinistic devices were Eugene Ysaye (1858-1931), Fritz Kreisler (1875-1962) and Mischa Elman (1891-1967). Ysaye, a gargantuan personality, represented the epitome of the uninhibited, free-wheeling romantic ethos, and his tempestuous fusion of passion and poetry rendered the Sarasate-Joachim syndrome archaic. Kreisler, who confounded the middle-European conservatives with the continual usage of his unique fingertip impulse vibrato, added new vistas of charm, grace and nobility of spirit to violin performance. Elman, first of a flood of Russian-Jewish violinists to emerge from "The Pale of

Mischa Elman, one of Auer's most celebrated students, circa 1909.

Eugene Ysaye, circa 1920.

Settlement" to win international fame, boasted a throbbing, lava-like tone of hypnotic opulence, abetted by a highly personalized fingertip impulse vibrato and a bow arm of prodigious sound production. Interestingly, he was the pupil of the Hungarian Leopold Auer (1844-1930), who succeeded in combining many of the best features of Joachim, Wieniawski and Sarasate with his own singular violinistic attitudes that came to represent the vanguard of the new Russian school. Violin art was truly moving into the 20th century, though the stellar pre-Heifetz protagonists still had one foot in the 19th.

In the wake of this joint onslaught, even the finest among those violinists who clung to standards of the past were summarily downgraded. The single new career of violinistic anachronism to reap great financial success was that of Jan Kubelik (1880-1935), who was dubbed "the heir to Paganini"—a specialist of bravura gymnastics whose residence in the top echelon was comparatively brief.

The turn of the 20th century enables us to hear many of the celebrated pre-Heifetz violinists through the miracle of phonograph recordings—an indelible, irrefutable testament. It is true that most of these are primitively engineered, that some of the artists were past their prime, that they were not really conditioned for playing into a microphone (or horn), as are our modern artists, that the surface noise obscures the quality of their tone. Yet, if we listen carefully, it is possible to judge such essentials as intonation, tempi, musical discipline (or lack of it), musical proportion, dynamic variety, general interpretation, and even, to a fair extent, tonal quality. For some reason, early violin recordings do not suffer to the degree of other musical mediums. In fact, some of the discs of the 'teen years offer surprisingly good fidelity of natural violin sound, when some of the most exquisite and exciting violin vignette performances of all time were made by Kreisler, Elman, and Heifetz. We are able to hear Sarasate at only 60, perhaps a bit below his peak, but not at all doddering

On April 25, 1925 Heifetz played at Leopold Auer's birthday celebration. Seated: Auer with Efrem Zimbalist. Standing, from left to right: Isidor Achron,

Jascha Heifetz, Ossip Gabrilowitsch, Sergei
Rachmaninoff, Josef Hoffman and Paul Stassievich.

with old age; Joachim, at 74, in the twilight of his career, but still younger than Heifetz at this writing; Ysaye at 54; Kubelik at 25; Vecsey at 18; Kreisler at 35; Elman at 25; Zimbalist at 25; Burmester at 42, and a sizeable legion of colleagues and would-be Heifetz rivals.

It is precisely through a comprehensive investigation of these recordings that we are best able to knowledgeably appraise the emergence of the young Heifetz in the **immediate** context of that period and in competition with his predecessors and older colleagues.

Even before the public debuts of Heifetz in world capitols, reports about a super-prodigy began to trickle out of Russia. Albert Spalding (1888-1953) tells of attending an Auer class (while on a concert tour) in St. Petersburg in 1913, where a group of other Auer star pupils *"were eclipsed by this miniature wizard in his early teens."* He describes the boy Heifetz's rendition of the difficult Ernst Concerto—.*"The first flush of fingered octaves was attacked with a kind of nonchalant aplomb; the tone was firm, flowing and edgeless, the intonation of fleckless purity. A kind of inner grace made itself felt in the shaping of the phrase. I completely forgot the tawdriness of the piece in the elegance and distinction of its delivery. . . while the boy was playing Auer strode nervously about the room, glancing at me now and then to appraise my reactions. His dark, restless eyes danced with delight as the wonder boy threaded his effortless way through the tortuous technical problems. He expected nothing less than paralyzed astonishment from me—nor was he disappointed. He would turn away with a helpless shrug of the shoulders, as if to say: 'Was there ever anything like it'?"* And it is reported that as early as four years before the 1917 New York debut, Kreisler, after hearing Heifetz in Berlin, told Zimbalist, *"You and I might as well take our fiddles and break them across our knees."*

Since then, lavish tribute to his phenomenal instru-

46

Heifetz, circa 1913.

From left to right: Max Rosen, Jascha Heifetz, Prof. Leopold Auer and Toscha Seidel, circa 1915.

mentalism has been paid by such stellar colleagues as Menuhin, Szigeti, Kogan, Primrose, Piatigorsky, Flesch, and a galaxy of violinists great and small, throughout the world for some three generations. David Oistrakh has said, *"There are many violinists. Then there is Heifetz."* Henryk Szeryng, in private, refers to him as "The Emperor." To *"play like a Heifetz"* was destined to become the professional's axiom to indicate performance perfection.

Of course, during his long career, like his revolutionary predecessor, Paganini, Heifetz has also been subject to adverse criticism—some valid, some apparently sensation-seeking. We shall examine these observations in due course.

Although Heifetz's playing in 1917 was not as highly charged in vibrance and drive as it became in the middle 1930's, all the ingredients of his instrumental

Nicolo Paganini is the only violinist with whom Heifetz can be compared in terms of his impact upon violin playing.

A distinguished group listens to violinist Henryk Szeryng who calls Heifetz "the Emperor." From left to right: Samuel Applebaum, Walter Piston, Paul Paradise, Dorothy Bales, et al, at his 1974 concert in Boston.

equipment were fully developed—those remarkable abilities that excited awe in his fellow professionals then, as now.

What are these qualities, and how are they manifested in the early recordings of Heifetz as compared, say, to the recordings of Sarasate, Kubelik and Vecsey, who (aside from their individual interpretative proclivities) were considered elite technical masters of their instrument?

First of all, the muscular coordination and reflexes of Heifetz are faster and more responsive than those of any other famous violinist. He might be likened to the first athlete to run the mile in under four minutes, though in his case, the performance is more the equivalent of three-and-a-half minutes. His high-wrist bow position, abetted by the Auer bow grip, and a closer-to-the-bridge stroking line, lends a scarcely-rivalled sonority to his sound in the live concert hall. He possesses a fingertip impulse vibrato generally akin to those which characterized the tones of Kreisler, Elman and Seidel. This sound might best be described as virile, as opposed to the one-dimensional wrist-or-arm-impelled sweet-tone vibrato of other players.

His crackling bow salvos, his ability to sustain bowed sound, the crisp clarity of his spiccato, the explosive bite of his up-and-down-bow staccatos, and his singular knack for split-second unity of finger intensity with aggressive bow attack, have never been matched. His technical dominance embraces not only agility, speed and intonation of a purity unequalled by any violinist, but every facet of tone production. The uncanny Heifetz ability to maintain the intensity of vibrato from one end of the fingerboard to the other, in all positions, with all fingers, has elevated the singing propensities of the violin to their fullest potential. But there is yet another capability that places the basic equipment of Heifetz in a class by itself. **Like a mighty custom-built limousine with multiple, ineffably fluid gear gradations, Heifetz can diversify the speed of his vibrato from**

Jan Kubelik was considered as one of the greatest violinists of his time until Heifetz came on the scene with his superior playing. Many violinists celebrated Heifetz's debut by retiring from the concert stage, circa 1928.

zero to incredible finger intensity—with all points in between—so that his sound represents the quintessence of tonal variety. Of all the superb violinists who have gained renown since 1917, not one has this ability to anywhere near the extent of Heifetz.

Closely related to this is the singular Heifetz mastery of the left hand *horizontal* movement of the fingers. Many marvelous modern technicians (and interpretative artists) have extraordinary control of the *vertical* up-and-down finger contact, but are limited to *varying* degree in the horizontal movement, *as it applies to stylistic finger position changes for expressive effect* (not, of course, in technical finger shifting). While his daredevil willingness to go-for-broke, irrespective of technical difficulties involved, may be emulated by a few other bravura-type players, none can really challenge the immaculate exactness of pitch, clarity of articulation and impeccable bow control of Heifetz in live unedited performance. His is the ultimate blend of tension and flexibility, in violin and bow technique.

The first Heifetz recordings date from 1917; the main group of Sarasate's, 1904; the better discs of Kubelik and Vecsey, somewhere in between; Ysaye's were made in 1912; Kreisler and Elman have numerous excellent specimens from the teen decade. Thus—making all due allowances for the engineering, as well as the playing conditions of the artists, it is possible to make some direct comparisons from the discs, without having to rely on written or oral evaluations which are so often either unknowledgeable or biased. Sarasate's facility at 60 was still excellent. Ysaye, at 54, was already a bit past his prime, but in any circumstances, the elements of eccentricity in his playing, and its inconsistency, would seem to mitigate against disc reproduction of his finest performance. Admittedly, he would have to be heard live in his best years, to be adequately assessed. The others were in their prime.

Sarasate is easily the best of the Sarasate-Kubelik-Vecsey virtuoso triumverate. He exhibits striking audacity and drive. But in such pieces as his own *Habanera, Zapateado, Zigeunerweisen* and *Introduction et Tarentelle*, though the playing has both fluency and polish, his consistently low-keyed sound and cool minimal vibrato have no sparkle. The G-string tone is dry and devoid of either opulence or sensuality; the bowing, sleek, but lacking any detonative bite. One has only to hear the repeated high G-string D's midway through the *Tarentelle* as exploded by the boy Heifetz to recognize the demise of the 19th century and the nascence of the 20th. In the Chopin-Sarasate *Nocturne No. 2 in E-Flat*, the glassy tone and impersonal projection of Sarasate are worlds away from the suave velvety vibrance of Heifetz.

Heifetz, Rubinstein and Feurman during a recording session.

Kubelik, "heir to Paganini," fares much worse in direct confrontation with the boy Wizard of Vilno. His dull, typewriter-like facility, chaste, metronomic musicality, scarcely vibrant tone and atrocious slides in Sarasate's *Zigeuneweisen* and *Zapateado,* and Bazzini's *Round of the Goblins,* are woefully inadequate compared with the glittering young Heifetz versions. And in the strictly technical ordeal of Paganini's *Moto Perpetuo,* the finger and bow dexterity of the adolescent newcomer compared to those of the "heir" are monumentally faster, cleaner and more effervescent

Vecsey's quasi-salon style in the Moszkowski-Sarasate *Guitarre,* with its gauche slides, and his slow one-dimensional vibrato, pales before the Heifetz rendition, which already reflects that polished sophistication that proclaims the 20th century. The Vecsey recording of the Schubert-Wilhelmj *Ave Maria,* which, aside from its ungainly slides, is a respectable performance, is no match for that of the young Heifetz, whose sustained G-string vibrance, glossy octaves and singing doublestops are obviously of another, later era.

The legendary uniqueness of Ysaye is reflected, to some degree, in his recordings, but his swashbuckling romanticism, hyper-personalized musicality and many faceted emotional communication, are inextricably bound to a bygone era of permissiveness, quite alien to the demands of our time. **Nor did his violinistic equipment, in any particular, challenge that of Heifetz.** Ysaye shunned the rigors of the Tchaikovsky Concerto, and only essayed the Brahms Concerto late in his career. As a romanticist incarnate, he handled the classical repertoire with elastic license.

In the years immediately prior to 1917, with Ysaye past his zenith, Kreisler and Elman were vying for supremacy with the public. Elman eventually became a victim of the Heifetz ascendency, but Kreisler, Ysaye, had (and still has) a host of adherents who greatly prefer his music-making, within its own connotation, to that of any other violinist—including Heifetz. Yet, in terms of instrumental sovereignty, neither could be considered a competitor of Heifetz.

Mischa Elman (standing) was 33 years younger than Eugene Ysaye but both lost their careers to Heifetz's superior violin playing. Though Ysaye had already passed his prime, Ysaye and Elman played a joint concert in New York in November, 1919 at the Hippodrome in New York at the same time Heifetz played at Carnegie Hall. Both concerts filled the house.

The standards of instrumental mastery, introduced by Heifetz in 1917, have never been surpassed, and his influence upon violinists the world over, either directly or indirectly, has been staggering—including those whose musical persuasions lie in utterly different directions. **And this hegemony has nothing whatsoever to do with whether one does, or does not prefer the Heifetz style and interpretations to those of other celebrated violinists.** Since 1917, audiences have come to take the Heifetz performance perfection for granted, indeed, in some, the familiarity has unaccountably bred a measure of contempt. But in 1917, such perfection was not only unknown, it was undreamed of, and it was a revelation. Even in his "salad years," Heifetz conferred new horizons of suavity, sophistication and—yes—glamour to violin art.

In one fell swoop, the boy Heifetz eliminated the traditional artificial separation between so-called bravura technicians, lyric-oriented players and specialized stylists. He was all three in one. And a long list of concert calibre violinists, including elite pupils of his own teacher, Auer, along with leading lights from the studios of Hubay, Sevcik, Flesch, Ysaye, Kneisel, et al., were instantly downgraded following his sensational debut. Symphony orchestras and conservatories everywhere were the ultimate beneficiaries of the Heifetz suzerainty. **It is reasonable to assume that without his example, violinistic instrumental standards would be appreciably lower.**

The earliest Heifetz recordings are all vignettes or single movements of larger works, due to the time limitations imposed by the old 78 rpm discs. Yet, despite the surface noise of the reproductions from the acoustically engineered platters, they are still astonishing, and many of them pinpoint facets of the enormity of the young Heifetz instrumental superiority with dramatic effect, even though the repertoire, musically, is lightweight. They also reveal some of the more controversial aspects of his playing.

Tone production mastery is strikingly exhibited in the lush G-string sound and vibrant doublestops in the 1918 Mendelssohn-Achron *On Wings of Song*, (as in *Ave Maria*), and the 1919 *Andante* from Lalo's *Symphonic Espagnole* contains most of the piquant stylistic subtleties of Heifetz's later years. In digital bravura and rivalling the incredible accuracy of the 1918 Paganini *Moto Perpetuo*, are the quicksilver gymnastics of the 1917 Bazzini *Round of the Goblins*, with its pristine double-harmonics and uproarious left-hand finger pizzicatos, the icily diabolical fingered octaves of the 1917 Beethoven-Auer *Chorus of Dervishes*, and the flawless 1917 Wieniawski *Scherzo-Tarantelle* and 1918 Sarasate *Introduction et Tarantelle*. In this vein also is the 1924 Sarasate *Carmen Fantasy* (a truncated Lento Assai, a slightly-cut Allegro-moderato and complete Moderato finale). The first two episodes are hectically suave, but the finale, faster and cleaner than any other violinist, attains an acceleration so cyclonic that the musical pulse is obliterated—a prime example of a Heifetz misuse of his singular ability and penchant for blinding speed.

Also outstanding among the endearing morceaux morsels are the exquisite *d'Ambrosio Serenade*, the 1917 Elgar *La Capricieuse*, with its peerless staccatos, and several nearly forgotten mini-gems by Achron, sparked by the 1924 *Hebrew Dance*, a scintillating showpiece brimming with captivating Eastern European inflections. The 1924 Scott *Gentle Maiden* exhibits the seraphic Heifetz lyricism and augurs the melting Crowther *Gweedore Brae* of 1945. Lili Boulanger's *Cortege* is invested with demonic propulsion, and her *Nocturne* contains thrilling intensity of E-string sound (1924). Heifetz's earliest *Havanaise* (1924, with piano) has not quite the grand gesture and sinuous mellifluence of his later versions, but the super-rapid passage-work is awesome. The above are but a small sampling of the first Heifetz discs (recently re-released on LP's by RCA Records) that swiftly won top prominence among violin recordings.

On the debit side among them are his youthful indiscretions in comically fast caricatures of the Mozart-Kreisler *Rondo* and Mendelssohn Concerto finale (both 1920), and the Schubert-Kreisler *Rondo* (1926), in which a melding of haste and drive violates the gentle spirit of the music in the outer sections, while the lyric middle, smooth as silk, lacks affection. (His 1946 version is a mite more relaxed, but essentially the same.) The 1917 Achron *Hebrew Melody* reflects the freshness of youth and has remarkable articulation in the rapid passages. Yet, the emotion is more from the finger than the heart. Tchaikovsky's *Serenade Melancholique* (the 1920 first version) pulsates with rich sound, but is not very "melancholique."

A dozen of the early brevities were remade with electric engineering in the latter '20's and '30's. The sound, of course, is better; the performances much the same. However, the earlier versions have a certain pubescent charm that is so in keeping with the juvenile essence of the music itself, that they are preferable. For all their age and drawbacks, the body of early Heifetz discs is dotted with performances that no other violinist has ever approached—then, or now.

PART 2
"THE MUSICAL PERSONALITY"

Apart from his revolutionary contribution in creating pinnacle standards of violin instrumental mastery, Heifetz is one of a handful of violinists entitled to be called a "Great Personality of the Violin." This means that in addition to being a superb violinist (as are many), **his sound and style are utterly unique unto himself.** No knowledgeable violin fancier can easily mistake the playing of Heifetz for another. In fact, it is this very overwhelming personalization that is unattractive to those who believe that highly personalized interpretations have no place in modern instrumental performance.

58

Pablo de Sarasate, circa 1892.

Dating from early in his career, Heifetz has been charged with being "cold." This accusation has been applied both to his platform image and his playing. How valid are these charges? Let us first discuss the "cold" platform image.

Audiences are made up of people. While they are perfectly willing to worship an idol (we see it in the political arena and the entertainment world, both pops and classic every day), they prefer a human element in their idols—some evidence that the idol is subject to at least a slight measure of the stresses to which they themselves are vulnerable. The winning runner who crosses the finish line breathless, agonized of visage, collapsing into an exhausted heap, instantly incurs more sympathy than the disdainful champion who wins without seemingly drawing a long breath. In the concert hall, audiences are prone to adore maestros who possess a greater or lesser degree of "Terpsichorean" talent—who sweat and strain and generally show wear and tear in the consummation of their chores. The majority in the audience have never been averse to a little "ham" in their adored ones—pianists who lustily *stomp* the pedals, flourish their arms heroically, or sing to themselves audibly while playing. Nor have violinists been immune to such idiosyncrasies as swaying to-and-fro, a plentiful repertoire of facial grimaces, diverse violin and bow posturings, and heavy obstreperous breathing.

Enter Heifetz, who stands erect, invariably holds his violin high, registers no facial contortions or emotings whatsoever, *imperturbable*. Together with the infallible perfection of his performance, the combination projects a super-human aura. And irrespective of how he may affect individuals in his private relationships, the man-on-the-platform conveys an overpowering sense of aloofness. In his late years, Heifetz has tried to overcome this image by cracking an occasional smile and talking to his audience. But the "cold" image, so long established, is not easily divested. And no matter how hard he may try, the stern Heifetz of the olympian

60

Heifetz, circa 1936.

instrumentalism and implacable countenance, is not
readily transformable into a hail-fellow-well-met "Mr.
Congeniality."

But what does a platform image have to do with
the actual sound-and-effect of music? Much, it would
appear to some. It is reported that several years ago a
psychologist made an experiment in which a group of
listeners heard recordings by various violinists who were
identified. Asked for their "emotional" reactions, Heifetz's playing was called "brilliant," "cold," "unemotional," "dry." But when the experiment was repeated
and the violinists were *not* identified, the artist inducing

61

the most gut impact was Heifetz. However, it does seem odd that a group who knew enough about violin playing to be pre-conditioned by the Heifetz "cold" label, did not recognize his inimitable sound and style, identified or not. Such a test actually proves little, though admittedly, those who are prone to be biased by the visual can obviously react more objectively to the aural magnetism of Heifetz's recorded performances.

It is futile to try to pinpoint what is "cold" or "not cold," since coldness or warmth must inevitably reside in the ear and emotional response of the individual auditor—and he most certainly has the right to his opinion, whether he be layperson or professional. **Yet, the critic should be wary of making blanket evaluations of Heifetz's ability for emotional communication. A comprehensive survey of his recordings can be quite surprising in that area, and arouse a dichotomy of feelings in the objective listener.**

Heifetz, circa 1960.

It has long been apparent that traits of an artist's personality (*not his character as a human being!*) can be mirrored in his playing. Heifetz has never been one to "wear his heart on his sleeve," on or off stage. But it is palpably *ridiculous* to accuse him of playing without feeling. One has only to hear his opening phrase of the Glazounov Concerto or Bruch *Scotch Fantasy*, the plaintive strains of Crowther's *Gweedore Brae* or the tittilating lilt of Herbert's *A la valse*—among a long list of his choice items—to realize the fallacy of such a charge.

It has been noted that the very perfection of Heifetz's playing can convey a sense of detachment—an expression that somehow the Heifetz "inner man" has left the stage for a coffee break, leaving the incomparable machine to continue the playing, while the man himself returns and departs at will.

A perennial ingredient in the Heifetz musical character is his manner of applying his artful slides and position changes to the same beautiful effect in all of his playing, whether or not this interferes with the structure or ethos of the composition. On the other hand, his willingness to risk a difficult finger manipulation in order to achieve a totally unorthodox, and often beguiling nuance (where others will opt for the easier traditional fingering), emphasizes the striking degree of his artistic personalization and independence. Some purists find these indulgences intolerable, yet who among them can know for certain that were the deceased composer to hear the effect he might, more often than not, say, *"Keep it in—I like it."* All this is particularly vivid in his novel performance of Mozart's *Concerto No. 5 in A*, in which the classical rules are often "bent," but the interpretation is marvelously bright and buoyant, vitiated only by the super-hectic Turkish theme in the finale.

Like any other musical personality, that of Heifetz does not equally embrace every facet of the emotional gamut. The timbre of his tone is ravishingly soprano, limpid purity of exquisite smoothness ennobles his lyric utterances, but tenderness (in the sense of heart-warm-ing gentleness) is not one of his endemic assets. The obdurate steel of his self-discipline, the irrepressible propulsion of his inner drive, his insatiable monomania in an eternal quest for perfection, have not been conducive to encouraging the expression of those emotions which are generally associated with human frailties, introversion or self-effacement. The Heifetz "songfulness" reflects the adamantine radiance of a rare diamond, not the dulcet sweetness of gushing sentiment. For all the fire of his sound, the romanticism of Heifetz projects an aura of passion that is controlled, reserved, decorous, and at times, impersonal.

Despite his compulsion for perfection, it is not true that Heifetz has never fallen below his own standard. He, himself, describes a period of violinistic retrogres-

Heifetz, circa 1960.

Heifetz, circa 1960.

sion. "And now I'm going to confess something. There came a time when my disinclination to practice caught up with me. After a certain New York recital, W.J. Henderson, the music critic of the "Sun," hinted in his review that I was letting the public and him down, and that I had better watch my step. Though it was hard to hear, *the warning came in the nick of time. I began to take a good look at myself. I started to practice seriously. I curbed my youthful extravagances. I shall always be grateful to Henderson. He jolted me out of my complacency and put me on the right path. Critics can sometimes be very helpful.*" The reproof must have served its purpose, because since that period, the performance consistency of Heifetz has exceeded that of any of his colleagues in living or "record*ing*" memory. His fanatical insistence on maintaining his own maximal standards, decade after decade, in contrast to some of his noted younger colleagues, deserves the respect of all violin partisans. **With Heifetz, the violin has always come first—a most hazardous choice, considering the complex demands of the human condition.** And where certain of his colleagues have sought to combine their violinistic careers with other provocative activities—resulting in greater or lesser disadvantages to their playing—Heifetz has remained the living, unmitigated symbol of violinistic dedication.

PART 3
"THE MUSICIAN-INTERPRETER"

Although the Heifetz instrumental hegemony has long been conceded, on occasion, he has been censured vehemently, sometimes cruelly, in his role as a musician-interpreter. He has been accused of approaching *"every piece of music he plays with the notion that it was fashioned by the composer to serve him as a performer,"* of *"misguided musicianship,"* of *"a certain lightness of mind commonly known as bad taste,"* of being a purveyor of *"Silk Underwear Music."* These scattergun charges merit investigation because of the stature of the professional critics who made them. Perhaps the ultimate approach to the matter would be an in-depth examination of the Heifetz repertoire, lightweight, middleweight and heavyweight.

William Primrose, Jascha Heifetz and Gregor Piatigorsky recording the Beethoven Trio in D, Opus 8. Circa 1960.

Heifetz would earn about $5000 during the 1940-1950's for a single, sponsored radio broadcast, circa 1943.

But why not make these performance evaluations with some semblance of reasonableness rather than vitriolic doctrinaire opinion or flip featherhead aspersion? Which criticisms are inextricably bound up with the subjective tastes and preferences of the individual; which can be considered valid musical shortcomings? How far can overwhelming personalization be tolerated? At which point do we demand that an individualist of Heifetz's stamp depersonalize his musical-making— at least in the masterworks—and to what degree? We can discuss these matters, formulate decisive opinions, and prove nothing. Ultimately, **all of our opinions are subjective,** but in the process of investigation, we may be able to clarify some of our own attitudes.

In this regard, it may be profitable to look into the complaints of Virgil Thomson, who with his myrmidons, has been a highly vocal spokesman for the minority anti-Heifetz cabal.

Mr. Thomson has written, *"I confess to a not great taste for violin recitals myself, because the Baroque instrument has somehow not managed to inspire our best composers to do their best work. At least, not since the invention of the oversensitive Tourte bow made the playing of it a pure virtuoso job."* This intimates that Mr. Thomson would willingly write off the best of the noble violin declarations of Tartini, Mozart, Viotti and Spohr, the beguiling, entertaining (oh, horrors!) romanticism of Vieuxtemps, Wieniawski, Bruch and Lalo; and **above all, indicates that he considers the violin concertos of Beethoven, Mendelssohn, Brahms, Tchaikovsky and Prokofiev, along with the sonatas of Beethoven and Brahms to be inferior products of their creators.** He thinks the Tourte bow (made about 1780) is "oversensitive." Does he then imply that he would prefer a return to the old "mushy" pre-Tourte bows of the Baroque era so that the last 200 years of violinistic glory and accomplishment could be summarily castrated? If the violin masterworks of Beethoven and Brahms cannot satisfy the musical taste buds of Mr. Thomson, what can?

And if he disdains *both* these and the violin pieces of light entertainment, either we must accede to the demise of the violin, as we know it, or await the day that Mr. Thomson, himself, elevates the repertoire with his own compositions—a revelation that the world of violin playing has yet to experience.

However, the arrant snobbery that Mr. Thomson exhibits in his role as the "hanging judge" of the violin and its traditions is most archly vested in his heading to a 1940 Heifetz recital, titled, *"Silk Underwear Music."* One might be tempted to allow the epithet to slip by with the kind of transient titter reserved for those smart-aleck quips that titillate blase readers of quasi-intellectual journals, except that it has been specifically concocted to artfully and totally denigrate an instrumentalist of Heifetz's historic stature.

It seems that Mr. Thomson is not consistent. If he has such a low estimate of music and performances that entertain and delight, why then does he squander his own talents in writing such folk-oriented (and not at all significant, in its metier) genre music as the score for *The Plow That Broke the Plains?* One should not, for example, castigate his music as "cornbelt claptrap," simply because it does not equate with the masterworks of Bach, Beethoven and Brahms, since it *does* have a function to serve in the overall musical scheme of things. Even featherweight "Silk Underwear" cinema scores, such as his, if played with slick professional eclat, have a relevance of their own, though they may be (to borrow a phrase from Mr. Thomson) *"affected, frivolous and picayune."* And who, by the way, can prove that a jolly Rondo finale from a Beethoven violin-piano sonata, or a "dancy" Gavotte from a Bach Solo Partita is, or is not, more meaningful musical communication than the reverential Schubert-Wilhelmj *Ave Maria* or songful Chopin-Sarasate *Nocturne?* **Or that one syndrome can, or should, replace the other?** But unwittingly, with his "Silk Underwear" mot, Mr. Thomson poses an inquiry into a phase of violin exper-

70

tise that cannot be fully understood and appreciated by any writer who does not have intimate knowledge of the techniques of violin playing. If we can—for the moment —admit that the entirety of respectable violin art is not vested *solely* in a relative handful of masterworks—that appetizers, soups, pastas and desserts have a rightful, if lesser place in the violinistic banquet, we will discover that "Silk Underwear" violin music, as catered by a Heifetz, demands technical resources that can be signally different from those required in baroque and classical opuses. Any competent orchestra can easily give a first-class performance of *The Plow That Broke the Plains* and similar cinematic "Silk-undies." But many a respectable, yes, even world-renowned interpreter of baroque and classical violin masterworks does not possess the vibrant beauty of sound, the fluid, expressive lyricism, and the finger and bow flexibility and coordination to play viands of the romantic repertory to outstanding effect.

Violinists collectively, have toiled incessantly for more than *three centuries* to attain the instrumental versatility epitomized by Heifetz. Naturally, **the intellectual and musical requirements for supreme interpretations of the masterworks are far more profound than those needed for melodic and bravura audience-pleasing vignettes. But the point is—the art of making the violin both "sing and sizzle" in these vignettes involves technical skills that are different. Different in the sense that they represent an epochal extension of the totality of violinistic technique**—and not even Mr. Thomson can turn back the clock. Call it "Silk Underwear Music" or ear tickling diversion, this new element of violin art has become an integral part of the concert scene in our century, beloved by audiences the world over. It may be depreciated, even temporarily shelved (when violinists permit themselves to be brow-beaten by commentators of Mr. Thomson's persuasion), but never completely eradicated.

Enough of regression! Let us get right to the heart of the matter—in the musical stratosphere—with Bach. How often have we heard the allegation, *"Heifetz is an incredible fiddler, but he can't play Bach"*? How inane! Heifetz can play anything. What is meant is that Heifetz does not perform Bach to the taste of some individual listener—a prerogative of choice to which we are all entitled. The crux of the matter lies in the personalization of Heifetz's art and the era from which he derives.

It is true that Heifetz's sound and style are emblazoned on every bar he plays. This also applies to such stellar figures as Casals, Kreisler, Landowska, Rachmaninoff and many others. The art of these giants was built on the premise that the sought-after ideal of instrumental performance was a sublime blending of the creative urge of the composer with the individualized personality of the artist. Neuterization of the artist in favor of some amorphous goal which has, in recent years, become popularized as "playing music the way the composer intended," would be an anathema to them. (And only the anointed, of course, are blessed with absolute revelation of the intentions of long-deceased composers). **When it is pointed out that of the finest dozen performances of the Bach Solo Sonatas (and Beethoven Concerto and Sonatas), each is strikingly different from the other, the pundits are strangely silent.** (Will the real Mr. Bach and Mr. Beethoven please stand up!)

Inasmuch as the question of playing Bach authentically, as it was played in Bach's time (before the invention of the modern arched bow, vibrato, and altered violin bass-bars and fingerboards) is purely academic, we must perforce view the Heifetz interpretations in the context of modern performance. (So much for "pur-

Left to right: Artur Rubinstein, Jascha Heifetz and Emanuel Feuermann during a break while practicing. While Heifetz is essentially extremely controlled while performing, he has a charming laugh and a warm sense of humor, circa 1940. Feuermann died in 1942 during a routine operation.

ism," in the ultimate sense, as it applies to the Bach Solo Sonatas!) **However, one cannot sluff off the matter of whether an artist does, or does not perform music in the general spirit of the age in which it was conceived.** The ethos and tempo of life of the "ancient" in the powdered wig are not those of the swaggering romantic dandy with the waxed moustache—and neither equates with the ever-urgent, coolly perfectionist atomic age man.

74

In the Heifetz 1952 (RCA) recordings of the Bach Solo Sonatas, the "purist" listener can doubtless pinpoint tussles for hegemony between violinist and composer, but Heifetz has obviously made a sincere effort to pay his respects to Bach, insofar as the dictates of his own rugged musical personality will permit. Let us remember that Heifetz emanates from a violinistic school that considered beauty of sound to be paramount. But his interpretations, while certainly not metronomic (neither were those of Casals!) are strongly disciplined. Except for the Allemande of the *Partita No. 2 in D minor*, which is played considerably faster than the Andante marking—thereby sacrificing the maximum sense of breadth—the Heifetz penchant for superspeed is, for the most part, admirably held in check. And whether one does, or does not find aesthetic satisfaction from the performances, it must be admitted that his sense of personal involvement with the music seems to be sustained throughout. **The sheer violin playing itself, is magnificent.**

In the *Sonata No. 1 in G minor*, the Adagio is broadly ariose; the Fugue has scrupulous thematic delineation in the chord batteries; the Siciliano is mildly "Heifetz-y," but fluent and angelic in sound; the quicksilver detaches of the Presto, reined to a crisp medium pace.

The Allemande of *Partita No. 1, in B-minor* is a bit too urgent and "light" on serenity, but powerful in authority and daring in fingering selection; the several Doubles and Corrente are brilliant, if occasionally "slick"; the Sarabande, stately and beautiful in sound; the Bourree, fast, perhaps not exactly a model of "courtly" grace, but exact in rhythmic pulse.

The Grave of *Sonata No. 2, in A-minor*, is quite personalized, never blandly literal, and Heifetz often seeks for dramatic effect in the higher positions in preference to maintaining an unvarying aura of simplicity; the Fugue is mildly propulsive, with spectacular bowed chord playing that always accentuates the correct melodic note register, ending with a thrillingly vibrant broken chord; the Andante Sostenuto strives a mite overmuch for lyric effect, but it is indubitably "Bach that sings;" the finale Allegro is remarkably articulated and has much variety of bowing strokes.

Following the superspeed Allemande from *Partita No. 2, in D-minor*, the Corrente is somewhat mannered, and the Sarabande is not for those who insist on rhythmic punctilliousness, though both contain some interesting forays into the higher positions; the Gigue is reasonable in pace and has excellent dynamic variance; the mighty Chaconne (much like the 1935 recording; considerably better than the 1970 version) projects some original ideas, is boldly conceived, alertly rhythmic (which, as a dance form, it should be) and inimitably "Heifetz."

In *Sonata No. 3, in C-major*, the Adagio is organ-like and grandiose, with the theme notes nobly emphasized by "backlash" bow thrusts (unlike some noted colleagues who, in their discs, "take the easier way out" by ending every chord on the E-string note, whether or not it happens to be the thematic one!); the Fugue is a heroic display of violin virtuosity; the Largo is glossy and not sufficiently ingenuous in spirit; the Allegro assai is a dextrous finger-and-bow tour-de-force.

The familiar Preludio of *Partita No. 3, in E-major* is pellucidly etched, the tempo, logical, the bowing, flawless; the Loure, somewhat stoic; the Gavotte and Rondo, well-paced, with good dynamic contrasts and modal variety; the two Menuettos, slightly "libertine," but the "piano" repetitions of the theme are exceptionally sensitive; the Bourree and Gigue sport an occasional mannerism, but are tastefully paced, and in the Gigue, spiccato bowing is smartly employed in the service of diversified nuance.

Thus, in the aggregate, we find Heifetz's Bach Solo Sonatas less highly personalized than most vehicles of his repertoire, even though his sound is so immediately recognizable that one is apt to say *"That's Heifetz,"* at least as soon as he will say *"That's Bach."* Yet, more than a few listeners who will extoll the Bach playing of Casals, Landowska or Kriesler despite all of their exceptional personalizations, will bridle at the slightest deviation from impersonal literalness by Heifetz. It is a curious inequity. **Perhaps it is because the Heifetz sound and mannerisms are so unequivocally identifiable with the 20th century ethos, as distinct from the more romantically inclined Bachian idiosyncrasies of his older colleagues. In any case, those who demand little or no personalization (does this latter exist?) in Bach Solo Sonatas must seek elsewhere.** However, it might be fruitful for them to give this Heifetz set another unprejudiced hearing. They may sometimes find Heifetz at odds with musicological dogma—but his playing is scarcely "dry."

Heifetz, circa 1940.

The 1953 recordings of the two Bach Concertos (RCA, Wallenstein, Los Angeles Philharmonic) are valid interpretations that are often beset by a lack of spiritual repose. In *No. 1, in A-minor,* only the third movement projects a feeling of haste; the first movement is sensitive, and unlike the remainder, relatively free from a sense of over-urgency. *No. 2, in E-major,* is generally comparable in mood, though the opening movement is keenly alert to dynamic contrast. We again see, in these works, an interpretative negation of the innate pulse of Bach's age, though not to any harrowing degree. The sound, of course, is consistently beautiful and varied in color.

Bach's *Concerto for Two Violins and Orchestra, in D-minor,* with Erick Friedman (1961, Sargent, New Symphony Orchestra of London) is most convincing in the slow movement. Though Heifetz dominates in the playing (as he would if paired with any violinist) and, it would appear, the engineering balance, the similarity in general sound and style between him and Friedman results in some smoothly limned interplay. The opening Vivace is unconscionably fast, as established by Sargent.

Least attractive among Heifetz's Bach offerings are the ill-conceived *Double Concerto* recording, in which he plays both parts himself (RCA, Waxman, RCA Chamber Orchestra, 1946)—a presentation which sorely lacks the vital contrasts that can be provided by a well-selected partner—along with several transcribed "over-pretty" excerpts from the *English Suites* (with piano, 1934 and 1946) and the patently self-indulgent *Minuets 1 and 11* from *Partita No. 3* (1925). All of these latter performances have provided grist to those who steadfastly assert that *"Heifetz can't play Bach."*

How does Heifetz fare with Beethoven? In 1940, one of the all-time most highly publicized recording collaborations of an instrument masterwork, took place. Heifetz and Toscanini (or was it Toscanini and Heifetz; which Mohammed; which The Mountain?) recorded the mighty *Beethoven Violin Concerto* (NBC Sym-

Heifetz, circa 1947.

phony). Many still consider the results to be the greatest of all Beethoven concerto interpretations. Others cannot abide it. The first movement performance comes under most fire. In live concert, this movement is often disappointing, as even many of the finest violinists are not fully "warmed up" until somewhere around the cadenza. In this movement, it is apparent that Heifetz and Toscanini got along better with each other than with Beethoven. Everyone is thoroughly "warmed up," but in the "Allegro, ma non Troppo," the "ma non Troppo" is summarily displaced by a "Troppo" Allegro that precludes that sensitive flexible introspection which can

Heifetz and Arturo Toscanini recording the Beethoven Violin Concerto, circa 1940.

Heifetz with Brooks Smith, circa 1958.

transport this music to exalted heights. The Auer and Joachim cadenzas are smashingly brilliant, of course. The Larghetto, conversely, is gloriously pure and sleek, and the Rondo, ebullient and suave. The 1955 version with Munch and the Boston Symphony has better engineered sound, as to be expected, but the interpretation is much the same. (**The earlier and later versions of all the Heifetz concerto repertoire reveal few interpretative changes**).

As always, the Heifetz personalization is ever powerfully in evidence, but Beethoven offers the opportunity for the many-faceted Heifetz tone to "sing" in a way different from the more expressively restrictive polyphony of Bach, and hence is often devastatingly effective. This latter is particularly impressive in the *Romances in F and G* (1951, Steinberg, RCA Symphony). These two winsomely classical works, standards of the repertoire, are potentially tedious for all their munificent pedigree, and have never been outstanding audience-pleasers, even within the classical context. But the Heifetz spectrum of sound and his ineffable polish more than compensate for his (in this instance) minimal mannerisms, and the *Romances*, ennobled with a cool grace, are delectable to the ear.

In the Beethoven violin-piano sonatas, we encounter Heifetz as a chamber-music player, albeit only in the duo perspective. One would never know these works are essentially a wondrous example of instrumental parity and co-existence by perusing the album spine of the *"Beethoven-Violin Sonatas-Heifetz"* (as it reads). The album front says *"Heifetz—The Beethoven Sonatas for Violin and Piano—Complete"*—still no mention of a pianist-collaborator. Not until we pore into the enclosed brochure, do we find the names, in small print, of Emanuel Bay (who plays nine of the ten) and Brooks Smith (who plays the *Kreutzer*). The recordings are from RCA, made between 1947 and 1960.

82

Heifetz, circa 1947.

To some degree, this one-sidedness is reflected in the performances—yet—they are not to be taken lightly, since many of the sonatas offer some prime music-making. *Sonata No. 7, in C-minor, Op. 30, No. 2,* sometimes referred to as the *Winter,* is strangely relaxed and chastened for Heifetz, with nicely-honed tempos and tasteful delineation of the varied moods. **It must be pointed out that if one listens to the Heifetz readings of these ten sonatas with music in hand, his fidelity to the printed dynamic markings and shadings is remarkably constant—a clear indication of his homage to the composer.**

83

What might be considered surprising, considering the impetuous Heifetz temperament, is his sensitivity and care in dealing with the delicate intimacies of the unorthodox *Sonata No. 10, in G-major, Op. 96*. Again, we find his tempos salubrious—and the hazardous problems of tone control in the Adagio Expressivo are made to order for the Heifetz "multi-geared" sound. At one point, he hits a high C on the A-string with a rapturous vibrance no other violinist could negotiate—and academicians be damned! It is ravishing, and logical, too.

The difficult-to-communicate first two movements of *Sonata No. 3, in E-flat major, Op. 12, No. 3* are cannily burnished, and the Rondo cavorts brightly. In *Sonata No. 1, in D-major, Op. 12, No. 1,* the Andante con moto approximates a Moderato, but the overall performance is affable, and the Rondo finale, pristinely grateful.

Less satisfactory is *Sonata No. 8, in G-major, Op. 30, No. 3.* Again, the finale, Allegro Vivace, romps merrily at a realistic clip, but the Allegro assai and tempo di Menuetto are imbued with an air of "impatience" and muscularity that jars the blithe essence of the music. *Sonata No. 5, in F-major, Op. 24 (Spring),* despite some radiantly vibrant tone in the opening Allegro, suffers even more from this misfeasance.

The Heifetz rendition of the titanic *Sonata No. 9, in A-major, Op. 47 (Kreutzer)* is another of those interpretations calculated to arouse more than the usual amount of controversy. As a sort of "concerto-sonata," the largest of the ten canvases, the very nature of the work invites the heroic ministrations of a Heifetz, yet, particularly in the second movement variations, solicits a discreet reflectiveness that mitigates against overpersonalization. Heifetz has recorded the *Kreutzer* twice; first, in 1951, with pianist Benno Moiseiwitsch; later with pianist Brooks Smith in 1960 (RCA). While he tends to dominate both pianists, the violin-piano rapport (with Smith) and the engineering are better than

Heifetz departs for London to take part in the "Festival of London" where he will play with the London Philharmonic Orchestra under Sir Malcolm Sargent. With him are Mrs. Heifetz and works by Stradivari and Guarneri del Gesu (violins in the double case)! May 11, 1951.

those of the 1951 recording, though the playing is a trifle more mannered than the earlier collaboration with the amiable, conscientious playing of Moiseiwitsch. In the faster episodes, Heifetz conquers all with bravura extroversion, which he also applies to the discursive embellishments of Variation II of the Andante con Variazioni—a disputatious procedure. But interpretative tastes aside, again we find that the many-nuanced tone of Heifetz lends a special quality to the ariose aspects of the work, and overall, it is difficult to resist the blandishments of this glistening, galvanic reading. Recently, a highly respected critic of the younger generation, who abhors subjective, individualized performances, admitted to me in private that he was "bowled over" by a "live" Heifetz performance of the *Kreutzer* he had heard.

In nine of the Sonatas, piano collaborator Emanuel Bay plays with sure-fingered, discriminating musicality and miniscule self-assertion, as is the traditional lot of the hired accompanist. And it has been little different with Kreisler, Elman, Menuhin, Oistrakh, Stern, Milstein, or even Szigeti! Only when great violinists collaborate with "name" solo pianists, is the balance altered—to any appreciable extent.

Two Mozart Sonatas, *No. 15, K. 454* and *No. 10, K. 378*, convey performance traits similar to those of his Beethoven. The former flirts with and sometimes achieves sparkling transparency, but is often hard-edged, and the slow movement is over-effusive. It is almost as if Heifetz was trying too much to charm. The latter work, more elfin in nature, is played with more relaxation and something akin to warm cordiality—hence, is more convincing. Both are with the discreet partnership of Brooks Smith (RCA, 1954).

The Brahms Violin Concerto of Heifetz is a glamorous affair, enhanced by his own hair-raising cadenza, one of the most technically demanding ever penned (RCA, Reiner, Chicago Symphony, 1955). For sustained tension, sheer virtuoso excitement and smoothness of delivery, it is unequalled, and wholly in affinity with his temperament. Those who recall the Heifetz performance in his prime will scarcely deny the thrilling effect of his "live" unedited Brahms in the concert hall. (One is apt to forget this in listening to a plethora of edited "souped-up" modern recordings). The recording with Koussevitsky (Boston Symphony, Auer cadenza, 1939) is not comparable in the engineering, but little different in the performance. **In fact, the vibrance, tension and perfection of Heifetz was never greater than in the mid-30's, and was sustained since that time well into the decade following his retirement from the international concert stage.**

The lyric beauty of Brahms' *Sonata No. 2, in A, Op. 100* is made to order for the Heifetz tonal spectrum, and while the 1936 recording with Bay reveals certain over-usage of slick slides, especially in the first movement, his superior intensity of sound enlivens a sonata which (unlike *No. 3, Op. 108*) is not really a sure-fire audience pleaser.

Among the remaining popular concertos of the standard repertory, several stellar Heifetz performances come immediately to mind. The Tchaikovsky D-major, recorded three times (1937, 1950, 1957), apart from its immaculate delivery, dramatically points up the multifarious nuances of the Heifetz vibrato in the grand melodic statements. There have been more than a few exceptional performances of this concerto in the last three or four decades, but none can rival the phenomenal constancy of the Heifetz sound. The three performances are similar, except for the advancement of engineering techniques, but the 1937 version (Seraphim Records, Barbirolli, London Philharmonic) is a sentimental favorite with many professionals. It is interesting to note that the earliest recording features the Auer passages of thirds and tenths that twice replace the original pedestrian endings of the two principal sections (first movement). But in the succeeding discs, Heifetz, in an effort to attain even more climactic excitement, applies an

Mr. and Mrs. Jascha Heifetz departing for England on the Queen Mary. October 11, 1947.

extra helping of dazzling doublestops to further spice up the stroganoff, a ploy which merely succeeds in "cluttering up the kitchen." This effort is somewhat symbolic of the Heifetz strivings, through the years, to elevate a brilliance which was already incredible. Frustrating!

The Mendelssohn E-minor, Op. 64, recorded in 1949 (Beecham, Royal Philharmonic, Seraphim Records) and 1959 (Munch, Boston Symphony, RCA) is geared to rapidity, but contains many a glint of comparative repose, within its own context. The limpid Andante, burnished with varied speeds of vibrato, sings seraphically. The 1959 version seems a trifle more mellow and less intense than that of 1949, but the finales in both, though paced at super-speed, are slower than the juvenile single 78 cut of this movement made in 1920 (which was, incidentally, much less vibrant in tone). One may wish to dispute the Heifetz outer movement tempos, but the performance is nevertheless scintillating.

The Sibelius D-minor (Beecham, London Philharmonic, 1935, Seraphim Records; Hendl, Chicago Symphony, 1959, RCA) has long been a choice Heifetz acquisition, and he is largely responsible for the great popularity the concerto has achieved since 1935. Several other top violinists have produced interpretations of outstanding merit, but none projects the gelid luminescence of the Northern star, the indomitable ruggedness of the Finnish ethos, to a degree rivalling Heifetz.

One of the less heard Heifetz performances is his *Symphonie Espagnole*, recorded in 1951 (Steinberg, RCA, Symphony, "Intermezzo" movement omitted)—a stunning delivery, permeated with suave, subtle Latin flavor. The simmering Scherzando which is rarely exploited to its fullest potential in terms of arch inflection and tonal variety, is instilled with a unique vitality-languorous, yet wonderfully chipper. The Andante, and the sensuous triplet theme of the whirlwind finale, are swathed in lush sound, and all is exquisitely polished.

A matchless exhibition of concerto violinistics is the

Heifetz with Gregor Piatigorsky (1960) his lifelong friend and accompanist (cello). Piatigorsky died of lung cancer in 1976. His piano accompanists included Benno Moiseiwitsch (left) and William Kapell (right).

Heifetz Elgar B-minor, Op. 61 (Sargent, London Symphony, 1949, RCA), a performance of one of the most massive and demanding vehicles of its kind—calculated to induce other violinists either to stand up with hats doffed, or quail in disbelief.

There is a cluster of works in the standard repertoire, both full and medium length that are essentially the "personal property" of Heifetz, opuses of intensely violinistic nature—uncomplicated, musically, but unfailingly effective. Few would dispute his supremacy in the concertos of Glazounov, Conus, Vieuxtemps Nos. 4 and 5, Spohr No. 8 *Gesangsscene*, Bruch *Scotch Fantasy* and Concerto No. 2, together with the violin-piano sonatas of Richard Strauss, Saint-Saens, Bloch Nos. 1 and 2 (*Poeme Mystique*), the Saint-Saens *Introduction and Rondo Capriccioso* and *Havanaise*, Sarasate's *Zigeunerweisen* and the Sinding *Suite in A-minor*. And many would insist upon including in this broad grouping the Bruch No. 1 and Wieniawski No. 2 concertos, the Ravel *Tzigane*, and the Debussy and Faure, Op. 13 sonatas.

Another domain in this rarified category comprises contemporary concertos either expressively composed for or popularized by Heifetz. There is the Prokofiev No. 2, its blend of saucy badinage and ethereal melody seemingly created for Heifetz; the *Concerto, Op. 47* of Louis Gruenberg, an Americana jazz-tinted work of sparkling sophistication, fashioned specifically for the Heifetz style and awesome technical arsenal, and so difficult, no other leading violinist has yet attempted its performance; the concerto of Erich Wolfang Korngold, with its rapturous cinematic panorama; the sweeping biblical incantations of *Concerto No. 2* (*The Prophets*) by Mario Castelnuovo-Tedesco; the intensely rhapsodic concerto of William Walton; the lusty rhetoric of the concerto by Miklos Rosza. Shorter standouts of this contemporary vintage are Castelnuovo's *Figaro* (Paraphrase on *Largo al Factotum* from Rossini's *Barber of Seville*) and his airily vivacious rondo, *The Lark*, along with Franz Waxman's inflammatory *Carmen Fantasy*.

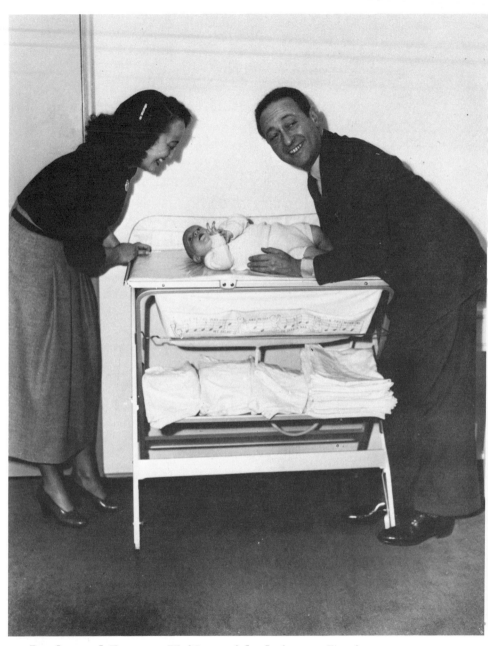

Jascha and Frances Heifetz with their son Jay (age three months). January 11, 1949.

For all the Russian genesis of his art, Heifetz has been the personification of the American idiom as it applies to classical violin playing. His innate gift for rhythmic exactitude, insidious syncopation and "jazzy" inflection enable him to play virtuoso jazz-oriented Americana in a unique style. That distinctive manner of playing, referred to as "commercial" (intense in sound, designed for emotional response, ear-titillating), familiar to millions through motion picture recordings made by other violinists, has been immensely influenced by Heifetz. He has also displayed a marked penchant for French music—Saint Saens, Debussy, Ravel, Poulenc and Ibert. Although Heifetz does not play these genres with the sensual Gallic perfumery of the arch-type French violinists (Thibaud, Francescatti, Merckel, et al.), his cool incandescence and glistening sophistication conjure up an aromatic bouquet of sound inimitably his own—as in Debussy's *La plus que lent* and *Beau Soir*. His most controversial interpretation in the Gallic repertory is possibly that of the Chausson *Poeme* (Solomon, RCA Symphony, 1952), in which, despite occasional phrases that might be accepted as "poetic" by Heifetz partisans, the drive and "muscle" of his playing can be onerous to those auditors who see the *Poeme* as exuding reverie and an aura of mystery.

The history of violin playing is rife with examples of celebrated violinists who shunned certain works, particularly those of composers who were their contemporaries, because they felt the music to be alien to their own *specific* violinistic and musical styles. Often, they "ducked" a work simply because they realized their equipment could not meet its challenges, either on the sound production or technical level. And apparently such concertos as the Bartok Nos. 1 and 2, Stravinsky, Schoenberg, Prokofiev No. 1, Hindemith (1939) and *Kammermusik No. 4*, and Berg have not appealed to Heifetz. **But does anyone seriously doubt that he could have performed them masterfully, if he so desired?** It is easy to perceive how the anti-melodic abrasiveness of some of these works would be untempting to the Heifetz musical palate. In any case, the elite violinists have *always* sought out those vehicles that they felt would show them off to best advantage—unlike younger artists who, in the effort to build a career, are often forced to learn and perform works for which, privately, they have little or no affection, merely because the newness of these works will help them to obtain engagements!

In view of his peerless technical equipment, it might seem odd that Heifetz has not exploited the bulk of Paganini's music, the theme-and-variations show-pieces, as well as the concertos. But while Heifetz has never been loath to emphasize his technical superiority, he has not made a fetish or specialty of circus gymnastics, that is, of blatantly flaunting his technique in the service of vaudevillean sensationalism, as have other super-technicians. **He has not had to, inasmuch as his technique-tone production supremacy extends infinitely beyond the confines of simplistic one-dimensional Paganiniana.** But in his four recorded Paganini items, no one has equalled his *Moto Perpetuo*, the melodic grace and suave stylings of Caprices Nos. 13 and 20, or the spine-tingling bravura of the Auer violin-piano setting of Caprice, No. 24. He did perform the Paganini-Wilhemj Concerto in his early career.

PART 4
"THE TRANSCRIBER"

The transcription of short encore pieces from other musical mediums has long been an avocation of violinists, great and small. The practice achieved its greatest popularity in the transcriptions (and pseudo-transcriptions) of Kreisler. Heifetz, also an able pianist, has been the logical successor to Kreisler in this metier, and is said to have made in excess of 150 short violin-piano settings. His transcriptions are well-conceived, bold in instru-

Heifetz, circa 1949.

mental contrivance, and harmonically ingenious. But changing fashion in the make-up of violin recitals has reduced the potential of his success in this field. For the past two or three decades, under the relentless pressure of "purist" academicians, violin recitals have been purged of fun entertainment delicacies, and graduated into joyless, if erudite, affairs. Often four, or even five violin-piano sonatas are programmed, in which a first-rank violinist is paired with a competent, experienced, but essentially lesser rank pianist-accompanist. These chamber music menus are called violin recitals (?). We are constantly warned by the academicians against yielding to the temptation of enjoying sentiment or sentimentality in musical selection via confection pieces— precisely the ingredient that once provided so enchanting a leavening to recital programs *as a balancing supplement to masterworks.*

The transcriptions of Heifetz came into prominence shortly before the new trend became widespread —a trend which has been an important factor in plummeting public interest in violin recitals to a low ebb. But recently, thanks to younger artists like Spivakov, Perlman, Zukerman and Fodor, some of the old showpieces and transcriptions are beginning to appear on the second half of violin recital programs. Hopefully, the best of the Heifetz transcriptions will eventually receive their share of the "play."

Heifetz himself has recorded some 62 of his own violin-piano settings. Most of his transcriptions cannot readily be bandied about by students and non-professionals as can, for example, Kreisler's *Old Refrain.* They are too violinistically demanding, and, *collectively*, are not calculated to equal those of Kreisler in mass saleability.

As with all violin transcribers, the transcriptions strongly reflect the violinistic idiosyncrasies of their creator. In order to creditably perform Heifetz transcriptions, a violinist must have some affinity, however slight, with the Heifetz violinistic vocabulary—con-

Heifetz, circa 1951.

trolled intensity of tone, a knack of negotiating suave (and vibrant) finger slides and position changes, the ability to "sing" in doublestop combinations of every device, and a commanding facility. The artfulness and variety of the Heifetz transcription doublestops and harmonic embellishments rival, and in some instances, even transcend those of Kreisler, and are eminently contemporary in concept—an irrefutable testament to the age in which Heifetz has lived and performed.

Among the most popular are his settings of Godowsky's *Alt-Wien*, a Viennese-type strudel in which Heifetz concocts his own brand of "gemutlichkeit," and the Dinicu *Hora Staccato*, which, in its days of prime popularity, raised the staccato consciousness of violinists everywhere to an acute pitch. Both have been mass audience disc favorites. Also highly favored are the six transcriptions of songs from Gershwin's *Porgy and Bess*, topped by the luscious *Bess, You Is My Woman Now* and the sultry, whimsical *It Ain't Necessarily So*, both prime Heifetz recordings. The Gershwin *Three Preludes* transcriptions are also widely played, and like the *Porgy* selections, have been featured in discs by Soviet players (Kogan, Bezrodny, etc.), demonstrating the geographical extent of the Heifetz influence.

Two Prokofiev transcription records, *Masques* (from *Romeo and Juliet*) and *March in F-minor* are a smidgeon below the Heifetz top standard of performance perfection. But the traditional spiritual, *Deep River*, with its searing G-string and doublestop vibrance, constitutes legendary violin playing, and Albeniz's *Sevillianas*, is a pert, peppery paella. The Ponce *Estrellita* may not exactly "smile" when it twinkles, but the glowing performance reflects an urbane, sophisticated charm. And the Dvorak *Humoresque* again points up the singular Heifetz audacity as, among other ornamental devices, he chooses to incorporate a wide open doublestop fifth in a delicate melodic phrase ending.

If a general revival of violin recital "encore" numbers comes to pass, the Heifetz transcriptions offer a rich potential to enterprising violinists, and in historical perspective, they merit an esteemed niche in their metier.

PART 5
"THE COLLABORATOR"

Historically, the role of the elite virtuoso violinist as a collaborator with other musicians has had more

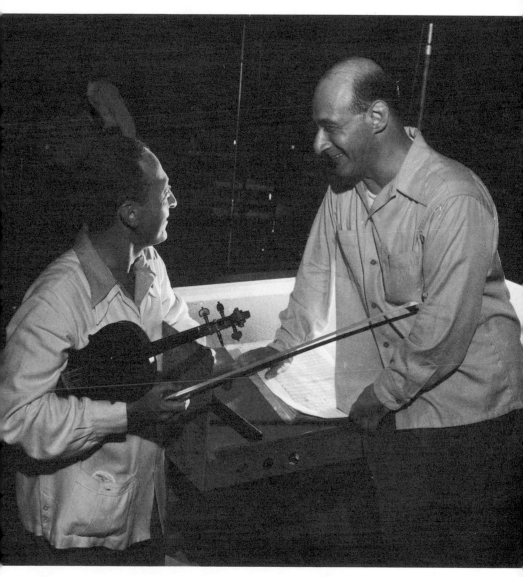

Heifetz with William Steinberg. Circa 1947.

Heifetz recording the Scottish Fantasy of Bruch with
William Steinberg conducting the RCA Symphony
Orchestra. Circa 1947.

"downs" than "ups." Even stellar artists of their day like Spohr and Joachim, both noted for their dedication to serious, cerebrated musicality, had their problems and deficiencies in this medium. Spohr, who wrote a plethora of chamber music works in which he was featured as a sort of soloist with "accompanying" musicians, deemed himself lucky when he could find other professional (or non-professional) musicians who could simply negotiate the notes, as he toured the smaller cities and hamlets of Europe. And he constantly had to bear this in mind and cater to the situation as he composed the music. Judging by statements from his "Autobiography," one can easily imagine the execrable level of many of these performances. **But the significant point is that Spohr admittedly thought of his chamber music compositions as vehicles to be used as a medium through which he could showcase his own talent and technical skills, even when he played with musicians of respectable caliber.** The concept of equalized "team" playing was by no means an unequivocal tenet of his musical commitment.

Karl Flesch says of Joachim's chamber music playing, *"The Joachim Quartet. . . left a great deal to be desired as an ensemble. . . .Altogether the quartet consisted of a solo violin with three instruments accompanying—a style which is diametrically opposed to the aims of our own time's quartet playing. . .".* He describes the instrumental weaknesses of Joachim's partners, Halir, Wirth and Hausmann, and adds, *"The leader's (i.e. Joachim's) personality would indeed have towered above even far greater instrumentalists than were his colleagues."*

Ysaye is described by Flesch as having given an "unforgettable" performance of the Franck Sonata in 1892. The piano collaborator is not even mentioned, a clear implication that the violinist dominated the proceedings. Flesch also tells of a performance in about 1902 of Tchaikovsky's *A Minor Trio,* in which Ysaye *was still in every respect superior to his partners* who

101

were Busoni and Becker. He adds, "Ysaye devoted himself to quartet playing only occasionally, whereas he joined with Raoul Pugno, the extraordinarily musical pianist, in regular performances of sonatas. In this, as in his solo work, he was above all original and creative, limited only by his personality." Again we find the "personality" of a stellar violinist a deleterious factor in collaborative playing.

The famous Heifetz scorn (below) shows his displeasure at being photographed without permission when he played in Beersheba, Israel. After the main portion of the concert, as Heifetz was taking his bows, a fanatic rushed at him with an iron bar and tried to break his violin. Heifetz raised his right hand to protect the fiddle and had it bruised but no bones broken. The protest was over Heifetz playing Richard Strauss, a German composer accused of Nazi connections. The photo on the facing page shows him immediately before the attack.

Kreisler played chamber music in private with Ysaye, Casals, Thibaud, Enesco and other leading artists—as do just about all instrumental stars to this day, as an enjoyable, musically profitable and satisfying avocation. However, the recording of the *Kreisler Quartet in A*, played by *The Kreisler String Quartet* (Kreisler, Petrie, Primrose, Kennedy) made in 1935, reveals Kreisler's chamber music playing to be as highly personalized as anything Heifetz has ever done in that area. And the sonatas he recorded with Rachmaninoff (Grieg No. 3, Schubert Op. 163, Beethoven No. 8), and the complete Beethoven Sonata cycle, recorded with Franz Rupp, though respectful to the spirit of the music, are still exceedingly strong in personalization and, to a considerable degree, stylistic idiosyncrasies.

Mischa Elman organized *The Elman String Quartet*, a group with a fluctuating personnel which performed with serious purpose and amicable rapport. But

Circa 1953

in the final analysis, the ensemble's chief blandishment was the famed "Elman tone," and, of course, his presence.

Later chamber music performances, both live and recorded, featuring such vivid violinistic personalities as D. Oistrakh, Menuhin and Stern, manifest their marked dominance over their collaborating artists in all but a few instances—even when these artists are of excellent calibre.

The crux of the difficulty resides in three elements. First, since at least the heyday of Ysaye (and probably before, even though the extremely personalizing device of the vibrato was still either non-existent or only in the elementary stage of development), **the "Great Personalities of the Violin" have stood above their lesser colleagues by virtue of the individualized violin sound they produce.** Second, is the factor of an individualized style, a manner of playing that makes a unique impression upon, and communicates with the listener, **plus a certain spiritual quality emanating from "within" the artist himself.** Third, **and until comparatively recent times, of lesser importance,** is the matter of musicianship—fidelity to the printed score, the period in which the music was composed, and the general ethos of the music itself. In chamber music, the very existence of the soloist sound-style uniqueness is in itself a definite obstacle to completely equitable collaboration with other musicians—as compared to the equitable balance inherent in first-class concertizing chamber ensembles without individual "stars." The stronger the soloist's individuality, the greater his difficulty in blending with other musicians. And if his musicianship is at all slovenly or too self-indulgent, so much the worse!

Like all "Great Personalities of the Violin," Heifetz, as a chamber music collaborator, has been confronted with these problems. And the number of chamber works that he has recorded for posterity, well exceeds, thus far, the output of any celebrated violinist since the dawn of recorded musical performance. This,

104

Jascha Heifetz (protesting the photograph with a Heifetzian scorn), takes a break with Piatigorsky and Rubinstein while they practiced at the home of Max Epstein. August 29, 1949.

in itself, leaves him particularly vulnerable to criticism as compared to his colleagues. Though his repertoire as a collaborator is sizeable, Heifetz has wisely left the string quartet form to the organized string quartet ensembles, whose players are instrumentally, musically and psychologically attuned to "team" playing and unhampered by the possession of the (necessary) soloist ego.

We must immediately single out the violin-piano sonata and the instrumental duo forms as being in a different category from the forms embracing three or more players. **In the two-artist vehicles, it is possible for two striking musical personalities to fully exercise their individual traits (within reasonable limits, of course) to gainful advantage.** In various violin-piano sonatas,

*While it looks as though Heifetz disagrees with
Piatogorsky's instructions to Rubinstein (facing page),
the "attack" above has never been fully explained!
In any case, the usual Heifetz cool is far from evident!
Circa 1949.*

though Emanuel Bay and Brooks Smith have provided Heifetz with admirable partnership (indeed, I have heard Smith in live performance wax exceedingly feisty), they were still "hired hands" who were not paid to exert their musical personalities in a manner that could in any way "steal the thunder" from their mighty employer. (As if *any* instrumentalist could!)

But if no instrumentalist can steal the thunder from Heifetz, several artists (not violinists, naturally) have manfully "stood up" to Heifetz in collaborations of ex-

Immediately prior to their recording session, Heifetz, Rubinstein and Piatigorsky relax. . . quite in contrast to their stormy (see facing page) rehearsals! Circa 1949.

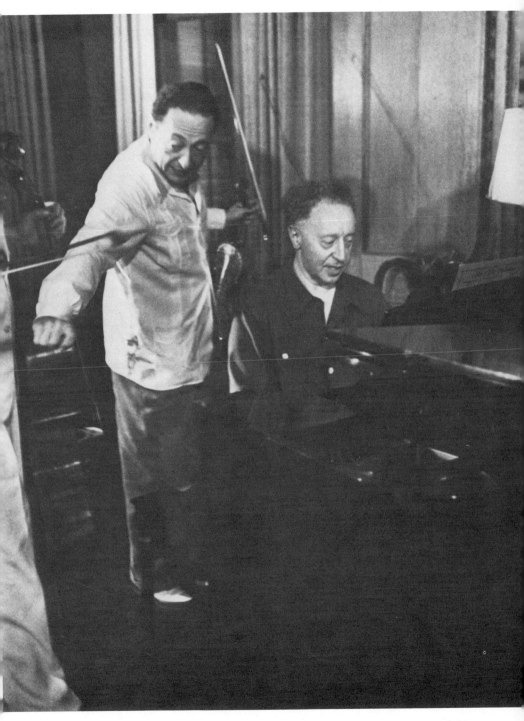

traordinary merit. At least seven duo works register outstanding disc performances. The Franck *Sonata in A,* recorded in 1937 (now on Seraphim Records), with Artur Rubinstein, is a historic performance, full of fire, yet pensively reposed in the poetic Recitativo-Fantasia. The sheer sonal assault of the vibrant violin often thrusts that instrument into the forefront, but the dynamism of Rubinstein tends to keep matters on an even keel. Both personalities are prominently conspicuous and successfully integrated. This Franck recording, incidentally, is quite superior to the Heifetz-Smith "live concert" recording made in 1972. A similar type of relationship is evinced in the 1950 recording with the late pianist, William Kapell, in Brahms' *Sonata No. 3 in D-minor, Op. 108.* It is highly-charged Brahms; the opening Allegro has some over-indulgent violin slides but is nonetheless exciting; the Adagio G-string and doublestop intensity is in the finest Heifetz fettle. Meanwhile, young Kapell refuses to be abashed as he attacks with full strength, articulating and shaping his phrasing to coincide with those of the violin. The engineering, too, is evenly balanced—tempos are brisk, but logical; dynamics, carefully observed.

Two duos with Piatigorsky contain superb virtuosity by both violinist and cellist—choice performances of their type—the eminently rhapsodic Kodaly *Duo for Violin and Cello, Op. 7,* and Martinu's *Duo for Violin and Cello,* with its furious Rondo finale. As the principal collaborator of Heifetz, by virtue of the many discs issued through "The Heifetz-Piatigorsky Concerts," (as well as in live concerts and private musical soirees), Piatigorsky has apparently worked out his own method of coping with the Heifetz phenomenon. In the best of their collaborations, he sturdily asserts his own massive personality, yet, he scrupulously avoids any instrumental slugging matches. His attitude seems to be one of gentle, affectionate, permissive forebearance toward an esteemed, precocious, willful brother.

It is interesting to compare the two recordings of

110

Miklos Rozsa, musical director of the Young Musicians Foundation, is discussing a score with Heifetz at the University of Southern California (Los Angeles). May, 1960.

111

the Brahms *Concerto for Violin and Cello in A-minor, Op. 102*, one made with Emanuel Feuermann in 1939 (Ormandy, Philadelphia Orchestra), the other, with Piatigorsky in 1960 (Wallenstein, RCA Symphony). Feuermann, too, stands his own ground with Heifetz, but like Piatigorsky, avoids conflict. Though Feuermann is not dominated, the general aggressiveness and intense vibrance of Heifetz (the opening G-string theme of the violin in the Andante fairly blazes) invariably precipitates the violin into the foreground. The 1939 version was considered outstanding at the time, but the 1960 discing is both superior as an ensemble performance, and, of course, in the engineering. In contrast with the earlier disc, Heifetz has seemingly mellowed, the Adagio burns a bit less fiercely, and he listens to his partner more intently. And the basic timbre of the Piatigorsky tone is somewhat more in affinity with that of Heifetz than the tone of Feuermann.

*The photographer Myron Davis, associated with
Time-Life Picture Agency, was lucky enough to be
invited to the apartment home of Max Epstein to take
these photographs of the greatest trio the musical world
had known since Casals-Thibaud-Cortot. Circa 1949.*

The publicity shot for the Heifetz-Rubinstein-Piatigorsky recordings issued by RCA. During August, 1950 RCA released the Tchaikovsky Trio in A minor, Opus 50; the Mendelssohn Trio in D minor, Opus 49, and the Ravel Trio in A Minor, Opus 1915. The recordings were received with mixed emotion. None of Heifetz's chamber concerts are as staggering in their greatness as many of his solo performances. Circa 1949.

A particularly convincing collaborator of Heifetz is the great violist, William Primrose, an artist who never "takes a backward step" in any of their performances. Indeed, those ensemble records in which Primrose participates are unusually strong in instrumental balance. The Primrose tone is exceptionally sumptuous in Arthur Benjamin's *Romantic Fantasy for Violin, Viola and Orchestra* (Solomon, RCA Symphony, 1956), a fetching, readily listenable contemporary opus of resplendent instrumental interplay and lush textures, aptly titled. The balance of the orchestra with the solo violin and viola is sometimes less than ideal, but the Heifetz-Primrose match-up is dashing and ornate in sound.

Another exceptional pairing of this duo is in Mozart's *Sinfonie Concertante in E-flat, K. 364*, also with Solomon and the RCA Symphony, 1956. The interpretation is all air and light, the playing, ineffably silken and mercurial. Yes, one can single out occasional unilateral Heifetz slides, or a bravura-type whiplash into a climactic note. And the free-moving Adagio exudes angelic transparency rather than the bittersweet sentiment implied in the music. But for all that, it is a definitive interpretation, and effervescent music-making.

One of the superlative Heifetz performances is the 1941 disc of Chausson's *Concerto for Violin, Piano and Quartet in D. Op. 21*, with pianist Jesus Maria Sanroma and the Musical Art Quartet. The lissome Heifetz style with its ever insinuating nuances, is made to order for this work. There is, however, a certain instrumental imbalance, as Sanroma, a sensitive, conscientious stylist, is too small-scaled an artist to be matched one-on-one with a sovereign instrumentalist like Heifetz, and tends to become part of the background with the quartet. It is unfortunate that Heifetz never recorded it again with a heavyweight pianist like Rubinstein, Kapell or Gilels.

Four of the finest Heifetz chamber music collaborations were recorded in 1941, three with Rubinstein and Feuermann. The Heifetz mannerisms are in low profile in an uncommonly relaxed (for him) version of Beetho-

Piatigorsky, Primrose and Heifetz (left to right) discuss their appointments at the Institute of Special Musical Studies at USC with Dr. Norman Topping, President of the University. Primrose left the faculty very quickly. October, 1971.

ven's *Trio in B-flat, Op. 97 (Archduke)*, a robust Brahms *Trio in B, Op. 8*, and a glistening, yet seductively dulcet reading of Schubert's grateful *Trio in B-flat, Op. 99, D. 898*. The piano and cello are beautifully balanced with the violin, both in performance and engineering. The fourth of this vintage is a *trenchant* performance, unequalled in its brilliance of Dohnanyi's *Serenade in C. Op. 10*, with Primrose and Feuermann, in which Primrose, his tone fervidly vibrant and sonorous, amply demonstrates once again that he was certainly the premier violist of his time.

116

A 1950 recording of Tchaikovsky's *Trio in A-minor, Op. 50*, with Rubinstein and Piatigorsky, has the violin and piano vying heroically for primacy—neither champion inclined to give an inch—with the cello decidedly under-miked. For all that, it contains some epic playing from all three in the grand Slavic manner.

Even in Heifetz's moments of most affable concurrence with his partners, the listener is hard put to forget, throughout every bar and phrase, that he is being wooed by a supreme virtuoso. It is not only the incursiveness of his attack, the singularity of his sound, and his liberal usage of personalized slides and position

Heifetz and Piatigorsky appeared in concert at Hancock Auditorium in April, 1972.

changes, **but the fact that he indiscriminately uses these "Heifetz-y" slides and position changes while his string partners do not—in repetitive and interchanging phrases.** In certain types of music—and according to the degree of such misapplication—the overall group performance is vitiated. Those listeners who are inclined to resent these intrusions will find them particularly overt in the recordings of such transparent works as Boccherini's *Sonata in D for Violin and Cello,* (with Piatigorsky, 1964), Beethoven's *Serenade, Op. 8 (Trio in D,* with Primrose and Piatigorsky, 1960), and Mozart's *Quintette in G-minor, K. 516* (with Primrose, Piatigorsky, Baker and Majewski, 1961). Brahm's *Piano Quartette in C-minor,* though thicker in instrumental texture, also contains more than the norm of these indispositions, albeit the piano performance of Jacob Lateiner, bountiful in color and shadings, deserves special mention (Piatigorsky, Lateiner, Schonbach, 1965).

Three more Heifetz disc ensemble performances merit singling out—the scintillating Mendelssohn *Octette in E-flat major, Op. 20,* in which his personal virtuosity, plus the vigorous, strongly-etched collaboration of his partners, adds up to a performance of surpassing brilliance (with Piatigorsky, Primrose, Baker, Belnick, Stepansky, Majewski, Rejto, 1961); Dvorak's *Piano Quintette in A* (Piatigorsky, Lateiner, Baker, De Pasquale, 1964), a reading of thrilling lyricism; and Mendelssohn's *Trio No. 2 in C-minor, Op. 66* (with Piatigorsky, Pennario, 1963), a buoyantly felicitous romp. These memorable recordings may well set the standard for these works for a long time to come.

A number of additional ensemble performances featuring Heifetz, Piatigorsky and "guests," reflect similar positive and negative features, to one degree or another. Thanks to recordings, future generations will have the privilege of hearing these performances and placing them under microscopic surveilance. And while they may note that Heifetz, the peerless virtuoso, is not the ultimate "team player," time and time again, he

William Primrose (left) with Heifetz, pianist Leonard Pennario and Piatigorsky as they are about to rehearse for a "Summit Meeting of the Strings," held in Hollywood's Pilgrimage Theater. The Pilgrimage is an outdoor bowl suitable for chamber music. August 8, 1961.

creates stunning effects that all the finest "team players" in the world—if rolled up into one—could never achieve. Criticisms aside, had these records never been made, the world of music would be considerably the poorer. (All the above ensemble recordings are by RCA except when otherwise noted).

• • • • •

No violinist who ever lived has been "all things to all men" in every type of music—not Paganini, Joachim, Sarasate, Ysaye, Kreisler, Elman, Oistrakh, Szigeti, Francescatti, Szeryng, Menuhin, Stern, Grumiaux, or any other. But no one ever expected it of them. Only Heifetz has been criticized for not being the embodiment of that "impossible dream." The very demands made upon him by certain critics and observers are in effect a sort of reverse tribute to the man—an admission to his special stature as a violinist. People have come to expect perfection from Heifetz, and where the foibles of other violinists are often overlooked or excused, his tend to be emphasized—another reverse tribute. Expecting Heifetz to never misuse his prodigious gifts is like asking the world's richest man to never exploit the power vested in his wealth—it is too much to ask of any human being.

Does Heifetz "serve the music," or does the music serve him? The totality of his recordings indicate time and time again that the answer is—both. The violinistic and musical style of Heifetz has reflected the spirit of his time and place as vividly as any artist who ever lived, in any medium. He has dared to seek out new violinistic effects, and if they have not been successful in every instance, they are eminently provocative and unique unto himself. His commanding position in the pantheon of violin art is assured.

Meanwhile, let us correct those who sometimes refer to Heifetz as "The Paganini of the 20th Century." More properly, he is "The Heifetz of the 20th Century," and controversies notwithstanding, he is a *nonpareil*.

120

Heifetz and Piatigorsky, circa 1974. This is the most recent photograph of the two together. Piatigorsky died of lung cancer in 1976; one lung was removed in 1975. As a heavy smoker he was always concerned about lung cancer and mentioned it frequently. . . though he continued to smoke heavily.

Dagmar Godowsky, daughter of the composer to Heifetz's right, with Charlie Chaplin and Samuel Chotzinoff to his left, circa 1919.

HEIFETZ

by Jascha Heifetz

This chapter is based upon a series of interviews starting with Heifetz's first in-depth interview in 1918.

I am often asked about practicing. In my early years I did not believe in the "all-work-and-no-play" theory. I do not think I could ever have made any progress if I had practiced six hours a day. In the first place, I never believed in practicing too much. . . it is just as bad as practicing too little! And then there are so many other things I like to do. I am fond of reading, and I like such sports as tennis, golf, bicycle riding, boating, swimming, etc. Often, when I am supposed to be practicing hard, I am out with my camera, taking pictures! I have now become (May, 1918) what is known as a *camera fiend.* And just now I have a new car which I have learned to drive, and which takes up a great deal of my time. I have never believed in grinding. In fact, I think that if one has to work very hard to get a particular piece in shape, it will show in the execution of the piece.

To interpret music properly, it is necessary to eliminate and overcome technical difficulties; the audience should not feel that the artist is struggling with what are considered difficult passages. You must practice the difficult passages more intensively so that they will not be difficult when you execute them before the public.

I hardly ever practice more than three hours a day on an average, and I usually keep my Sundays free, though sometimes, I also take an extra holiday. As to some people saying that I practice six or seven or eight hours a day, that is ridiculous. I would not have been able to live under such circumstances.

Of course, you cannot take me too literally, when I talk about practicing three hours a day. . . or not practicing six or seven hours a day. There are times when you have a new piece, and it is very interesting, and you just want to practice that much. Please do not think that because I do not favor over-practicing, that I can do without ever over-practicing. There are times when a lot of practicing is what you *want* to do, and not what you *have* to do.

However, speaking for myself, I have never found where more than three hours a day was necessary, as far as keeping in condition. There is a happy medium.

I suppose, when I play in public, it looks very easy. It is only very easy because before I ever came to the concert stage, I worked very, very hard. And, of course, practice makes a difficult piece easy.

Practicing for me is a combination of putting two things together. First, I *study* the piece. I call this *mental* work. Then, I start to practice the piece. I call this physical work. I have to combine the two before I reach any goal. And don't forget, when a certain amount of effort is expended in practice, like in everything else, you then have to relax. So even though I may practice three hours a day, it is certainly not three hours consecutively, but rather three hours with frequent intervals for relaxation in between.

As far as technique is concerned, people say that I have a natural technique because it looks as though I did not have to work very hard to get it. *This is not true!* I had to develop it, to assure it, and to perfect it. If you start playing the violin at three, as I did, with a little violin one quarter of the size of a normal violin, I suppose the violin becomes second nature in the course of time. I was able to play in all seven positions within the first year of my playing the violin, and I could play the Kayser Etudes also in that time. But that does not mean to say I was a virtuoso by any means!

My first teacher was my father. He was a good violinist and Concertmaster of the Vilna Symphony Orchestra in Lithuania. I made my first appearance in public in an overcrowded auditorium of the Imperial

Heifetz, circa 1974.

124

Music School in Vilna, when I was not quite five. I played the Fantaisie Pastorale with piano accompaniment. Later, when I was six years old, I played the Mendelssohn Concerto in Kovno, also to a full house.

I did not have any stage fright when I appeared at these concerts. As a matter of fact, I never had stage fright. Of course, something might have happened to upset me before a concert, and perhaps there are times that I did not feel quite at ease when I first got on the stage. Such things might have to do with changes in time, not sleeping or not eating properly, or having an upset stomach, but I certainly would not call it "stage fright."

At the Royal School of Music in Vilna, and before that time, I worked at all the things every violinist studied. I think that I played almost everything! I did not work too hard, but I worked hard enough. After I left my father's teaching, I began studying with Ilya Davidovitch Malkin, who was a student of Prof. Auer.

I graduated from the music school when I was still only seven years old! Since Malkin was a pupil of Prof. Leopold Auer when I graduated from the Vilna School, Malkin took me to play for Auer. I was not immediately accepted to Prof. Auer's class as many people think. I had to wait a little while before Auer finally accepted me as his *personal* student.

Prof. Auer was a wonderful and incomparable teacher. I do not believe that there is any teacher in the world who could possibly approach him. Don't ask me how he did it, for I would not know how to tell you, for he is completely different with each student. Perhaps that is one reason that he was such a great teacher. I think that I was with Prof. Auer about six years. I had both class lessons and private lessons from him, though towards the end, my lessons were not very regular. I never played exercises or technical works of any kind for the Professor, but outside of the big things—the Concertos and Sonatas, and the shorter featured pieces which he would let me prepare, I often chose what I wanted.

126

During World War I, Prof. Leopold Auer took his better students to Norway for a musical holiday. Standing, left to right: Eddie Brown, Jascha Heifetz, Max Rosen, Toscha Seidel and an unidentified young lady. Circa 1915.

Prof. Auer was a very active and energetic teacher. He was never satisfied with a mere explanation, unless certain it was understood. He could always demonstrate for you by picking up his own violin and bow, and playing. He was very talented. The Professor's pupils were supposed to have been sufficiently advanced in technic that they only had to depend upon the Professor for his wonderful lessons in interpretation. Yet, there were all sorts of technical finesses which he always had up his sleeve; any number of fine, subtle points in playing, as well as in interpretation, which he would disclose to his students as it became necessary. What was very important was that the more interest and ability the pupil showed, the more the Professor gave of himself. He was a very great teacher!

Heifetz, circa 1946.

Take bowing, for example. The true art of bowing is one of the greatest things in Prof. Auer's teachings. I know that when I first came to the Professor, he showed me things in bowing that I had never learned in Vilna. It is hard to describe in words how I am able to hold my right arm so high with unstrained movements of the arm and the wrist, but I suppose you can see it as you watch me play.

But bowing, as Prof. Auer teaches it, is a very special thing. The movements of the bow become easier, much more graceful and less stiff.

In Prof. Auer's class, there were usually between twenty-five and thirty students. While we each gained individually from the Professor's criticisms and corrections, it was interesting to hear the others who played before your turn came. Then, we would get all kinds of hints from what Prof. Auer told them. I know I always enjoyed listening to Poliakin, a very talented violinist, and Cecile Hansen, who attended the classes at the same time I did. The Professor was a stern, strict, and very exacting teacher, but at the same time, he was very sympathetic. If our playing was not just what it should be, he always had a fund of kindly humor upon which to draw. He would anticipate our stock excuses and say: "Well, I suppose you have just had your bow rehaired!" Or, "These new strings are very trying" or "It's the weather that's against you again, is it not?" Or something like that.

Prof. Auer's examinations were not easy. We had to show that we were not only soloists, but also sight readers of difficult music.

It is very difficult for me to tell you that one technical difficulty was more of a problem for me than another. I do know that I had trouble playing staccato. To get a good staccato, when I first tried, seemed very difficult when I was in my 'teens. Really, at one time I had a very poor staccato. But then one morning, I do not know just how it was, I was playing the cadenza in the first movement of Wieniawski's F-sharp minor Con-

Eugene Fodor won the top Tchaikovsky Prize in Moscow, 1974. In the final round he played both the Tchaikovsky and Sibelius violin concerti. He studied both concerti with Heifetz. Along with Erick Friedman, Fodor gained international recognition as a virtuoso student of Heifetz.

130

certo. It is full of staccatos and double stops, the right way of playing staccato came to me quite suddenly, especially after Prof. Auer had shown me his method. (Eugene Fodor, one of Heifetz' top soloist students, remarked that during his lessons Heifetz would always make him play staccatos for fifteen minutes, while the Maestro slowly circled him, studying his technic for down-bow staccato carefully, so he could teach it to other students. Heifetz insisted he play the very same cadenza in the Wieniawski Concerto from which he himself learned staccato. This is evidence of Heifetz' dedication and seriousness as a teacher. Fodor is, of course, famous for his execution of the up-bow and down-bow staccato.)

To master the violin means, to me, the ability to make the violin a perfectly controlled instrument, guided by the skill and intelligence of the artist to compel it to respond in movements to his every wish. The artist must always be superior to his instrument. It must be his servant, one that he can do with what he will.

It appears that mastery of the technique of the violin is not so much of a mechanical accomplishment as it is of a mental nature. It may be that scientists can tell us how, through persistency, the brain succeeds in making the fingers and arm produce results with an infinite variety of inexplicable vibrations. The sweetness of tone, its melodiousness, its legatos, octaves, trills, and harmonics, all bear the mark of the individual who uses the strings on his violin like his own vocal chords. When an artist is working over his harmonics, he must not be impatient and force purity, pitch or the right intonation. He must coax the tone, trying it again and again, seeking for improvements in his fingering as well as his bowing at the same time.

Sometimes, he may be surprised how, quite suddenly, at the time when he least expects it, the results arrive! More than one road leads to Rome!!

The fact is that when you get it, you have it, that's all!! I am perfectly willing to disclose to the musical pro-

131

fession all the "secrets" of the mastery of violin technique, but are there any "secrets" in the sense that some of the uninitiated take them? If an artist happens to excel in some particular skill, he is at once suspected to knowing some "secret" means of doing so. However, that may not be the case. He does it just because it is in him, and as a rule, he accomplishes this through his mental faculties more than through his mechanical abilities. I do not intend to minimize the value of great teachers who prove to be important factors in the life of a musician; but think of the vast army of pupils that a master teacher brings forth, and listen to the infinite variety of their spiccatos, octaves, legatos and trills!

For the successful mastery of violin technique, let each artist study carefully his own individuality, let him concentrate his mental energy on the quality of pitch he intends to produce, and sooner or later he will find his way of expressing himself. Music is not only in the fingers or in the elbow. It is in the mysterious *ego* of the man; it is his soul; and his body is like his violin. . . nothing but a tool.

Of course, the great master must have the tools that suit him best, and it is the happy combination that makes for success.

Each individual violinist may be recognized by the vibrations and modulations of the notes, as easily as people can be recognized by their voices. Who can explain how the artist harmonizes the trilling of his fingers with the emotions of his soul? The way my violin sounds is the way I feel inside. It is a very personal feeling. A great artist will never become great through mere imitation, and never will he be able to obtain the best results only by methods adopted by others. He must use his own initiative, although he will surely profit by the experience of others. Of course, there are standard ways of approaching the study of violin technique, but they are too well known to dwell upon them here. But the niceties of the art, that which separates good violinists from great violinists, that must come from within. You can make a *violinist,* but you cannot make an *artist!*

132

The late Jack Benny playing a duet with Jascha Heifetz. August 17, 1942.

Critics are always directing their attention to repertory and programs. Every violinist, of course, likes to play those works which they like the best. Each work has its own beauties. Naturally, one likes best what one understands best. I prefer to play the classics, like Brahms, Beethoven, Mozart, Bach, Mendelssohn, etc. However, I played Bruch's G-minor in 1913 at the Leipzig Gewandhaus with Nikish, where I was told that Joachim was the only other violinist as young as myself to appear there as soloist with the orchestra.

133

Then there is the Tchaikovsky Concerto which I played in Berlin in 1912 with the Berlin Philharmonic Orchestra, also under Nikish. Also Bruch's G-minor and many more. I played the Mendelssohn Concerto in 1914 in Vienna with Safonoff as conductor. Last season (1917) I played the Brahms Concerto in Chicago with a very fine and elaborate cadenza by Prof. Auer. I think the Brahms Concerto for violin is like Chopin's music for piano, in a way, because it stands technically and musically for something quite different and distinct from other violin music. Chopin does this for piano music. The Brahms Concerto is not technically as hard as, say, Paganini, but in interpretation, it is of course much more complex.

I find a simplicity in the Beethoven Concerto, a kind of clear beauty which makes it far harder to play than many other things technically more advanced. The slightest flaw, the least difference in pitch, in intonation, and its beauty suffers.

Of course, there are some Russian concertos besides the Tchaikovsky. There is the Glazounov and others. I understand that Zimbalist was the first to introduce it in this country, and I expect to play it here next season.

Of course, I cannot only play concertos, and I cannot always play Bach or Beethoven. And that's what makes it so hard to select programs. The artist can *always* enjoy the great music of his instrument, but an audience wants variety. At the same time, an artist cannot play only just what the majority of the audience wants. I have been asked to play Schubert's *Ave Maria* or Beethoven's *Chorus of the Dervishes* at every one of my concerts, but I simply cannot play them *all the time*. I'm afraid if program-making were left altogether to audiences, the programs would become far too popular in character. But then too, audiences are just as different as individuals.

I try hard to balance my programs, so that everyone can find something to understand and enjoy. I expect to prepare some American compositions for next

134

season (that would be 1919). Oh, no, not as a matter of courtesy, but because they are really fine, especially some smaller pieces by Spalding, Cecil Burleigh, and Grasse.

However much my life seems to be dedicated to music, and however much I love music, I cannot help feeling that music is not the only thing in life. I really cannot imagine anything more terrible than always to hear and think and make music! There is so much else to know and appreciate, and I feel that the more I learn and know of other things, the better artist I will be.

Mrs. Frances, son Jay and Father Jascha bid the photographer farewell in this public relations photo. September 8, 1952.

MY FAVORITE VIOLIN
by Jascha Heifetz

While it is not, of course, true to say that a good violin makes a good violinist, there is some relationship between the two. Even the best players would be severely handicapped by a poor instrument, just as a pianist would be by an inferior piano. Moreover, they have their preferences for particular kinds of instruments, just as pianists have. That is not difficult to

Heifetz with his Guarnerius del Gesu, circa 1940.

Heifetz with his Strad and del Gesu in a double case, circa 1960.

understand when one considers how enormously violins differ in tone and everything else. For some years I had a Stradivarius, and it seemed all that I desired, yet the time came when I longed for a Guarnerius, which I thought would suit me better still. I play one of these today.

But let me go back to the beginning, which, I am afraid, means going back to a very early age, for I was only three years old when I began to play the violin. I do not say that everyone should begin so young as that, but in my case it has apparently done no harm. My instrument at that time was quarter size, a thing of a few inches in length, yet quite large enough for me to shoulder.

My father gave me my first lessons, and though I do not remember being made to practice, I think there were times when I would have preferred something more playful. Let us say that my father "persuaded" me to practice; and I am glad that he did.

For my first public appearance at the age of seven, I was promoted to a half-size in violins. Two years later I was given a three-quarter size instrument, and at 13 I became the proud possessor of a violin of full regulation size.

But if I had reached the top of the tree in that respect I had not in others. I longed for an instrument made by one of those master craftsmen whose art has been for centuries the envy of the world, and probably always will. But the price of them! And the difficulty of finding them!

When I made my debut in New York, I was using a Tononi. Very soon afterwards I had a romantic stroke of fortune. Someone who had admired my playing came to see me and told me that he had a Stradivarius, which he would be pleased to lend me, and I could retain it as long as I liked.

In 1937 Jascha Heifetz bought a Stradivarius violin for $30,000. This same violin is worth more than $250,000 today.

138

I thanked him most gratefully, and for a long time I used this instrument at all my concerts. It was magnificent, as every Strad is, and I was proud to have the privilege of playing on it. After two years I decided that I could not continue to avail myself of the lender's generosity, and as the means made it possible, I bought the instrument.

Time passed, and then I gradually began to feel that, wonderful as the Strad was, my style of playing, my individuality, would be suited better by a Guarnerius. I felt that this would give me more power, more tone, and in a hundred subtle ways, respond more perfectly to my moods and temperament. But Guarnerius violins are more rare today than Strads, for the number made was two or three hundred fewer.

My father kept a lookout for one in Germany, and at last he was able to send a telegram to me in New York that he had been successful. I telegraphed back that if I was satisfied with it after seeing it I would buy it. The next time I was in Germany I saw the Guarnerius and became its owner.

It is dated 1742, and had lain in a family safe for several years. It was once in the possession of Wilhelmj, a great violinist, who arranged some of Chopin's Nocturnes for the violin, as well as Schubert's *Ave Maria*. Ferdinand David, another famous musician, also possessed this instrument at one time, and, in fact, it is named after him.

Another essential for a violinist is a good bow. I keep seven or eight in use, including a Kittel, presented to me by Professor Auer, my former tutor.

I am often asked whether I consider that English people are musical. Let me relate a story. During one of my recent visits I was lunching with a leading novelist and I suggested that afterwards we should go to a cer-

Heifetz with his pride and joy, the Guarnerius del Gesu of 1742. This violin has a current value of $500,000.

142

tain concert. He stared aghast at me, said he did not care much for music, and would prefer to be excused.

But I pressed him, and he went. He was frankly bored by the first item, faintly interested in the second, "sitting up" to hear the third, and all agog with enthusiasm for the fourth. He was cured, I hope, of his dislike for music, and is now, I believe, one of its admirers.

A story, to close with, of how I was once offered a big contract in Paris. I was in one of the humbler cafes of the French capital one evening, when it was suggested that I should give a violin solo. I did not want to do so, but the leader of the orchestra came and offered to lend me his violin. He asked me if I knew any of Chopin's Nocturnes? I pretended that I was ignorant of them, whereupon he went into ecstacies concerning their beauties.

At the end of his discourse I said I would play Schubert's *Ave Maria.* I think I created an impression, for the manager afterwards offered me a hundred francs a night to stay!

Luthier Koodlach repairing one of Heifetz's fiddles! Heifetz is so attached to his Guarnerius del Gesu of 1742, that he has refused all offers to sell it and has kept it close to him at all times. The attachment that violinists have for their instruments is closer, in many cases, than they might have to another human being. Guarnerius del Gesu owners usually treat their instruments reverently.

In 1934 Heifetz returned to Russia for a concert tour.
He said that he found his original quarter-size fiddle in
Russia at his Uncle's house! May 10, 1934.

144

DR. JEKYLL AND MR. HEIFETZ
by Constance Hope, Publicity Manager

From *Publicity is Broccoli*, copyright 1941 (renewed 1969).

Jascha Heifetz doesn't need anybody to tell the world how great he is. He has been doing just that, and quite convincingly too, with his own two hands and a fiddle, since he was seven. Lunching with a group of friends one day he casually mentioned that he has been earning his own living ever since, and Harpo Marx, a very fast man with a gag at all times, turned to him and snapped: "And I suppose before that you were just a bum!"

Standing on the very pinnacle of success, he is the dream come true of every young musician who ever drew a bow or blew a breath. A prodigy of fantastic talent in childhood, he is a supreme artist in maturity. About him clings every appurtenance of success— jammed concert halls, his fabled Stradivarius and Guarnerius, a charming and famous wife and two lovely children, a sprawling handsome country place, a collection of first editions, a beautiful boat, and all about him witty and gay friends.

Is it any wonder that the layman is often surprised to learn that an artist of Heifetz' stature retains a publicity representative? It's unquestionably true that a successful artist can seldom dispense with a publicity representative of some sort. In the first place, it is said representative's job to guard against that bugbear of everyone in public life—being misquoted. Secondly, there may be a certain impression of himself and his work which the artist wants conveyed to the public, or which his publicity adviser feels it is desirable to convey. And finally, the representative may be on hand for a little pure and simple space-grabbing. All three are important.

The greater the person, the greater his need for someone who will act as a liaison for him in his dealings with press and public. Even President Roosevelt has his Steve Early.

A friend of mine who learned that I had sold Jascha Heifetz on retaining me to handle his press relations sneered, "There's a tough job for you. All you have to do is explain to the people how Heifetz manages to take a bow and fiddle, make it look so easy, and sound so good."

He was wrong. Our problem was in a subtler and more delicate field of public relations. I considered it my job to spike the persistent but completely unfounded legend that Jascha Heifetz is cold.

Now this is a very peculiar legend because audiences all over the world have been throwing their hats over the flagpole every time Heifetz lifts a bow ever since Teddy Roosevelt was beating various and sundry corporations over the head with a big stick.

It is even more peculiar in view of the fact that to hundreds of our best people Heifetz is a host at parties, and a practical joker of note. He will also drop everything but a Mozart concerto to whale the tar out of unsuspecting guests at ping-pong. In fact the only time his famous poker face is in evidence off the stage is when Mother No. 4,978 begins that famous conversational *faux pas:* "Mr. Heifetz, if you would only listen to my Jerome, for just one number ————."

The people who are most amused at the "cold Heifetz" legend are his fellow musicians and his intimates. Those who were fortunate enough to attend a now-celebrated gala in the tiny theatre atop the Chanin Building a year or two ago have a vivid recollection of a perspiring figure, garbed in short trousers (above the knee) and a Buster Brown collar, fiddling away for dear life while the audience howled. It was Heifetz, playing his part in a travesty based on life in the Chatham Square Music School, in which Toscanini himself played a part, by the way. And others, who have attended parties sponsored by deserving charities, and found Heifetz rigged up in some outlandish garb auctioning off rare treasures with more vigor than skill, can't entertain the thought that J.H. is a cold one without laughing at the idea.

146

Left to right: Michael Yurkevitch, Heifetz and Luthier Rosenthal. Seven American violinmakers sent violins to Heifetz when he had a contest for determining who made the best fiddles in America. The contest was held in 1942 at the offices of Rudolph Wurlitzer in New York. The judges included Heifetz, Jay C. Freeman, a connoisseur, and Sascha Jacobson, a violinist. Yurkevitch's violin was judged to be the best for tone, workmanship and accuracy of measurement. It was a full-size copy of a Guadagnini made in Milano, Italyin 1747. Rosenthal took third prize while B.F. Phillips of Pittsburgh took second place.

Heifetz and wife Frances posing for a publicity shot in 1938.

Ever since Heifetz crawled out from behind velvet pants and a quarter-sized fiddle, he has been the big moment of any gal who could tell Bach from Palestrina. But it wasn't until the summer of 1925, when I made my first trip to Europe, that I actually met the great man. In one of those delightfully accidental meetings (it had taken me two days to plan it), I was talking to Isidor Achron, Heifetz' accompanist at that time, when the violinist came over and joined us. They soon turned aside and began an animated conversation in Russian, unaware, of course, that I was brought up in a Russian-speaking household and understood what they were saying.

I eavesdropped with increasing indignation, for Heifetz inquired: "I say, Isidor, who's that girl?" "Oh, a friend of mine from New York. Nice little thing, isn't she?" (I was furious at this, fancying myself at sixteen a grown-up young lady.) "She's not my type," said Heifetz critically. Then the two of them began to appraise me in earnest, discussing my good and bad points like a couple of New York State farmers sizing up a prize Holstein at a county fair.

Presently Heifetz left for fairer company. I turned to Achron and said in vindictive Russian: "Humph! A fine way to talk in front of a young girl."

Achron's jaw dropped. Then he scurried across the deck after Heifetz. "Hey, Jascha, she knows Russian!" Achron gasped, and the two of them collapsed against a lifeboat, suffocating with laughter.

Many people, though, whose only contact with the violinist has been at bow's length across the footlights, labor under the delusion that his natural reserve indicates a lack of emotion. This fact was uppermost in our minds about four years ago when Heifetz' then personal representative, Rudy Polk, approached us on the subject of publicizing Heifetz.

We felt that it was unfortunate that the public should have such an erroneous impression of this great artist. For this reason, as soon as we took over the ac-

Heifetz prepares for a tennis game before he departs for Israel. May 5, 1950.

150

count we resolved to present Jascha Heifetz to the musical public as the charming, gay and vigorous person that he really is.

If you're past the age that thinks Lana Turner is the first Hollywood glamour girl, you undoubtedly know that Heifetz is married to the former Florence Vidor, the screen star. They have two delightful children, Josepha and Bobby, whose pictures invariably turn out to look like magazine covers (and Jascha just as invariably refuses to let them be photographed).

When I saw the impeccable Mr. Heifetz in his California home, sailing a boat in as disreputable a pair of dungarees as ever graced a forecastle, making a soapbox auto for Bobby, or playing the accordion at a beach barbecue, I realized that this was just what Dr. Gallup ordered. I knew that a candid picture layout on life *chez* Heifetz was just my dish. I also knew that news-hungry feature editors would drool delightedly over the picture of a million dollars worth of talent frying an oyster.

But, as happened more than once in the early stages of our association, I had reckoned without Mr. Heifetz. More than once I was to sit down glumly holding my barked shins because of the perverse streak in his nature which prevents even a genuine dyed-in-the-wool swami from predicting what his reaction to a given situation or project will be.

And not infrequently Mr. Heifetz, with Machiavellian glee, would hold out on me. Weeks after he had done something that was good for space in the papers when it happened, he would tell me about it in an offhand way. What made me furious was that he always seemed to be smiling when he told me about it.

For Mr. Heifetz, it might be inserted for the record, has a mind of his own. And one paradoxical fact about this man of many paradoxes is that although he is extremely warm and frank with his friends, with the general public he feels that certain things, such as his family life, his hobbies, his interests off the concert stage, are of no great interest to anyone but his immediate circle of friends.

Jascha's father, Rubin Heifetz, was the boy's first teacher, in Russia. Among other things which the elder Heifetz impressed on his gifted son was this: It is undignified and rather cheap showmanship for an artist to let his face express anything while he is playing. Let the violin convey the emotions you feel, said Heifetz pere; and Jascha learned his lesson well.

In line with his feeling that all his musical emotions should be expressed through his violin, Heifetz believes that so far as the public is concerned, the artist should be in full evening dress at all times. He doesn't think it is of too much importance to his listeners that he has a farm in Connecticut and is fond of sailing a boat. He sees no particular reason why anyone should be interested in the fact that he likes to use his valuable hands for sharpening an ax or digging in the garden. The main thing, he feels, is that the hands perform properly when he steps out on the concert stage.

Now let me ask *you* a question: Did I get my candid shots of Heifetz at play? Answer: It took me two years to do it—but I did it.

The funny thing about it is that once Heifetz did drop his reserve on the concert stage, and it happened accidentally. He was once engaged to play a concert in Philadelphia at the debut of a conductor in the Robin Hood Dell. When he arrived at the Dell, he found his conductor with a Grade A case of nerves.

Heifetz knew the young conductor had a fine talent, but it was immediately obvious to him that the cause of the nerves was overanxiety to have everything go right in his debut with the men of the Philadelphia Orchestra and with Heifetz. Jascha turned on all of his famous charm to put the young conductor at his ease— he told amusing stories, trotted out all the gags he knew, even mimicked the great conductors to illustrate to his young conductor what not to do. His gay mood infected the young conductor, who relaxed and began to enjoy
152

A typical Heifetz stance during a concert, circa 1951.

himself. Heifetz did such a good job in getting the conductor in a good mood that when the time came to go
onstage, he himself walked on still smiling at a final bit
of horseplay. The mood of conductor and soloist quickly
spread itself across the footlights, and the evening's concert was a sensation.

Heifetz carries the question of secrecy about his
personal likes and dislikes to rather peculiar lengths.
Leonard Lyons, Broadway columnist of the New York
Post, tells this characteristic story about Heifetz. The
violinist had arrived from California a few days before
and was riding in a taxi with his brother-in-law, S.N.
Behrman, the playwright. One of Behrman's plays had

153

Heifetz and son Jay, with Mrs. Frances Heifetz, at their home in Beverly Hills, California. January 13, 1949.

*Heifetz gives Jay his first lessons on October 10, 1951.
Jay did learn to play the violin, but he never achieved
any degree of proficiency. The violin seems too large for
Jay!*

just opened the week before. To make conversation, Behrman politely asked Heifetz if he had seen any plays since he had been in town. Jascha gave him a quizzical look and then answered softly: "Wouldn't you like to know?"

One of the musical experiences that must be gone through to be enjoyed is to sit through a Heifetz concert alongside a good violinist, and watch his face. He will sit first in enthusiasm, then amazement, and finally in goggle-eyed wonder as Heifetz rips off tricky cadenzas as if they were light airy trifles. I don't think Jascha has ever played a less-than-perfect concert in his life. He has a deep and passionate sincerity in his music-making that makes careless playing a crime of the first order.

He carries that same sincerity over into his outside life, and it can be another source of trouble for his publicity representative. He will never sign a ghosted article. It must always be "by Jascha Heifetz as told to Joseph Doques." If his name goes on a story, it must be something which he has written in its entirety. This, of course, flouts all the traditions. It is enough to get a man thrown out of the "Publicity Employers Protective Association," because Rule Three of the code says that an artist must never acknowledge that at any moment he cannot sit down and whip up a three or four thousand word bit of whimsy on any subject at all. It was also a handicap to some extent with the magazines, for Jascha's name on an article is a strong selling point.

And it was our conviction at that stage in Jascha's career that articles in national magazines would be of more value from the standpoint of prestige than almost anything else we could do. For that reason we concentrated to some extent on national magazine publicity.

Even the old lady in Dubuque must know that a good many of the stories in our national magazines are publicity inspired. Most of our captains of industry or ball players, or tennis stars, or even senators do not tie themselves to their dens at regular intervals to produce articles that are the joy of editors. A good many are

Heifetz told Benno Rabinoff that violinists should always be happy! Benno said to Heifetz: "Jascha, aren't you happy when you play? You never seem to smile!" "Benno, every violinist should be happy when he plays. He should be happy because he's playing well. If he's not playing well, he should be happy because it will soon be over!" Circa 1958.

ghosted, a large part are inspired by the editors (and then ghosted), and a fair share come from the minds of publicity men. The usual approach to these not unimportant media is to think up an "angle" (involving our client of course) and then suggest it as a possibility to one of the numerous free-lance writers who make a specialty of doing magazine articles. The free-lancer then submits an outline to editors of various magazines, who either toss the writer out or invite him to submit a completed article.

This procedure is standard. Sometimes a writer will get his own angle, and approach you for material on your client. Or, in rare cases, the magazine itself will ask you for information. As a general rule, however, magazine articles, especially stories about a personality, are inspired.

For instance, *Harper's Magazine* was interested in an interview with Jascha, called "Radio—American Style," based on Heifetz as a radio artist here and abroad. *Life* did a picture story on "Music Under the Stars," basing the story on Jascha's appearance in the Lewisohn Stadium; and a story on amateur participation in music by Jascha Heifetz as told to George Albee won the seal of approval from *Good Housekeeping*.

Jascha is no respecter of the anguish of a publicity man seeing a good story going to waste. When he is intensely interested in a cause, he often forbids me to capitalize on it from a publicity standpoint. For example, Heifetz sponsored a contest for violin makers. He believed that by establishing the reputations of a number of first-class violin makers in this country, he would not only perform a notable service for music, but would serve to encourage the development of skilled American workmen. Heifetz believed so deeply in the cause and felt so sincerely that it was a good thing for America, that he was desperately afraid that someone would think it was just a publicity stunt. He gave me blunt and categorical orders to keep my ink-stained fingers off the contest. I averted my eyes in horror and did what I was told—but I will never be the same, even though he finally permitted me to announce the results of the contest.

One of the most important factors in any successful publicity campaign is a complete understanding between you and your client. You're stymied until the client is convinced that you're not completely mad every time you make a suggestion, and that there are valid reasons for everything you do. Often it is months before such an understanding is reached.

As time passed and Jascha came to a better understanding of what our goal was in handling his publicity our task became progressively easier. On our part, we were better able to anticipate his reaction to any given situation and were therefore better able to speak authoritatively for him. For example, we know that Jas-

Heifetz with wife Frances and son Jay, late 1952.

cha is usually sympathetic to any project where children are concerned. One day, we learned that the Children's Aid Society was sponsoring a "freckles" contest at one of their settlements. Jascha's picture, *They Shall Have Music*, had just opened, and he was due East for a Lewisohn Stadium concert. The Children's Aid was tickled at the thought of having Heifetz for a judge. We wired him and to our delighted astonishment a wire shot back from Jascha saying he was flying in for the contest. And fly in he did, alighting from the plane carrying a huge magnifying glass which, he gravely assured us, was the only scientific method of judging a freckled-face contest. We quickly finished our publicity photos and turned to leave, but not Mr. Heifetz. The last time we saw him that afternoon he was buying ice-cream cones all around and having the time of his life. And that with a taxing performance of the Beethoven violin concerto scheduled for the same evening.

A good illustration of how happily this understanding between client and publicity representative can work happened another time when Jascha was interviewed in Chicago, where he had gone for a concert appearance. As part of our regular advance publicity, we had sent announcements and press books to all the papers. A press book, you may recall, is a mimeographed folder of material about your artist, including a dozen or more stories of general interest that can be used anywhere.

Included among them was a story in which Heifetz made several very innocuous statements about the audience's participation in a concert. The story had been making the rounds of all the tour towns that year, and nobody had been very excited about it.

In preparing for the interview we had suggested, however, the Chicago reporter had seen something in the story which gave him an idea. He interviewed Heifetz and the next day a darn good piece, "Hiss Me If You Don't Like Me, Says Heifetz," was in the Chicago paper and being flashed from coast to coast via wire services

Heifetz, circa 1953.

and the syndicates. The reporter's obvious interest in the subject had roused Jascha's also, and in this enthusiasm he had given a rattling good interview. But despite my most earnest protestations, Jascha has remained convinced that I had engineered the whole thing—one of the few times a client has given me more credit than was due.

I have always felt that it is a mistake to oversell a client on the things your publicity service can or cannot do. To take one vivid example, if you have ten people doing publicity for you, they can't get you good notices about your concerts unless you yourself have the goods. I prefer to tell the client this, very frankly, and also to warn him in advance that there may be certain bitter pills which he will have to swallow. Once this is made clear, it is easier for him to understand your objectives. He can realize that every picture and every story which goes out from your office, no matter how large or how small, is part of a general picture which you are creating in the public's mind. Little by little the mosaic of picture layouts, features, canned-outlet stories and news items fits together until at last you can present a smooth picture of your client which you feel shows him to best advantage.

Often a good part of a public-relations job can be accomplished simply by telling the client himself of some unconscious error in human relations, rather than by spadework in the field. Sometimes you may wear your knuckles raw on editors' doors simply because your client has unconsciously put himself in the wrong light with press and public. I have seen a campaign which failed to click simply because a certain prima donna adopted an over-arrogant air to cover up her feeling of inferiority. If your client, without meaning to, makes the newspaper boys sore, your picture and story material are useless unless you can spot the trouble.

One day we approached Heifetz with an idea for a story. In fear and trembling I told Jascha the title now used as the subtitle of this chapter. Instead of showing his annoyance, he grinned and told us that we had his unqualified approval.

Then, somewhat to our surprise, he revealed that he was aware of the poker-face legend and that he approved of the steps we had been taking to overcome it.

An ink stain on a sofa in my living room is a reminder of another facet of Heifetz' personality that we, in our publicity activities, have sought to bring across to the American public. For in my apartment one wintry day two years ago Jascha had his first and only mass interview with the scholastic press.

Heifetz, Rubinstein and Feuermann, circa 1941.

The students of today are the concert audiences of tomorrow, and consequently we maintain close touch with the editors of hundreds of high-school and college publications throughout the country. In New York City alone there are more than fifty such journals, and on the

Standard Oil Company had three teen-age guests (without their mothers!!!) spending a "Weekend with Music" in New York City. Heifetz greeted the youngsters after his performance at Carnegie Hall. From left to right: Dorothy Satcher, Carson City, Nevada; Priscilla Steele, Wellesley, Massachusetts and Ralph Ladnier of Biloxi, Mississippi. March 28, 1949.

afternoon that Jascha received the scholastic press there were about sixty reporters present. Which makes me think that there might have been a couple of ringers there too, just for the opportunity to visit with the great man.

I remember the afternoon well, because it was one of the few times I arrived late for an appointment with a client. But late I was, and when I rang the doorbell of my apartment Jascha himself answered it. He had arrived early and had been receiving the visitors—ushering them in from the foyer, providing chairs, and making them comfortable. It wasn't until I introduced him that the majority of the kids knew that it was Heifetz who had been serving as the receptionist.

Even though he didn't show it, Jascha was as nervous as a cat, more so, I'll wager, than at any concert he's ever given. Yet the kids took to him from the start. He gave straightforward answers to straightforward questions, and believe me, there were no holds barred. Jascha held his own, for the most part, but one or two questions really floored him.

He groped for words when one persistent youngster calmly inquired if Heifetz was satisfied with himself, but recovered long enough to answer with a flustered smile, "How do you think *I'm* going to answer that?"

He shook his head mournfully when another reporter asked him how his children felt about having him for a father, and finally replied, "They'll probably soon express themselves on that point."

The final question was a portent of things to come.

"And how, Mr. Heifetz, do you feel about autograph hounds?" queried one young miss, fumbling innocently in her purse.

"I feel fine, so far," smiled Jascha complacently.

It was like a prearranged signal. I can still see Jascha, surrounded by a milling group of youngsters, each with a fountain pen and pad, eyes alight, with the scent of the kill in their nostrils—and Jascha, grinning like a schoolboy, harassed but happy.

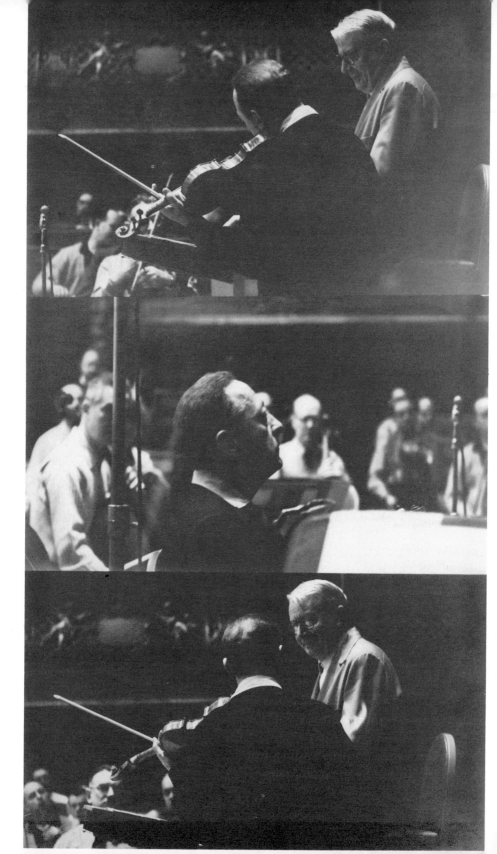

A JASCHA HEIFETZ
Discography

compiled by John Anthony Maltese

In the following discography I have listed only those recordings by Jascha Heifetz which have been released publicly, either through major recording companies, or through private sources. Of the latter, mention should be made of a new Rococo release, No. 2071, the contents of which were not known when the discography proper was prepared. It includes a new pressing of the Mendelssohn Concerto, with Cantelli and the New York Philharmonic, previously on Penzance #33. Other works are the *Havanaise* by Saint-Saens (orchestra unidentified), *Garden Scene* by Korngold (Emanuel Bay, piano), and the slow movement from the Bruch Concerto in D Minor. This disc, called "Jascha Heifetz in Concert," complements the previous Rococo LP, No. 2070, titled "Jascha Heifetz in Performance," listed in the discography (Beethoven Concerto, Brahms Hungarian Dance No. 1, and the 2nd movement from the Sibelius concerto).

In several instances works have been listed which, while recorded with the intention of being released, for one reason or another have never been incised on disc. Such recordings for the most part are not planned for future release unless it has been indicated next to the work in the discography: "To Be Issued."

So-called "live performances" have not been included unless they are either already publicly issued or slated for future release. To try to list all the rest of Heifetz's unissued "live" material now in the tape underground would be nearly impossible, but may I say here that such irresistible items as Novacek's *Perpetual*

Heifetz recording the Mendelssohn Concerto with Charles Munch, 1959.

Motion, the Mendelssohn and Brahms concertos with Toscanini, a rendition of MacDowell's *To A Wild Rose* with Jack Benny, Hubay's *Zephyr*, and many others are known to exist if one has ambition enough to go after them.

Prof. George Zazofsky had Heifetz's permission to take these photos (see also previous and following pages) while Heifetz recorded both the Mendelssohn and the Prokofiev Concertos with Charles Munch and the Boston Symphony Orchestra. The photos on the facing page show him listening to a playback of the Mendelssohn. Jack Pfieffer, the producer, sits between Heifetz and Munch in the top photo, circa 1959.

In the session after the actual recording, the artists listen to the playback, studying the score so they can mark the spots where they must re-tape. An apprehensive Jack Pfieffer sits between Heifetz and Charles Munch. Finally, Heifetz approves!! Circa 1959.

In October 1972 Heifetz gave yet another rare solo recital in Los Angeles. The program was given in honor of his tenth anniversary at the University of Southern California, and all proceeds from it were given to the University's scholarship fund. The program included Franck's A Major Sonata; Richard Strauss' E-flat Major Sonata; three movements from Bach's Partita in E Major for Unaccompanied Violin; *Nigun* by Bloch; *La Plus que Lente* by Debussy; *Etude-Tableau* by Rachmaninoff; *Nana* by de Falla; *La Chasse* by Kreisler; *Tzigane* by Ravel; and an encore, *Sea Murmurs*, by Castelnuovo-Tedesco. At the end, he made a short curtain speech in which he stated that he was "pretty much tired." Reviews of the event once again made it clear that Heifetz was right up there with the best of them. Daniel Cariaga said in *The Los Angeles Times* that ". . . Heifetz still commands the most silken, unpressured, and resonant tone within memory. His legato is seamless not in effect or illusion, but in fact. And his music-making moves forward at all times in inexorable but unhurried action. If his playing of the Franck Sonata was never a dialogue, but rather a soliloquy, who could mind, given this articulation and projected sense of line?. . ." In the *Herald Examiner* Karen Monson wrote, ". . . A strenuous program, but Heifetz took it all in his stride. He admits no dramatic histrionics to his performing; everything is very business-like, very much in place. . . . The violin speaks with natural airy beauty— Heifetz even looks most comfortable when he's in a playing position, satisfied that the music is flowing easily. But there are moments—moments Monday evening that drew to mind the sheer wonders of music. Heifetz doesn't always turn a phrase perfectly, but when he does, the effect is unsurpassed. In the finale of the Franck Sonata, for instance, there were such moments of virtual perfection, and in Debussy's *La Plus que lente* . . . At one point in the evening it looked as if (accompanist Brooks Smith) had given up and gone home. When Heifetz finished his three Bach movements, he

173

On the previous page Heifetz and Munch listen to the replay of their recording of the Prokofiev Violin Concerto. The photographer, George Zazofsky was a musician in the orchestra. He had permission to take the photos and he caught Heifetz in some of the most candid shots ever made of the Master.

It makes one wonder if Heifetz's face is not a perfect mirror of his heart. Perhaps that's why he doesn't show his emotions while he is performing. Yet the photo on the facing page shows him pleased with his performance . . . while the photo above shows him delighted. Heifetz is precise and unpredictable. Circa 1959.

stayed on-stage, waiting for the pianist to join him in *Nigun* by Ernest Bloch. Smith may have taken a turn around the block; it took Heifetz's sounding of an A-major tuning chord on the piano to summon back the collaborator."

The Associated Press reported some things that Heifetz himself had to say about the concert. About the donation of money raised: "That is essential. The Eastern schools are able to draw away our best pupils by offering several thousand dollars in scholarships. Now at last we will be able to provide the same incentive of what some people call the almighty dollar. Myself, I don't call it that. To me there is only one almighty and that is God. . . The audience may have been the worst behaved and most enthusiastic on record. There was applause, catcalls and cheers, and all this was recorded for a possible album. I haven't heard it yet, so I don't know whether it will be released." (*Editor's note: Heifetz has approved the concert for release and it has been announced that Columbia is issuing it in 1977.*)

Benjamin Britten and Serge Koussevitzsky. Heifetz played the Beethoven Violin Concerto with Koussevitzsky in Los Angeles in 1950.

PART I — 1917 through 1920

NOVEMBER 9, 1917

Chorus of Dervishes (Beethoven-Auer). Andre Benoist, pf. RCA.

La Capricieuse (Elgar). Andre Benoist, pf. RCA.

Ave Maria (Schubert-Wilhelmj). Andre Benoist, pf. RCA.

Scherzo-Tarantelle (Wieniawski). Andre Benoist, pf. RCA.

Valse Bluette (Drigo). Andre Benoist, pf. RCA.

DECEMBER 19, 1917

Hebrew Melody (J. Achron). Josef Pasternack, cond. orchestra. RCA.

La Ronde des Lutins (Bazzini). Andre Benoist, pf. RCA.

Turkish March (Beethoven-Auer). Andre Benoist, pf. RCA.

Meditation (Glazounov). Andre Benoist, pf. RCA.

Malaguena (Sarasate). Andre Benoist, pf. RCA.

OCTOBER 3, 1918

Sicilienne et Rigaudon (Kreisler). Andre Benoist, pf. RCA.

Guitarre (Moszkowski-Sarasate). Andre Benoist, pf. RCA.

Moto Perpetuo (Paganini). Andre Benoist, pf. RCA.

Romance (Wieniawski). Andre Benoist, pf. RCA.

OCTOBER 4, 1918

Nocturne in Eb, Op. 9, No. 2 (Chopin-Sarasate). Andre Benoist, pf. RCA.

Minuet in the Style of Porpora (Kreisler). Andre Benoist, pf. RCA.

On Wings of Song (Mendelssohn). Andre Benoist, pf. RCA.

Caprice No. 20 in D Major (Paganini-Kreisler). Andre Benoist, pf. RCA.

Zapateado (Sarasate). Andre Benoist, pf. RCA.

OCTOBER 13, 1919

Widmung (Schumann-Auer). Samuel Chotzinoff, pf. RCA.

Scherzo (Tchaikovsky). Samuel Chotzinoff, pf. RCA.

Zigeunerweisen (Sarasate). Samuel Chotzinoff, pf. RCA.

OCTOBER 14, 1919

Slavonic Dance, Op. 46, No. 2 (Dvorak-Kreisler). Samuel Chotzinoff, pf. RCA.

Symphonie Espagnole (4th movement) (Lalo). Josef Pasternack, cond. orchestra. RCA.

Zigeunerweisen (Sarasate). Samuel Chotzinoff, pf. RCA.

Valse (from Serenade in C) (Tchaikovsky). Josef Pasternack, cond. orchestra. RCA.

178

OCTOBER 28, 1919
Serenade (d'Ambrosio). Samuel Chotzinoff, pf. RCA.
Minuet (Mozart-Burmeister). Samuel Chotzinoff, pf. RCA.

SEPTEMBER 16, 1920
Hungarian Dance No. 1 (Brahms-Joachim). Samuel Chotzinoff, pf. RCA.
Slavonic Dance, Op. 72, No. 8 (Dvorak-Kreisler). Samuel Chotzinoff, pf. RCA.
Valse (Glazounov-Heifetz). Samuel Chotzinoff, pf. RCA.
Berceuse, Op. 28, No. 3 (Juon). Samuel Chotzinoff, pf. RCA.
Concerto in E Minor—Finale (Mendelssohn). Samuel Chotzinoff, pf. RCA.
Rondo (From Haffner Serenade) (Mozart). Samuel Chotzinoff, pf. RCA.
Caprice No. 13 (Paganini-Kreisler). Samuel Chotzinoff, pf. RCA.

SEPTEMBER 17, 1920
Waltz in D (Godowsky-Heifetz). Samuel Chotzinoff, pf. RCA.
Concerto in A Minor: Andante (Goldmark). Josef Pasternack, cond. orchestra. RCA.
Concerto in D: Canzonetta (Tchaikovsky). Josef Pasternack, cond. orchestra. RCA.

SEPTEMBER 18, 1920
Serenade Melancolique (Tchaikovsky). Josef Pasternack, cond. orchestra. RCA.

PART II — 1921 through 1929

OCTOBER 19, 1922
Hebrew Lullaby (J. Achron). Samuel Chotzinoff, pf. RCA.
Grand Adagio (Glazounov-Zimbalist). Samuel Chotzinoff, pf. RCA.
Andaluza (Granados-Kreisler). Samuel Chotzinoff, pf. RCA.
Vivace (Haydn-Auer). Samuel Chotzinoff, pf. RCA.

OCTOBER 20. 1922
Nocturne in D-Flat (Chopin-Wilhelmj). Samuel Chotzinoff, pf. RCA.
Slavonic Dance in Em, Op. 72, No. 2 (Dvorak-Kreisler). Samuel Chotzinoff, pf. RCA.

SEPTEMBER 24, 1924
Hebrew Dance (J. Achron). Isidor Achron, pf. RCA.
Stimmung (J. Achron). Isidor Achron, pf. RCA.

SEPTEMBER 25, 1924

Nocturne in F Major (N. Boulanger). Isidor Achron, pf. RCA.

DECEMBER 18, 1924

Cortege (N. Boulanger). Isidor Achron, pf. RCA.

Habanera (Sarasate). Isidor Achron, pf. RCA.

The Gentle Maiden (Scott). Isidor Achron, pf. RCA.

DECEMBER 19, 1924

Havanaise (Saint-Saens). Isidor Achron, pf. RCA.

'Carmen' Fantasy (Sarasate). Isidor Achron, pf. RCA.

DECEMBER 29, 1925

Minuets I & II (Bach). Unaccompanied. RCA.

Les Petits moulins a vent (Couperin-Press). Isidor Achron, pf. RCA.

La plus que lent (Debussy-Roques). Isidor Achron, pf. RCA.

DECEMBER 29, 1926

La Fille aux cheveux de lin (Debussy-Hartmann). Isidor Achron, pf. RCA.

Scherzo-Impromptu (Grieg-Achron). Isidor Achron, pf. RCA.

DECEMBER 31, 1926

Hebrew Melody (Achron-Auer). Isidor Achron, pf. RCA.

Zapateado (Sarasate). Isidor Achron, pf. RCA.

Ave Maria (Schubert-Wilhelmj). Isidor Achron, pf. RCA.

Rondo (Schubert-Friedberg). Isidor Achron, pf. RCA.

MAY 8, 1928

Valse Bluette (Drigo-Auer). Isidor Achron, pf. RCA.

Jota (de Falla-Kochanski). Isidor Achron, pf. RCA.

Sonata in C Minor: 2nd Movement (Grieg). Isidor Achron, pf. RCA.

Puck (Grieg-Achron). Isidor Achron, pf. RCA.

On Wings of Song (Mendelssohn-Achron-Heifetz). Isidor Achron, pf. RCA.

Estrellita (Ponce-Heifetz). Isidor Achron, pf. RCA.

PART III — 1930 through 1939

DECEMBER 23, 1932

Sea Murmurs (Castelnuovo Tedesco-Heifetz). Piano Accompaniment (2 takes). Private recording.

Largo in C Minor (Clerambault-Dandelot). Piano Accompaniment. Private recording.

Hora Staccato (Dinicu-Heifetz). Piano Accompaniment. Private recording.

Alt Wien (Godowsky-Heifetz). Piano accompaniment. Private recording.

Flight of the Bumblebee (Rimsky Korsakoff-Heifetz). Piano accompaniment (2 takes). Private recording.

FEBRUARY 3, 1934

Sea Murmurs (Castelnuovo-Tedesco-Heifetz). Arpad Sandor, pf. RCA.

Alt Wien (Godowsky-Heifetz). Arpad Sandor, pf. RCA.

Rondo in E-flat Major (Hummel-Heifetz). Arpad Sandor, pf. RCA.

Flight of the Bumblebee (Rimsky Korsakoff-Heifetz). Arpad Sandor, pf. RCA.

FEBRUARY 6, 1934

Sarabande (Bach-Heifetz). Arpad Sandor, pf. RCA.

Impromptu No. 3, in G Major (Schubert-Heifetz). Arpad Sandor, pf. RCA.

Sonata in E-flat Major, Op. 18 (Strauss). Arpad Sandor, pf. RCA.

Tzigane (Rhapsodie de concert) (Ravel). Arpad Sandor, pf. RCA.

FEBRUARY 1934

Sevillanas (Albeniz-Heifetz). Arpad Sandor, pf. RCA.

Largo in C Minor (Clerambault-Dandelot). Arpad Sandor, pf. RCA.

L'Enfant prodigue: Prelude (Debussy-Heifetz). Arpad Sandor, pf. RCA.

La Capricieuse (Elgar). Arpad Sandor, pf. RCA.

Holzapfel und Schlehwein (March) (Korngold). Arpad Sandor, pf. RCA.

Sumare (Milhaud-Levy). Arpad Sandor, pf. RCA.

Concerto No. 5, in A Major, K. 219 (Turkish) (Mozart). John Barbirolli, cond./London Philharmonic. RCA.

Caprice No. 24, in A Minor (Paganini-Auer). Arpad Sandor, pf. RCA.

Sonata No. 2, in A Major (Vivaldi-Busch). Arpad Sandor, pf. RCA.

Scherzo-Tarantelle (Wieniawski). Arpad Sandor, pf. RCA.

MARCH 1934

Ruralia Hungarica (Andante Rubato) (Dohnanyi-Kreisler). Arpad Sandor, pf. RCA.

Heifetz and Rubinstein. Circa 1941.

(Top facing page.) Heifetz with Eugene Ormandy. Circa 1937. (Bottom facing page.) Setting the microphones for the trio recording sessions (with Feuermann and Rubinstein). Circa 1941.

Concerto in A Minor, Op. 82 (Glazounov). John Barbirolli, cond./London Philharmonic. RCA.

Meditation (Glazounov). Arpad Sandor, pf. RCA.

Guitarre (Moszkowski-Sarasate). Arpad Sandor, pf. RCA.

Caprice No. 13, in B-flat Major (Paganini-Kreisler). Arpad Sandor, pf. RCA.

Caprice No. 20, in D Major (Paganini-Kreisler). Arpad Sandor, pf. RCA.

An einsamer Quelle (Strauss-Heifetz). Arpad Sandor, pf. RCA.

FEBRUARY 24, 1935
Concerto in D Major, Op. 77 (Brahms) (1st & 2nd move.). Arturo Toscanini, cond./N.Y. Philharmonic. Live.

MARCH 1935
Introduction & Rondo Capriccioso (Saint-Saens). John Barbirolli, cond./London Philharmonic. RCA.

Concerto No. 4, in D Minor, Op. 31 (Vieuxtemps). John Barbirolli, cond./London Philharmonic. RCA.

Concerto No. 2, in D Minor, Op. 22 (Wieniawski). John Barbirolli, cond./London Philharmonic. RCA.

NOVEMBER 1935
Concerto in D Minor, Op. 47 (Sibelius). Sir Thomas Beecham, cond./London Philharmonic. RCA.

DECEMBER 1935
Sonata No. 1, in G Minor (Bach). Unaccompanied. RCA.

Partita No. 2, in D Minor (Bach). Unaccompanied. RCA.

Sonata No. 3, in C Major (Bach). Unaccompanied. RCA.

JANUARY 30, 1936
Sonata No. 3, in E-flat Major (Beethoven). Emanuel Bay, pf. RCA.

Sonata No. 7, in C Minor (Beethoven). Emanuel Bay, pf. RCA—unissued.

JANUARY 31, 1936
Sonata No. 8, in G Major (Beethoven). Emanuel Bay, pf. RCA.

Sonata No. 2, in A Major (Brahms). Emanuel Bay, pf. RCA.

FEBRUARY 3, 1936
Sonata in B-flat Major, K. 378 (Mozart). Emanuel Bay, pf. RCA.

Sonata in C Minor, Op. 45 (Grieg). Emanuel Bay, pf. RCA—unissued.

FEBRUARY 7, 1936
Sonata in G Major, Op. 13 (Grieg). Emanuel Bay, pf. RCA.

FEBRUARY 10, 1936
Sonata No. 1, in A Major (Faure). Emanuel Bay, pf. RCA.
Sonata in B-flat Major, K. 454 (Mozart). Emanuel Bay, pf. RCA.

MARCH 1937
Tallahassee Suite (Scott). Emanuel Bay, pf. RCA.
Concerto in D Major, Op. 35 (Tchaikovsky). John Barbirolli, cond./London Philharmonic. RCA.
Polonaise Brilliante No. 1, in D Major (Wieniawski). Emanuel Bay, pf. RCA.

APRIL 1937
La Ronde des Lutins (Bazzini). Emanuel Bay, pf. RCA.
Hora Staccato (Dinicu-Heifetz). Emanuel Bay, pf. RCA.
Sonata in A Major (Franck). Artur Rubinstein, pf. RCA.
Mouvements Perpetuels No. 1 (Poulenc-Heifetz). Emanuel Bay, pf. RCA.
Havanaise (Saint-Saens). John Barbirolli, cond./London Philharmonic. RCA.
Zigeunerweisen (Sarasate). John Barbirolli, cond./London Philharmonic. RCA.

DECEMBER 20, 1937
Concerto No. 2, in G Minor (Prokofiev) (1935). Serge Koussevitzky, cond./Boston Sym. Orchestra. RCA.

APRIL 11, 1939
Concerto in D Major, Op. 77 (Brahms). Serge Koussevitzky, cond./Boston Sym. Orchestra. RCA.

DECEMBER 21, 1939
Double Concerto in A Minor, Op. 102 (Brahms). Eugene Ormandy, cond./Philadelphia Orch., Emanuel Feuermann, cello. RCA.

1939
Hora Staccato (Dinicu-Heifetz). Emanuel Bay, pf. Film.
Concerto in E Minor, Op. 64 (Mendelssohn) (3rd move.). California Junior Symphony Orchestra. Film.
Estrellita (Ponce). Emanuel Bay, pf. Film.
Introduction & Rondo Capriccioso (Saint-Saens). Unidentified orchestra. Film.

PART IV — 1940 through 1949

MARCH 11, 1940
> *Concerto in D Major, Op. 61* (Beethoven). Arturo Toscanini, cond./NBC Symphony Orchestra. RCA.

FEBRUARY 18, 1941
> *Concerto in B Minor* (Walton) (1939). Eugene Goossens, cond./ Cincinnati Symphony Orchestra. RCA.

MAY 22, 1941, and AUG. 29, 1941
> *Duo No. 2, in B-flat, K. 424* (Mozart). William Primrose, violist. RCA.

MAY 22, 1941
> *Passacaglia* (Handel-Halvorsen). William Primrose, violist. RCA.

MAY 28, 1941
> *Concerto in D Major, Op. 21* (Chausson). Jesus Maria Sanroma, pf/Musical Art Quartet. RCA.

SEPTEMBER 8, 1941
> *Serenade in C Major, Op. 10* (Dohnanyi). William Primrose, viola/Emanuel Feuermann, cello. RCA.

SEPTEMBER 9, 1941
> *Divertimento in E-flat, K. 563* (Mozart). William Primrose, viola/Emanuel Feuermann, cello. RCA.

SEPTEMBER 11-12, 1941
> *Trio in B Major, Op. 8* (Brahms). Artur Rubinstein, pf/Emanuel Feuermann, cello. RCA.

SEPTEMBER 12-13, 1941
> *Trio in B-flat Major, Op. 97* (Beethoven). Artur Rubinstein, pf/ Emanuel Feuermann, cello. RCA.

SEPTEMBER 13, 1941
> *Trio in B-flat Major, Op. 99* (Schubert). Artur Rubinstein, pf/ Emanuel Feuermann, cello. RCA.

FEBRUARY 13, 1942
> *Concerto in D Major, Op. 77* (Brahms) (1st move.). Eugene Goossens, cond./New York Philharmonic. Live.

MARCH 2, 1942
> *Valse Bluette* (Drigo). Emanuel Bay, pf. Live.
> *To a Wild Rose* (MacDowell). Jack Benny, violin/piano accompaniment. Live.

186

MARCH 12, 1942

Concerto No. 5, in A Major, K. 219 (Mozart). Efrem Kurtz, cond./orchestra. Live.

JANUARY 3, 1943

Concerto No. 5, in A Major, K. 219 (Mozart) (1st move.). Efrem Kurtz, cond./orchestra. Live.

APRIL 9, 1944

Concerto in E Minor, Op. 64 (Mendelssohn). Arturo Toscanini, cond./NBC Symphony Orchestra. Live.

JANUARY 14, 1945

Concerto in D Major, Op. 61 (Beethoven). Artur Rodzinski, cond./New York Philharmonic. Live.

NOVEMBER 26, 1945

Golliwogg's Cake-Walk (Debussy-Heifetz). Emanuel Bay, pf. Live.

Allegro (from *Divertimento, K. 219*) (Mozart-Heifetz). Donald Voorhees, cond./Bell Telephone Orchestra. Live.

Perpetual Motion (Novacek). Donald Voorhees, cond./Bell Telephone Orchestra. Live.

Cello Sonata (Rachmaninoff-Heifetz) (3rd move.). Emanuel Bay, pf. Live.

DECEMBER 17, 1945

Concerto, Op. 47 (Gruenberg) (1944). Pierre Monteux, cond./San Francisco Symphony Orchestra. RCA.

CIRCA 1945

Huella (Cancion Argentina) (Aguirre-Heifetz). Emanuel Bay, pf. Decca.

Deep River (Negro Spiritual) (Anonymous-arr. Heifetz). Milton Kaye, pf. Decca.

Jamaican Rumba (Benjamin-Primrose). Milton Kaye, pf. Decca.

Hexapoda (5 Studies in Jitteroptera) (Bennett). Emanuel Bay, pf. Decca.

White Christmas (Berlin-Heifetz). Salvador Camerata, cond./orchestra. Decca.

Hungarian Dance No. 7, in A Major (Brahms-Joachim). Emanuel Bay, pf. Decca.

Giant Hills (Burleigh). Emanuel Bay, pf. Decca.

Moto Perpetuo (Burleigh). Emanuel Bay, pf. Decca.

Figaro (Rossini-Castelnuovo Tedesco). Emanuel Bay, pf. Decca.

Nocturne in E-flat, Op. 55, No. 2 (Chopin-Heifetz). Emanuel bay, pf. Decca.

Gweedore Brae (Crowther). Milton Kaye, pf. Decca.

Beau Soir (Debussy-Heifetz). Milton Kaye, pf. Decca.

Clair de lune (Debussy-Roelens). Emanuel Bay, pf. Decca.

Golliwogg's Cake-Walk (Debussy-Heifetz). Emanuel Bay, pf. Decca.

Humoresque (Dvorak-Heifetz). Milton Kaye, pf. Decca.

Florida Night Song (Dyer). Emanuel Bay, pf. Decca.

I Dream of Jeannie with the Light Brown Hair (Foster-Heifetz). Emanuel Bay, pf. Decca.

Old Folks at Home (Foster-Heifetz). Emanuel Bay, pf. Decca.

From the Canebrake (Gardner). Milton Kaye, pf. Decca.

A Woman Is a Sometime Thing (Gershwin-Heifetz). Emanuel Bay, pf. Decca.

Bess, You Is My Woman Now (Gershwin-Heifetz). Emanuel Bay, pf. Decca.

It Ain't Necessarily So (Gershwin-Heifetz). Emanuel Bay, pf. Decca.

My Man's Gone Now (Gershwin-Heifetz). Emanuel Bay, pf. Decca.

Summertime (Gershwin-Heifetz). Emanuel Bay, pf. Decca.

Tempo di Blues (Gershwin-Heifetz). Emanuel Bay, pf. Decca.

Three Preludes (Gershwin-Heifetz). Emanuel Bay, pf. Decca.

Melodie (Gluck-Kreisler). Emanuel Bay, pf. Decca.

Berceuse (from *Jocelyn*) (Godard). Bing Crosby, vocal/Victor Young, cond./orchestra. Decca.

Viennese (Godowsky-Heifetz). Milton Kaye, pf. Decca.

Waves at Play (Grasse). Emanuel Bay, pf. Decca.

A la Valse (Herbert). Milton Kaye, pf. Decca.

Dance No. 4 (Krein-Heifetz). Emanuel Bay, pf. Decca.

Where My Caravan Has Rested (Lohr & Teschmacher). Bing Crosby, vocal/Victor Young, cond./orchestra. Decca.

March (from *The Love for Three Oranges*) (Prokofieff-Heifetz). Emanuel Bay, pf. Decca.

Masques (from *Romeo and Juliet*) (Prokofieff-Heifetz). Emanuel Bay, pf. Decca.

Piece en forme d'habanera (Ravel-Catherine). Milton Kaye, pf. Decca.

Le Cygne (*The Swan*) (Saint Saens-Heifetz). Emanuel Bay, pf. Decca.

Vogel als Prophet (*The Prophet Bird*) (Schumann-Heifetz). Emanuel Bay, pf. Decca.

Prelude in C-Sharp Minor, Op. 34, No. 10 (Shostakovich). Emanuel Bay, pf. Decca.

Prelude in D-Flat, Op. 34, No. 15 (Shostakovich). Emanuel Bay, pf. Decca.

Melodie (Tchaikovsky). Emanuel Bay, pf. Decca.

Ao pe da fogueira (Valle-Heifetz). Emanuel Bay, pf. Decca.

Moderato assai (Weill-Frenkel). Emanuel Bay, pf. Decca.

Levee Dance (White). Milton Kaye, pf. Decca.

OCTOBER 14, 1946 and OCTOBER 19, 1946

Concerto in D Minor for 2 Violins (Bach). Franz Waxman, cond./RCA Chamber Orchestra. RCA. (Note: Heifetz plays both solo parts.)

OCTOBER 16, 1946

Tango (Castelnuovo Tedesco-Heifetz). Emanuel Bay, pf. RCA.

La Chevelure (Debussy-Heifetz). Emanuel Bay, pf. RCA.

Fairy Tale in B-flat Minor, Op. 20, No. 1 (Medtner-Heifetz). Emanuel Bay, pf. RCA.

Presto in B-flat Major (Poulenc-Heifetz). Emanuel Bay, pf. RCA.

Gavotta, Op. 32, No. 3 (Prokofieff-Heifetz). Emanuel Bay, pf. RCA.

March in F Minor, Op. 12, No. 1 (Prokofieff-Heifetz). Emanuel Bay, pf. RCA.

Daisies, Op. 30, No. 3 (Rachmaninoff-Heifetz). Emanuel Bay, pf. RCA.

Etude-Tableau, Op. 39, No. 2 (Rachmaninoff-Heifetz). Emanuel Bay, pf. RCA.

Oriental Sketch, Op. 2, No. 2 (Rachmaninoff-Heifetz). Emanuel Bay, pf. RCA.

Valses nobles et sentimentales Nos. 6 and 7 (Ravel-Heifetz). Emanuel Bay, pf. RCA.

OCTOBER 17, 1946

Tempo di Valse (Arensky-Heifetz). Emanuel Bay, pf. RCA.

Gavottes I & II (Bach-Heifetz). Emanuel Bay, pf. RCA.

Mediterranean (Bax-Heifetz). Emanuel Bay, pf. RCA.

Folk Dance (Beethoven-Heifetz). Emanuel Bay, pf. RCA.

Nocturne in E Minor, Op. 72, No. 1 (Chopin-Auer). Emanuel Bay, pf. RCA.

Pantomime (de Falla-Kochanski). Emanuel Bay, pf. RCA.

Danza de la Gitana (Halffter-Escriche). Emanuel Bay, pf. RCA.

Scherzo (from *Trio in D Minor*) (Mendelssohn-Heifetz). Emanuel Bay, pf. RCA.

Corcovado (Milhaud-Levy). Emanuel Bay, pf. RCA.

Cantilena Asturiana (Nin). Emanuel Bay, pf. RCA.

Tango (Poldowski). Emanuel Bay, pf. RCA.

OCTOBER 18, 1946

Sea Murmurs (Castelnuovo Tedesco-Heifetz). Emanuel Bay, pf. RCA.

La Fille aux cheveux de lin (Debussy-Hartmann). Emanuel Bay, pf. RCA.

La plus que lent (Debussy-Roques). Emanuel Bay, pf. RCA.

Jota (de Falla-Kochanski). Emanuel Bay, pf. RCA.

Valse Bluette (Drigo-Heifetz). Emanuel Bay, pf. RCA.

Alt Wien (Godowsky-Heifetz). Emanuel Bay, pf. RCA.

Estrellita (Ponce-Heifetz). Emanuel Bay, pf. RCA.

Flight of the Bumblebee (Rimsky Korsakoff-Heifetz). Emanuel Bay, pf. RCA.

Romanza Andaluza (Sarasate). Emanuel Bay, pf. RCA.

Rondo (Schubert-Friedberg). Emanuel Bay, pf. RCA.

OCTOBER 19, 1946

Hebrew Melody (Achron-Auer). Emanuel Bay, pf. RCA.

Zapateado (Sarasate). Emanuel Bay, pf. RCA.

Ave Maria (Schubert-Wilhelmj). Emanuel Bay, pf. RCA.

NOVEMBER 8, 1946

Carmen Fantasy (Waxman). Donald Voorhees, cond./RCA Symphony Orchestra. RCA.

NOVEMBER 11, 1946

Prelude, Gavotte and Gigue (Bach). Violin unaccompanied. Live.

1946

Sonata No. 3, in D Minor, Op. 108 (Brahms). Benno Moiseiwitsch, pf. Live.

SEPTEMBER 12, 1947

Scottish Fantasy (Bruch). William Steinberg, cond./RCA Symph. Orch. RCA.

NOVEMBER 8, 1947

Concerto No. 5, in A Minor, Op. 37 (Vieuxtemps). Sir Malcolm Sargent, Cond./London Symphony Orchestra. RCA.

NOVEMBER 10, 1947

Concerto No. 4, in D Major, K. 218 (Mozart). Sir Thomas Beecham, cond./Royal Philharmonic. RCA.

DECEMBER 16, 1947

Sonata No. 1, in D Major (Beethoven). Emanuel Bay, pf. RCA.

Sonata in C Major, K. 296 (Mozart). Emanuel Bay, pf. RCA.

DECEMBER 17, 1947

Sonata No. 2, in A Major (Beethoven). Emanuel Bay, pf. RCA.

Sonata No. 5, in F Major (Spring) (Beethoven). Emanuel Bay, pf. RCA.

Banjo and Fiddle (Kroll). Emanuel Bay, pf. RCA.

Sweet Remembrance (Mendelssohn-Heifetz). Emanuel Bay, pf. RCA.

DECEMBER 18, 1947

Gartenszene (Garden Scene) (Korngold). Emanuel Bay, pf. RCA.

Vocalise, Op. 34, No. 14 (Rachmaninoff-Press). Emanuel Bay, pf. RCA.

Menuet (Ravel-Roques). Emanuel Bay, pf. RCA.

Danse Fantastique (Shostakovich-Glickman). Emanuel Bay, pf. RCA.

Berceuse (from *Firebird*) (Stravinsky-Dushkin). Emanuel Bay, pf. RCA.

Mouvement Perpetuel (Tansman). Emanuel Bay, pf. RCA.

1947

Concerto in D Major, Op. 35 (Korngold) (radio premiere). Efrem Kurtz, cond./New York Philharmonic. Live.

Concerto No. 5, in A Major (Turkish), K. 219 (Mozart). Efrem Kurtz, cond./New York Philharmonic. Live.

Concerto in D Minor (Sibelius) (2nd movement only). Unidentified conductor and orchestra. Live.

FEBRUARY 16, 1948

Romance in F Major, Op. 50 (Beethoven). Donald Voorhees, cond./Bell Telephone Orchestra. Live.

Romanza Andaluza (Sarasate). Donald Voorhees, cond./Bell Telephone Orchestra. Live.

Zapateado (Sarasate). Donald Voorhees, cond./Bell Telephone Orchestra. Live.

APRIL 19, 1948

Jota (de Falla). Donald Voorhees, cond./Bell Telephone Orchestra. Live.

JASCHA HEIFETZ

First Records by this
Brilliant Genius *of the* Violin
who is under exclusive contract with
the Victor Talking Machine Company

The brochure that Victor issued with the first Heifetz records is reproduced on this and the following pages.
192   *November 27, 1917.*

GENIUS is a word not lightly to be used in these days when super-talent is the gift of many. Yet what other word can be applied to Jascha Heifetz, who began to play the violin when but three years old, and at five drew an audience from miles around musical Vilna to hear him? At six he was playing the Mendelssohn concerto—a virtuoso work. At seven he had graduated from the Royal School of Music at Vilna, and at nine he astonished Petrograd; so much so that Leopold Auer, teacher of a score of famous players, pronounced him one of the most astonishing violinists he had ever heard, and made him one of his chosen disciples. In 1911 Heifetz astounded musical Europe. On October 27, 1917, this boy played at Carnegie Hall, New York, before a houseful of the most distinguished of musicians and reviewers in the United States, and it is they who have used the word "genius" in connection with Jascha Heifetz.

It is not that Heifetz has merely a phenomenal technique—an exquisitely beautiful tone, complete mastery of bow and control of finger—but he has innate musicianship. He is playing as Mozart might have played, because the stream of consciousness within him is a fountain of music, and his violin is spokesman of his dreams. Whatever his teachers could tell him he has absorbed almost unconsciously, as one absorbs food and drink. No one could teach him to play with genius, however, and if he has learned to do so from outside sources it has been from the songs of the birds, the call of the winds in the trees, and perhaps a little from the voice that crooned him to sleep in the shadowy twilights of babyhood—a voice that sounded so sweet in his ears that he thought of the world into which he had come as one in which music was the natural speech, and so made it his own.

74563   Ave Maria   Schubert-Wilhelmj 12-inch $1.50

Schubert's "Ave Maria" is one of the loveliest of all the melodies in the realm of music—a tune sent from heaven as surely as to heaven it rises. Small wonder that Wilhelmj, one of the greatest of all violinists, saw in this perfect song a melody of unbelievable beauty for the violin. Violinists, like singers, strive for a perfect "cantilena," or singing tone, held for long tones, swelling and diminishing at will. Wilhelmj was especially famous for a lovely fullness of tone, and assigned the melody to the silver-wound G string. This is the lowest in pitch of the four strings to a violin, and at the bidding of a master will produce a tone of singular richness and purity, not unlike the high notes of a perfect tenor. Nothing more exquisite can be imagined than the tone obtained by Jascha Heifetz in this cantilena melody. The "second verse" is played an octave higher and with "double-stopping"—that is, playing on two strings at once. Here again an exquisite tone is produced, a tone so sweet that it seems as though the heavenly melody had been wafted from earth to remote regions of ethereal infinity, far removed from the pains and passions that darken the color of human song. And so marvelous is the strain that it draws the soul of the listener on its upward flight, and permits a moment at least of that spiritual ecstasy which is of heaven itself.

74562   Scherzo-Tarantelle   Henri Wieniawski, Op. 16 12-inch $1.50

The word "scherzo" means "playful," and was applied first by Beethoven to an idealized minuet of his invention, and a tarantelle is a wild Italian dance used in olden times, it is said, as a cure for the tarantula's bite, the sufferer dancing until exhausted. A piece of music combining these characteristics engages the imagination at the outset. It is music in headlong flight, myriad notes flying from the nimble fingers and wand-like bow of the performer. A great deal of this piece is played "staccato"—that is, detached, moving, or rather springing the bow slightly from the string between each note. This means that in addition to the delicate up-and-down motion of the right wrist, there is an infinitesimal pressure and release of finger and thumb, to which the flexible bow responds like a live thing. As a mere gymnastic feat this is difficult enough, and one might forgive a slight roughness of tone, but there is no roughness here. Indeed, Heifetz produces a quality of tone that is pure violin, yet is unlike that of any other violinist. There is a sheen upon it, a silvery gloss that radiates from every note, no matter how swiftly they fly past. Notes? These are not notes that fly from a violinist's bow, they are points of light, sparkling and flashing in obedience to a magic wand. Close your eyes as you listen, and it will seem as though some wandering spirit of the night had thrown a cluster of stars upon the darkness.

64758 Valse Bluette   Richard Drigo   10-inch $1.00

"Valse Bluette" is an "air de ballet," but Russian Ballet is what is meant, and there is none of the artificial theatrical quality with which one usually associates the word ballet. It is a free, spontaneous waltz movement, beginning as a pure legato melody, but later breaking into a glittering pyrotechnical display of flashing notes that dazzle the imagination. Richard Drigo, the composer, is an Italian by birth, but has been for many years conductor of the Ballet at the Royal Marinsky Theater in Petrograd. He has therefore had a hand in the developing of the extraordinary modern Russian Ballet, in which the art of the dance has taken on a new significance. The present violin transcription was made by Leopold Auer, the teacher of Jascha Heifetz, and is an amazing test of the young violinist's powers. Not only does he overcome all the difficulties, but they actually seem not to exist, and through it all he preserves the remarkable, lustrous tone quality which has captivated the world's keenest critics of violin tone. There is, moreover, a happy poetic fancy about the interpretation which assures us that Heifetz is not merely a great violinist but is a great artist. His music has sunshine in it—the warmth, the happiness, the pliant sympathy of youth.

64759 Chorus of Dervishes   Ludwig von Beethoven   10-inch $1.00

"The Ruins of Athens," from which the "Chorus of Dervishes" is transcribed for violin by Leopold Auer, is a dramatic piece by Kotzebue to which Beethoven wrote incidental music, and was produced in Pesth, 1812. Dervishes (also called Fakirs) are a religious sect of Mohammedans who seek, as an act of worship, to get into an ecstatic state, and accomplish this by hashish and other physical and mental stimulants. While under this excitement they perform the dance of the "Whirling Dervishes," gyrating at an incredible speed, developing amid weird shouts, through all stages of delirious frenzy, spinning like tops till they fall exhausted to the ground. The extraordinary tone-picture of one of these dances which Beethoven drew in "The Ruins of Athens" has been transformed into a violin "étude" or study-piece by Leopold Auer, demanding the most amazing virtuosity of the performer. A great deal of the time the performer is called upon to play in octaves. Octaves are formed on the violin mainly by placing the forefinger on one string and the fourth finger on the other, and drawing the bow across the two strings. For every change the hand has to be shifted, and, moreover, the relative position of the fingers has to be altered slightly to conform to the fact that the notes draw closer together as the hand travels up the violin keyboard. To play octaves on the violin absolutely in tune is at any time difficult; to play them at the pace Jascha Heifetz plays them is an incredible act of virtuosity. But even while doing this he does not lose sight of Beethoven's conception, nor does he develop any roughness in tone, and the onward rush of the dance fairly carries the listener off his feet. Here is surely one of the most amazing violin records ever made.

4021—RJQA—11-27-17

DECEMBER 12, 1948

Caprice No. 24, in A Minor (Paganini-Auer). Donald Voorhees, cond./Bell Telephone Orchestra. Live.

Chaconne (Vitali). Donald Voorhees, cond./Bell Telephone Orchestra. Live.

MARCH 21, 1949

Hungarian Dance No. 7, in A Major (Brahms-Joachim). Donald Voorhees, cond./Bell Telephone Orchestra. Live.

Sweet Remembrance (Mendelssohn-Heifetz). Donald Voorhees, cond./Bell Telephone Orchestra. Live.

APRIL 22, 1949

On Wings of Song (Mendelssohn-Achron-Heifetz). Emanuel Bay, pf. RCA.

JUNE 6, 1949

Concerto in B Minor, Op. 61 (Elgar). Sir Malcolm Sargent, cond./London Symphony Orchestra. RCA.

JUNE 10, 1949

Concerto in E Minor, Op. 64 (Mendelssohn). Sir Thomas Beecham, cond./Royal Philharmonic. RCA.

SUMMER 1949

Hungarian Dance No. 7, in A Major (Brahms-Joachim). William Steinberg, cond./Hollywood Bowl Sym. Orch. Live.

Hora Staccato (Dinicu-Heifetz). William Steinberg, cond./ Hollywood Bowl Symphony Orchestra. Live.

Concerto in D Major, Op. 35 (Tchaikovsky). William Steinberg, cond./Hollywood Bowl Symphony Orchestra. Live.

1940's

Jamaican Rumba (Benjamin). Donald Voorhees, cond./orchestra. V-Disc.

Ruralia Hungarica (Andante Rubato) (Dohnanyi). Howard Barlow, cond./orchestra. V-Disc.

Romanza Andaluza (Sarasate). Donald Voorhees, cond./ orchestra. V-Disc.

Zapateado (Sarasate). Donald Voorhees, cond./orchestra. V-Disc.

Impromptu No. 3, in G Major (Schubert). Donald Voorhees, cond./orchestra. V-Disc.

Bygone Memories (from *Tallahasse Suite*) (Scott). Donald Voorhees, cond./orchestra. V-Disc.

La Ronde des Lutins (Bazzini). Orchestra/Lionel Barrymore, host (2 versions). Armed Forces Broad.

Jim Jives (from *Hexapoda*) (Bennett). Orchestra/Lionel Barrymore, host. Armed Forces Broad.

196

Hungarian Dance No. 1, in G Minor (Brahms-Joachim). Orchestra/Lionel Barrymore, host. Armed Forces Broad.

Hungarian Dance No. 1, in G Minor (Brahms-Joachim). Piano/ Lionel Barrymore, host. Armed Forces Broad.

Concerto No. 2, in D Minor, Op. 44 (Bruch) (2nd move.). Orchestra/Lionel Barrymore, host. Armed Forces Broad.

Concerto No. 2 (I Profeti) (Castelnuovo-Tedesco) (2nd move.). Orchestra/Lionel Barrymore, host. Armed Forces Broad.

Figaro (Rossini-Castelnuovo Tedesco). Orchestra/Lionel Barry- more, host (2 versions). Armed Forces Broad.

Nana (de Falla-Kochanski). Orchestra/Lionel Barrymore, host. Armed Forces Broad.

Ruralia Hungarica (Andante Rubato) (Dohnanyi). Orchestra/ Lionel Barrymore, host. Armed Forces Broad.

Waltz in D Major (Godowsky-Heifetz). Orchestra/Lionel Barry- more, host. Armed Forces Broad.

Introduction & Rondo Capriccioso (Saint-Saens). Orchestra/ Lionel Barrymore, host. Armed Forces Broad.

Zapateado (Sarasate). Orchestra/Lionel Barrymore, host. Armed Forces Broad.

Bygone Memories (from *Tallahasse Suite*) (Scott). Orchestra/ Lionel Barrymore, host. Armed Forces Broad.

Concerto No. 2, in D Minor (Wieniawski) (2nd move.). Orches- tra/Lionel Barrymore, host. Armed Forces Broad.

Ave Maria (Schubert-Wilhelmj). Orchestra. Armed Forces Broad.

Vogel als Prophet (Schumann-Heifetz). Orchestra/Lionel Barry- more, host. Armed Forces Broad.

Poeme (Chausson). Donald Voorhees, cond./Bell Telephone Orchestra. Live.

Nana (de Falla). Donald Voorhees, cond./Bell Telephone Orch. Live.

Beau Soir (Debussy-Heifetz). Donald Voorhees, cond./Bell Telephone Orchestra. Live.

Valse Bluette (Drigo). Emanuel Bay, pf (Bell Telephone Hour). Live.

Meditation (Glazounov). Piano accompaniment. Live.

Alt Wien (Godowsky). Donald Voorhees, cond./Bell Telephone Orchestra (2 versions). Live.

Viennese (Godowsky-Heifetz). Donald Voorhees, cond./Bell Telephone Orchestra. Live.

Concerto in A Minor (Goldmark) (2nd move.). Donald Voor- hees, cond./Bell Telephone Orch. Live.

Waves at Play (Grasse). Donald Voorhees, cond./Bell Tele- phone Orchestra. Live.

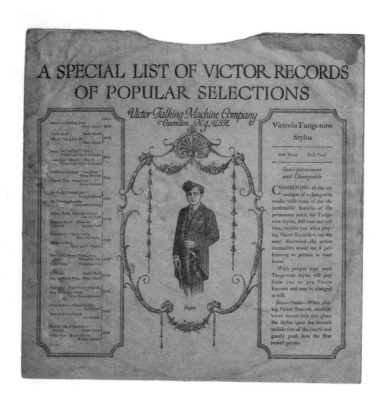

The first record envelopes which featured Heifetz's sketch on them. Circa 1917.

Famous Violin Selections by Some of the Greatest Violinists of the World

Heifetz makes records for the Victor Company exclusively

Before the Victor and Victor Records were available, only the great musicians and most diligent students could find the time for the years of close study necessary to become familiar with the compositions of all the great masters. To-day the Victor and Victrola bring all this beautiful music into your home for you to enjoy, to study and to understand.

		Number				Number
Rigoletto (Morosgny) (Violin)	Mischa Elman	64201	Fiorell's Serenade (Alberto Randegger, Jr.) (Violin)	Jan Kubelik	74256
Serenade (Gloucienski) (Op. 15, No. 1) (Violin)	Maud Powell	64281	Thais—Meditation (Massenet) (Violin)	Mischa Elman	74341
Serenade Espagnole (Chaminade-Kreisler) (Violin)	Fritz Kreisler	64503	Spanish Dance (Sarasate, Op. 26, No. 8) (Violin)	Jan Kubelik	74356
Valse Bluette (Riccardo Drago) (Violin) Jascha Heifetz		64756	Harlequin's Serenade (From "La Millions d'Arlequin") (Drigo) (Violin)	Efrem Zimbalist	74457
Capriccioso (Edward Elgar, Op. 17) (Violin)	Jascha Heifetz	64760	Ave Maria (Schubert-Wilhelmj) (Violin)	Jascha Heifetz	74563

Victor Talking Machine Company, Camden, N. J., U. S. A.

A LIST OF VICTOR RECORDS SPECIALLY RECOMMENDED
by
Victor Talking Machine Co.
Camden N. J. U. S. A.

For Best Results Use

VICTROLA TUNGS-TONE NEEDLES

On All Victor Records

Gartenszene (Garden Scene) (Korngold). Emanuel Bay, pf. (Bell Telephone Hour). Live.

Londonderry Air (arr. Kreisler). Emanuel Bay, pf. (Bell Telephone Hour). Live.

Tambourin Chinois (Kreisler). Orchestra. Live.

Concerto in E Minor, Op. 64 (Mendelssohn) (2nd-3rd move.). Donald Voorhees, cond./Bell Telephone Orch. Live.

Concerto No. 4, in D Major, K. 218 (Mozart) (2nd move.). Donald Voorhees, cond./Bell Telephone Orch. Live.

Estrellita (Ponce). Donald Voorhees, cond./Bell Telephone Orchestra. Live.

Concerto No. 2, in G Minor (Prokofiev) (1935) (2nd move.). Orchestra. Live.

Havanaise (Saint-Saens). Orchestra. Live.

Introduction & Tarantelle (Sarasate). Donald Voorhees, cond./ Bell Telephone Orchestra. Live.

Ave Maria (Schubert-Wilhelmj). Donald Voorhees, cond./Bell Telephone Orchestra. Live.

Serenade Melancolique (Tchaikovsky). Orchestra. Live.

Mairzy Doats (Drake & Hoffman & Livingston). Donald Voorhees, cond./Bell Telephone Orchestra. Private recording.

Concerto in D Major, Op. 35 (Tchaikovsky) (1st move.). Fritz Reiner, cond./orchestra. Film.

PART V — 1950 through 1959

FEBRUARY 7, 1950

Humoresque (Dvorak-Heifetz). Donald Voorhees, cond./Bell Telephone Orchestra. Live.

Habanera (Sarasate). Donald Voorhees, cond./Bell Telephone Orchestra. Live.

APRIL 5, 1950

Sonata in B Minor (Respighi) (1917). Emanuel Bay, pf. RCA.

APRIL 6, 1950

Sonata No. 7, in C Minor (Beethoven). Emanuel Bay, pf. RCA.

Sonata No. 3, in G Minor (Debussy). Emanuel Bay, pf. RCA.

APRIL 7, 1950

Sonata No. 1, in D Minor (Saint-Saens). Emanuel Bay, pf. RCA.

JULY 19-20, 1950

Concerto in D Major, Op. 35 (Tchaikovsky). Walter Susskind, cond./Philharmonic Orchestra. RCA.

JULY 26-27, 1950

Concerto in B Minor (Walton) (1939). William Walton, cond./
Philharmonia Orchestra. RCA.

AUGUST 4, 1950

Chaconne in G Minor (Vitali). Richard Ellsasser, organist.
RCA.

AUGUST 23-24, 1950

Trio in A Minor, Op. 50 (Tchaikovsky). Artur Rubinstein, pf/
Gregor Piatigorsky, vlc. RCA.

AUGUST 25, 1950

Trio in D Minor, Op. 49 (Mendelssohn). Artur Rubinstein, pf/
Gregor Piatigorsky, vlc. RCA.

AUGUST 28, 1950

Trio in A Minor (Ravel) (1915). Artur Rubinstein, pf/Gregor
Piatigorsky, vlc. RCA.

SUMMER 1950

Concerto in D Major, Op. 61 (Beethoven). Serge Koussevitzky,
cond./L.A. Philharmonic. Live.

NOVEMBER 29-30, 1950

Sonata No. 3, in D Minor, Op. 108 (Brahms). William Kapell,
pf. RCA.

1950

La Fille aux cheveux de lin (Debussy-Hartmann). Emanuel Bay,
pf. RCA.
Hora staccato (Dinicu-Heifetz). Emanuel Bay, pf. RCA.
Polonaise Brilliante No. 1, in D Major (Wieniawski). Emanuel
Bay, pf. RCA.
Scherzo-Tarantelle (Wieniawski). Emanuel Bay, pf. RCA.

CIRCA 1950

Prelude (Bach). Unaccompanied. Film.
Scherzo (from *F.A.E. Sonata*) (Brahms). Emanuel Bay, pf.
Film.
La Fille aux cheveux de lin (Debussy-Hartmann). Emanuel Bay,
pf. Film.
Hora Staccato (Dinicu-Heifetz). Emanuel Bay, pf. Film.
Melodie (Gluck-Kreisler). Emanuel Bay, pf. Film.
Trio in D Minor, Op. 49 (Mendelssohn) (1st & 3rd move.).
Artur Rubinstein, pf/Gregor Piatigorsky, vlc. Film.
Sweet Remembrance (Mendelssohn-Heifetz). Emanuel Bay, pf.
Film.

201

THE BELL SYSTEM

presents

THE TELEPHONE HOUR

February 16, 1948

JASCHA HEIFETZ—*Guest Soloist*

DONALD VOORHEES AND THE

BELL TELEPHONE ORCHESTRA

FLOYD MACK AND TOM SHIRLEY, *Announcers*

Rakoczy March, from "The Damnation of Faust"..*Berlioz*
ORCHESTRA

Romance in F Major (Opus 50) .... *Beethoven*
JASCHA HEIFETZ AND ORCHESTRA

En bateau .... *Debussy*
ORCHESTRA

a. Romanza Andaluza .... *Sarasate*
b. Zapateado .... *Sarasate*
JASCHA HEIFETZ AND ORCHESTRA

THE PROGRAM IS SUBJECT TO CHANGE

A program, autographed by Heifetz, shows a typical hour-long radio program to which the public was invited. Courtesy John Maltese. February 16, 1948.

Caprice No. 24, in A Minor (Paganini-Auer). Emanuel Bay, pf. Film.

March (from *The Love for Three Oranges*) (Prokofiev-Heifetz). Emanuel Bay, pf. Film.

Trio in B-flat, Op. 99 (Schubert) (excerpt). Artur Rubinstein, pf/Gregor Piatigorsky, vlc. Film.

Polonaise Brilliante No. 1, in D Major (Wieniawski). Emanuel Bay, pf. Film.

Scherzo-Tarantelle (Wieniawski). Emanuel Bay, pf. Film.

JANUARY 22, 1951
Capriccio-Valse, Op. 7 (Wieniawski). Emanuel Bay, pf. (Bell Telephone Hour). Live.

APRIL 1, 1951
Concerto in D Minor, Op. 47 (Sibelius). Dimitri Mitropoulos, cond./N.Y. Philharmonic. Live.

MAY 14-15, 1951
Sonata No. 9, in A Major (Kreutzer) (Beethoven). Benno Moiseiwitsch, pf. RCA.

MAY 18, 1951
Concerto No. 1, in G Minor, Op. 26 (Bruch). Sir Malcolm Sargent, cond./London Symphony Orchestra. RCA.

MAY 29-30, 1951
Concerto No. 5, in A Major, K.219 (Turkish) (Mozart). Sir Malcolm Sargent, cond./London Symphony Orchestra. RCA.

JUNE 12-13, 1951
Symphonie Espagnole, Op. 21 (Lalo). William Steinberg, cond./RCA Symphony Orchestra. RCA.

JUNE 15, 1951
Romance No. 1, in G Major, Op. 40 (Beethoven). William Steinberg, cond./RCA Symphony Orchestra. RCA.

Romance No. 2, in F Major, Op. 50 (Beethoven). William Steinberg, cond./RCA Symphony Orchestra.

JUNE 16, 1951
Zigeunerweisen (Sarasate). William Steinberg, cond./RCA Symphony Orchestra. RCA.

JUNE 18, 1951
Havanaise, Op. 83 (Saint-Saens). William Steinberg, cond./ RCA Symphony Orchestra. RCA.

JUNE 19, 1951
Introduction & Rondo Capriccioso (Saint-Saens). William Steinberg, cond./RCA Symphony Orchestra. RCA.

NOVEMBER 19, 1951

Ave Maria (Bach-Gounod). Donald Voorhees, cond./Bell Telephone Orchestra & Chorus. Live.

I Dream of Jeannie with the Light Brown Hair (Foster-Heifetz). Donald Voorhees, cond./Bell Telephone Orchestra. Live.

Banjo and Fiddle (Kroll). Donald Voorhees, cond./Bell Telephone Orchestra. Live.

Concerto in D Minor, Op. 47 (3rd move.) (Sibelius). Donald Voorhees, cond./Bell Telephone Orchestra. Live.

DECEMBER 9, 1951

Concerto in D Major, Op. 77 (Brahms). George Szell, cond./New York Philharmonic. Live.

1951

Stimmung (Achron). Emanuel Bay, pf. Live.

Zephyr (Hubay). Emanuel Bay, pf. Live.

OCTOBER 15, 1952

Sonata No. 3, in E-flat Major (Beethoven). Emanuel Bay, pf. RCA.

Sonata No. 4, in A Major (Beethoven). Emanuel Bay, pf. RCA.

OCTOBER 16, 1952

Sonata No. 6, in A Major (Beethoven). Emanuel Bay, pf. RCA.

Sonata No. 8, in G Major (Beethoven). Emanuel Bay, pf. RCA.

OCTOBER 16-17, 1952

Sonata No. 10, in G Major (Beethoven). Emanuel Bay, pf. RCA.

OCTOBER 21 & 29, 1952

Sonata No. 1, in G Minor (Bach). Unaccompanied. RCA.

OCTOBER 22, 1952

Partita No. 3, in E Major (Bach). Unaccompanied. RCA.

OCTOBER 22 & 29, 1952

Sonata No. 3, in C Major (Bach). Unaccompanied. RCA.

OCTOBER 23 & 29, 1952

Partita No. 1, in B Minor (Bach). Unaccompanied. RCA.

OCTOBER 24, 1952

Partita No. 2, in D Minor (Bach). Unaccompanied. RCA.

OCTOBER 24, 25, & 29, 1952

Sonata No. 2, in A Minor (Bach). Unaccompanied. RCA.

DECEMBER 3, 1952

Concerto in E Minor (Conus). Izler Solomon, cond./RCA Symphony Orchestra. RCA.

JANUARY 10, 1953
Concerto in D Major (Korngold). Alfred Wallenstein, cond./
Los Angeles Philharmonic. RCA.

NOVEMBER 30, 1953
Sonata in D Major, Op. 1, No. 13 (Handel). Emanuel Bay, pf.
RCA.
Sonata in E Major, Op. 1, No. 15 (Handel). Emanuel Bay, pf.
RCA.

DECEMBER 1, 1953
Sonatina No. 3, in G Minor (Schubert). Emanuel Bay, pf. RCA.

DECEMBER 2, 1953
Sonata No. 1 (Bloch). Emanuel Bay, pf. RCA.

DECEMBER 6, 1953
Concerto No. 1, in A Minor (Bach). Alfred Wallenstein, cond./
Los Angeles Philharmonic. RCA.
Concerto No. 2, in E Major (Bach). Alfred Wallenstein, cond./
Los Angeles Philharmonic. RCA.

DECEMBER 8, 1953
Tzigane (Ravel). Alfred Wallenstein, cond./Los Angeles Phil.
RCA.

DECEMBER 9, 1953
Hungarian Dance No. 7, in A Major (Brahms-Joachim). Alfred
Wallenstein, cond./Los Angeles Philharmonic. RCA.
Suite in A Minor (Sinding). Alfred Wallenstein, cond./Los
Angeles Philharmonic. RCA.

MARCH 14, 1954
Concerto in E Minor, Op. 64 (Mendelssohn). Guido Cantelli,
cond./New York Philharmonic. Live.

MARCH 30, 1954
The Lark (Poem in the Form of a Rondo) (Castelnuovo-Tedesco). Emanuel Bay, pf. RCA.

OCTOBER 28-29, 1954
Concerto No. 2 (I Profeti) (Castelnuovo-Tedesco). Alfred Wallenstein, cond./Los Angeles Philharmonic. RCA.

OCTOBER 29, 1954
Serenade Melancolique (Tchaikovsky). Alfred Wallenstein,
cond./Los Angeles Philharmonic. RCA.

NOVEMBER 2, 1954
Concerto No. 2, in D Minor, Op. 44 (Bruch). Izler Solomon,
cond./RCA Symphony Orchestra. RCA.

NOVEMBER 3, 1954
Concerto No. 8, in A Minor, Op. 47 (Spohr). Izler Solomon, cond./RCA Symphony Orchestra. RCA.

NOVEMBER 5, 1954
Concerto No. 2, in D Minor, Op. 22 (Wieniawski). Izler Solomon, cond./RCA Symphony Orchestra. RCA.

DECEMBER 8, 1954
Sabre Dance (Khachaturian-Heifetz). Brooks Smith, pf. RCA.
Sonata in B-flat Major, K. 378 (Mozart). Brooks Smith, pf. RCA.

DECEMBER 9, 1954
Sonata in B-flat Major, K. 454 (Mozart). Brooks Smith, pf. RCA.

DECEMBER 10, 1954
Serenata Napoletana (Sgambati). Brooks Smith, pf. RCA.
Sonata in E-flat, Op. 18 (Strauss). Brooks Smith, pf. RCA.

FEBRUARY 21-22, 1955
Concerto in D Major, Op. 77 (Brahms). Fritz Reiner, cond./ Chicago Symphony Orchestra. RCA.

NOVEMBER 25, 1955
Concerto in D Major, Op. 61 (Beethoven). Charles Munch, cond./Boston Symphony Orchestra. Live.

NOVEMBER 27-28, 1955
Concerto in D Major, Op. 61 (Beethoven). Charles Munch, cond./Boston Symphony Orchestra. RCA.

DECEMBER 15, 1955
Sonata No. 2, in G Major, Op. 13 (Grieg). Brooks Smith, pf. RCA.

DECEMBER 15-16, 1955
Sonata in A Major, Op. 13 (Faure). Brooks Smith, pf. RCA.

DECEMBER 16, 1955
Cod Liver 'Ile (Shulman). Brooks Smith, pf. RCA.

DECEMBER 16-17, 1955
Sonata No. 2 (Poeme Mystique) (Bloch). Brooks Smith, pf. RCA.

DECEMBER 17, 1955
Song Sonata (Bennett). Brooks Smith, pf. RCA.

FEBRUARY 12, 1956
Concerto in D Major, Op. 61 (Beethoven). Dimitri Mitropoulos, cond./New York Philharmonic. Live.

MARCH 27, 1956

Concerto, Op. 24 (Rozsa). Walter Hendl, cond./Dallas Symphony Orchestra. RCA.

APRIL 14, 1956

Caprice No. 13, in B-flat Major (Paganini-Kreisler). Brooks Smith, pf. RCA.

Caprice No. 20, in D Major (Paganini-Kreisler). Brooks Smith, pf. RCA.

OCTOBER 1, 1956

Romantic Fantasy (Benjamin). Izler Solomon, cond./RCA Symphony Orchestra. William Primrose, viola. RCA.

OCTOBER 2, 1956

Sinfonia Concertante in E-flat Major, K. 364 (Mozart). Izler Solomon, cond./RCA Symphony Orchestra. William Primrose, viola. RCA.

MARCH 27, 1957

Trio in G Major, Op. 9, No. 1 (Beethoven). William Primrose, vla/Gregor Piatigorsky, vlc. RCA.

MARCH 28-29, 1957

Trio in E-flat Major, Op. 3 (Beethoven). William Primrose, vla/Gregor Piatigorsky, vlc. RCA.

MARCH 29-30, 1957

Trio in C Minor, Op. 9, No. 3 (Beethoven). William Primrose, vla/Gregor Piatigorsky, vlc. RCA.

APRIL 19, 1957

Concerto in D Major, Op. 35 (Tchaikovsky). Fritz Reiner, cond./Chicago Symphony Orchestra. RCA.

FEBRUARY 23 & 25, 1959

Concerto in E Minor, Op. 64 (Mendelssohn). Charles Munch, cond./Boston Symphony Orchestra. RCA.

FEBRUARY 24, 1959

Concerto No. 2, in G Minor, Op. 63 (Prokofieff). Charles Munch, cond./Boston Symphony Orchestra. RCA.

HUMAN RIGHT'S DAY 1959

Concerto in D Major, Op. 61 (Beethoven). Paul Paray, cond./Detroit Symphony Orchestra. Live.

CIRCA 1959 (UCLA MASTER CLASSES)

MR. HEIFETZ PERFORMS

Concerto in D Minor for Two Violins (Bach) (2nd-3rd move.). Erick Friedman, vln/Brooks Smith, pf. Film.

Concerto in A Minor (Bach). Carol Sindell, vln/Jascha Heifetz, pf. Film.

Quartet No. 5, in A Major, Op. 18, No. 5 (Beethoven) (1st move.). Carol Sindell, vln/Erick Friedman, vln/Rosen, vlc. Film.

MR. HEIFETZ INSTRUCTS:

Polonaise Brilliante No. 2 (Wieniawski). Varoujon Kodjian, vln/Brooks Smith, pf. Film.

Ao pe da fogueira (Valle). Varoujon Kodjian, vln/Brooks Smith, pf. Film.

Concerto in D Major, Op. 77 (Brahms). Erick Friedman, vln/ Brooks Smith, pf. Film.

Etude No. 5 (Dont). Claire Hodgkins, vln. Film.

Poeme, Op. 25 (Chausson). Claire Hodgkins, vln/Brooks Smith, pf. Film.

Concerto in D Major, Op. 35 (Tchaikovsky). Robert Witte, vln/ Brooks Smith, pf. Film.

Sonata in G Minor (Bach) (Adagio & Fugue). Erick Friedman, vln. Film.

Concerto (Khachaturian) (1st movement). Elizabeth Matesky, vln/Brooks Smith, pf. Film.

Sonata in A Major (Franck) (1st movement). Erick Friedman, vln/Brooks Smith, pf. Film.

Partita No. 2, in D Minor (Bach). Varoujon Kodjian, yln. Film.

MAY 19-20, 1960

Double Concerto in A Minor, Op. 102 (Brahms). Alfred Wallenstein, cond./RCA Victor Symphony Orchestra. Gregor Piatigorsky, cello. RCA.

AUGUST 15, 1960

Sinfonia No. 9, in F Minor (Bach). William Primrose, vla/ Gregor Piatigorsky, vlc. RCA.

AUGUST 15 & 22, 1960

Serenade (Trio in D, Op. 8) (Beethoven). William Primrose, vla/Gregor Piatigorsky, vlc. RCA.

AUGUST 16, 1960

Sinfonia No. 4, in D Minor (Bach). William Primrose, vla/ Gregor Piatigorsky, vlc. RCA.

AUGUST 16 & 22, 1960

Trio No. 2, in B-flat Major (Schubert). William Primrose, vla/ Gregor Piatigorsky, vlc.

AUGUST 17 & 22, 1960
Trio in D Major, Op. 9, No. 2 (Beethoven). William Primrose, vla/Gregor Piatigorsky, vlc. RCA.

AUGUST 18, 1960
Sinfonia No. 3, in D Major (Bach). William Primrose, vla/ Gregor Piatigorsky, vlc. RCA.

SEPTEMBER 20-21, 1960
Duo, Op. 7 (Kodaly). Gregor Piatigorsky, cello. RCA.

SEPTEMBER 22-23, 1960
Sonata No. 9, in A, Op. 47 (*Kreutzer*) (Beethoven). Brooks Smith, pf. RCA.

MAY 15 & 22, 1961
Scottish Fantasy, Op. 46 (Bruch). Sir Malcolm Sargent, cond./ New Symphony Orchestra of London. RCA.
Concerto No. 5, in A Minor, Op. 37 (Vieuxtemps). Sir Malcolm Sargent, cond./New Sym. Orchestra of London. RCA.

MAY 19-20, 1961
Double Concerto in D Minor (Bach). Sir Malcolm Sargent, cond./New Symphony Orchestra of London. Erick Friedman, violin. RCA.

AUGUST 21-22, 1961
Quintet in F Minor (Franck). Leonard Pennario, pf/Israel Baker, vln/William Primrose, vla/Gregor Piatigorsky, vlc. RCA.

AUGUST 24-25, 1961
Octet in E-flat, Op. 20 (Mendelssohn). Israel Baker, vln/Arnold Belnick, vln/Joseph Stepansky, vln/William Primrose, vla/ Virginia Majewski, vla/Gabor Rejto, vlc/Gregor Piatigorsky, vlc. RCA.

AUGUST 28-29, 1961
Sextet in G Major, Op. 36 (Brahms). Israel Baker, vln/Virginia Majewski, vla/William Primrose, vla/Gabor Rejto, vlc/ Gregor Piatigorsky, vlc. RCA.

AUGUST 29-30, 1961
Quintet in G Minor, K. ??? (Mozart). Israel Baker, vln/William Primrose, vla/Virginia Majewski, vla/Gregor Piatigorsky, vlc. RCA.

NOVEMBER 30-DECEMBER 1, 1961
Quintet in C Major, Op. 163 (Schubert). Israel Baker, vln/ William Primrose, vla/Gregor Piatigorsky, vlc/Gabor Rejto, vlc. RCA.

MAY 14 & 16, 1962

Concerto No. 1, in G Minor, Op. 26 (Bruch). Sir Malcolm Sargent, cond./New Symphony Orchestra of London. RCA.

Concerto No. 4, in D Major, K. 218 (Mozart). Sir Malcolm Sargent, cond./New Symphony Orchestra of London. RCA.

JUNE 3-4, 1963

Concerto in A Minor, Op. 82 (Glazounov). Walter Hendl, cond./RCA Symphony Orchestra. RCA.

OCTOBER 6, 1963

Concerto No. 5, in A, K. 219 (Turkish) (Mozart). Chamber Orchestra. RCA.

OCTOBER 7, 1963

Tema con Variazoni (Rosza). Chamber Orchestra/Gregor Piatigorsky, cello. RCA.

OCTOBER 10, 1963

Concerto in B-flat, Op. 22, No. 2 (Vivaldi). Chamber Orchestra/Gregor Piatigorsky, cello/Malcolm Hamilton, harpsichord. RCA.

OCTOBER 14 & NOVEMBER 12, 1963

Passacaglia (Handel-Halvorsen). Gregor Piatigorsky, cello. RCA (Col.).

Suite Italienne (Stravinsky). Gregor Piatigorsky, cello. RCA (Col.).

OCTOBER 17, 1963

Trio in D Minor, Op. 32 (Arensky). Leonard Pennario, pf/ Gregor Piatigorsky, vlc. RCA.

NOVEMBER 6, 1963

Trio in D Minor, Op. 35 (Turina). Leonard Pennario, pf/ Gregor Piatigorsky, vlc. RCA.

NOVEMBER 7-8, 1963

Trio in C Minor, Op. 66 (Mendelssohn). Leonard Pennario, pf/ Gregor Piatigorsky, vlc. RCA.

NOVEMBER 11, 1963

Trio in F Minor, Op. 65 (Dvorak). Leonard Pennario, pf/ Gregor Piatigorsky, vlc. RCA (Col.).

MARCH 23, 1964

Trio in E-flat, Op. 1, No. 1 (Beethoven). Jacob Lateiner, pf/ Gregor Piatigorsky, vlc. RCA.

MARCH 26-27, 1964

Quintet in C Major, K. 515 (Mozart). Israel Baker, vln/William

Primrose, vla/Virginia Majewski, vla/Gregor Piatigorsky, vlc. RCA.

NOVEMBER 9-10, 1964

Quintet in A Major, Op. 81 (Dvorak). Jacob Lateiner, pf/Israel Baker, vln/Joseph de Pasquale, vla/Gregor Piatigorsky, vlc. RCA.

NOVEMBER 11, 1964

Trio in C Major (Francaix) (1933). Joseph de Pasquale, vla/ Gregor Piatigorsky, vlc. RCA.

NOVEMBER 18, 1964

Sonata in D Major (Boccherini). Gregor Piatigorsky, cello. RCA.

Duo, Op. 39: Prelude (Gliere). Gregor Piatigorsky, cello. RCA Col.).

Duo (Martinu) (1927). Gregor Piatigorsky, cello. RCA.

APRIL 13, 1965

A Woman is a Sometime Thing (Gershwin-Heifetz). Brooks Smith, pf. RCA.

Bess, You Is My Woman Now (Gershwin-Heifetz). Brooks Smith, pf. RCA.

It Ain't Necessarily So (Gershwin-Heifetz). Brooks Smith, pf. RCA.

My Man's Gone Now (Gershwin-Heifetz). Brooks Smith, pf. RCA.

Summertime (Gershwin-Heifetz). Brooks Smith, pf. RCA.

Tempo di Blues (Gershwin-Heifetz). Brooks Smith, pf. RCA.

Three Preludes (Gershwin-Heifetz). Brooks Smith, pf. RCA.

APRIL 14, 1965

Beau Soir (Debussy-Heifetz). Brooks Smith, pf. RCA.

Golliwogg's Cakewalk (Debussy-Heifetz). Brooks Smith, pf. RCA.

La Chevelure (Debussy-Heifetz). Brooks Smith, pf. RCA.

Le Petit ane blanc (Ibert-Heifetz). Brooks Smith, pf. RCA.

Valses nobles et sentimentales: Nos. 6 & 7 (Ravel-Heifetz). Brooks Smith, pf. RCA.

Le Cygne (The Swan) (Saint Saens-Heifetz). Brooks Smith, pf. RCA.

APRIL 16, 1965

Divertimento, Op. 37, No. 2 (Toch). Gregor Piatigorsky, cello. RCA.

AUGUST 17-18, 1965

Quartet in C Minor, Op. 60 (Brahms). Jacob Lateiner, pf/

Sanford Schonbach, vla/Gregor Piatigorsky, vlc. RCA.

APRIL 4, 1965
Concerto in D Minor for 2 Violins (Bach). Chamber Orchestra/
violin soloist. Live.
Octet in E-flat Major, Op. 20 (Mendelssohn). With students
from U.S.C. Live.

APRIL 4, 1965
Divertimento, Op. 37, No. 2 (Toch). Gregor Piatigorsky, cello.
Live.
Concerto in B-flat, Op. 22, No. 2 (Vivaldi). Chamber Orches-
tra/Gregor Piatigorsky, cello. Live.

FEBRUARY 7, 1966
Sonata No. 1, Op. 2 (Ferguson) (1931). Lillian Steuber, pf.
RCA.

FEBRUARY 8, 1966
Sonata in G Minor, Op. 1 (Khachaturian). Lillian Steuber, pf.
RCA.

OCTOBER 15, 1966
Double Concerto in A Minor, Op. 102 (Brahms). Orchestra/
Gregor Piatigorsky, cello. Live.
Concerto in E Minor (Conus). Orchestra. Live.

MAY 2-3, 1967
Sonata in D Minor, Op. 75 (Saint-Saens). Brooks Smith, pf.
RCA.

MAY 4, 1967
Jota (de Falla-Kochanski). Brooks Smith, pf. RCA.
Nana (de Falla-Kochanski). Brooks Smith, pf. RCA.
Daisies, Op. 30, No. 3 (Rachmaninoff-Heifetz). Brooks Smith,
pf. RCA.
Oriental Sketch, Op. 2, No. 2 (Rachmaninoff-Heifetz). Brooks
Smith, pf. RCA.
Capriccio-Valse, Op. 7 (Wieniawski). Brooks Smith, pf. RCA.

JUNE 24-25, 1968
Double Quartet in D Minor, Op. 65 (Spohr). Israel Baker, vln/
Pierre Amoyal, vln/Paul Rosenthal, vln/Milton Thomas, vla/
Allan Harshman, vla/Gregor Piatigorsky, vlc/Laurence
Lesser, vlc. RCA.

JULY 1-2, 1968
Trio in E Minor, Op. 90 (Dumky) (Dvorak). Jacob Lateiner, pf/
Gregor Piatigorsky, vlc. RCA.

SEPTEMBER 19-20, 1968

Fantasie in C Major, Op. 159 (Schubert). Brooks Smith, pf.
RCA.

PART VII — 1970 to date

JULY 8, 1970

Serenade Melancolique, Op. 26 (Tchaikovsky). Chamber
Orchestra. RCA.

JULY 10, 1970

Valse (from *Serenade in C*) (Tchaikovsky). Chamber Orchestra.
RCA.

SEPTEMBER 15, 1970

La Fille aux Cheveux de Lin (Debussy-Hartmann). Brooks
Smith, pf. Film-RCA.

It Ain't Necessarily So (Gershwin-Heifetz). Brooks Smith, pf.
Film-RCA.

Garden Scene (Korngold). Brooks Smith, pf. Film-RCA.

Rondo (from *Haffner Serenade*) (Mozart-Kreisler). Brooks
Smith, pf. Film-RCA.

March (*Love for Three Oranges*) (Prokofiev-Heifetz). Brooks
Smith, pf. Film-RCA.

Daisies, Op. 30, No. 3 (Rachmaninoff-Heifetz). Brooks Smith,
pf. Film-RCA.

SEPTEMBER 16, 1970

Chaconne (from *Partita No. 2*) (Bach). Unaccompanied. Film-
RCA.

SEPTEMBER 1970

Scottish Fantasy, Op. 46 (Bruch) (abridged). French National
Orchestra. Film.

Passacaglia (Handel-Halvorsen) (excerpt). Pierre Amoyal, viola.
Film.

OCTOBER 23, 1972

Prelude, Lourre, & Gigue (from *Partita No. 3*) (Bach). Unaccompanied. Live-Col.

Nigun (from *Baal Shem*) (Bloch) (1923). Brooks Smith, pf. Live-
Col.

Sea Murmurs (Castelnuovo Tedesco-Heifetz). Brooks Smith, pf.
Live-Col.

La Plus que Lent (Debussy-Roques). Brooks Smith, pf. Live-
Col.

Nana (de Falla-Kochanski). Brooks Smith, pf. Live-Col.

Sonata in A Major (Franck). Brooks Smith, pf. Live-Col.

La Chasse (In the Style of Cartier) (Kreisler). Brooks Smith, pf. Live-Col.

Etude-Tableau, Op. 33, No. 4 (Rachmaninoff-Heifetz). Brooks Smith, pf. Live-Col.

Tzigane (Rhapsodie de Concert) (Ravel). Brooks Smith, pf. Live-Col.

Sonata in E-flat Major, Op. 18 (Strauss). Brooks Smith, pf. Live-Col.

Castelnuovo-Tedesco, Beverly Hills, California, 1950.

Jascha Heifetz, Violinist, In His Only Broadcast This Year Will Be Heard Today as Soloist With a 60-Piece Symphony Orchestra Directed by Bruno Walter. The New York Outlet Is WJZ From 6 to 7 P. M.

Leonard Bernstein, the musical genius who breathed new life into the New York Philharmonic Orchestra, did not get along too well with Heifetz. Circa 1947.

REVIEWS FROM NEW YORK NEWSPAPERS

The following pages contain a majority of the reviews which appeared in the New York papers during Heifetz's reign as the supreme violinist. The reviews are published as they appeared, with variations in spellings of composers' names, and with credits as they appeared in the press releases. A few reviews have been shortened to remove extraneous or unimportant material. A few reviews may be missing since many of the original New York papers have ceased publication and the "morgue" did not contain copies suitable for copying.

Jascha Heifetz the week of his debut. October, 1917.

OCTOBER 27, 1917
CARNEGIE HALL

"HATS OFF, GENTLEMEN, A GENIUS!"
APPLIES TO HEIFETZ, IN DEBUT

Russian Lad Called a Transcendentally Great Violinist — "Element Almost Preternatural Envelopes His Art" — "Plays With a Tone Lustrous and Silken, Fragrant, Intoxicatingly Sweet. . . an Illimitable Technique" — Huge Audience Seemed to Hold Every Violinist of Note Within Radius of Two Hundred Miles — Hearers Transported with Joy

JASCHA HEIFETZ, VIOLINIST, RECITAL, CARNEGIE HALL, AFTERNOON, OCT. 27. ACCOMPANIST, ANDRE BENOIST.

THE PROGRAM: Chaconne, Vitali; Concerto in D Minor, Wieniawski; "Ave Maria," Schubert; "Menuetto," Mozart; Nocturne in D Major, Chopin-Wilhelmj; Chorus of Dervishes, "Marche Orientale" from the "Ruins of Athens,". Beethoven-Auer; "Melodie," Tchaikovsky; Capriccio, No. 24, Paganini-Auer.

It may not be that the greatest violinists now browsing in these fertile pastures are quite serious in their rumored decision to shut up shop, burn their fiddles and withdraw to distant wastes or sombre forests to invite oblivion because Jascha Heifetz has come upon us. The power and the glory of the newcomer may not be as ruthlessly destructive as all that. Nevertheless, this Russian boy of seventeen summers is beyond all possibility of cavil a divinely inspired marvel, whom advance report has belied only by undervaluation, and the most breathtaking, the most crushing, the supremest genius of the violin that has confronted us in the past decade or perchance even more. His American debut last Saturday afternoon was one of those extraordinary occasions that stifles skepticism at its source and that carries away upon a tidal wave of seething enthusiasm the common boundary marks of moderation. A few strokes of a flame-tipped bow over strings become vocal with a fabulous sweetness sufficed to tell the story of a triumph that will reverberate through the extent of the land these months to come. The force and fervency of the general delight, which grew as the afternoon advanced, were of the sort that make an event historic. There was a huge audience which included, it seemed, every violinist within a radius of two hundred miles. And their enthusiasm amidst the general delight was not the least. No one, for that matter, seemed more transported than Maud Powell, who stayed to applaud frantically till the very last encore.

A True Genius

Jascha Heifetz is a transcendentally great violinist; and more, a very great artist—one who, saving the comparison, can stand in the presence of a Kreisler and not be ashamed. Between the measure of his art and the tenderness of his years there can be no relative considerations whatsoever. Heifetz at forty may—and probably will—be a more superlative executant and expositor than he is today. But were he twice his age the wonder and admiration at what he now encompasses would be undiminished.

Villiers de Ll'Isle-Adam exclaimed once of Richard Wagner: "He is cubic; he comprises all." In a sense, such a definition is applicable to Heifetz. He embodies a concentration of the supernal violinistic and musical traits—virtuosity purged of every element of grossness or vain display and the instinct for beauty carried to the very poignancy of loveliness. His pro-

219

Jascha Heifetz, the young genius who startled New York on October 27, 1917 with the finest violin playing the city had ever heard. October, 1917.

gram last week was in large degree commonplace and superficial; on the whole, unilluminating in its intellectual requisitions. Of what great issues Mr. Heifetz is capable in music imposing demands for deeper mental processes, for profounder emotional soundings and more consuming passions we must forbear for the moment to divine. But the intelligence, the emotion, the sensibilities and aspirations are there and in the manner of their exploitation the present and potential greatness of the artist stands overpoweringly vindicated. The tawdriest music which he essayed last week he invested with a loftiness, dignity and sheer ecstasy of beauty that lent it the illusion of surpassing worth—veritable re-creation, transfiguring past belief. But where the question was of greater music the accent became as that of luminous prophecy, magnificently effortless in its expression. In truth, an element almost preternatural envelopes the art of Jascha Heifetz. Heine once drew a comparison between the pianists of his time, defining Thalberg as a king, Liszt as a prophet and Doehler as a— pianist. Almost one is tempted upon encountering Heifetz to invoke Heine's classifications in respect to living violinists—in which case Kreisler is king, Heifetz prophet and—but the candidates for the third distinction are too numerous for record. A mere child, there proceed from this newest visitant the streaming splendors of maturest vision, a seer-like quality of divination, a dream-wrought fabric of poesy beyond words transporting, puissant, inevitable. The whole phenomenon is of a kind before which the accomplishment of the most talented artists among us—save one—pale their ineffectual fires. In his superb and poise and modest, gentlemanly bearing the boy exacts no less amazement. As if entranced in a celestially impelled business, his attitude is one almost of indifference to his audience. He acknowledged its tempestuous applause on Saturday with a few perfunctory bows and in some cases not at all. When some clamored immoderately for encores he returned to the stage and forthwith attacked the next group on his program. While playing his demeanor is as free from mannered affectations as his performances.

A Glorious Artistic Entity

A conscientious chronicle is assumed to involve a more or less categorical enumeration of an artist's specific virtues. With Heifetz the total impression is so complete, so overwhelming and indivisible that a reviewer must long rather to expatiate on the glorious artistic entity than to dissect and particularize. It may, however, be proper to point out that the newcomer plays with a tone so lustrous and silken, so fragrant, so intoxicatingly sweet that only the molten gold of Fritz Kreisler can be conjured up in comparison. But though it wrings the tears from the eyes by its lambent beauty, its vibrancy and infinite play of magical color, its nature bespeaks a singular aristocratic purity rather than an unrelieved sensuousness, though its power of emotional conveyance and suggestion is unparalleled. And, however forcible the vigor of Mr. Heifetz's superb, sweeping bowing, not the minutest impurity of any other sort mars its ceaseless enchantment. From the pitch the violinist never wavers by the breadth of even a hair. In his rhythm he is unfaltering, in his musicianship unchallengeable.

A technique is his transcendent, illimitable. A technique, however, contemptuous of its own colossal, all-embracing prowess, spiritualized and addressed at all times solely to idealistic ends. But if one barely notices it for its own sake, one is ever and anon reminded that nothing is impossible to it.

Heifetz. Circa 1921.

Heretical as the assertion may seem, we greatly doubt if Ysaÿe, at the height of his powers, ever played the Vitali Chaconne with a greater breadth and elevation of style, a more sculpturesque, plastic quality or a firmer grasp of its import than did Mr. Heifetz last week. A hazardous statement, but let it stand! The faded and battered Concerto of Wieniawski passed through a veritable rebirth. Mozart's Minuet proved delicacy incarnate, Wilhelmj's Chopin translation a closer approach to its poetic original than we have ever known it to be in this form. Professor Auer's intrinsically uninteresting Beethoven arrangement bits of gem-like witchery. Of the Paganini Caprice he made an etherealized tone poem. His most notable encores were the Tartini-Kreisler Theme and Variations and Cui's "Orientale," this last made inimitably atmospheric. A transcription of one of Popper's whirling 'cello pieces showed, as did many other numbers on the program, Mr. Heifetz's passage work to be as exquisitely wrought as finest golden filigree.

Andre Benoist, latterly with Albert Spalding, provided accompaniments worthy of the newcomer's art. In the Vitali Chaconne Frank L. Sealy was the organist.

H.F.P.

OCTOBER 27, 1917
CARNEGIE HALL

BOY VIOLINIST WINS TRIUMPH
Jascha Heifetz Casts Spell of Amazement Over Critics at Carnegie Hall

The American debut of Jascha Heifetz yesterday will go on record as one of the most notable incidents in the recent musical history of New York.

This Russian youth is said to be only sixteen years old, though he might be eighteen or nineteen to judge from his appearance, and forty to judge from his extraordinary poise. Yet already his mastery of the violin is such that one can compare him only to the greatest virtuosi of the present and the past.

Comparisons are often dangerous but the writer for *The American* does not hesitate to assert that in all his experience he has never heard any violinistic approach as close to the loftiest standards of absolute perfection as did Jascha Heifetz yesterday.

It was an occasion never to be forgotten, this sweeping triumph of a boy who, without pose or affectation, cast a spell of utter amazement over every professional listener.

To dilate upon the mechanical proficiency Jascha Heifetz has obtained on his instrument—to discuss in detail the extraordinary dexterity and precision of his slender fingers, the lightness, elasticity and supple firmness of his bowing—seems almost superfluous, when it can be described by one word: *perfection*. Verily, his command of the technics of the violin is nothing short of transcendental.

The tone he draws from the strings—a tone exquisitely pure and precise to the pitch at all times—is not only mellow, vibrant, intense, but breathes a delicately refined expressiveness that can only come from the soul of a poet.

223

Heifetz.
November, 1917.

Andre Benoist,
Heifetz's first
accompanist.

Such was the general impression made yesterday by Jascha Heifetz in a programme that comprised Vitali's Chaconne; Wieniawsky's Concerto in D minor; Schubert's "Ave Maria;" Mozart's "Menuetto;" the Chopin-Wilhelmj Nocturne in D major; transcriptions by Auer of Beethoven's "Chorus of Dervishes" and "Marche Orientale" from "The Ruins of Athens," a "Melodie" by Tchaikovsky; Auer's elaboration of Paganini's Capriccio No. 24, the Popper-Auer "Spinning Wheel," and Faust's "Serenade."

OCTOBER 27, 1917
SATURDAY, 2:30
CARNEGIE HALL

HEIFETZ PROVES GREATNESS QUIETLY
Nothing Spectacular, Sensational About Youthful Violinist in New York—
He Wins Victory Without Flourish or Appeal

By Max Smith

Of what violinist who has visited America in the last score of years can it be said as truly as of Jascha Heifetz: "He came, he saw, he conquered?" Yet there was nothing spectacular, nothing sensational, about the debut of this youthful musician in Carnegie Hall. He won his victory without any flourishes, without any appeals to the gallery, devoting himself simply to the task of playing his instrument just as well as he knew how.

As the writer has remarked before, there is happily more than one way of achieving impressive results in any given branch of interpretative music. For every performer whose talents and accomplishments are of a high order has a personality of his own, has individual traits that stamp themselves unmistakably on his art. And no less varied than the traits of the performers are the tastes of his listeners.

So, too, you may be more responsive to the appeal of a Kreisler than to that of a Jascha Heifetz. But you might have some difficulty in proving that Nikisch was a greater conductor than Toscanini or Kreisler a greater violinist than Heifetz.

Greater in some respects, no doubt, one is than the other; fortunately for us, nature never duplicates exactly. Yet scarcely each is great in his special way, and no less so because his excellences and imperfections do not coincide precisely with the excellences and imperfections of his rivals.

A Great Violinist

There can be no question, even though one's judgment is based necessarily on only one recital, that Jascha Heifetz takes a place among the leading violinists of the world. Despite his extraordinary youth he already has acquired a mastery of his instrument that probably is not surpassed by any other living virtuoso. But amazement at his precocious technical proficiency and musical intelligence and taste should not make one forget that he may still disclose shortcomings which were not evident at first nor should they induce one to underrate the achievements of fellow-artists whose powers have been completely revealed to us.

From a purely technical point of view this young master seems to have approached astonishingly to perfection. The slender fingers of his left hand solve the most difficult problems with incredible precision and dispatch. His bowing is nothing short of marvelous in its elasticity, its

lightness, in its supple adjustment of pressure and motion; in its smooth and fluent transition from the downward to the upward stroke, and vice versa.

The tone he draws from the strings, pulsating under the influence of an almost flawless vibrato, has a peculiar ethereal beauty. Never saturated with the fat of sensuality, never impregnated with purely animal passion, it has yet a penetrating sweetness and intensity of expression that carries its message, even in the loftiest and most tonal altitudes.

So exquisitely balanced a control, indeed, does Heifetz exercise over the finger board and the bow that the minute mechanical defects, which even the most distinguished men of his profession are rarely able to avoid entirely, seem to be totally eradicated from his playing. In his performance a little over a week ago, at any rate, the present writer failed to detect the least deflection from the correct pitch, the slightest semblance of a rasp, the faintest unintentional buzzing of the strings under the impact of his fingers.

Heifetz Musicianship

As for the musicianship and the taste displayed by Heifetz, it appeared to be as faultless as his technique. There was no attempt at exaggeration, no affectation, no pose. From first to last his phrasing fulfilled the most exacting demands.

Still, it must be conceded that the programme Heifetz had chosen for his American debut—a programme made up almost entirely of numbers other violinists had played here frequently—offered a better opportunity to measure the more palpable merits of his art than to gauge his musical penetration and grasp. Before we can form a perfectly comprehensive estimate of this remarkable young Russian, therefore, we must hear him in music that puts a heavier burden on his youthful shoulders, in music that makes demands on the emotions as well as on the intellect, that requires temperamental energy and fire as well as technical finish and delicacy.

To judge from his first recital, Jascha Heifetz is prone to be academic rather than romantic. Most musicians of his age would be in their period of storm and stress, or at least on the threshold of that period. Yet he seems to have already sailed safely through the danger zone and to have reached the placid harbor of mature manhood.

Perhaps he will never have the energy, the vigor, the nervous vitality of a Kreisler. It was interesting for those who heard the Viennese violinist twenty-four hours after Heifetz had been playing in the same hall, to draw comparisons between the two—the one quiet, reposeful, almost abstracted as he stood with motionless body, his profile toward the spectators; the other, alert, eager, quickly responsive, all a-tingle with temperament, as he manipulated his violin, facing the audience squarely.

But here we come again to the point emphasized at the outset. The public is fortunate in having a Kreisler, a Heifetz, an Elman and a Zimbalist. And fortunate it is, indeed, for all of us, that those masters of fiddle and bow are not cast in the same mold.

Heifetz, circa 1917.

One of the first Victor publicity photographs of Jascha Heifetz. Circa 1917.

DECEMBER 1, 1917
2:30 P.M.
CARNEGIE HALL

HEIFETZ STIRS 3000 TO WILD APPLAUSE
Unassuming Young Russian Wins Spectacular Success in Carnegie Hall

Jascha Heifetz, the young Russian violinist, whose American debut at Carnegie Hall in October was one of the sensations of the musical season, gave a recital in the same auditorium on the afternoon of Dec. 1 before an audience of 3000 persons, who greeted the young artist with a demonstration of enthusiasm which has not been equaled since the first American appearance of Paderewski in the early 'nineties.

The audience, which included many critical musicians, remained for a half hour after the end of the program, while the player gave seven encores, and would probably have stayed as much longer had not sheer fatigue compelled Mr. Heifetz to decline to play any more.

The prevailing characteristic of Mr. Heifetz's playing continues to be his utter lack of self-consciousness, a rare quality among violinists, and the seriousness with which he takes his art. He accepted all of the applause not as a personal tribute and gave his extra numbers with the air of one who was glad to play for people who wanted to hear him.

The Handel D Major Sonata was given in true classical style, and the Saint-Saens Third Concerto, utterly different in every respect, brought forth all the versatility of which Mr. Heifetz is obviously capable. The Bach Chaconne was also a beautiful piece of work and a group of short numbers all splendidly done, each in its individual way. The Wieniawski Polonaise roused the audience to a pitch of excitement, which was a climax to the former demonstrations.

JASCHA HEIFETZ HEARD IN SECOND RECITAL HERE

Jascha Heifetz's second recital in New York, which marked the young Russian violinist's fourth public appearance in this city, attracted a huge audience to Carnegie Hall yesterday afternoon. Even the stage had to be used to accommodate the crowd.

As before, Leopold Auer's extraordinary pupil fascinated his listeners through the beauty of his tone, the marvelous perfection of his technique and the quiet assurance and repose of his manner. His programme, however, might well have been chosen more wisely. Saint-Saen's Concerto No. 3 is quite ineffective without orchestra, and surely ought not to have been sandwiched between Handel's Sonata in D major, No. 4, and Bach's Chaconne.

Performed with a well-nigh incredible mastery of its manifold mechanical difficulties, though hardly with a complete grasp of the spirit of the music, this great work by Bach represented perhaps the most astonishing achievement of the afternoon—at least in the opinion of the cognoscenti. Strange enough, Heifetz actually drew from the E string in Wagner's "Albumblatt" an altitudinous C sharp that did not quite reach the true pitch, whereas, his intonation in the grueling chord-formations of the Chaconne was always impeccable.

Wilhelmj's transcription of the Wagner piece also disclosed, by the way, that Heifetz is not romantically inclined. His performance was far from temperamental. It was academic.

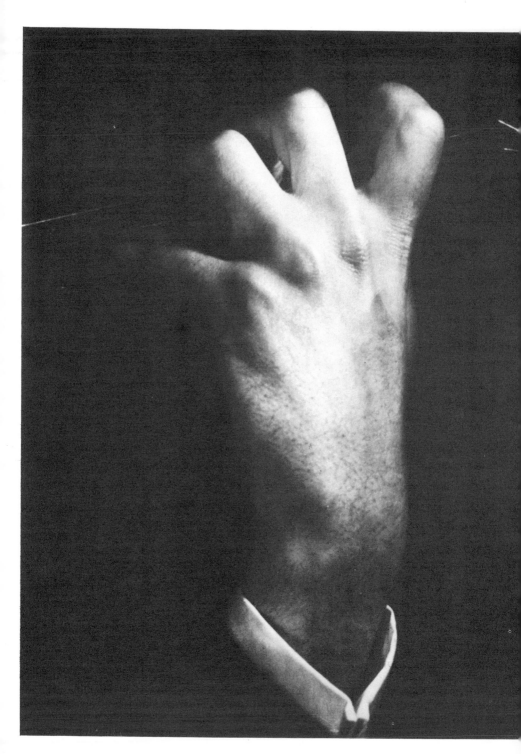

JANUARY 1, 1918
TUESDAY, 3:00 P.M.
CARNEGIE HALL

HEIFETZ RAGE OF CONCERT WORLD

By Max Smith

That Jascha Heifetz is the rage in the concert world was quite apparent at the young Russian violinist's third local recital yesterday afternoon in Carnegie Hall. Yet the demonstrations of the big gathering which applauded him so frantically after every selection on the programme in no way ruffled the equanimity of this extraordinary youth. Despite tumultuous demands, he refused to depart from his plan of giving encores only after the fourth group of pieces and at the close. And throughout the afternoon, he played as one whose every faculty was held unswervingly under absolute control.

A more amazing exhibition of technical mastery than Heifetz offered in such works as Paganini's Caprices Nos. 20 and 13, and Fritz Kreisler's gruelingly difficult version of that arch-virtuoso's "I Palpiti" variations would be impossible to imagine. Professional violinists sat agape as he made his revelations and gasped in amazement at the close when he shook out of his sleeve, as it were, the most dazzling strings of octaves at incredible speed.

It must be confessed, however, that this wizard of the bow failed to disclose the slightest rift in his shell of self-possession and placity, did not voice a single phrase with anything approaching temperamental zest or abandonment.

The Prelude, Sicilienne, Gavotte and Gigue in ancient style from a Suite by Josef Achron (pupil of Leopold Auer, too) he played delightfully. But Mozart's Concerto in A major could well have borne a little more emotional vigor and emphasis; and the Brahms-Joachim Hungarian Dance No. 7, given with a truly mathematical calculation of every effect, including the rubatos, was drained of every ounce of emotional throb and passion.

The accompaniments were admirably performed by Andre Benoist.

HEIFETZ INTERPRETS MOZART SUBLIMELY
Concerto in A the Jewel of Violinist's Third Recital Program

Mr. Heifetz has serious need of imitating the example of a well-known talcum powder manufacturing company hereabouts, which "couldn't improve the powder, so it improved the box." This phenomenal young violinist can probably not improve his playing—the Gods themselves cannot transcend perfection, the divine quantity—but he can and, indeed, must better his programs. Whatever he has so far touched has become sublimated by the golden fire of his genius. Still, excepting the Bach "Chaconne," he has hitherto consistently neglected music of a kind to glorify it; music commensurate in its message with the splendor of his expressive medium. He has limited himself, in the last analysis, to superficialities, amiable and eloquent as they sometimes were. To read from out the musical book of life has now become an obligation he imperatively owes his greatness.

The left hand of Heifetz, circa 1917.

231

His New Year's Day matinee in Carnegie Hall exhibited him in only one work of anything like the dignity and extent desired by those who most profoundly admire Mr. Heifetz. This was Mozart's A Major Concerto, his performance of which epitomized all things that enter into the absolute embodiment of Olympian classicism. Carved with a Praxitelean purity of outline, patterned with a sensitiveness and delicacy of phrase—formation akin rather to the most mysterious perfections of nature than to the subtlest artifice of convention, suffused with the impalpable, elusive tintings of a rainbow of moonbeams and with a poetry too etheral, almost, to apprehend, this interpretation recreated Mozart in the very essence of his thought. It dwarfed what preceded and followed—a very violinistic but musically trite "Suite in the Ancient Style," by a certain Josef Achron, said to be an Auer pupil; a Chopin transcription, a Brahms "Hungarian Dance," two Paganini caprices and the "Palpiti." All were wonderfully done and the glacial weather respected Mr. Heifetz's strings with surprising solicitude. The vast audience—part of it disposed on the stage in a sort of internment pen—received him ecstatically. When, however, are music lovers, finally to hear Heifetz in a Beethoven, a Brahms, a Franck sonata—when?

Andre Benoist assisted the violinist peerlessly.

H.F.P.

JANUARY 3, 1918
ACADEMY OF MUSIC

HEIFETZ IN BROOKLYN
Violinist Given Clamorous Welcome in Recital At Academy of Music

Jascha Heifetz gave his first Brooklyn recital on Thursday evening, January 3, in the Opera House of the Academy of Music. For some unaccountable reason, probably due to the fact that Brooklynites are clinging to their firesides these cold nights, the house was not especially well filled.

This disappointment was partially atoned for, however, by the extremely enthusiastic welcome accorded the young virtuoso. From the time he opened the program with Handel's Sonata in E Major, played with rare nobility of style and depth of feeling, the audience ecstatically applauded him. Handel's "Larghetto," Auer's arrangement of a Mozart "Gavotte," Bazzini's brilliant "La Rondo des Lutins" were played with such facile technique, exquisite bowing and artistic finish as fairly to take one's breath away. Mendelssohn's beautiful "Auf Flugeln des Gesanges" was very well received, as were also two delightful Spanish Dances by Sarasate. The encores, given generously to rapturous clamor, included "Valse Bluette" of Drigo, Cui's charming "Orientale," March from "Ruins of Athens," Rubinstein-Auer, and the "Tambourin Chinois" of Kreisler.

A.T.S.

Heifetz at age 16.
He became an
American citizen in
1925. Circa 1917.

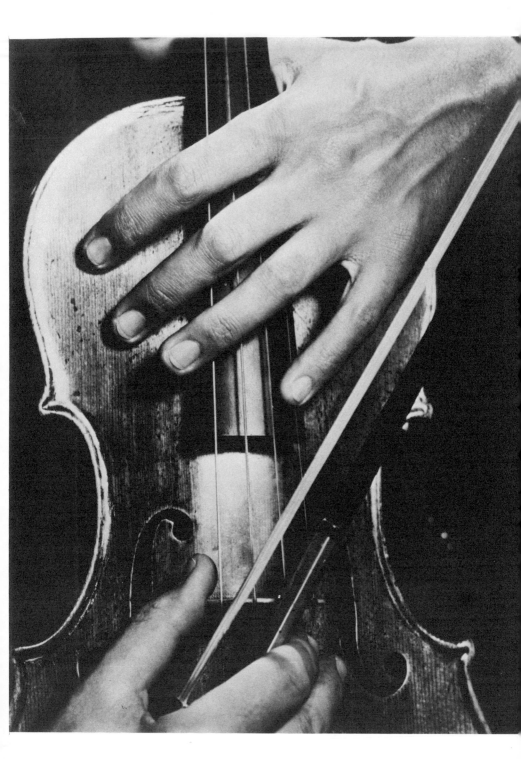

HEIFETZ IN POSTPONED RECITAL

In place of his recital on last New Year's Day Jascha Heifetz's recent illness postponed the young violinist's hearing until yesterday, when a Carnegie Hall audience, superlatively large, gathered to front and rear of him to listen to his playing. The small but all perfect tone of his instrument and the utter flawlessness of his use of it gained him another of those uproars of enthusiasm which are the mile posts of his career.

The Heifetz programme is never remarkably chosen. There is rarely grace in it that is not put there by his playing. That's perhaps because of the oneness of all programmes chosen by the younger Auer pupils. The Chopin Nocturne in E flat major and Tchaikovsky-Auer "Andante Cantabile"—no one will deny their grace and beauty, and indeed no one has for the last fifteen years. His playing made them heavenly, to be sure— but why infuse with humanity works so long divine? And the "Souvenir de Moscow"—well, a Heifetz audience will always crave for Wieniawski toward the close of the afternoon, and this particular audience revelled in its brave dullness. But artistically it was a denouement and not a climax.

Ernst's in F sharp minor was the portion of concerto Heifetz chose. It is such a concerto as suits his sounding undulations and smooth style especially well; seldom enough heard, for the reason that Ernst himself could not always overcome its technical difficulties, there is a nobility and yet a cleverness to it which prove the literature of the violin the loser for Ernst's comparatively early silencing. It was in the "Devil's Trill" of Tartini (they are all doing it nowadays) and in the Bach "Siciliano" and "Presto" that young Heifetz was at his most magnificent. His work on the G string just preceding the cadenza of the first—and indeed the cadenza itself—were glorious to hear. And the Brahms dances—and yes, the nocturne and andante cantabile, too—were truisms upraised to the realm of beauty's truth.

Heifetz Returns to Concert Stage After Illness

Jascha Heifetz, recovered from the illness which withdrew him temporarily from the concert stage, appeared again in violin recital in Carnegie Hall yesterday afternoon. An audience which, in spite of the numerous counter attractions which the city offered, filled every inch of available space in the auditorium assembled to hear him, and was tumultuous in its demonstrations of approval.

Mr. Heifetz seemed in full command of his powers, playing with greater freedom of style than he has sometimes displayed. His programme was such as to please a variety of tastes, ranging from the florid F sharp minor Concerto of Ernst, to a Sicilian and Presto of Bach, played without accompaniment. Other numbers were the Tartini "Devil's Trill," a Chopin "Nocturne," two Brahms dances, the Tchaikovsky "Andante Cantabile," Wieniawski, besides a Bach "Gavotte," Grasse's "Waves at Play" and "Vogel als Prophet," a Kreisler waltz and other short pieces played as encores.

The sincerity of this young artist is beyond praise, and gives distinction even to trivial numbers. His beautiful tone is an unfailing joy. Mr. Andre Benoist played admirable accompaniments.

Heifetz's hands and violin, circa 1918

HEIFETZ PLAYS GRIEG SONATA GLORIOUSLY
Violinist Demonstrates Command of This Type of Music in Recital

JASCHA HEIFETZ, VIOLINIST. RECITAL, CARNEGIE HALL, AFTERNOON, APRIL 6. ACCOMPANIST, ANDRE BENOIST.

THE PROGRAM:

Sonata for Violin and Piano in C Minor, Op. 45, Grieg; Concert No. 8, "Gesangscene," Spohr; Romance in G Major, Beethoven; Minuet, Porpora-Kreisler; "Hebrew Melody," "Hebrew Dance," Joseph Achron; "Lithuanian Song," Chopin-Auer; "Scherzo-Tarantelle," Wieniawski.

At last Jascha Heifetz, yielding to the importunities of his warmest and most judicious admirers, has played a modern sonata. So persistently has he avoided compositions of this exacting nature on his various appearances here that some timorous minds conceived the belief that he lacked the necessary intellectual and artistic maturity to elucidate the profundities or intimacies of the sonatas of Beethoven, Brahms, Franck or others—this regardless of the commanding qualities of mind and spirit he has steadily manifested in everything else. One movement of Grieg's superb C Minor Sonata sufficed to kill this preposterous notion. It showed what every observer of Mr. Heifetz's art should have implicitly realized—that he can be great along great lines even as in small things. It added confirmation to what his God-like reading of the Bach "Chaconne" made plain. A more inspiring delivery of this surpassingly poetic sonata than this youthful marvel, ideally seconded by his virtuoso accompanist, Andre Benoist, provided last week has not been put forth in a cycle of seasons. That Heifetz's share was tonally ravishing in the highest degree need scarcely be explained. And rhythmic life, which is indispensable in projecting the spirit of this masterwork, made the first movement and the Norwegian finale electrical. Perhaps even Jascha Heifetz has done nothing else here that denoted so consummately his intuitive appreciation of design, the plastic sense which he can suffuse so satisfyingly with the spirit of poetry and the continence of lofty, finely felt emotion.

The program on Saturday, though not ideal, scarcely pandered to lower tastes. Spohr's "Gesangscene" allowed Mr. Heifetz to show his necromancy in sublimating for the moment inferior music. It is sufficiently tiresome and antiquated stuff but, in the halo of a glorified cantilena which the violinist cast about it, assumed virtues not inherent in it. Of the shorter pieces it is not necessary to speak in detail, except it be to signalize the uplifting and noble performance of Beethoven's G Major Romance. Those members of the crowd that packed the auditorium and stage of Carnegie Hall who came for technical tid-bits had to content themselves with the Wieniawski "Scherzo-Tarantelle" when the more musical business of the afternoon was disposed of.

H.F.P.

Heifetz, circa 1918.

OCTOBER 26, 1918
CARNEGIE HALL

HEIFETZ AT HIS BEST IN OPENING RECITAL
Carnegie Hall Filled to Hear Young Violinist—
Displays Fullest Artistic Resources

Jascha Heifetz, whose first American appearance in this country last winter was among the exceptional accomplishments of a notable musical year, gave his introductory New York recital of the present season yesterday afternoon in Carnegie Hall. The auditorium was filled.

Heifetz has offered programmes of larger musical mould than that of yesterday, but it has not been often that opportunity arose permitting this supremely gifted violinist to display his fullest artistic resources to their utmost. Parts of the Tartini G minor sonata and of the D major concerto of Mozart were the exceptions.

As in previous performances, Heifetz revealed his mastery as a musician and technician. In the moulding of a phrase, the coloring of various moods in a composition, and the smooth delivery of the melodic line, Heifetz gave absolute satisfaction.

His style, noticeably in the lighter compositions, appeared warmer than last season, and this must have been gratifying to those of his admirers who have wanted more in this respect than it has been the violinist's custom to give.

Such violin playing as Heifetz supplied yesterday is heard seldom, and by only a few. Appreciation was manifested frequently by the audience, which applauded with enthusiasm and spontaneity.

OCTOBER 26, 1918
CARNEGIE HALL

HEIFETZ'S ART AS WONDROUS AS EVER
Violinist Gives First Recital of Season and
Again Rouses Amazed Admiration

JASCHA HEIFETZ, VIOLINIST. RECITAL, CARNEGIE HALL, AFTERNOON, OCT. 26. ACCOMPANIST, ANDRE BENOIST.
THE PROGRAM:
Sonata in G Minor, Tartini; Concerto in D Major, Mozart; Romance in F Major, Minuet, Beethoven; "Bird as Prophet," Schumann; "Guitarre," Moszkowski; "L'Alouette," Glinka-Auer; Polonaise in D Major, Wieniawski.

It is doubtful whether Heifetz has played with more spiritual beauty, regard for nuance and phrasing, dazzling technique than he disclosed at this recital, his first of the present season in New York. Last year, when this violin genius first amazed the concert-going element of this country with the uncanny perfection of his playing, the critical fraternity opened their bag of superlatives and "went the limit." And the glowing praise that was heaped upon this youth was unquestionably deserved. This year Heifetz's playing is no whit less godlike, his art is quite as distinguished, the heights he scales are fully as dizzy. Indeed, he is even a step further on the way toward the rainbow, perfection.

From left to right: Heifetz (age 18), Efrem Zimbalist, Mrs. Alma Gluck Zimbalist and Fritz Kreisler at the home of Mrs. Zimbalist at Fisher's Island, Connecticut. Circa 1919.

OCTOBER 26, 1918
CARNEGIE HALL

HEIFETZ GIVES FIRST RECITAL
Violinist's Extraordinary Technical Proficiency
Pleases Big Audience àt Carnegie Hall

by Max Smith

Before an audience that filled Carnegie Hall, Jascha Heifetz gave his first local recital of the season yesterday afternoon.

Heifetz opened his recital with Tartini's Sonata in G minor. Mozart's Concerto in D major came next in order, leading over to a group of pieces comprising Beethoven's Romance in F major and Minuet, Edwin Grasse's "Waves at Play," the Schumann-Auer "Bird as Prophet" and Moszkowski's "Guitarre." A pretty "Serenata Napoletana," by Sgambati and Wieniawski's Polonaise in D major brought the programme to a close.

As in the past Heifetz's playing was distinguished by extraordinary technical proficiency and impeccable artistic taste. Andre Benoist gave excellent assistance at the piano.

DECEMBER 1, 1918
CARNEGIE HALL

HEIFETZ, NOVAES AND GRAVEURE IN RECITALS
Violinist, Pianist and Baritone Draw Large Audiences
at Week-End Concerts

Jascha Heifetz, the young man whose beautiful violin tone and suave certainty in manipulating it have wooed New York to his recitals in much the same numbers and quite the same mood as occurs in the outpourings to listen to the Galli-Curci, within Carnegie Hall on Saturday afternoon. But, perhaps, the reference to the Galli-Curci is not quite fair to Heifetz, for he at least has the externals of his art as close to the measure of perfection as the thing is imaginable. Nevertheless, externals, even in perfection, pale in their interest. One cannot write interminably of a rainbow, perfect as it may be, nor are one's "Ohs!" and "Ahs!" at vision of it very robust later than early youth. The rainbow indeed, is merely the road to Walhalla, and young Mr. Heifetz, as so often happens to the gods, appears to remain stuck on the road.

Perhaps this sets forth the matter in bold and brusque fashion, appearing to begrudge its due to the wondrous thing the youth does in consideration of the more wondrous thing he does not. Yet one wishes to withhold nothing of praise for the one, merely to record a natural exasperation at the lack of the other—whereby the marvel of marvels does not yet abide with us. Young Mr. Heifetz, in instance, played a Tartini sonata with classic elegance and the Mozart concerto in D with elegant classicism; even dash entered into his account of a Wieniawski Polonaise. But always there was the impression one acquires from a wintry Belasco interior and its roaring fire of red light bulbs.

The thing wants the reality that escapes a mere magical apparition, that lodges only in human content. For this last, in the end, is the test of tests. And the human thing is some mixture, some amalgam of sympathy and vicarious stir of emotion and a vague touch of the spirit. And the amalgam has not yet been welded upon Heifetz's handling of his fiddle.

To Mr. Frederick H. Marten
Cordially your
Jascha Heif...
May 27th 1918.

C.
MISHKIN

APRIL 6, 1919
CARNEGIE HALL

HEIFETZ CLOSES HIS SEASON BRILLIANTLY

JASCHA HEIFETZ, VIOLINIST, RECITAL, CARNEGIE HALL, AFTERNOON, APRIL 6, ACCOMPANIST, ANDRE BENOIST.
THE PROGRAM:
Sonata in D Minor, Brahms; Suite, Sinding; "Walter's Prize Song" from "The Mastersingers," Wagner; "L'Alouett," Glinka-Auer; "Moto Perpetuo," Paganini; "Carmen" Fantasie, Sarasate.

Soft breezes and bland skies possessed no charms for Jascha Heifetz's adoring followers last Sunday afternoon. The God-like gifts of this famous youth attracted an overflow audience to Carnegie Hall. The hall was jammed, the stage was jammed, everywhere were listeners at this the violinist's sixth and farewell recital of the season in New York. And it was a rapt audience, greatly interested in some things than in others.

For instance, the Brahms D Minor Sonata, which began the program, was easily the musical highlight of the afternoon. It was beautifully played, too, by Heifetz and his superb accompanist, Andre Benoist. Yet it received far less applause than Paganini's "Perpetual Motion," a glittering show-piece devoid of emotional import or musical nobility. The Brahms sonata (to come back to genuine music) was interpreted with rare art. Its finely chiselled lines were traced with loving care by both artists, and the classical feeling that the score demands was not lacking.

Of Heifetz's tone or technique nothing need be said at this day. The first was as velvety, the second as dazzling as ever. But the artist looked tired—as well he might. after the exigencies of such a season as his has been. He needs a prolonged rest; for next season will undoubtedly be at least as taxing for him as this one has been.

Of course there were numerous encores. Audiences are proverbially greedy, too often inconsiderate. Heifetz gave extra numbers generously and with his habitual impassivity.

A rare recital, but joy was not unalloyed, perhaps. Spring was out-of-doors, and his call was music, too.

B.R.

APRIL 6, 1919
CARNEGIE HALL

TYPICAL AUDIENCE AT SUNDAY RECITAL— INTERESTING STUDY OF EMOTIONS AROUSED BY THE ART OF VIOLINIST HEIFETZ. GRADATIONS IN APPLAUSE. VIEWED FROM TWO POINTS THE EVENT AT CARNEGIE HALL PROVES PLEASING

The hardened professional attendant at musical performances is frequently more interested in the demeanor of an audience than in the art of the musician. In the case of such a performer as Jascha Heifetz, the violinist, who gave a recital yesterday afternoon in Carnegie Hall, the art may be taken for granted. But just how does a Sunday afternoon audience, composed largely of those who are held up to us as the true music lovers, comport itself in the presence of his playing?

242

There could be little doubt yesterday. When Mr. Heifetz and Mr. Benoist played the Brahms sonata in D minor for piano and violin, the applause expressed an honorable regard for the seriousness of the undertaking. The sonata was beautifully played, especially the slow movement, in which Mr. Heifetz demonstrated that he was quite equal to a noble and deeply felt reading of one of the most poetic creations of the composer.

The suite of Sinding, which followed, called for less concentration on the part of the listener and a more palpable display of technical agility on the part of the violinist. The applause had a firmer and more certain note. The time had now arrived for encore numbers, and when the artist responded with the slow movement of Tchaikovsky's E flat quartet arranged as a solo, happiness was unconcealed.

The prize song from "The Mastersingers" (thus carefully translated on the programme), Auer's transcription of Glinka's "L'Alouette" (not translated) and a moto perpetuo by Paganini comprised the third group. The breathless speed and unerring accuracy of the delivery of the last evoked storms of approval. More encores. Sarasate's "Carmen" fantasia was the finale. More encores. It was a typical Sunday afternoon recital and the audience matched it.

OCTOBER 25, 1919
CARNEGIE HALL

The weekend brought another treat to music lovers. At Carnegie Hall on Saturday afternoon Jascha Heifetz, one of the galaxy of young violinists who were graduated from the school of that master teacher, Leopold Auer, gave his first recital of the season here. His sun is in the ascendant. For the production of pure tone he is unrivaled. His technique is well-nigh perfect. He has poise. His assurance is tempered with modesty. Something lacking now in emotional temperament is sure to come with years and experience. Meanwhile it is a pleasure to hear him and a vast audience showed its appreciation of the fact by generous applause. Mr. Heifetz began his programme with Cesar Franck's Sonata in A minor, assisted by Samuel Chotzinoff at the piano. Then he played the Bruch "Scottish Fantasie." His smaller numbers included compositions by Godowsky, Dvorak, Rachmaninoff, Paganini, Wieniawski and Cecil Burleigh's "Moto Perpetuo."

And when they speak of Jascha Heifetz's purity of tone, they need not mean a cool serenity that recoils upon the listener. He plays simply with a detached perfection that is more potent than furious abandon.

Young people, young artists, are often like overgrown children. Must a boy pretend to the experience and maturity of middle age? Heifetz is not making the mistake. He was entirely himself on Saturday afternoon. He used his flawless technique with that dignified nonchalance that only comes from a knowledge of power, never from vanity. It is his and he can do as he pleases.

A season which early began to pour violinists gave New York the two most renown in one weekend. On Saturday afternoon the golden youth of Jascha Heifetz had its day in Carnegie Hall. The slim, fair chap personifies, somehow, the essence and attractiveness of his own playing. Nothing outrageously dramatic, nothing tremendously powerful or hulking. But in all he stands for, over all he plays, a seraphic sense of perfection and young beauty. Hearing him play, thousands who thronged Carnegie Hall had Heaven across their eyes as surely as he has it at his fingers' ends.

Whether or not he should have chosen Cesar Franck's violin and piano sonata will bear wise men's debating. Yet if he has not yet attained that period of storm and stress where mystics are made clear and depths of feeling plumbed, there is mysticism enough in his mere possession of such a tonal beauty and technique. Yes, these are only attributes of honest musicianship—all transparent enough—yet why should he of all the youths alone so glory in them?

• • • •

With the sounds of Kreisler's playing still in one's ears, perforce, one turns to one of the youngsters, Jascha Heifetz, who came forward for the first time in the new season at Carnegie Hall on Saturday afternoon. Mr. Heifetz is not yet out of swaddling clothes, as to programs, and it was one of those ready-made affairs that he presented—Cesar Franck's Sonata at the outset, Bruch's Fantasia on Scotch Airs to follow, and, thereupon, the usual grouping of odds and ends.

Mr. Heifetz's swaddlings are, however, chosen to fit him the better the more he settles down in them. His programs, in a word, contain something that he thinks he can do and does excellently well. Accordingly, the Franck Sonata was a very loose fit indeed. One could have slipped two or three Heifetz's between him and this music and still have found space for a lack of expression of its fundamentals in soaring feeling. But, thenceforth, Heifetz presented the Heifetz perfection of technic and the Heifetz sonority of tone. But there are considerably more things in heaven and earth than technic and tone.

OCTOBER 25, 1919
CARNEGIE HALL

BLIND PLAYER RIVALS HEIFETZ
Crowd Entering Carnegie Hall for Recital Hears
Impromptu Sidewalk Violinist

by Max Smith

There was music on the sidewalk in front of Carnegie Hall yesterday afternoon—and pretty good music at that—long before Jascha Heifetz, famous Russian, opened his first recital of the season within the packed auditorium.

The impromptu maker of music—a blind man, with smooth-shaven face and black hair that reached to his shoulders—also wielded fiddle and bow, and he reaped something of a harvest from the compassionate crowd.

The remarkable part of it all was that the wandering musician who, it seems, claims to be a relative of Ysaye, played remarkably well to judge from his performance of Schubert's "Ave Maria," a Hungarian dance by Brahms, and Raff's "Cavatina"—considerably better, in fact, than some men and women who have given recitals in Aeolian Hall in recent years. If his rhythm was extremely free, not to say erratic, his tone, at any rate, was good and his intonation, even in difficult double-stopping, absolutely pure.

As for Heifetz, youthful master of the violin, it goes without saying that he evoked thunderous outbursts of applause. His reputation is such that he need not fear a cool reception. Yet it cannot be said that he was heard at his best. Indeed, if he had been, critical opinion, no doubt, would have been somewhat divided.

To be sure, his playing from a purely technical point of view was marvelous even if not quite as impeccable as usual. In the final movement of Bruch's Scotch Fantasie, for example, it made many a listener gasp with astonishment.

Underneath the smooth exterior, however, there was little to grip the feelings. Franck's famous Sonata in A Major, as presented by him, had been polished off with emery. It carried no emotional message. It had no pathos, no passion, no dramatic accents.

The opening "Allegretto" was performed with an innocuous delicacy that made the music almost insipid. The middle movement was more satisfactory. Here the young violinist's eloquent tone was nobly in evidence. But the "Allegro poco mosso" he took at a pace altogether too fast.

Heifetz performed the Bruch Fantasie in much the same style, although he achieved impressive results at times. Generally his playing did not penetrate below the surface of the musical shell. Moreover, the objectionable Auer slide into higher positions on the finger that reaches for the loftier note, was altogether too much in evidence.

Two groups of pieces made up the rest of the programme. They included Dvorak's "Slavonic Dance" in G major, No. 3; Cecil Burleigh's "Moto Perpetuo;" Godowsky's "Legende," Wieniawski's "Saltarello Caprice," in E-flat major; Rachmaninoff's "Vocalize;" Ficco's "Allegro," and Paganini's "Non piu mesta."

Burleigh's "Moto Perpetuo," played at terrific speed—a tour de force —had to be repeated.

Samuel Chotzinoff assisted at the piano.

OCTOBER 25, 1919
CARNEGIE HALL

The name of Jascha Heifetz has become one to conjure with. On Saturday Carnegie Hall was filled to overflowing with the admirers of this young master of the violin and he gave his listeners the thorough satisfaction they expected.

Mr. Heifetz looks little older than when he first appeared before a New York audience. Tall, personable, free from all affectation, he is a pleasant figure to watch, and even pleasanter to listen to, for while he himself keeps his very youthful aspect, his art has matured and broadened. The first stroke of his bow across the strings at his debut proved to connoisseurs that here was a talent which promised greater things. For a time, indeed up to the present, he has seemed to stand still. Evidently he was going through one of those periods of subconscious growth after which an artist makes a forward stride, sometimes a great one. Mr. Heifetz quite rationally still plays like a youth, but now one feels that his development will be along the lines of real art, rather than mere virtuosity. His tone is more emotional. It is in this that his growth betrays itself most strikingly. He has always possessed a remarkable technique and exquisite certainty of intonation, but the fresh, adolescent coolness of his tone left the hearer proportionately unmoved. Mr. Heifetz has a long road still ahead of him, but he has taken the first arduous steps toward the goal so few may reach. Everyone who heard him on Saturday must wish him a safe arrival at the heights that so few attain.

His performance of both the Cesar Franck Sonata and the Bruch Fantaisie was on a high level of excellence. The two Dvorak Slavonic Dances, especially the beautiful one he played as an encore, gave much pleasure to his audience. Godowsky's pretty "Legende" and Rachmaninoff's "Vocalise"—far better suited to the violin than to the human voice—were also greatly appreciated. Mr. Heifetz astonished and delighted his hearers by a marvelous exhibit of the dazzling and difficult harmonies in a piece by Paganini. For him, however, harmonics are still but a virtuoso's display. Will he ever learn the magic of making them sounds of heavenly beauty, as Fritz Kreisler does? One hopes so, after Saturday's recital for one feels the sincerity of this gifted youth and his natural leaning toward the beautiful rather than the meretricious in the playing of his instrument. Mr. Chotzinoff deserves praise for his excellent accompaniments.

OCTOBER 25, 1919
CARNEGIE HALL

HEIFETZ DISPLAYS HIS GENIUS ANEW
Young Master Makes First Appearance of Season At Carnegie Hall

Jascha Heifetz made his first appearance of the season last Saturday afternoon in Carnegie Hall, before an ecstatic audience that jammed every corner of the auditorium and the stage. The occasion escaped being one of almost celestial delights only by reason of the atrocious air in the hall, which made breathing difficult and drowsiness inevitable and which forced a number of persons to forego regretfully the last part of an unforgettable exhibition of an art futilizing comparison.

This heaven-inspired youth played once more in a style that eludes analysis and mocks laborious description. Wagner's royal protector, Ludwig II, once asseverated that "a genius like Richard Wagner never has been before and will never come again." There are moments in Jascha Heifetz's playing which, saving hyperbole, sorely tempt the ravished and conquered listener to say exactly the same thing. He may not this time have done better than last year or the year before that. But how shall perfection transcend itself.

Heifetz has not been without his detractors, of course. Mistaking his miraculous poise and mystic aloofness, some of these have charged him with temperamental incapacity and coldness. But if last Saturday his magical tone and transfiguring style were not suffused with a poetic emotion of the most sublimated order then poetry and emotion, fancy and fervor, are no longer of this earth.

He showed the seriousness of his artistic purpose by beginning his program with Cesar Franck's Sonata, which as much as anything one knows, strips bare the soul of a player, exalts him as a seer or exposes him as a pretender. Together with his admirable accompanist, Samuel Chotzinoff (whose playing is entirely worthy of his great colleague's) he gave it with a beauty at times altogether poignant, a rendering rather of lyrical idealization than vigorous accent and large proportion. It differed in kind rather than in degree from the equally overpowering interpretation of Albert Spalding, which is laid out more weightily on a plane of tragic distinction. It sang to high heaven, and not a tonal blemish marred the joyous agitation of the last moment.

246

Heifetz with his teacher, Prof. Leopold Auer.
Prof. Auer died in 1930. Heifetz played at his
funeral in what some observers say was his
most touching performance, circa 1921.

After the sonata the wonderweaving boy lifted above its very dullness the long "Scotch Fantasie" of Bruch. Then came brevities by Dvorak, Burleigh, Godowsky, Rachmaninoff, Fiocco, Paganini and many extras. The gold in these was gilded and refined but not vainly; and the dross shimmered in transient and illusory splendor.

H.F.P.

NOVEMBER 16, 1919
CARNEGIE HALL

THREE VIOLIN PLAYERS IN CONCERTS
Jascha Heifetz Heard in Carnegie Hall, While Mischa Elman and the Veteran Ysaye Delight a Big Crowd in the Hippodrome

By Max Smith

Three of the world's greatest violinists played yesterday to approximately ten thousand men and women, most of whom belonged to the Slavic population of Greater New York.

In the afternoon Jascha Heifetz gave his second recital in Carnegie Hall—an auditorium that has seats for three thousand. But chairs for three or four hundred had been placed on the stage; and in the rear of the parquet stood a throng of enthusiasts who rushed helter-skelter down the aisles, as soon as the famous fiddler had played his last promised contribution, in order to enjoy at short range the inevitable extra numbers.

In the evening the veteran Ysaye and Mischa Elman, who is young enough to be his son, appeared jointly in the Hippodrome before a monster gathering, numbering at the very least six thousand. There, too, the stage was used to accommodate the overflow, and ever so many had to turn away disappointed from the box office.

People of Russian origin, especially those with an infusion of Semitic temperament in their blood, have a devouring passion for music, and for music played on the violin in particular. They are willing to make sacrifices, too, for what to them is more than mere pleasure—as S. Hurok seems to have been one of the first to discover.

Except for the press reservations, every seat and all standing room privileges in Carnegie Hall and in the Hippodrome had been bought with good money. And most of this money had been drawn from hard-earned savings.

That Heifetz was in excellent form yesterday became apparent soon after he had opened his programme with Vieuxtemp's A minor Concerto, Samuel Chotzinoff, as usual, assisting at the piano. He played a beautiful "Grave" by Friedemann-Bach with big, vibrant tone, and in the following Vivace disclosed the agility of his fingers and the electric energy of his bow-arm wrist.

Tchaikovsky's tenderly appealing "Melodie," Opus 42, No. 3, preceded by Smetana's "Aus der Heimat," aroused a tumult of applause, which Mr. Heifetz acknowledged by repeating the piece. The same composer's animated Scherzo (No. 2 from the same opus) also delighted the crowd, and the violinist, after several recalls, added two unannounced selections from his repertory.

Cesar Cui's "Lullaby," played "con sordino," and Auer's not altogether respectful adaptation of Paganini's Caprice No. 24 (here, for once, Heifetz's usually impeccable intonation left something to be desired, notably in the octave passages) brought the matinee to its formal close. But,

248

Eugene Ysaye, circa 1893.

as already suggested, the young virtuoso generously prolonged his recital for the benefit of his implacable admirers.

NOVEMBER 16, 1919
CARNEGIE HALL

HEIFETZ PLAYS TO STUPENDOUS AUDIENCE
Second Recital by Russian Violinist Again Draws
Vast Throng of His Worshippers

Before an audience that filled all available space, including the entire stage except the extreme front, and as much standing room as the fire department allows, Jascha Heifetz gave his second recital of the season at Carnegie Hall on the afternoon of November 16.

Criticism of an artist of Mr. Heifetz's caliber, is almost an impertinence, but it must be said that the program itself was not one of intense interest, nor was its performance characterized by monumental inspirational appeal. Technically, it was, of course, flawless. From beginning to end, intonation was impeccable and the phrasing something to marvel at. Singers especially high and lowly, should hear Heifetz and learn just what phrasing can be—and seldom is.

The Vieuxtemps A Minor Concerto with which the program began, is not the most interesting of violin numbers and is calculated to please the violinist rather than the ordinary listener. A "Grave" by Bach, arranged by Auer, followed, and a merry "Vivace" by Haydn. A "Melodie" by Tchaikovsky, was exquisitely given and was re-demanded by the audience. Cui's "Lullaby" was also delicately played, and the program closed with Auer's variations on a theme by Paganini, of monumental difficulty even as Brahm's variations for piano on the same theme. In this, Mr. Heifetz did unbelievable things with apparent unconcern, so that the audience swarmed to the front of the hall and demanded encore after encore.

J.A.H.

JANUARY 11, 1920
CARNEGIE HALL

HEIFETZ'S ARTISTRY EVOKES REVERENCE
Bach Chaconne and Other Works Played in Rare Style at His Recital

When Jascha Heifetz plays, the behounded critic draws a sigh of relief for more reasons than the greatest one. No need is his to search through a vocabulary worn thin by use. Anything expressing praise will do, from "amazing" to "zenith-touching" inclusive. Apparently anyone who has heard Heifetz, or has heard someone that has heard Heifetz, needs but to be told now that on Sunday afternoon last, for instance, Jascha Heifetz played at Carnegie Hall. The rest is, or should be, the silence of wonderment and of a reverent joy.

Heifetz was a "camera-fiend" during his early life. Circa 1917.

250

It may be of interest, however, further to record that he played the Grieg Sonata in G, with Samuel Chotzinoff, and that the latter sustained the piano part well; that the Bach Chaconne for violin alone stood out among his other feats of the afternoon like a single peak among the Himalayas; that the heavenly simplicity of it and of his playing of the Grieg apparently held applause in a comparative restraint; that the slighter works, such as Achron's "Coquetterie," Juon's "Waltz Mignon," and the Popper-Auer "Fileuse," unchained the gallery's wilder joy; and that the young master repeated these three and played six encores after the Rachmaninoff "Romance" and the Paganini "Witches Dance" to a stage-besieging shouting crowd.

Finally, that a gentle hint on the part of the management conveyed by way of removing the piano and turning off the lights, ultimately induced the worshippers to go home.

• • • •

Every time Jascha Heifetz appears in recital or with orchestra he cements the adoration of his old followers and collects new admirers. And that is as it should be, because the wonder-child is growing up and playing his violin better every week. Yesterday he played a typical violinist program in Carnegie Hall, beginning with the Grieg Sonata and ending with the Paganini "Witches Dance" (in addition to some seven encores). There is no worn melody that Heifetz cannot paint with fresh colors, and no passage that does not spring from his bow a miracle of beauty.

• • • •

The afternoon, for example, had sold out even the standing room of Carnegie Hall some days ago. For Jascha Heifetz, the violinist, played there; played the Grieg concerto, for one thing, and followed with a programme which, however delightful, kept valiantly to an artistic course. The Bach Chaconne he played with that impenetrable gloss which is his, and the lighter melodies of such as Achron, Stojowski and Paul Juon reaped a proportionately heavy applause. Rachmaninoff's "Romance" and Paganini's bedazzlements completed an afternoon which, though it started tardily, swung to speedy capture.

• • • •

Every seat sold, stage filled, standing room jammed—this was the audience which greeted Jascha Heifetz at Carnegie Hall yesterday afternoon. He offered an interesting programme, first the Grieg Sonata in G, then Bach's "Chaconne" for violin alone, and after these pieces de resistance the dessert, two groups of short pieces by Godowsky, Stojowski, Rachmaninoff, Paganini and others.

Mr. Heifetz found in Grieg's second sonata a work particularly suited to his style and individuality. It possesses the qualities of youth and buoyancy and also the tenderer side of Grieg's genius, which are eminently fitted to this youth beloved of the Gods. His tone in the slow movement was indescribably lovely, while the more brilliant portions of Grieg's work received the full measure of their beauty under his fingers. Let us hope that Mr. Heifetz will at some early day play the third sonata, which is even more beautiful than the second, as well as a riper expression of Grieg's genius and of the soul of the North.

JASCHA HEIFETZ'S LAST RECITAL

Jascha Heifetz gave the last of his numerous New York violin recitals yesterday afternoon in Carnegie Hall, when his remarkable popularity was shown again by the enormous audience that occupied every place in the hall that could accommodate people. It was tumultuous in its applause, especially for the lighter things of lesser musical value, with which his program was over-well provided, in unfortunate imitation of distinguished predecessors.

Mr. Heifetz is at the end of a long and arduous season, and it is not surprising that he was not always in his best condition nor that he played sometimes with a little less than that amazing perfection which is his. He began with four movements from Bach's E major solo suite. The brilliant prelude was played with a remarkable dash; it was not impeccable either in accuracy of intonation or rhythm; but there was marvelous beauty, breadth and repose in the other movements.

He followed this sonata with Jules Conus's E-minor Concerto, a piece that appeals to violinists because of its brilliancy, its effectiveness, its conformability with the nature of the instrument. These are qualities which it shares with other concertos written by violinists, as Vieuxtemps, Ernst, De Beriot; and while it is, of course, more modern in its facture, in the style of its decoration it is not more musically valuable than such concertos that have beguiled violinists in the past. Mr. Heifetz flung it off without sign of labor or effort and with enormous brilliancy.

He pleased greatly in two of Mr. Godowsky's Viennese waltz movements, one of which he had to repeat, as well as Paul Juan's muted "Serenade." Wieniawski's caprice he took at a breathless pace and with the lightness of a summer breeze—but it was not accurately intoned throughout. The program ended with Sarasate's fantasy on Bohemian airs.

• • • •

Bach figured also on Heifetz's programme. He was represented by four movements from the Sixth Sonata for violin alone. The other contributions, all performed with characteristic technical finish, and with nothing to show that a Saturday evening's revel at the Metropolitan in the music of "Boris Godunoff" had been a fatiguing experience, embraced Jules Conus's Concerto in E minor; Godowsky's "Viennese" and "Valse;" Paul Juan's "Berceuse;" Wieniawski's Caprice in A minor and Sarasate's "Bohemian Airs." Samuel Chotzinoff played the piano accompaniments.

• • • •

This will be Mr. Heifetz's last appearance here for two years, as he will go to England and will later tour as far as Australia. His audience filled all available space in the auditorium. His programme comprised the prelude, minuet, bourree, gavotte and rondo from Bach's sixth Sonata for violin alone, the Concerto in E minor by Jules Conus, a group of smaller pieces and Sarasate's "Bohemian Airs."

Mr. Heifetz played the concerto with a master hand. His tone was superb and his technic brilliant. His programme, save the first number, did not put to fullest test the taste either of the player or his listeners but that the latter were absorbed in his beautiful art.

253

Heifetz returns to Europe aboard the steamship "Imperator" after conquering America. October 7, 1920.

APRIL 4, 1920
CARNEGIE HALL

HEIFETZ GIVES A 'FAREWELL' RECITAL
Russian Violinist is Again Idol of Immense Throng in Carnegie Hall

After delighting New York audiences almost to the point of satiety for over two years, with his extraordinary art, Jascha Heifetz is about to withdraw from our midst to carry his gospel of perfect playing to other lands. His last recital for a while, was given in Carnegie Hall on the afternoon of April 4, before an audience that jammed every available space in the auditorium and on the stage.

The program itself was one of uneven interest. Beginning with four numbers from Bach's Sixth Suite for violin alone, he gave an altogether satisfactory piece of playing. The Loure and the Gavotte were the best of these. Following was Jules Conus' E Minor Concerto. In this Mr. Heifetz surpassed himself, doing some things on his G string that gave one a new idea of the potentialities of the instrument. The following group was of less interest. Two rather pianistic pieces for violin by Godowsky, Juon's muted Berceuse and the Godowsky Valse had to be repeated to satisfy the insistent clamoring of the groundlings, in this case the Gods of the gallery. The Caprice was taken at an appalling tempo, light as a feather, but in it the impossible occurred, his intonation faltered, but only momentarily.

The final number, Sarasate's "Bohemian Airs," was another triumph of technique, child's play for this artist. The young things, especially of the feminine gender, surged forward with the last note and kept Mr. Heifetz busy for another twenty-five minutes. He would probably be playing still if the lights had not been turned out. Samuel Chotzinoff was the accompanist.

J.A.H.

Mr. Heifetz also attempted some of the violin music of Bach—four movements from the E major suite (erroneously called the sixth sonata on the program) written for the unaccompanied instrument, but not played in the sequence intended by Bach. Mr. Heifetz's fiddling without a piano background was exceedingly good to listen to, and it would have been even better to listen to had the music not been that of Bach. Mr. Heifetz's reverence for what he was playing seemed to raise his ordinary placidity to the nth power—and Bach's violin music requires more spirit and intensity than any other. However, the packed house and the violinist both got their real innings when the latter proceeded to the concerto of Jules Conus (during the playing of which it is necessary to think of nothing at all) and, finally, to the usual type of pretty-pretties with which all violin recitals, apparently, must end.

There have been times when his playing has sounded a trifle cold, or when there has been a suggestion of listlessness. But yesterday was not one of those times. Superb playing was heard through a long programme containing music good and indifferent, Bach and Jules Conus. Paul Juon and Sarasate. No one could say that his playing lacked fire. He was as temperamental as he was perfect technically. He was as sure of his difficult passages as he was of his beautiful tone. It was a recital to please the most exacting tastes. Heifetz will be missed from New York's musical life next season.

DECEMBER 17, 1921
CARNEGIE HALL

AUDIENCE MARVELS AT HEIFETZ'S VIOLIN

Heifetz, child prodigy, has grown up. After nearly two years abroad he has returned a mature man, a mature musician, and, though he has broadened his shoulders and his musicianship, he remains the greatest technical master of the violin now living. Perhaps there are others who play with more fire, who have deeper emotional expressiveness, but if there are, they are very few. Heifetz is not merely a fiddler, a trickster who startles thousands because he can play faster and more accurately than any other violinist. He is now a seasoned interpreter of the best type of music.

Yesterday afternoon he gave a recital in Carnegie Hall, and he played with the dignity of a veteran and with admirable musicianship a sonata of Beethoven. There has come into his playing a delicacy, a super-refinement greater than that of former years. Wonderful shadings of tone and remarkable sureness in rhythms were played as few artists have the courage to play, in the manner of an intimate recital. There were no exaggerations, done for effect, no stunts or distortions. He played only to bring out what was in the music, submerging his own personality behind Beethoven.

But in the Wieniawski concerto, which followed, he changed his tactics. So brilliantly did he play that the somewhat threadbare themes sounded like great music. So cleverly did he execute this trick music that it seemed to be really fine. He took the audience out of their seats at the close of the first movement with a marvelous rush of technical display.

The audience yesterday was as large as Carnegie Hall would accommodate. Hundreds were turned away and many of them remained outside the hall till the programme was over to beg seat checks from those who left, that they might enter to hear the encores.

DECEMBER 17, 1921
CARNEGIE HALL

HEIFETZ ACCLAIMED AFTER YEAR ABROAD
Violinist's Art Transcends Quality of His Return Program

JASCHA HEIFETZ, VIOLIN RECITAL, CARNEGIE HALL, DECEMBER 17, AFTERNOON; SAMUEL CHOTZINOFF, ACCOMPANIST.
THE PROGRAM:
Sonata in G Opus 30, No. 8, Beethoven; Concerto in D Minor, Wieniawski; Nocturne in D Major, Chopin; "Coqueeterie," Joseph Achron; "Wienerisch," Godowsky; "Fileuse," Popper-Auer; "Othello Fantasie," Ernst.

After a season's absence, the young God of the violin found Carnegie Hall too small to house all the New Yorkers who hungered to hear him play. Not only was every seat taken, and the stage requisitioned for row on row of additional chairs, but room was found for a number of standees at the back of the auditorium.

The Athenian beauty, poise and refinement of Mr. Heifetz's art have not altered during his year abroad. He did not look in the best possible physical trim, but he played divinely well, even though here and there was an unwonted blemish of quality or of exact intonation. The slow movement of the Beethoven sonata was of unforgettable loveliness of tone and purity of style; and when he flashed through the fiddlers' fireworks of the Allegro Moderato of the Wieniawski Concerto there was a drumfire of applause such as no other violinist of the season has received.

Yet it was, withal, an indifferent, even a tawdry program. How little violin music (at least, how little that finds its way to the recital halls) is worthy of an art so fraught with spirituality as that of Heifetz! He does not play sugary trifles as entrancingly as some other and more earth-earthy virtuosi; and his marvelous technique, which apparently enables him to surmount the thorniest obstacles with the same placidity that is his when he intones a serenely lyric phrase, only emphasizes the tawdriness of pieces written for display.

The violinist, though recalled an uncounted number of times, re-served his extras until the end of the program. He was still playing them when the writer left the hall. His accompaniments were admirably played by Mr. Chotzinoff, who shared in the applause after the sonata.

O.T.

• • • •

Jascha Heifetz, the marvelous boy of 1917, returned to us Saturday, after a season's absence, in an afternoon recital in Carnegie Hall. The continuing might of the Heifetz name and fame was evident from one glance at the audience. It occupied every seat in the hall, it crowded the standing room, and it filled most of the stage. Sometimes celebrities play or sing to empty benches, no less celebrities for the loneliness of their un-attended majesty. Not so in the Jascha Heifetz case. The capacity of the room he plays in is the only limit to the size of the audience that hears him.

The programme offered by Mr. Heifetz on this occasion is open to objection. The first and musically most important number was Beetho-ven's eight sonata for violin and piano (the pianist here, as elsewhere, was Samuel Chotzinoff). But sonatas for violin and piano, no matter who plays them, cannot produce their full effect in a hall the size of Carnegie. Then came Wieniawski's D minor concerto, all very well in its way, but not the sort of thing that makes a concert highly significant. After that a group of the trivialities for which violinists have gone in so heavily during the last decade had its turn, and finally an old-fashioned virtuoso piece, the "Othello" fantaisie of Ernst. On the whole a pretty unsubstantial offering for a great artist.

Mr. Heifetz, looking a trifle more mature than when he had played here before, entered with his habitual dignity and calmness of demeanor and set about the business of the Beethoven sonata in highly serious fashion. But, though indisputably Messrs. Heifetz and Chotzinoff played the sonata well, either because of the undue size of the hall or because the violinist felt a little nervous over his return (despite his eternal imperturb-ability), the piece fell rather flat.

The Heifetz that we remembered, the Heifetz who was wont to soar serene and archangelic above the ills and accidents of our little planet, came back in the Wieniawski concerto. Here was the tone that ravished through its bigness, richness, and utter smoothness; here was the high celestial disdain of anything so of the earth, earthy as a mere mechanical obstase; here was the broad and easy flight as if poised on infallible and unfluttering wings; here was the satisfying perfection of an inevitable rhythm. The audience, which had received the sonata politely, stormed its applause after the first movement of the concerto and that demonstration was only the first in a series of ovations eagerly accorded the super-fiddler.

And yet the story would be offered incomplete without the admission that on the glistening surface of a masterly performance the suspicion of a flaw did here and there mar the absolute perfection. More than once the miraculous bow as it swept triumphant across the strings did just hint at a scratch; more than once there was an appreciable deviation from the 100 per cent purity of the stopping. In a lesser technician than Jascha Heifetz these tiny flaws would pass unnoticed. But when an artist chooses as his standard nothing less than perfection, by that inexorable standard must he be judged.

Nevertheless, and notwithstanding, Jascha Heifetz, if less a boy, is still a marvelous violinist. When he offers another programme here of more substantial musical worth it will be time to dig more deeply into the subject of changes and modifications that his art may have undergone and to appraise the effect on it of his maturing years.

JANUARY 2, 1922
CARNEGIE HALL

— HEIFETZ —

A vast audience which filled not only every seat and corner of the auditorium but also the entire platform greeted Jascha Heifetz at his second recital of the season in Carnegie Hall on the afternoon of January 2. Mr. Heifetz presented the Goldmark A Minor Concerto, three excerpts from the Bach Second Sonata, the "Havanaise" by Saint-Saens and other works. The young Russian played as brilliantly and as rapidly as on previous occasions; there were several lapses from pitch, demonstrating that the young violinist is a human being after all and not a marvelous automaton. He played some of his pieces at such a dizzy rate of speed that it was practically impossible for the ear to follow the melodic line. The great throng applauded their idol frenetically and compelled him to pile encore on encore. Samuel Chotzinoff's accompaniments were admirable.

C.F.

JANUARY 2, 1922
CARNEGIE HALL

HEIFETZ PLAYS

Those captious concertgoers who complain of the detached, impersonal Heifetz must have been converted to another opinion if they were in Carnegie Hall yesterday afternoon when he played the Goldmark concerto. In the andante his tone was warm, it even glowed. And in the unaccompanied Bach suite his cool, perfect technique was supported by evidence of growing temperament.

There was the usual crowd on the stage and the regular excited surging forward at the end, with demands for encores which he gave generously, beginning with that study in harmonics, "Zephyr."

HEIFETZ PLAYS AGAIN

Jascha Heifetz came back to Carnegie Hall yesterday afternoon to
give his second New York recital of the season. He had, of course, a full
holiday house, to which he played a program evidently suitable and satisfying. It began with Bach and the Goldmark Concerto in A minor, then
sloped away to such grades as the "Meistersinger" prize song, Saint-Saen's
"Havanaise," Lensky's air from "Eugene Onyegin" and the like. Aside
from the musical importance of such numbers, Mr. Heifetz played them
with the pluperfect ease which brings him today to the brink of being
quite uninteresting. Stylistic and tonal smoothness are not always anti-
dotes for fire and thought. Especially when such smoothness is sometimes
not present.

The Listener

• • • •

At his second recital, heard by a huge audience yesterday afternoon
in Carnegie Hall, Jascha Heifetz presented a programme distinctly more
acceptable than his previous one.

Of course Mr. Heifetz played marvelously well and was duly appreciated by those who are conversant with the difficulties of the fiddle. One
noted the transparent beauty and smoothness of his tone, the clean-cut
perfection of his technique, the purity of his unaffected style.

Yet somehow this amazing wielder of the bow failed to stir the
feelings deeply and keep the interest tense. Several violinists far less
accomplished than he, could be named, indeed, who are capable of
affording profounder satisfaction.

One admired his repose, his distinction, his straightforward simplicity. But there was something about his carefully ironed manners and
methods that breathed diffidence.

JASCHA HEIFETZ

Carnegie Hall was not large enough to hold all who desired to hear
Jascha Heifetz in this third New York recital this season. The chief works
of his program were unfamiliar—Joseph Achron's Sonata, Op. 29, which
contains much fine music and some that is commonplace, and Spohr's
Eighth Concerto. In the Achron Sonata, the violinist, who was assisted at
the piano by the composer's brother, Isidor Achron, made much of the
rich material of the second movement, and imparted great delicacy to the
third, where sometimes the piano was rather aggressive. Samuel Chotzinoff was the pianist in the Spohr Concerto and the remainder of the pro-

gram, which contained miscellaneous groups by Smetana, Spalding, Juon, Popper, Tchaikovsky and Paganini-Auer in which the polished technique of Mr. Heifetz was brilliantly revealed.

P.J.N.

JANUARY 7, 1922
CARNEGIE HALL

HEIFETZ PLAYS UNFAMILIAR SONATA

Jascha Heifetz presented an unfamiliar sonata by Joseph Achron, assisted by the composer's brother, Isidor Achron, at the violinist's fourth recital of the season in Carnegie Hall yesterday afternoon. There followed the infrequently heard Concerto No. 8 of Spohr, as if Mr. Heifetz sought to put his admirers to the test of more serious matters than have sometimes filled his more popular programs. He gave satisfaction in his closing groups of short pieces and arrangements by Paganini-Auer, Tchaikovsky, Smetana, Popper, Juon and a graceful "Berceuse" by Albert Spalding.

• • • •

Mr. Heifetz with consummate technical skill presented a rather diverting novelty, a sonata by Joseph Achron. The Spohr Concerto No. 3 and unhackneyed works of Smetana, Albert Spalding, Juon and Popper were among the most appealing numbers of his programme. Heifetz was at his best yesterday and that brought him abundant applause.

FEBRUARY 13, 1922

JASCHA HEIFETZ AGAIN

For his third recital of the season Jascha Heifetz chose a program of music more worthy of his genius than he has often been known to do. And the size and enthusiasm of his audience showed that his choice was as wise from the business point of view as from the artistic.

First came the Bruch "Scottish Fantasy," followed by an unaccompanied Bach "Chaconne." Then there was a group comprising a Beethoven "Romance," Brahms' Hungarian Dance No. 12, and two Spanish pieces of Sarasate. A melody from Gluck's "Orfeo" and Auer's arrangement of a Paganini caprice completed the formal program, to which Samuel Chotzinoff provided accompaniments.

The strong human appeal of the violinist's tone rather than his style was the most notable feature of his playing. His technical sureness survived the intricate demands of the Paganini, which was a brilliant gem of virtuosity, but the sweep of his legato and the unusual breadth of his muted tone were features dearer to the great audience, and hundreds rushed down toward the stage to demand encores. These were given with apparent reluctance, but were received with acclaim.

Is Heifetz then greater—as a violinist, than Casals is as a 'cellist? Certainly he is not. In fact, at the present time the elder man outranks the youngster in musicianship and artistry, if not in purely technical skill.

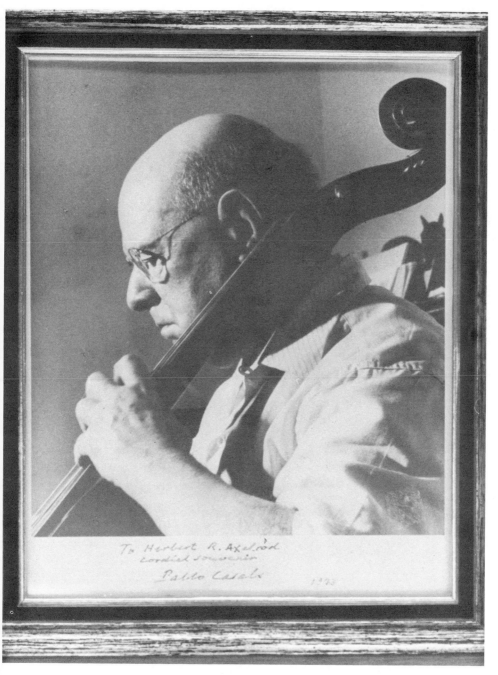

One reviewer wrote that Heifetz was surpassed in musicianship, artistry and technical skills by Pablo Casals. Circa 1972.

JASCHA HEIFETZ

Holiday music patrons exhausted all tickets for the third recital this season by Jascha Heifetz, given Monday afternoon at Carnegie Hall. The program was one of the best contrived Mr. Heifetz has played in New York and had more musical merit than some of its predecessors. Those who have not been quite satisfied of late that Mr. Heifetz's playing was the same as of yore, could find little to cavil at on this occasion. There was the old tonal velvet, the old technical surety and brilliance, the old serenity and purity, the old elegance and poise. Beginning with Max Bruch's "Scotch Fantasia" he passed to an impeccable performance of the Bach Chaconne and he illustrated every phase of the virtuoso's art in subsequent expositions of the G Major Romance of Beethoven, the Twelfth Hungarian Dance of Brahms, two Sarasate numbers, and a Paganini-Auer caprice. Samuel Chotzinoff accompanied. There was much excited and protracted applause.

O.T

LARGE AUDIENCE HEARS FOURTH HEIFETZ RECITAL

Carnegie Hall was filled yesterday afternoon for the fourth and last recital of Jascha Heifetz, and there was hardly room left for violinist and piano on the stage. He gave a well-balanced program beginning with a seventeenth century Chaconne by Tommasso Vitali, followed by Lalo's "Symphonie Espagnole," Bach's Air for G string, a Vivace from a Haydn Quartet, arranged by Auer; Rimsky-Korsakoff's "Hymn to the Sun" from the "Coq d'Or," a Wieniawski Tarantelle, and "Il Palpiti," by Paganini—this last a medium for spectacular display, with fearsome combinations of double-stop harmonics and high-speed pizzicati. This testified sufficiently to his technique, with his usual ability to produce apparently effortless cascades of notes, while there was the usual Heifetz purity and breadth of tone, still of a rather cool, detached perfection. The sensuous, melodious Lalo number, however, had warmth and feeling besides polish, and the audience waxed enthusiastic for half a dozen or more encores, including the Beethoven "Minuet in G" and the Tchaikovsky "Andante Cantabile."

JASCHA HEIFETZ FILLS CARNEGIE AT RECITAL
Young Russian Virtuoso Shows Marked Advancement in the Warmth and Vitality of His Well Nigh Impeccable Playing
By Max Smith

Appearing for the first time this season yesterday afternoon, Jascha Heifetz attracted the big crowd, somewhat to the disadvantage probably of contemporaneous recitals by Ossip Gabrilowitsch and Louis Graveure.

Carnegie Hall was not nearly large enough to hold all who wanted to hear the young Russian virtuoso, although most of the stage had been requisitioned. And the women ushers had no little trouble in managing the standees who packed the open space behind the last row of the orchestra, pressing their way into the aisles.

Heifetz began with Nardini's Concerto in E minor, with Samuel Chotzinoff at the piano. In excellent form from the start, he also played Mozart's Concerto in A major with that beauty and purity of tone, that precision, that perfection of technique in which he excels.

But why enlarge on this phenomenal violinist's traits, already so familiar and so frequently appraised? He is not losing his grip, as some would have had us believe a year ago. His command of the mechanics of the fiddle is still what it was, well-nigh impeccable. But is he broadening and developing in other respects? Is there more warmth of feeling, more vitality, more imagination in his playing than there used to be?

Among the smaller selections he contributed were Beethoven's Romance in F major; the Beethoven-Auer "Chorus of Dervishes," twice given; Grasse's "Waves at Play;" Wieniawski's Caprice No. 13 and Paganini's D major Caprice No. 20—not Wieniawski's as the programme had it.

A serenata by Sgambati and Wieniawski's Polonaise in D major completed the list. But, needless to say, supplementary numbers were added. For who could have resisted the demands of the enthusiasts thronging to the front?

• • • •

Heifetz, whose technique was always impeccable, is undoubtedly improving in his interpretation, which is simply saying that he is growing older and so is more experienced in his art. To me one of his best characteristics is his ability to make you feel absolutely at your ease. There are some violinists and indeed some singers, even artists of distinction, who cannot do that. As you listen to them, you feel uncertain. Will the violinist get over that passage all right? Will he finish that cadenza in good shape? Or will the singer reach that particular note that you feel he or she is aiming for? What is the result? The audience being in sympathy with the artist, naturally feels a certain anxiety. That anxiety destroys the ability to have perfect enjoyment of the music.

When some time ago I discussed with the great Auer, who was Heifetz's teacher, the precise standing of Heifetz, tried to draw him out, I told him—it was soon after Heifetz's debut in this country—that the young violinist had carried me away by his marvelous technique and the beauty of his tone, but that he had appealed rather to my intelligence than to my heart.

Auer replied: "Well, he took you out of yourself, didn't he? He made you forget everything but his playing, didn't he? You heard nothing but the music. You thought of nothing else."

"That is true," said I.

"Well, then," said the great Auer, "he did all that you should expect."

Today, however, I must admit that Heifetz is beginning to appeal to the emotional as well as to the intellectual.

Coming out after the concert, I could not help being impressed by a remark I heard made by an old lady. She said: "That young man only needs some great sorrow, some terrible disappointment to make him really wonderful, because he will then be more human. Today he suggests a disembodied spirit."

Those who believe in reincarnation would be inclined to add that perhaps it is a disembodied spirit that plays through the violin of Jascha Heifetz.

Mr. Heifetz, who has recently acquired a valuable new violin, played a programme of serious violin music. Less of the virtuoso type of music was heard than at most of his recitals. In Mozart's A major concerto he made a deep impression.

It takes a very good musician to play this old music and make it interesting, and that is what Mr. Heifetz did. In his playing there is a refinement of style, a delicacy, a rhythmic touch that fits this sort of composition admirably. Cadenzas with swift runs and double stopping were executed perfectly. The whole concert was a delight to the ears. A concerto of Nardini, a Beethoven Romance, Edwin Grasse's "Waves at Play" and several short Wieniawski pieces were featured on his programme.

OCTOBER 28, 1922
CARNEGIE HALL

JASCHA HEIFETZ

Jascha Heifetz gave his first recital of the season before the usual overflowing audience in Carnegie Hall on Saturday afternoon of last week, with Samuel Chotzinoff at the piano. His program included Nardini's Concerto in E Minor, Mozart's in A and shorter numbers by Beethoven, Grasse, Wieniawski and Sgambati. Of the two concertos, the Nardini was perhaps the more interesting as a whole, though the Mozart was given with the purest classical style, and technically both were, as indeed was the entire program, impeccable. The Beethoven Romance in F seemed somewhat chilly, but the Auer arrangement of the Dance of the Dervishes, from Beethoven's "Ruins of Athens," was played with such verve that the audience demanded a repetition. Grasse's "Waves at Play" was a trifle too impersonal to be of ultimate appeal, and the same might be said of Sgambati's Serenata. Two Caprices and the D Major Polonaise of Wieniawski were spirited in effect and brought prolonged applause.

The playing of Mr. Heifetz has altered practically not at all since his first appearance here. It is still the most highly polished, musically perfect playing that one can hear at the present time in the concert room, but still lacking in emotional and in any markedly intellectual appeal. Each composer is presented in perfection and the listener left to attach to each work what significance it may have in his own individual ear. But, after all, may not this be the perfection of art?

J.A.H.

NOVEMBER 25, 1922
CARNEGIE HALL

JASCHA HEIFETZ

The usual crowded house welcomed Jascha Heifetz at Carnegie Hall on Saturday afternoon. Brahms' Sonata in A, although a work which makes few emotional demands, received a curiously undistinguished performance, though played by Mr. Heifetz with great beauty of tone and flawless technique. This remarkable technique played its part in a thrilling performance of the Prelude to Bach's Sixth Sonata for violin alone, to which were added a Bourree, Minuets Nos. 1 and 2 and a Gigue, all equally well played. The program also included Tchaikovsky's Serenade Melancolique, a transcription by Auer of his Valse Scherzo, a Meditation and Valse by Glazounoff, Wieniawski's Saltarella, Wilhelmj's transcription of Chopin's Nocturne in D, Paganini's Perpetuum Mobile and numerous encores. Samuel Chotzinoff was an excellent accompanist.

B.H.

MARCH 15, 1925
CARNEGIE HALL

HEIFETZ THIRD RECITAL

Jascha Heifetz began his third violin recital in Carnegie Hall, on Sunday afternoon, March 15, with Georges Enesco's second Sonata for piano and violin, an early work of the Romanian composer which is remarkable for its fine continuity. The work was played with colossal brilliancy by Mr. Heifetz and Isidor Achron at the piano. At this point the program broke into a galaxy of popular short pieces ranging from an Eighteenth Century Madrigal of Aubert to a modern Hebrew Dance by Joseph Achron. Included in the first group were Debussy's "La plus que lente," Cecil Burleigh's "Clouds" and the more vigorous, virtuoso work of Castelnuovo-Tedesco, "Capitan Fracassa." Wagner's "Romance" opened the next group and was followed by a Capriccio from the fourth Suite of Ries. The high spirited work of the Rhenish violinist was perhaps the most finished and perfect of all of Mr. Heifetz' program. Paul Juon's Valse Mignonne, "Arva," came somewhat as an anti-climax, but Godowsky's charming "Legende" redeemed it. The "Legende," which is a romantic study in sixths, would be better unaccompanied, for the violin part is complete in itself, containing melodies and harmonies which do not require the support of the piano for their fullest meaning. Wieniawski's "Souvenier de Moscou" gave the usual brilliant climax and brought demands for numerous encores, which Mr. Heifetz gave generously, but with his customary reserve.

H.M.M.

MARCH 15, 1925
CARNEGIE HALL

JASCHA HEIFETZ'S THIRD RECITAL

Jascha Heifetz gave his third violin recital of this season yesterday afternoon in Carnegie Hall. The audience, as is usual at Heifetz entertainments, filled all the seats and crowded the standing room. The program, save a sonata for piano and violin by Georges Enesco at the start, made for the most part merely for popular appeal. Shorter pieces by some nine composers, several of which were familiar in the violinist's repertoire and several of lesser interest, formed the next two groups, and the list ended with a piece also favored here in the past by the player. A little music strictly classic would not have been amiss among the selections, and especially when the size of the audience was taken into account.

The Enesco sonata in F minor, opus 6, was almost a novelty. The distinguished Romanian composer, who has been heard here himself as a violinist this season, would undoubtedly lay little stress upon its value as being an early work. It was introduced here in 1910 by Mr. and Mrs. Mannes. The first two movements—"assez mouvemente" and "tranquillement"—are without any great beauty or life. The final movement carries traces of the composer's native folk songs and sustains interest. The score, not without unusual rhythmic difficulties, was played with rare finesse by Mr. Heifetz and his pianistic associate, Isidor Achron. There was much applause for the sonata, and for Mr. Heifetz in such pieces as Aubert's "Madrigal," Burleigh's "Clouds" and a capriccio from Reis's fourth suite, given with marvelous purity and beauty of tone and poetic taste. Other numbers included Joseph Achron's "Hebrew Dance" and Tedesco's "Capitan Fracassa."

*On the facing page, Heifetz strikes a
meditative pose (September 22, 1924).
Below, he plays his violin for the blind Helen
Keller. She said she felt the beautiful sound
by touching Heifetz's violin as he played for
her. June 21, 1924.*

Heifetz, circa 1925.

MARCH 15, 1925
CARNEGIE HALL

JASCHA HEIFETZ PLAYS

Jascha Heifetz, who is unquestionably one of the best living violinists, gave his third recital of the season in Carnegie Hall yesterday afternoon. There were many disappointed people turned away after every nook and corner of the big auditorium was filled to repletion. But that is only what happens every time this artist plays.

Heifetz had a well-balanced program, which he gave as probably only one other violinist could give it. Enesco's second sonata (for violin and piano) was the first and longest of the numbers, conveniently divided into three parts to allow seating of late comers, though there were fewer of that tribe present yesterday than usual.

Of the numerous short pieces following "La Plus Que Lente," by

268

Debussy, and "Clouds," by Cecil Burleigh, seemed to delight the audience the most. The old tried and true "Souvenir de Moscou" of Wieniawski, the bane of all but the best performers on the violin, finished the program and was played most capably in a style so easy that made it seem anything but difficult. Isidor Achron was the capable accompanist.

The ending of the printed program was the signal for the standees to rush down the aisles and clamor for more. Mr. Heifetz obligingly played until some thoughtful person turned out the light.

JANUARY 5, 1928
CARNEGIE HALL

HEIFETZ, BACK FROM TRAVELS, IS ACCLAIMED BY THRONG
Violinist Gives First Recital in Two Years Before Multitude in Carnegie Hall

By Herbert F. Peyser

Strongarm tactics were none too strong to propel ticket holders through the seething mob that made Carnegie Hall lobby the abode of desperation at 8:30 o'clock last evening. Once inside the house, it became another struggle to reach one's lawful seat. Aisles were jammed, standing room was pretty much wherever sitting room was not, and the stage all but vanished beneath the serried occupation of a motley host. As late as 10 o'clock a crestfallen multitude still besieged the outer doors, making it imperative to keep them shut and vigilantly guarded.

And all because Jascha Heifetz had come back from two years' wandering in the East and proposed to give his first violin recital of the season!

The erstwhile wonder-lad of the fiddle set himself the task of playing Beethoven's "Kreutzer" sonata (with Isidor Achron at the piano), Lalo's "Symphonie Espagnole," tidbits (arranged and otherwise) by Suk, Schubert, Debussy, Novacek and Paganini's "Palpiti." But to the clamorous, febrile cohorts the things he played were doubtless a very minor matter. It sufficed unto them that he stood there applying horse hair to catgut for the production of any sounds that might be.

Mounting Enthusiasm

Mr. Heifetz was cordially applauded after the successive movements of the Beethoven sonata and deliriously after the Lalo "Symphony." As usual in such cases the tide of enthusiasm burst into its most foaming crests as the evening drew to a close. The consecrated violinist looked urbane as usual, even bored. His playing was, to all intents, what it has been for some years past—charming, finished, delicate, unexciting.

The "Kreutzer" sonata came in for a pretty, small scale, sweetly diffident, even epicene performance. All cantilena Mr. Heifetz delivered with engaging purity and a prevailing grace. The more calculating and sentimental music of Lalo yielded readier results to a somewhat less tepid and more forthcoming treatment. The violinist successfully extracted the last ounce of sugar from its system and spread the syrup very thick, indeed.

But the cool, impassive, unconcerned virtuoso of last night is fundamentally a different being from that preternatural youth of ten years ago whose seemingly irrecoverable art, haloed with an other-worldly radiance, knew naught of the taint or grossness of earthly contacts and could for a passing moment, transfigure the ignoblest of music to the likeness of an unfoldment from on high.

Al grandioso Heifetz con mi admiración entusiasta

José G. Rocha

Mex.

Heifetz from a 1928 sketch by Jose G. Rocha done during his Mexican tour.

270

JANUARY 5, 1928
CARNEGIE HALL

HEIFETZ IN VIOLIN RECITAL AFTER TOUR OF THE WORLD

Jascha Heifetz played his first violin recital in Carnegie Hall last night since his return from a concert trip around the world, having been gone nearly two years. He received a welcome any conquering hero might have been proud of—a sold-out house, the stage so packed with admirers the artist had hardly elbow room, standing room at a premium and the box office besieged by hordes, who had to put their money in their pockets and go out into the cold disappointed.

No one will dispute that Heifetz is an artist of a higher order, and his wonderful reception last night proved he has many admirers. His program, however, was somewhat disappointing. It did not contain the fire and sparkle that one associates with genius. It was a remarkably well-played program, nevertheless.

The little heard Beethoven Sonata No. 9 for piano and violin (Kreutzer) opened the concert. The first and last movements were given a precise interpretation by the violinist, who played from his notes, and in the second section, with variations, he produced some exquisite tones, which brought much applause.

Lalo's "Symphonie Espagnole" came next and the andante movement seemed to receive the best treatment at Mr. Heifetz's hands. It was violin playing of the highest order. Four short pieces made up the third part of the program. "La Fille aux Cheveux de Lin," by Debussy and arranged by Hartman, was of the style the audience liked and the applause was so insistent it was repeated. "Perpetuum Mobile," by Novacek was in this group, as were Suk's "Chanson d'Amour" and Friedberg's arrangement of Schubert's "Rondo." The "Perpetuum" astonished by the amount of music possible to extract from one instrument in a given time.

The unusual printed program was brought to a close with Paganini's "Palpiti," executed in the same clear-cut style as the ones preceding it.

Heifetz received an ovation then that must have surpassed anything he had experienced in his trip around the world.

He was between two surging waves of humanity, behind him on the stage and before him across the footlights. Of course, he had to play many encores. But the pieces were all remarkable for their execution rather than their content. Heifetz is a great violinist, yet one cannot conceive him saying what another great violinist, strangely enough arriving yesterday from Europe, is reported to have said to a reporter: "Music with me is a passion. If it were prohibited and against the law I would be a criminal, for I must play; under such conditions I would be a criminal. My music would be a secret thing."

A.C.B.

JANUARY 5, 1928
CARNEGIE HALL

JASCHA HEIFETZ REAPPEARS

by Olin Downes

The enormous audience that wedged and pushed into Carnegie Hall last night showed that a long absence in foreign lands had not in any way affected the regard of the local public for the art of Jascha Heifetz. That wonderful violinist reappeared last night for the first time in two years in this city and appeared, if anything, a more perfect artist than ever. He played the Beethoven "Kreutzer" sonata; four movements of the Lalo "Symphonie Espagnole," smaller pieces by Suk, Schubert, Debussy, and Paganini's "I Palpiti." He played with his wonted, and, as it sometimes seemed, almost weary mastery. But perhaps this demeanor is only the reserve of an exceptionally sensitive and truly great artist. Some have claimed that Heifetz is merely a super-technician. It is an estimate which falls far short of his depth and distinction as an interpreter. It is true that he is often aloof from or at least outside of what he does. But this is not coldness, and it is anything but superficiality. The classicism of the Beethoven sonata was due to the music. If the variations seemed in some cases trivial and well nigh without end, it was because they are in fact trivial for the greater part, and no respectful and artistic interpretation could make them otherwise. Other violinists than Mr. Heifetz inject more of what is called "passion" into the first and last movement and some play as if they took seriously the absurd literary interpretation of Tolstoy. Heifetz speaks in this music with a finer sense of proportion; he leaves something to the imagination, and his supreme mastery is art itself, a thing of incomparable beauty of line, and all this with an ease and perfection of execution that is a perpetual marvel.

But if it could be objected that the Beethoven music was treated in too impersonal a spirit, such an objection could never apply to the playing of Lalo. This was a thousand miles, of course, from the style of Beethoven's sonata, which actually belongs, despite its date and its strong inner feeling, to the composer's classical period. The Lalo performance was an epitome of the sensuous, exotic spirit of the music. It was Latin in the grace but glowing and colorful. Sometimes, as in the slow movement, it took on a touch of nobility, when sensuous feeling was transformed by the interpreter into something greater than itself. And a temperament which is reserved in outward manifestations but, without doubt, intense as it is sensitive, touched this familiar but not outworn music, and the well-nigh miraculous technical accomplishment, with flame.

The art of Mr. Heifetz, which appears to us to grow more distinguished with the years, has back of it a true intellectuality and an aristocratic sense of style which disdains equally what is sentimental or insincere, or in any solicitations of superficial approval. We may take his phenomenal technic for granted. It would be superfluous and impertinent to discuss it. He is like no other violinist before the public, and it will be long before a violinist like him will be seen again. Others in the long future will enjoy success equal to his, but not for the same reasons. His art is now reaching its maturity, and a wonderful maturity it is.

Paganini wrote his own music to best show his style and skills. This concert poster appeared in 1833.

PAGANINI!

SIGNOR PAGANINI, grateful for the liberal Patronage he has experienced, begs respectfully to announce to the Nobility, Gentry, and Public resident in Manchester and its Vicinity, that in deference to the wishes of numerous Families who were unable to attend his Concerts at the Salford Town Hall, and in order to afford an opportunity to all classes who may be desirous of hearing his Performance, HE WILL GIVE A GRAND

Farewell Concert,

At the THEATRE-ROYAL,

On Wednesday Evening, September 4th, 1833,

BEING MOST POSITIVELY THE LAST TIME

He can possibly have the honor of appearing before them previous to his final departure for the Continent, on which occasion he has secured the services of those highly celebrated Vocalists,

MISS WELLS and MISS WATSON,

ALSO

MR. WATSON,

Composer to the Theatre Royal, Covent Garden, & English Opera House, & Member of the Royal Academy of Music.

PROGRAMME OF THE CONCERT.

ACT FIRST.

Aria, Miss WELLS, "Soave Immagine," .... Mercadante.
Song, Miss WATSON, "The merry Mountain horn," .... Bishop.
(BY DESIRE.)

The admired variazione upon the popular Neapolitan Canzonetta, "The CARNIVAL OF VENICE," descriptive of the Freaks and Vagaries of a Venetian Carnival, by SIGNOR PAGANINI . . . . } Paganini.

Ballad, Miss WELLS, "Comin thro' the Rye," .... Melodies.
Ballad, Miss WATSON, "Meet me by Moonlight," .... Wade.

Sonata Sentimale upon the Prayer in Pietro L'Ermita, followed by a Tema Variato, executed on One String only, (the 4th,) by SIGNOR PAGANINI } Paganini.

ACT SECOND.

Duet, Miss WATSON and Miss WELLS, "Lo! when showers descending," .... Bishop.
(BY PARTICULAR DESIRE.)

The humourous variations on the "Contradanza delle Streghe," or Dance of the Witches round the Walnut Tree of Benevento, by SIGNOR PAGANINI . . } Paganini.

Ballad, Miss WELLS, (by desire,) "Kate Kearney," .... Melodies.
Ballad, Miss WATSON, "The Swiss Drover Boy," .... Melodies.
By particular desire,—The favourite MELODY OF THE NORTH, "The KEEL ROW," Miss WELLS and Miss WATSON, (as sung by them at the Theatres Royal, Dublin, Edinburgh, Glasgow, Liverpool, &c. &c. having been called for & repeated three times on each Evening } Watson.
(BY DESIRE,)

The favorite National Air of St. Patrick's Day, arranged and executed on ONE STRING, (the 4th.) by SIGNOR PAGANINI . . . . } Paganini.

MR. WATSON WILL PRESIDE AT THE PIANO-FORTE.

Tickets to be had and Places for the Boxes taken (only) of Mr. SOWLER, St. Ann's-square.
BOXES, 5s.——UPPER BOXES, 4s.——PIT, 2s. 6d.——GALLERY, 1s. 6d.

No Places can be secured unless the Tickets are taken at the time.

DOORS WILL BE OPENED AT SEVEN AND THE CONCERT COMMENCE AT EIGHT O'CLOCK.

JANUARY 5, 1928
CARNEGIE HALL

HEIFETZ JAMS CARNEGIE HALL
Throng Acclaims Return of Violinist in Brilliantly Rendered Program

By W.J. Henderson

Jascha Heifetz, the violinist, has come back. He has been far, far away among the Orientals who gaped with wonder at the ravishing sounds issuing from his magic fiddle. The town knew he had been away. It was evidently sitting up waiting for him to come back and when he arrived it rushed to Carnegie Hall and bought all the seats in the house.

There was not an inch of space anywhere. The stage was crowded. The standing room was jammed. There were people on the sidewalk in the cold hoping that some would go away early and give them seats.

The audience seemed a bit chilly when the concert began. The reception of the artists was little more than sympathetic. But after the first number, the Kreutzer sonata, the applause acquired a different note. It was deep and persistent. The violinist was recalled half a dozen times. From that moment till he finally wearied of playing encores after the program, there was nothing but enthusiastic demonstration. All of which might mean nothing, for robustious audiences are rather common in this town. But last evening the excitement had significance. It may have been even that some of those present justly measured the growth of Heifetz's art.

He had a capable assistant in Isidor Achron in the Beethoven sonata and the two musicians made the worn work sound fresh and engaging. It was in this composition and particularly in the first movement that Mr. Heifetz disclosed a stronger grip on the emotional quality of his music. There was not an instant of impetuous energy, not a moment lacking in the control of the artistic intelligence; but in certain attacks and in the boldness and inner fire of certain passages one perceived the widening of the experience of the artist.

In the long suffering "Symphonie Espagnole," which followed, there was further evidence of the artist's increase in appreciation of the purely emotional lure of music. His Spaniards were all grandees, not peasants, but they languished and loved and touched with all the romance that lingers by the banks of the Xeni and the Darve. Mr. Heifetz's tone retains all its golden purity and his intonation its exquisite accuracy. His staccato ripples and glitters yet and his cantilena flows in a stream of luminous glory. But he is broadening and deepening. He is still a player of faultless finish, but he says more than he did. He is a commanding figure in the musical world; he promises to be more imperial. He may never be imperious, but he will rule and be loved.

JANUARY 5, 1928
CARNEGIE HALL

MR. HEIFETZ RETURNS

By Samuel Chotzinoff*

Returning to Carnegie Hall last night after a two year absence, Jascha Heifetz encountered the same vast audience he had commanded in New York since he made his memorable debut just about ten years ago.

274

Last night's audience, a little uncertain whether it would find Mr. Heifetz unchanged, leaned anxiously forward to catch the first phrases of Beethoven's "Kreutzer" Sonata for violin and piano with which the program began. These phrases came through clear and pure. In the "Presto" which followed, one found the same fingerboard accuracy, while the bow bit into the strings with the old finality, releasing streams of uncannily matched tones or wafting cantalina passages delicately tempered and refined. It was the same Heifetz, and one could afford to lean back, certain that everything the violinist undertook to do would come to pass with the highest ease and beauty.

So much for the virtuoso. The musician, as revealed in the "Kreutzer," was hardly on a plane with this sonata of Beethoven. Certainly there is more in the "Kreutzer" than ravishing beauty of sound, refinement of phrasing and an aristocratic reticence of sentiment, felicities in which Mr. Heifetz wrapped Beethoven's music. Granted that the "Kreutzer" is altogether innocent of those implications which made it in Tolstoy's hands a musical causation of a domestic tragedy. On the other hand it is more than the mere loveliness which Mr. Heifetz would have us believe it is. What it really is one can only apprehend, not explain. The printed score indicates passion, turmoil and conflict as well as beauty and repose. Mr. Heifetz showed us the serenity and loveliness, but only fitfully the more human emotions of the music.

The "Symphonie Espagnole" of Lalo was, on the contrary, a matter for the utmost satisfaction, both musical and violinistic for the listener last evening. The piece had a double appeal—the appeal of a dazzling technical and musical exposition that ran beautifully parallel. And, strange to relate, the passion that would not be summoned in Beethoven found expression in Lalo. It was distinctly Spanish in character, buoyantly rhythmical, proud in feeling, patrician in its gracefulness—a most accurate interpretation of its title.

The smaller matters, like Suk's "Chauson d'Amour," Schubert's "Rondo," Debussy's "La Fille aux Cheveux de Lin" and the Novacek "Perpetuum Mobile," were perfect impressions of the musical character of each. A perpetuum mobile with Heifetz is just that—a cascade of notes that, once set in motion, goes on quite by itself, ceasing only when the artist turns off the switch.

The Paganini "I Palpiti" came last. It is the fashion to decry the arrangements of Paganini as unworthy the attention of serious musicians. But it is nearer the truth to say that Paganini is so seldom played because there are so few violinists who can play him. One cannot live by profundity alone, and an exhibition of mere virtuosity such as Mr. Heifetz gave in "I Palpiti" must forever be a joy to those who are enthralled by the mystery of any perfect mechanism.

The concert as a whole was a memorable display of virtuosity combined with a musical intelligence beautifully clear and chaste. Mr. Achron, the assisting pianist, played well and discreetly.

* *Mr. Chotzinoff, who often accompanied the young Heifetz on the piano, married Mr. Heifetz's sister; she passed away in 1976.*

HEIFETZ HAS ANOTHER LOVE — CELEBRATED VIOLINIST IS ALSO A PASSIONATE COLLECTOR OF RARE BOOKS

By William Bridges

Books. Long tables ranged with books in serried rows. Books stacked in dusty piles under the tables, in forlorn battered heaps in the corners, banked against the walls, bright dustcovers calling attention to books on the bargain counter and somber, sober books packed by the thousands into shelves, corridors of shelves, miles of dusty shelves, almost, disappearing into the shadows at the back of the shop.

The second-hand bookshop was in Albany, the time was four or five years ago, and the only visitor one dismal autumn afternoon was an absorbed young man methodically working his way through the shelves and pausing now and then to draw a fat volume out, blow a fog of dust from its top, sneeze, thumb its brown-stained pages and move on after replacing it with tender solicitude for its age-brittle binding.

Three hours later it was closing time and the lights blinked twice in drowsy periods to warn any stragglers who might have tangled their consciousness in the mazes of old books. There was a shuffling sound far back in the shop and the young visitor of the early afternoon emerged, a single thin book clutched under his arm, dusting hands that could never be perfectly clean again.

"I'd forgotten you," grinned the clerk. "Find something?"

"Yes." The young man took a step nearer the door and tendered the book. "How much is it, please?"

Leisurely, the clerk took the gray old book between a thumb and forefinger, flipped open the cover and glanced at the title page.

"*Scarlet Letter*, eh? Oh, a dollar and a quarter I guess."

The exact change was in his hands so quickly he must have blinked his astonishment and an instant later the young man was streaking for the door. Fascinating folios in old calf beckoned to him but he did not stop to browse now. For Jascha Heifetz was scheduled to give a violin recital in Albany in a little more than an hour—and he was Jascha Heifetz. And the book hugged ecstatically to his breast was the rare first issue of the first edition of Hawthorne's *The Scarlet Letter*, worth $1.25 to the bookstore that didn't suspect its nature, but worth about $1,500 to any collector who did. Heifetz had two very good reasons for not wasting time.

That's a picture of one of the greatest violinists the world has ever known in one of the supreme moments of his life—a moment that only inveterate book collectors can savor with him to the fullest. To find an unappreciated treasure, a flawless jewel cast aside as worthless by its owner—in other words, a rare and valuable book that a careless bookseller is willing to part with for practically nothing; that is the thing which every collector dreams about in his happy and well-fed and contented moments—and achieves but once or twice in a lifetime if ever. The supreme moment visited Jascha Heifetz in his book-collecting days.

No wonder he's a book-collecting enthusiast, no wonder his library in his Park Avenue penthouse is one of the dearest, most satisfactory spots he has ever known. It is filled with treasures, lined with biblio-jewels that he and every collector who sees them appreciates with the keenest delight.

"I began collecting books in 1919," Mr. Heifetz told a visitor from *The Sun* the other evening. He sat behind a littered desk, tapped a cigarette on the space-bar of a portable typewriter, and let his eye rove around the small, book-lined room. "Samuel Chotzinoff really started me. As a boy in Russia, of course, I'd read a lot—Dickens and Tom Sawyer and Thackeray and Shakespeare and Byron. Byron especially. He's very popular in Russia—or was.

"But some ten years ago I was with Chotzinoff while I was playing and he infected me with a love of those familiar books all over again. I saw his books and I thought I'd like to see what they looked like in the original. First editions, you know.

"Collecting is already a habit. Ever since I was a boy in Russia I've always been collecting something. But I was in Sydney, on a concert tour in Australia, when I first began to collect books. I didn't care about condition then. They could be battered and torn—in fearful condition—but I didn't know any better and I bought them."

"What sort of things do you collect—English literature, modern first editions, fine press books?"

"Everything," Mr. Heifetz said and smiled his sudden illuminating smile. "Just everything. Fine press books—yes, some. But mostly the substantial things of English literature. I've most of Dickens in the original parts, just as the books were published in small magazine form. And come here—you must see my George Moore collection."

He ran his finger along a ledge of books and then unlocked a wall panel, disclosing high tiers of tightly packed volumes.

"That's the rest of them. I think it's one of the finest Moore collections in the country—possibly the best. Everything he wrote. All in first edition and almost every volume autographed. I must show you my *Pagan Poems*. It's fascinating—fascinating. There's a whole page on the flyleaf in Moore's autograph."

Out of the bathroom he dragged a little white stool and climbed up to extract the thin *Pagan Poems* from the top shelf.

"I didn't pick that up at a bargain as I did the *Scarlet Letter*, you may be sure. Oh, not at all. The price of that was fully known and appreciated. But I got it with most of the other Moore books—I bought an almost complete set and finished it as I could."

He stepped down and ran his hand across a deep shelf at the bottom.

"Here are some of the books that will interest you—the Kelmscott *Chaucer*, my poor Shakespeare Fourth Folio—too bad it isn't a First Folio, isn't it?—Beaumont and Fletcher, 1679, and —"

He grinned and plucked at a tall thin volume lying across the tops of the half-dozen volumes that in themselves were worth a small fortune.

"This you doubtless know—Peter Arno's *Hullabaloo*. You know it, eh? Yes, I'll admit it's rather out of place. But it's getting to be a problem where to store my books."

As perfectly at home among his beloved books as among the mazes of a violin composition, Jascha Heifetz moved from bookshelf to bookshelf, pulling down a volume here and there, indicating others with a sweep of his arm. He pointed out a magnificent *Don Juan* in a slipcase, *Treasure Island* with Stevenson's autograph nonchalantly stuffed away beside some brown little volume he treasured because it was one of the first books he bought, an 1866 *Alice In Wonderland*, with Tenniel's unsurpassed illustrations that caused Heifetz to laugh as he opened to the title page, a long sequence of Stevenson, of Goethe, of Hardy, a few of Conrad, many of Kipling's most famous books, the regal forty volumes of the Tudor Translations standing in frozen Christmas splendor of white vellum behind a panel.

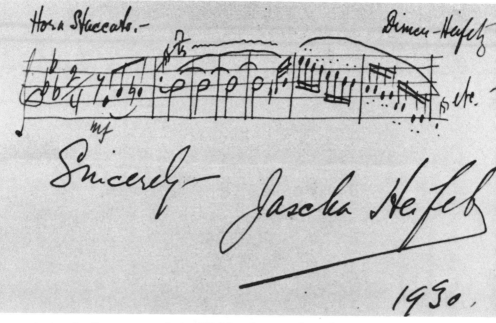

Horn Staccato.–   Dimer–Heifetz

mf

Sincerely–   Jascha Heifetz

1930.

A musical autograph in Heifetz's own hand, owned by John Maltese.

He knew them all, intimately. He had arranged them on the shelves himself. No one else was allowed to move them, possibly to disarrange the order or handle them with less loving care. He knew their dates, their issues and editions, where he had bought them and when.

"But I don't collect now as I once did," he mourned. "Partly it's time, partly because the books I want have become so expensive. A Kilmarnock Burns at fifteen thousand dollars—it is no sport for anyone but a millionaire. And you never know when to stop. You find yourself wondering if maybe you could afford a Gutenberg Bible! When one does that it surely is time to stop.

"So now, for a time, I am collecting coins. No, it isn't a joke. Gold coins—I have become a numismatist. I have traveled around the world, and I thought it would be interesting to know something about the currency of each country—I have been in practically every country on the globe. So I began with France and collected first the Louis d'or, then the older gold coins. Then in England I did the same, and in other countries I visited. It's interesting. I have always loved the color of gold, anyway."

But he was back on books. "You know," he said, "I am sure there is wonderful book-hunting to be done in New York—yes, even in cynical, sophisticated, self-conscious New York, where the dealers know all about books. They know a great deal in Paris, but I found a Voltaire "first" once. A most interesting book on his theory of music and numbers. For seventy-five francs I carried it away. And one can still do that in New York, I'm certain."

He fell to musing for a moment. "I wonder," he said, half to himself, "I wonder if I will have time next Monday afternoon to go down on Fourth Avenue?"

278

VARIED PARIS PROGRAMS
Berlin Philharmonic—Ysaye, Kreisler, Heifetz and Virtuosity

By Henry Prunieres

The Berlin Philharmonic Orchestra, under Wilhelm Furtwangler, has triumphed for the fourth time here in Paris. Formerly I did not think that a conductor who had reached the highest degree of technical perfection was still able to go ahead. Furtwangler, however, during the past year has discovered the means of surpassing himself. The audience was completely bowled over by the two concerts. As I search my memory I cannot recall equal delirium in the hall, except perhaps when Arturo Toscanini and the New York Philharmonic came here a year ago. Furtwangler found himself forced to return to the platform twenty times to acknowledge the acclaim and applause of the auditors who seemingly had not thought of quitting the hall. On the first evening he was obliged to add excerpts from Berlioz's "La Damnation de Faust" and on the second the overture from Wagner's "Die Meistersinger."

I will not expatiate upon the technic of this great conductor. No exaggeration, and not a single unnecessary gesture. A left hand of incredible independence. Gesticulation of great reserve, of delicacy and of expressiveness. He plays upon his orchestra as upon an instrument, and a superb instrument it is indeed. I confess that from the point of view of tone quality only the great American orchestras are its superiors. The strings are truly marvelous. The contrabasses especially have a velvety and dolce quality in their power which recalls to my mind the contrabasses of the Boston Symphony Orchestra.

Years ago Furtwangler was in the habit of sacrificing too much to obtain effects, and I recall a performance of Beethoven's Fifth that was not free from lapses in taste. Nothing of this remains today and one can only acquiesce fully in anything he does in the interpretations of the "Eroica," "Till Eulenspiegel," the Prelude A l'Apres-Midi d'un Faune," the "Tannhauser" overture, the C major symphony by Schubert or the Third Brandenburg by Bach.

The final impression is one of absolute perfection, but without that correctness lacking in warmth which is the result of pure orchestral virtuosity. What emotion, what heroic force, what delicate sensitivity, and what concentrated and rich lyricism! There is no doubt whatever that Furtwangler has placed himself today in the very first rank of orchestral conductors.

The parade of virtuosos has begun. I regret that I was not able to hear Kreisler. Although he seemed very tired, his success was great. I suppose that the death of Eugene Ysaye will have affected him deeply. Some years ago I recall having heard the Austrian violinist render enthusiastic homage to the Belgian genius, whom he proclaimed as his true master, although, strictly speaking, he had never studied with him. From the time that Kreisler left the Paris Conservatory with a brilliant premier prix at the age of 13 he relates that he worked alone, going to hear Ysaye every time the opportunity presented itself—Ysaye, whom he put at the head of all the virtuosos he knew.

It is Kreisler, in truth, who appears to be the heir and successor of the Belgian. To be found in him is that flame and that endless giving of himself which characterized and animated Ysaye. The Belgian, however, sacrificed less than does Kreisler to pure virtuosity. The superb sonata recitals of Ysaye and Pugno cannot ever be erased from the memory.

Ysaye founded the magnificent quartet which bore his name. It was this quartet which had the honor of presenting the premiers of Cesar Franck's and Debussy's quartets and of playing them in various musical centers of the world. He looked upon himself as a great servant of the music of today and of the past, and he did not feel it beneath his dignity to take part in a quartet or to play a sonata with a worthy collaborator.

Virtuosos of today hardly ever consent to play with orchestras, and rarely appear as soloists with anything else except modest accompanists. Among the virtuosos, I can discern only Thibaud, Casals and Cortot who have not become the slaves of their own virtuosity.

There is a real peril here for the art of music, and it is high time that the critic and public stage a revolution against the abuses of virtuosity. Is it not absurd for a pianist to think he has lost caste by accompanying a singer in public? I still recall with emotion the cycles of Schumann Lieder sung twenty years ago by Marya Freund, with Alfred Cortot playing heavenly accompaniments at the piano. Today no pianist of the second rank would dare follow his example.

All these reflections came to my mind as I heard the recital of Jascha Heifetz at the Opera. Here is undeniably a marvelous virtuoso. I feel that it is safe to say, without fear of contradiction, that the world has never had a violinist, not even Paganini, who played with such prodigious technique. Is it to be endured and tolerated that an artist of this rank plays such miserable programs as those he played here and contents himself with an accompanist of such mediocrity? To be scorned is a public which acquiesces in such revolting procedure. It will be objected that it was these very detestable transcriptions and the vulgarest tidbits of virtuosity which had the greatest success and which were encored. This is no excuse. A true artist ought to have respect for himself and for his art and ought to guard himself from flattering the lowest tastes of the public. Though he evoked the enthusiasm of the auditorium by the magic of his incomparable bowing, he revolted, at the same time, a great number of people of taste, many of whom left the hall before the end of the concert.

Throughout the whole program hardly anything except the "Tzigane" by Ravel was to be tolerated. Not that I like particularly this piece, whose musical content is very anemic, but we must recognize that it achieves its purpose perfectly. In this piece are brought together themes and rhythms which are dear to the gypsies of Hungary. In it are to be found the most formidable technical difficulties which a virtuoso is called upon to surmount. Apart from this brilliant piece, we heard only some transcriptions of the most despairing mediocrity; the tedious "Scottish Fantasy," by Max Bruch, and a new composition by Castelnuovo-Tedesco, "The Lark," which disconcerted me with its insignificance, a series of etudes and exercises of virtuosity lacking in organic continuity and vital force.

Heifetz played this program with a supreme ease which ignored difficulties. But how frigid is this dazzling playing! Let us recognize that it was difficult to play with warmth and emotion music which does not possess these qualities. Years ago I heard Heifetz interpret very agreeably music by Mozart. We must admit that he plays very well, but a little in the manner of a miraculous automaton which might execute the most diabolically difficult compositions with an infallible sureness and with a ravishing tone-quality. It is a paradox that an artist who possesses such

280

Isaac Stern has, unfortunately been compared to Heifetz during his entire career. Circa 1947.

perfection of technique does not prevent us from becoming tired of him. Obviously there is lacking in him that which illuminated the playing of Ysaye and that which comes to us from a Kreisler—namely, a great soul.

I must point out the very fine recital given at the Theatre des Champs Elysees by the violinist Zino Francescatti. Of all the young men, he seems to me to best represent the French school of violin playing. In his playing are to be found the best qualities of Jacques Thibaud, the fullness of tone, the intimate and deep warmth, the brilliant shading and the suppleness of execution, all matched with a moving spirituality. He has splendid technique, but he knows how to make his hearer forget it. He is already a finished artist and one of whom the world will soon talk.

Zino Francescatti was Europe's answer to Heifetz. He is a magnificent artist and a warm, gracious person. Circa 1975.

282

OVATION TO HEIFETZ

By Olin Downes

When Jascha Heifetz played for the first time in two years in this city last night in Carnegie Hall, he found an audience which had exhausted the capacity of the hall and which flowed into every available nook and cranny of the auditorium awaiting him. Mr. Heifetz, a monarch returning to his own, performed with that complete authority, technical mastery and sense of form and proportion which are always, and sometimes in a miraculous degree, his attributes.

He played the Grieg sonata in C minor for violin and piano; the Mozart A major concerto; the Adagio and Fugue from the Bach unaccompanied sonata in G minor; small pieces by Hummel-Heifetz and Rimsky-Korsakoff, and the printed program ended with the Ravel "Tsigane." The pianist was Isidor Achron. It is needless to say that Mr. Heifetz played encores, and that at the end of the program announced on the printed slip, a large number rushed down to the stage, to look, to breathe adoration.

The qualities which make Mr. Heifetz pre-eminent among all violinists were of course present last night. The audience recognized them and responded warmly. For some this was a new discovery, for others the pleasant incarnation of an old one. But if the audience had expected a new development of style or of feeling since the last season Mr. Heifetz appeared in this city, his playing did not reveal any. He started the Grieg sonata in dramatic style, perhaps with less care for sheer beauty and clarity of tone than is usual with him. This is perfectly in place in Grieg's work, so much more romantic, lyrical, in some moments impassioned, than it is an example of "sonata form" or other attributes of the classic German musical art—characteristics for which Grieg had so little sympathy or aptitude. There was the thought at the beginning that this music might reveal a more passionate and less contained player than the Heifetz of former years. But as the performance went on, very surely, very coherently and beautifully, too, it was evident that after all here was the old detachment.

Mr. Heifetz unquestionably feels deeply; he has innate taste and a horror of musical exhibitionism which would lead him, under any circumstances, to avoid as the plague the obvious or melodramatic. The Mozart concerto, a far greater work, and one more difficult to play well, is much more native to Mr. Heifetz's style. The cadenzas were, of course, fascinating for the clarity, poise and dignital resource with which they were delivered. The curious finale of the concerto, when Mozart, more inspired than Ravel, seems also inclined in the direction of the "Tsigane," was the culmination of an interpretation always edifying. Need it have been so objective?

For the writer the most interesting and the most moving performance of the evening was the movements from Bach's unaccompanied sonata. The music, in itself of infinite richness and sometimes of searching pathos, has particularly the quality of line, the intellectual design, the deep and contained feeling which Mr. Heifetz so fortunately conveys. His performance was almost sculptural, and this with the ease and mastery which should ever be present when a violinist undertakes such music. Up to that point in the program—and it is of interest as signifying the esteem in which Bach was held as well as Heifetz—the applause was the heaviest of the evening.

But it was even heavier for the trifle, the Hummel Rondo in Heifetz's transcription, and heaviest of all for that inane gimcrack, "The Bumble-Bee." When this piece, this ditty, is played as fast as Mr. Heifetz can play it, the imitation of a fly buzzing against a windowpane is perfect. Perhaps it is this close kinship to nature which delights an audience. Ravel's "Tzigane" was a more astounding feat, though hardly better music. At the end patrons were crowding and milling about the platform, rendering homage to Mr. Heifetz.

OCTOBER 15, 1932

MUSIC AND MUSICIANS

By W.J. Henderson

Listening to Heifetz on Tuesday evening, the writer found an old and sadly worn reflection forcing its way into his mind. Do artists ever feel the tremendous burden of their debuts? Surely they must. It is a serious matter for a young musician to make a first appearance and have the public impressed with the idea that he has already reached the climax of his development. Yet this is so often the case that this writer can never cease to wonder at it. Thirty years ago people were saying that Josef Hofmann was a tremendous virtuoso, but that he had no emotional communication. No matter how he plays, there are people who continue to repeat that estimate of his art.

Vladimir Horowitz came into our ken and we were told by high authority that he was not only the most amazing of all wizards of the keyboard, but that he was a master interpreter. Yehudi Menuhin, an immature child with a marvelous musical instinct and a more than ordinary mentality was declared to be an interpreter of the foremost rank. Horowitz, a very modest and serious young man, who has surely no fancy for

Herbert Gehr of Time-Life Pictures took this rare photo of Vladimir Horowitz and Heifetz. Circa 1935.

spending his life in the mere jugglery of tones, has made rapid strides in analytical power and synthesis of exposition. He grows normally, as an artist of his type should be expected to grow. But those who rhapsodized about him when he made his debut have now nothing more to say than they said then. He is still the same Horowitz, and if they live to hear him thirty years hence, he will not have changed for them.

To be sure no artist acquires a new individuality. Elman has radically modified his style and yet it is still the distinctively Elman style. But the erratic products of mere impulse have been relegated to a secondary position while the fruits of reflection and ripened understanding have become conspicuous. Fritz Kreisler still has some of the artistic characteristics of the Master Fritz who so many years ago made his debut in Boston as assisting artist at the concerts of Moriz Rosenthal. But these characteristics, while they help to mark the style, are by no means the distinguishing traits of Kreisler's art. The man Kreisler grew from the boy prodigy, but the man is decidedly a man, and not a boy.

Musical artists are just like other folk; they grow up.

The most succinct, complete and just criticism of the art of Heifetz, we think, is that written by Walter Wilson Cobbett in Grove's "Dictionary of Music": "He is not what is known as a temperamental player, his aspirations being toward an art entirely free from exaggeration; but nothing more subtle in expression or more perfectly balanced has been heard than his interpretations of the works which the great masters have written for the violin."

That, we think, puts the whole matter in the hollow of a hand. And we invite particular consideration to the author's use of the word "subtle." It is the subtlety of Heifetz's interpretative method that defies the mob and confounds the professional commentators who rejoice in martial challenge and flaunting banner. At the time of his debut this writer said that his delicate, polished and fastidiously tasteful style came directly down the line from Viotti and was removed as far as possible from the influence of Paganini which always furthered the development of virtuosity.

Viotti was the father of the modern school of classic violin playing. His art was perfectly poised, noble in repose, commanding in dignity. He was a true son of Corelli, guided by Pugnani. He would have had some difficulty in communicating his soul to this age of demonstration, in which any conduct governed by order and respect is likely to be condemned as austere or even ascetic. Heifetz suffers in the eyes of some music lovers because he is an exponent of the great Russian school. So is his friend and artistic associate, Efrem Zimbalist. These two violinists are the foremost living players of the school.

Temperament will always be a bone of contention. The fundamental meaning of the word is "individual peculiarity of physical and mental constitution." Doubtless pituitary and other glands have something to do with the matter. Musicians are frequently possessed of temperaments passionate and ill-controlled. When they play or sing, they reek with emotion, and when they reek with this they seldom reek with intellectuality. The musical artist who is captain of his soul is almost certain to be described as lacking in temperament. Yet it is indisputable that the greatest artists are those who know what they are doing and are always in perfect control of their powers. We believe that Horowitz will in time be one of these, though his intellectual force has not yet asserted its complete sovereignty. Heifetz is always in command and there is never a moment when the strong lines of his design are blurred. He is and will continue to be a master of form and style.

Efrem Zimbalist, one of Prof. Auer's favorite pupils, with one of his students. Zimbalist and Heifetz were close friends in the early days of Heifetz's career. Circa 1950.

A BIBLICAL CONCERTO HEARD AT THE PHILHARMONIC: SOME WAGNER MARVELOUSLY PLAYED.

2,883rd CONCERT OF THE PHILHARMONIC-SYMPHONY SOCIETY, ARTURO TOSCANINI, CONDUCTOR; ASSISTING ARTIST, JASCHA HEIFETZ, VIOLINIST; AT CARNEGIE HALL.

PROGRAM

1. Cherubini .... Overture to "Anacreon"
2. Castelnuovo-Tedesco .... Second Concerto
   ("The Prophets") for Violin and Orchestra, Jascha Heifetz, Violinist.
   (First performance anywhere)

Intermission

3. Wagner .... Prelude to Act I, "Parsifal"
4. Wagner .... Good Friday Spell, from Act III, "Parsifal"
5. Wagner .... Daybreak, and Siegfried's Rhine Journey, from "Goetterdaemmerung"

The amazingly generous Philharmonic-Symphony Society, not content with offering the town a Beethoven Cycle under Toscanini, has been presenting us, on the side, with a Heifetz Cycle, to the vast delight of those subscribers who have found themselves listening to Mr. Toscanini and Mr. Heifetz on the same program. Thursday night, for the fourth time in a week, the renowned violinist stood beside the Maestro's podium and conferred upon an appreciative audience the benison of his honeyed virtuosity.

Mr. Heifetz did not, as before, regale his listeners with an established masterwork. Having disposed of so familiar and cherished a matter as the Brahms Concerto a week ago, he accomplished last evening a "world premiere" of a brand-new piece for violin and orchestra, the first performance anywhere of a concerto by the Florentine composer, Castelnuovo-Tedesco, whose Overture to "The Taming of the Shrew" has recently been heard here under Mr. Toscanini's direction. The concerto is dedicated to Mr. Heifetz.

In his new work, Castelnuovo-Tedesco has turned from Shakespeare to the Old Testament for inspiration. His concerto has a title, "The Prophets," but this, he explains, is not to be understood as implying a precise and detailed program. It is intended to give merely an indication of what he calls the "ethnical environment" of his music. The composition, he tells us, "is supposed to be a kind of Biblical concerto, an evocation of times in the glorious past."

It seemed to Mr. Castelnuovo-Tedesco that "the choice of a solo violinist in the midst of the varied utterances of the orchestra might suggest the flaming and fanciful eloquence of the ancient prophets among the surrounding voices: voices of the people, voices of nature."

For the principal themes of his concerto, the composer informs us that he has resorted to traditional Jewish melodies, or fragments of melodies.

The imaginative plan chosen by Castelnuovo-Tedesco as the framework for his concerto is one that is peculiarly suited to musical treatment; and the composer has given us an effectively planned and admirably contrasted series of mood pictures and characterizations, conceived in those general terms of poetic and dramatic implication which; as he wisely perceived, were best fitted to his scheme. His organization of the thematic material that he has selected is skillful and ingenious; the musical tissue is both delicate and firm; the instrumentation is brilliant.

It is only fair to recognize the fact that Castelnuovo-Tedesco was hampered by the difficulty inherent in his choice of subject. The Prophets, as they exist for us in the Old Testament, have spoken for themselves with a splendor and sublimity which must necessarily futilize an attempt at any sort of musical transmutation.

"The whole earth is at rest, and is quiet." . . . "Thy pomp is brought down to the grave, and the noise of thy viols." . . . "I will exalt my throne above the stars of God." . . .

Magic such as that, magnificence such as that, must leave any music-maker, save another Bach, another Handel, fainting and gasping in the rear. No music on such a subject, except the very greatest could possibly avoid afflicting us with an uncomfortable awareness of the immense disparity between the imaginative theme and its musical treatment.

Castelnuovo-Tedesco should be applauded for his bravery, at least; and also for his musicianship.

The solo part of the concerto imposes taxing problems on the player, but Mr. Heifetz solved them easily and, on the whole, delightfully.

"When half-gods go so the gods arrive"; and so it was Thursday evening. The talented Mr. Castelnuovo-Tedesco was succeeded on the program by Wagner at his most subduing. It was not surprising, therefore, that the latter half of the concert erased, for a time, all memory of that which had preceded it—especially as Mr. Toscanini improved the occasion by giving us such a disclosure of the "Parsifal" Prelude and Good Friday music and the Daybreak-Rhine Journey excerpt from "Gotterdammerung" as even he has seldom achieved.

Only those whose privilege it has been to hear "Parsifal" at Bayreuth under Toscanini can know what he makes of the work—what prodigies of recreation he achieves on every page of that profound and complex and infinitely subtle score. But such interpretations of the Prelude and Good Friday scene as were vouchsafed to us last evening give us the essence of the matter.

They are not to be described. It must suffice for the moment to say that they are marvelous for their sensitive penetration into the deepest secret of this music's significance and beauty, and their inexplicable power of laying bare the heart of that secret.

We heard Thursday night, in the passage prefatory to the Good Friday Spell, the music that Wagner wrote for the scene in which, after Parsifal baptizes Kundry, she—the grave and humble penitent, who through the ages and her many incarnations could only tempt and laugh and mock—now bows her head and weeps. In this episode there is an incomparable passage in which the muted violins and violas are accompanied by five soft pizzicati notes of the cellos and double-basses. Some of us had never realized what Wagner meant by those throbbings of the string basses, and by the succeeding phrase of the violins, until we heard them as Toscanini directs that they shall sound.

Some veil was lifted from the inner ear and mind, and suddenly this music of effable compassion and unfathomable grief became a part of us, and turned the heart to water.

MR. HEIFETZ OPENS THE VIRTUOSO'S YEAR IN A NOTEWORTHY CONCERT OF VIOLIN MUSIC

FIRST APPEARANCE THIS SEASON OF JASCHA HEIFETZ IN A RECITAL OF MUSIC FOR VIOLIN AND PIANO, AT CARNEGIE HALL; ACCOMPANIST, ARPAD SANDOR.

PROGRAM

1. Sonatina .... Schubert
2. Sarabande, Gavotte, and Mesette .... Bach-Heifetz
3. Sonata .... Strauss
4. Concerto .... Conus
5. Hungarian Dance .... Brahms
6. El Puerto .... Albeniz-Heifetz
7. Alt Wien .... Castelnuovo-Tedesco
8. Molly on the Shore .... Grainger
9. Hebrew Dance .... Achron

The incomparable Mr. Heifetz opened the virtuoso's year last evening at Carnegie Hall with a recital of unusual interest and distinction. The circumstances of the occasion, taken at their face value, appeared to give the lie to the somewhat familiar assertion that we are in the depths of a depression and that music and musicians are bluer than the eagle that should be winging their hopes aloft.

To be sure, there were no auditors on the stage, and the house was not packed to suffocation; yet there was nothing conspicuously blue in the atmosphere of the affair except the smoke in the lobby during the intermission. Mr. Heifetz, looking like an advertisement for a sun-cure, faced a well filled house when he came upon the platform, bronzed, impassive, wrapped in his fabulous Buddhistic calm and what appeared to be an added layer or two of vacational well-being.

The audience greeted him with heartening fervor, and then settled into that mood of eager and alert responsiveness which is so characteristic and so flattering a trait of the gatherings that Mr. Heifetz draws to his music-making. For you will never find among these assemblies the type of listener prefigured by the immortal Mrs. Boffin, who (you will recall) at the beginning of Mr. Wegg's reading, "reclined in a fashionable manner on her sofa as one who would be part of the audience if she found she could, and would go to sleep if she found she couldn't." There are not doubtful Mrs. Boffins at Mr. Heifetz's recitals—or, if there are, they remain in discreet and shamed retirement.

One was especially grateful to Mr. Heifetz for giving us an opportunity to hear the relatively unfamiliar sonata in E flat major (op. 18) of Richard Strauss—a work which had not crossed my aural thresholds in many a year. The work, of course, is a product of the relatively youthful Strauss; it belongs to the same year, 1887, as the first of the tone-poems, "Macbeth"—which, it is good to learn, Mr. Bruno Walter is to conduct for us this season with the Philharmonic-Symphony Orchestra. The violin sonata antedated such full-bodied Straussian master-works as "Don Juan" and "Tod und Verklaerung" by only one and two years, respectively; and it is engrossingly suggestive of the master who was to come, despite its echoes of Schumann and of Brahms and its deficiency of thematic profile.

Jascha Heifetz celebrated his birthday on February 2, 1940 with his first wife, the former Florence Vidor, and their two children Robert and Josepha.

Castelnuovo-Tedesco with Piatigorsky in Switzerland, circa 1935.

Strauss was twenty-three when he composed the work. He had encountered, two years before, his esthetic awakener, Alexander Ritter, that embodied storm-wind, who, as Richard himself confessed, helped the nascent revolutionist to find himself as an individualist and a pathbreaker.

The sonata lacks thematic salience—it has little of the genius for significant line that was to blaze forth so soon in "Don Juan." The melodic invention is for the most part trite and sentimental. But the harmonic structure of the music betrays the coming master. Here is the Strauss who was about to entrain for the Liszt-Wagner encampment—who was, indeed, already on his way there. Here are hints and prophecies of the young lion who was stirring in the Brahmsian veldt, stretching his great muscles, muttering tonal thunder in that young and powerful throat which was to voice the startling utterances that shook the symphonic heavens of the dying '80's.

The sonata is not meat for fiddling youngsters. It offers problems of technic, especially in the Finale, with its intonational chevaux de frise, which require the skill and aplomb of a virtuoso. Mr. Heifetz traversed it unfalteringly, most musically, most revealingly, as he did the far simpler measures of the Schubert Sonatina in G minor (No. 3 of Op. 137). The elementary character of this work of Schubert's, by the way, has been exaggerated. When Schubert composed it, he had already written some of the supreme music of the world; and his inimitable voice speaks from these comparatively simple pages. Schubert himself did not give the three items of his Opus 137 their present title. He called them sonatas. The minimizing designation "Sonatinas" was not attached to them until Diabelli printed them in 1836, eight years after Schubert's death.

The music's fragrant loveliness and gayety, its innocence of the heart, was exquisitely felt by the violinist. This was among Mr. Heifetz's repeated achievements in the sensitive notation of style and sentiment and period, mood and manner. He reminded us continually, indeed, as he has so often done before, that he supplies a standard of musical taste and sensibility, and of all that is meant by a necromantic mastery of technic, beyond which it would be unreasonable to ask him to advance. His playing yielded us its old delights; in its exhibition of a various and poised exquisiteness; in the sensitive matching and contrasting tonal hues and patterns, the delicate bevelling of phrase, free and cleansed of the dust of ineptitude and slackness; in the gravity or the swiftness of the sure and confident craftsman, the effortless triumphs over a thousand pitfalls; in the strong flight of the poet's wings.

There is in this musician's art no sediment or excess. It has occasionally what seems almost like the ultimate touch, within its province and its control, of fine-grained loveliness and rectitude. It has genius, and it has felicity—those qualities which are so seldom harmoniously allied. It causes us again to realize that music is sometimes, as verse is always, "not the thing said, but a way of saying it." In his utterance of the substance of that which he would convey, this remarkable artist seems to have cherished the experiences of the mind and the imagination with an alembicated passion which gives to the union of emotion and of will the purity and the flame of poetry.

Heifetz playing tennis. May 4, 1950.

HEIFETZ GREETED AT CARNEGIE HALL
Violinist Gives a Masterful Interpretation of the Schubert Sonatina
AUDIENCE IS ENTHUSIASTIC
Artist Wins Much Applause for His Final Group—
Arpad Sandor, Accompanist, Praised

By Olin Downes

There is a legend of a Heifetz who cannot err, who, with thoughtful, impassive countenance, masters his audiences by the inscrutable perfection and finish of his playing. After listening to Mr. Heifetz last night in Carnegie Hall the auditor realized again the fallibility of legends, and the further fact that Jascha Heifetz, an extremely sensitive musician and man, is as changeable in mood and human of feeling as other great musicians.

He was well content, at first, to appear as a past master of ensemble performance. His program began with the delicious Schubert Sonatina, and this performance, by its fineness of texture, warmth of feeling, and supreme sense of beauty, was a model of intimate and poetical interpretation. The listener dreamed his dreams and saw visions with the lonely of soul, the shy and introspective Schubert.

Interpreting the sonatina, Mr. Heifetz was assisted by Arpad Sandor, a pianist of unusual gifts, including a tone which he aptly shades, a wide range of dynamics and capacity for bravura. At the same time the pianist missed some of the finest shades of the music that the violinist, with ease and mastery, encompassed. Accomplished and responsive as he is, Mr. Sandor required more objectivity when he collaborated with Mr. Heifetz in the performance of Schubert's music.

The Strauss sonata is of the stuff that went into the making of the tone-poem "Heldenleben." There is the swing and stride of the themes in the opening major key. There is the development that, often too elaborate, nevertheless bears everything forward on its swift current. Interpreting Strauss, Mr. Heifetz immediately broadened his style, at the same time that he gave the music a distinction which, with all its freshness and vigor, it may easily lack. It is virile if not great music, and its eloquence was heightened by the performance. And Mr. Sandor made much of a brilliant and difficult piano part.

The Conus concerto permitted of fire-works, and they were, of course, plentiful. They were less important, musically speaking, than the thematic material, the movements coming from the G minor English Suite for piano. The arrangement dispenses with Bach's wonderful ornamentations of his "Sarabande." The delicate foliations of the melody are omitted and it might be asked, why the tempo, surely too fast, of the "Sarabande?"

A final group of short pieces included Heifetz's arrangement of Albeniz's "El Puerto" and other small pieces, as announced, by Brahms, Castelnuovo-Tedesco, Grainger and Achron. The audience applauded these pieces to the echo and Mr. Heifetz added to the program.

294

Ping-pong is still one of Heifetz's favorite sports. Circa 1950.

HEIFETZ NOW APPROACHES THE "SPY" ANTICIPATING
NO TERRIFIC ORDEAL

Jascha Heifetz, when he brings his violin to the microphone this evening, does not anticipate the same "terrific ordeal" he encountered at his broadcast debut several years ago.

"I remember," he said, "with what fear I came before that dreadful little black box. It seemed a spy, waiting to take each sound as I played it, and send it, with no chance of recall, to a critical and unsympathetic audience. For the first minutes of playing for that first appearance before the microphone, it was a terrific ordeal. I should not want to repeat it again. I finished the concert physically exhausted. I will play this time in an entirely different spirit. The little black box will seem to me like meeting an old friend again. Experience tells."

As a listener, Mr. Heifetz finds hazards in the ether; the hazards are words. He contends there is entirely too much talking on the radio, which makes it very difficult for a willing auditor to concentrate on the program.

"I have tried very hard," said Mr. Heifetz, "to listen to good music over the radio. We seem invariably to be greeted by a flood of words, either explaining the music or totally irrelevant. This blah makes complete enjoyment almost impossible.

"I look forward to a time when great music will be heard uninterruptedly for a radio public which I am sure is as appreciative as a concert audience. When a composition is completed I should much prefer to have several minutes of silence—a period to enjoy once again the music which I have just heard. But instead, the music completed, we are greeted with a flood of words, words, and then more words.

"The first time I appeared before a radio audience two years ago," he said, "the sponsors of the program were amazed when I insisted upon using the procedure of the concert hall. I could not understand why I should be made to feel I was enclosed in a vault. I wanted to play as though a sympathetic, not a hostile audience were facing me.

"I insisted upon tuning my violin without having the power immediately turned off as though tuning the violin before my concert audience— why not before my unseen listeners, who are listening just as sympathetically, perhaps more intimately, in the parlors of their own homes.

"I understand that radio is slowly becoming used to the idea that the old formal method of broadcasting, when every sound and word was measured and weighed, is not necessarily the best. Intimacy, spontaneity, the newness that comes with each concert, are tremendously important.

"Each time I play I have the feeling I am making my debut. If everything were invariably cut and dried, I could not stand it. It would be insupportable. I want to feel as though I am giving a concert, not retracing a map."

The review above clearly states Heifetz's feelings about radio broadcasting. Circa 1951.

OCTOBER 17, 1934
CARNEGIE HALL

MR. HEIFETZ PLAYS GREAT MUSIC IN THE GRAND MANNER
By Samuel Chotzinoff

Having enchanted the Soviets, South America and Mexico with his fiddling, Mr. Jascha Heifetz returned to his New York public last night in a recital at Carnegie Hall. When artists are interviewed by the press, they are usually asked what they think of New York audiences. Last night Mr. Heifetz answered this inquiry in an unusual but none the less significant fashion. He played a program of music so severe and noble, and one so removed from the beaten track as to amount to the artist's belief in a revolutionary change in the taste of Manhattan's concert-going public.

The gesture was both a subtle compliment to our musical perceptions and an earnest of the violinist's own high-minded predilections. It is very gratifying to be made to feel that the best in the violinist's repertoire is none too good for us. But it is also good to see a puissant virtuoso find delight in a program of music that was created for a purely musical purpose. Ordinarily, a purely musical program is affected by executants who lack the flair for virtuosity, or by those who have lost that flair. But Mr. Heifetz was, and is, the foremost violin virtuoso of his time, perhaps of all time. No one can approach him in the technique of his instrument and in the consummate ease with which that technique is manipulated. For such an artist to put aside his superlative violinistic equipment and dedicate his great powers to the interpretation of musical masterpieces is something quite new in the annals of concert giving. That New York was ripe for so highminded an exhibition was evidenced by the full house that it drew, and the enthusiastic response of the listeners.

OCTOBER 17, 1934
CARNEGIE HALL

Many Recalls for Violinist in Program Marked by Warm and Brilliant Art
SONATAS BY THREE B'S
Emanuel Bay Collaborates in Playing of
Bach, Brahms and Beethoven Works

If any rubrics remain of the legend that for so long labeled Jascha Heifetz as a cold and unemotional player, the recital in Carnegie Hall last night, his first of the season, should forever dispel them. A certain reserve of bearing, a manner apparently unconcerned and aloof, kept this legend alive. Among those who listen more with their eyes than with their ears, long after it was apparent that the young man whose prodigious technical endowment amazed his auditors years ago had matured into an artist of rare depth of vision and intensity of feeling. No one could listen to last night's performance without knowing he was in the presence of greatness.

The program comprised Brahm's sonata in D minor, the Bach G minor sonata for violin alone, Beethoven's "Kreutzer" sonata and three shorter pieces; a Handel larghetto, a Scarlatti-Heifetz sonatine, and a Mozart-Kreisler rondo.

Although all three of the major compositions were played with consummate beauty, the performance of the Bach was epochal. Mr. Heifetz gave it a reading that one has never heard surpassed. The fuga is not actu-

Heifetz, with Emanuel Bay at the piano, and the composer Ottorino Respighi during the rehearsal in Buenos Aires for the Respighi sonata. Circa 1934.

ally written for two or three continuous polyphonic melodies but his playing produced the effect of a full fugue by setting the leading voice in exquisitely modulated color before the accompanying voices. This and other masterly outward encompassing of the work was not, however, its chief excellence. It was the fact that Mr. Heifetz had obviously passed long since beyond the composition's formidable technical frontiers into his inner life. Hence the opening adagio became (as it rarely becomes in performance) the passionate, yet untroubled, meditation of a great mind; a soliloquy wherein thought unfolded spaciously, unhurriedly, and the final Siciliano-Presto achieved the gorgeously free, vigorous sweep of movement that is too often obscured by the technical dazzle of its scales and passage work.

Throughout the Bach, the breadth and splendor of Mr. Heifetz's tone matched the subject he was expounding, and at its close the capacity audience drew him again and again to the stage in a fury of applause.

These same superlative gifts characterized the Beethoven. Its variations have often seemed rather dull under a less gifted bow. Last night's
reading, with its sensitive nuance, proved the fault has not been Beethoven's. The finale, taken at a breathless presto and with a brilliant, reckless
zest, again roused the audience to clamorous applause.

Only in the Brahms sonatas first movement—and part of the last did
one feel that the violinist's tone and treatment might have been more
ample, less exquisitely fastidious, for Brahms's canvas is here given broad,
vigorous brushstrokes. The adagio, on the other hand, lifted and melted
the heart by the tender and sustained loveliness of its portrayal.

Emanuel Bay, who accompanied, played with remarkable sensitivity
the second movement of the Brahms, and the finale of the "Kreutzer"
gave special evidence of his growth. Only occasionally in the Brahms did
he permit hardness to mar some of his forte passages. Such things, however, were unimportant details in an evening of great music greatly
recreated.

H.H.

DECEMBER 4, 1936

MUSIC

By Lawrence Gilman

HEIFETZ PLAYS THE CONCERTO OF SIBELIUS WITH THE PHIL-
HARMONIC 3246TH CONCERT OF THE PHILHARMONIC-SYM-
PHONY SOCIETY OF NEW YORK; JOHN BARBIROLLI,
CONDUCTOR; ASSISTING ARTIST, JASCHA HEIFETZ, VIOLI-
NIST.

PROGRAM

1. Liszt .... "Weinen, Klagen"
   Variations on a Motive of J.S. Bach; transcribed for Orchestra by Leo
   Weiner. (In commemoration of the 50th anniversary of the death of
   Liszt, July 31, 1886.) First time in New York.
2. Sibelius .... Concerto for Violin, in D minor, Op. 47
   I. Allegro moderato; II. Adagio di molto; III. Allegro ma non tanto
   JASCHA HEIFETZ

Intermission

3. Schubert .... Symphony No. 2, in B-flat major
   I. Largo—Allegro vivace; II. Andante; III. Menuetto-Allegro vivace;
   IV. Presto vivace (repeated by request)
4. Wagner .... Overture to "The Flying Dutchman"

Mr. Heifetz is quite likely to provide the major musical reward of any
orchestral program on which he is "assisting artist" (in the fine old phrase
of long Philharmonic tradition). But last night he was exceptionally in the
vein, exceptionally the master of beautiful sound and miraculous virtuosity and musicianly poise.

He had chosen to play the Sibelius Concerto, a work that is technically difficult and exacting out of all proportion to its essential musical
value. It has been called, indeed, "impossibly difficult." Yet Mr. Heifetz
played it with that Olympian detachment and repose which he brings to
all his performances.

300

During the lull in Heifetz's career, he hired a publicity agent and consented to interviews and publicity shots. Mary Plummer of the Associated Press is shown here interviewing Heifetz in his home. As Heifetz grew older, he became more and more detached from the general public. May, 1936.

Heifetz playing ping-pong, circa 1936.

What a figure is presented by this superlative virtuoso! He is dignified without pomposity, reserved without coldness, modest without pre-
tense. Always he is the scrupulous artist devoted with absorbed intensity
to the high task before him—the task of making real for others that image
of music which his mind has shaped and his imagination warmed.

There is neither room nor time for anything that would blur that
image or compromise that task; no room for adding to the music anything
that is not inherent in its form and substance and intention; no time for
exploiting an occasion. There is only a great and simple artist who has
become an instrumental voice, a vehicle of thought and meditation, a
quickening tongue that brings implicit beauty out of quietness.

Many things have happened in the world of music and of men since
that October day in 1917 when Jascha Heifetz, a Wunderkind of sixteen
who had journeyed from a war-torn Russia to New York by way of Siberia
and the Pacific, made his American debut in a recital at Carnegie Hall.
That occasion has become a legend. Mr. Heifetz is himself a legend, in
living process of formation, accretion, perpetuation. A day will come—
happily distant, in all likelihood—when the legend will become incredible. It will not be believed that music-making of so magical and conquering a sort could shape itself upon the web of time so quietly, with such
patrician calm, such deep integrity, in so uncalm and brazen and
treacherous an age.

Mr. Barbirolli provided a musicianly accompaniment for the soloist,
with some especially skillful-handling of rhythm in the problematical
Finale. He had previously taken his orchestra through an imposing performance of Leo Weiner's transcription of the "Weinen, Klagen" keyboard. Variations of Franz Liszt, performed in commemoration of the fiftieth anniversary of Liszt's death in the summer of 1886, when, in the
course of a festival at Bayreuth, the old and weary Abbe was seized with
mortal illness, turned his face to the wall, and murmured "Tristan" he
had remembered when, a quarter century before, he had conceived this
sensuous, impassioned treatment of Bach's theme of sacred grief!

DECEMBER 4, 1936
CARNEGIE HALL

HEIFETZ PRESENTS SIBELIUS CONCERTO
Brilliancy and Elan Mark His Playing With Philharmonic
at Carnegie Hall
TRIBUTE PAID TO LISZT
Barbirolli Directs Orchestra in Work by Schubert and
Overture by Wagner

By Olin Downes

The predominant and extremely exciting feature of the Philharmonic-Symphony concert last night in Carnegie Hall was Jascha Heifetz's
performance of the Sibelius violin concerto. This concerto has been long
in coming into its own, but little by little it advances to its proper position.
That Mr. Heifetz has included it in his repertory will further advance the
composition with the public, and this will be due to more than a celebrated musician's reputation. The audience applauded a performance of
singular brilliancy and elan. They also applauded the music, and were
greatly moved by its power and plenitude of inspiration, its legendary
spirit and wild nature harmonies and sullen grandeur.

By some this score is considered unidiomatic for the solo instrument. It is worthwhile to point out that for years Sibelius was himself enamored of the violin and planned his future as a virtuoso. That he has written difficult and unconventional passages is fairly obvious, but this is because of a style extremely original and eloquent in a new way. It is a kind of writing so free of precedent that it puts the concerto in a place wholly by itself, but it will be with this unique creation as with other unprecedented works of genius; once it is understood, there will be no complaint of its being either unviolinistic or ineffective.

We never heard Mr. Heifetz play with such sweep and splendor of tone. That his technic was more than adequate for every demand made upon it goes without saying, but he played with an earnestness and a spirit that embodied the virile and elemental quality of the music. That one listener differed with him in some details of pace and phrase is of importance only as it emphasizes a conception so compelling in its special logic that personal predilections were swept aside, and effects that had not been anticipated threw new light upon certain pages.

The performance also was characterized by a fine absence of sentimentality, which saved the slow movement from its one hint of weakness. For the long-drawn melody can easily become overripe in the hands of anyone disposed to linger over its measures.

Mr. Heifetz, of course, conceived this work orchestrally. It was evident that Sibelius's instrumentation sometimes overbalanced the solo part, as it should, with his full consent; indeed, he abetted Mr. Barbirolli. Here, again, as the secrets of a score difficult to properly balance become generally understood, the very balances which now obscure or bewilder the average musician will be treasured. Sometimes the orchestra goes beserk, and mounts in towering fury. In other places it mutters ancestral things, under the solo part, or provides passages of such special transparency as those that accompany the opening theme, or it broods and lies fallow while the violin rhapsodizes. The last movement is the most originally scored of them all, with the curuous persistent rhythms, the color scheme which is so dark and low, the scraps of dance motives flung about, the swirling of wind instruments; and the sudden change at the last to the wild shout, in the major key, of the brass, while the violin whirls chromatically, screaming like a banshee.

It was further characteristic of Mr. Heifetz that whatever his own emotion, it was held in control; that there was always a plenitude of strength back of the tone; the grip of a master; the clarity and form maintained, however mad the fantasy. This was sovereign art, and the invocation of great music.

Mr. Barbirolli directed the orchestra that supported Mr. Heifetz in a very sympathetic spirit, not always with clarity or precision of detail. These things are not easy to obtain with Sibelius's heavy instrumentation. But he responded to the soloist's thought; there was the effect of unity of ideas and of dialogue and not mere accompaniment for the violin on the part of the orchestra.

The purely orchestral compositions were Leo Wiener's instrumentation of Liszt's "Weinen-Klagen" variations on the celebrated theme of J.S. Bach; Schubert's Second symphony in B flat, and the "Flying Dutchman" overture of Wagner. The performance of the Liszt transcription was men-

Liszt at his home in Weimar shortly before his death.

Rosenthal   Mannsfeld

tioned on the program page as a commemorative observance of the fiftieth anniversary of Liszt's death in 1886. It must be said that there could hardly have been a more inadequate gesture toward the genius of Weimar and the prophet of so much of the music of the modern era. In the first place we had not Liszt, but a transcription of Bach: in the second place bad Liszt transcriptions; in the third place Wiener's tasteless orchestral treatment of Liszt's transcription. In the fourth place we had a very commonplace and undistinguished performance.

The best conducting of the evening was that of the delectable Schubert Symphony, which Mr. Barbirolli is to be thanked for bringing to the attention of this public. It is a jewel, full of Schubertian inspiration. The second theme of the first movement would stand high in any one of the greatest of Schubert's works. The whole composition goes with zest and felicity; its language is that of sheer beauty; there is little conventionality or padding. The instrumentation is astonishingly good for the Schubert of 1815, when he could have had but the smallest experience of the orchestra, but then it would be astonishing if Schubert did not astonish.

This was, as has been said, the best orchestral performance of the evening; best in tone quality, in technical finish and straightforward, enthusiastic interpretation. A noisy and exaggerated reading of the "Flying Dutchman" overture brought the end of the concert.

THE FABULOUS HEIFETZ HEARD IN PHILHARMONIC CONCERT
By Samuel Chotzinoff

As soloist with the Philharmonic-Symphony at Carnegie Hall last night, Jascha Heifetz gave a memorable performance of the Sibelius violin concerto. It was playing of an extraordinary sort in which all the faculties of the artist are alive to the occasion and there is the most perfect affinity between the hand, the heart and the brain. Before Mr. Heifetz's uncanny mechanism and what one might call his inspired will to interpretation, the Sibelius held back not a single moment of its twilight loveliness. Everything in it—its melancholy raptures, its noble broodings, its icily brilliant frenzies—was projected faultlessly and naturally, and with that improvisational air of a legendary story-teller, which the earlier creations of Sibelius quite definitely impose on an interpreter.

The concerto is a rhapsodic narrative, though the composer never divulged its story. One cannot help feeling its legendary and epic flavor, as one may apprehend the quality of a tale told by a great actor in a language which one does not know. Indeed, it would even prove fatal to know the program Sibelius had in mind, for the music is concerned with an emotional continuity rather than with a pictorial one, and the listener's experience is already satisfying and complete. Mr. Heifetz, who apprehends so magnificently the "absoluteness" of the classics of the violin was led, last night, by an unerring instinct to throw himself boldly into the rhapsodic northern vein, and his identification with the strange, dark and passionate legend gave the work its proper stature. For once it is important to speak of unerring technique, of beautiful tone, of noble phrasing, of exigent rhythm and of everything else that forms the base of interpretation. These were all present and in the highest degree. But one was aware only of a perfect re-creation of curiously searching music, mysterious yet near, vague, but emotionally definite.

Heifetz, May, 1936.

Mr. Barbirolli began the concert with a new transcription by Leo Weiner of Liszt's variations on Bach's "Weinen, Klagen," which forms the first chorus of the Leipzig Cantor's Twelfth Church Cantata. Mr. Weiner's orchestral version is an orthodox one in the matter of harmony, for which, I suppose, one ought to be grateful, when one considers the temptations of modern composers to add a little of the strange spices that are the harmonic staples of the day. Its orchestral garb is colorful and, as in most recent translations of old music, the brasses are not unduly neglected. I don't know why the piece did not make a greater effect than it did, unless it was that we have had a surfeit of transcriptions.

The conductor repeated (by request) Schubert's Symphony No. 2 in B flat major, which he introduced to Philharmonic-Symphony audiences recently, and ended the program with the overture to "The Flying Dutchman." His handling of the orchestral part of the Sibelius was in general praise-worthy. But the finish of the first movement was indecisive and rather muddy. If the orchestration is at fault at this point, Mr. Barbirolli should have exercised the prerogative of a general and achieved clarity by means best known to himself.

AUGUST 4, 1937
LEWISSOHN STADIUM

HEIFETZ'S TOWERING GENIUS ENCHANTS 17,000 AT STADIUM
Spellbinds Record-Sized Audience with Heroic Rendition of Mendelssohn Concerto

The most exquisite sounds which rose into space from this planet last night came from the wood of a tree which probably was growing in Italy at the time when Galileo invented opera glasses. This wood was made into a violin by Antonio Stradivari, who died in 1737, exactly two hundred years ago.

The sounds of which I write were slight of volume. Faintly they reached the extremes of the Lewissohn Stadium, and the people outside the gates, closed because there was no more room, had to strain their ears and listen attentively to catch them at all.

For sensory effect alone these sounds would have been enjoyed anywhere and everywhere, yet there is one country, Germany, where they must have been banned. The sounds, in the order of transmission, originated in the mind of Mendelssohn, now in musical exile from the land that he adored, and last night they were communicated by Jascha Heifetz as soloist with the Philharmonic-Symphony Orchestra.

The Nazi dictum that Jewish composers are debilitating was out of order, at this concert, because Mendelssohn as communicated through Heifetz seemed virile, patrician and altogether wholesome. He spoke with a concise eloquence. He was coherent and the introspective romanticism of his musical nature was tinged with the restraint of classicist.

It would be interesting to compare the performance of Mr. Heifetz on this occasion with a record of the concerto as he played it thirty years ago, when he was six years old but there isn't any such record. If there were we might have a partial answer to the perplexing question of how much the development of his personality has changed his playing.

No longer do people complain, as they did only a few years ago, that although his technique is incredibly superb, he lacks temperament and passion. No doubt his playing has matured, emotionally, but also I am in-

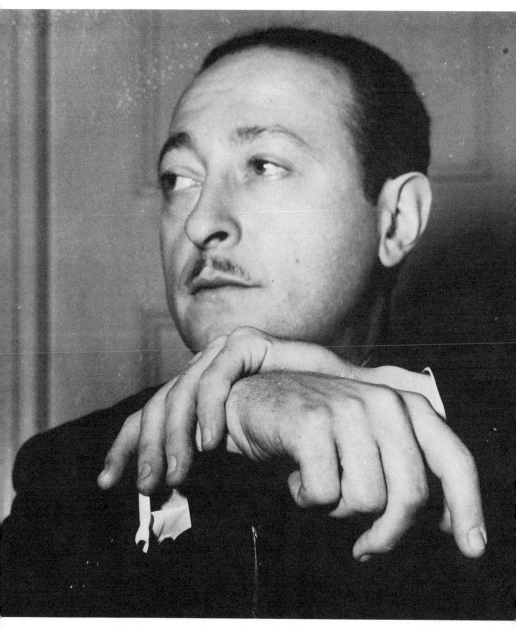

Heifetz after playing in Boston, February 7, 1937.

Heifetz "couldn't get music out of adding machine
buttons," so an inventor made a special accordion which
had two keyboards fashioned after a piano. Since
Heifetz plays the piano extremely well, the short
keyboard for the bass suited him perfectly and he was
able to play the accordion to his own satisfaction.
October 14, 1936.

clined to think that he and other artists of like integrity have been educating us, unwittingly, and without our knowledge. He has taught us to value the message inherent in a composition and to like it best when set forth simply, without any straining for effect.

In addition to sustaining his own solo part in the style of a master, he last night inspired the orchestra and dominated it. During the concerto the playing of the orchestra was quite superior to the playing at other times.

Mr. Heifetz also played with warmth and spirit the gay "Carmen" Fantasie of Sarasate, the Spaniard who, like Heifetz, was famed in his time as a violinist of purity and sweetness of tone and facility of execution, and like Mendelssohn was popular in England. As an encore he played the "Hora Staccato," which he picked up, I hear, in a Rumanian cafe.

The management estimated the audience at 17,000. I should have guessed that there were more. By 8:10 the Stadium itself, including the stairs, was crowded and ticket selling there stopped. The field was filled with chairs, all occupied. Many stood, and even the stairs of the Stadium were full and there were people out on the sidewalk, hearing what they could.

The program included the first Stadium performance of the overture to "Die Schweigsame Frau," by Richard Strauss; the Brahms Variations on a Theme of Haydn, and Tchaikovsky's Fourth Symphony. I can't honestly write complimentary words about the way they played, so let there be silence.

George King Raudenbush, conductor, whose brief term ends when Heifetz plays in the Tchaikovsky concerto, has scarcely had a chance to become acquainted with an orchestra which seems to be willing to play as well or as badly as a conductor insists.

His ability to inspire loyalty is apparent from his record in leading an orchestra in Harrisburg, Pennsylvania. Twenty or thirty people from there have been here during his week of conducting, attending all the concerts and sounding his praises as man and musician. His orchestra includes physicians, stenographers and persons of various occupations. There was even a department store credit manager who kept the orchestra books so straight that they have been straight ever since.

Henry Beckett

AUGUST 5, 1937
LEWISSOHN STADIUM

HEIFETZ PLAYS TCHAIKOVSKY'S CONCERTO DEDICATED TO AUER—AGAIN PACKS STADIUM FOR TOTAL OF 50,000 FOR THREE NIGHTS

The violin concerto which Tchaikovsky first dedicated to Leopold Auer was played last night by Auer's most-distinguished pupil, Jascha Heifetz, as soloist with the Philharmonic-Symphony Orchestra at the Lewissohn Stadium.

When this Concerto in D major was first performed, at Vienna in 1881, the soloist, Adolf Brodsky, to whom the work then was dedicated, received applause, but the concerto itself was hissed. Last night there was no hissing, but the applause was mainly for Mr. Heifetz. Faithful as he may be to the score, the suspicion arises, every time he plays it, that Heifetz somehow refines and intensifies the composition as conceived by Tchaikovsky.

311

In 1917, when he made a debut with orchestra at Philadelphia, this was the work that Mr. Heifetz chose to play, and the late James Huneker wrote that "the concerto by his fellow-countryman and long considered hopeless for any except a supreme virtuoso, was, literally, child's play for this extraordinary young man."

Since then he has played the concerto in various places, including the Stadium, and now the prevailing attitude would be that although it is a delight to hear Mr. Heifetz play anything, the Tchaikovsky concerto is scarcely worthy of his bow any more.

Of course I am sure that Heifetz does not feel that way. Being the virtuoso musician that he is his range of interest is wide and he can find substance and esthetic nourishment in compositions which lesser men disdain because they lack perception.

This week, on three successive nights, including the one when rain stopped the concert, Mr. Heifetz has drawn to the Stadium a total of 50,000 people or more, to hear him in the works of two composers who nowadays are scoffed at by a great many self-appointed authorities on relative values in music.

Mendelssohn they call "insipid," Tchaikovsky, "vulgar." Well, Mendelssohn is insipid when some choir leader without taste gives a sentimentalized performance of "The Elijah," and Tchaikovsky was a vulgar caricature of himself when his Fourth Symphony was played at the Stadium on Tuesday, but when the violin of Heifetz was heard in the concertos the adjectives seemed entirely inappropriate.

It is true, though, that neither concerto is in keeping with the extremely dissimilar characteristics of the two composers, as disclosed in life and works. Mendelssohn is thought of as a wholesome, easily successful, happy, sweet-spirited extrovert, and Tchaikovsky as an unwholesome, frustrated, melancholy and morbid introvert. The German Jew wrote music for the Lutheran Church and the Slav wrote for the Russian Orthodox Church.

Heifetz and Rubinstein photographed at lunch by John Maltese. Circa 1937.

312

Much of Mendelssohn's violin concerto, however, is like the fair revery of one more detached from worldly affairs than Mendelssohn was, whereas the Tchaikovsky concerto dances and sparkles and glows with brilliant sensuousness.

George King Raudenbush last night ended his term as conductor. He has taken his impossible task with fine spirit and his devoted friends from Harrisburg should not fret because he has had little praise. A conductor is not disgraced because he fails to meet the standards of an orchestra which still is associated, in memory, with history's noblest medium for the works of the immortals.

And why should a conductor of Scotch-Irish and Pennsylvania Dutch ancestry be expected to make Rimsky-Korsakoff's "Scheherazade" sound any more Oriental than Babylon, Long Island?

Henry Beckett

DECEMBER 2, 1937
CARNEGIE HALL

JASCHA HEIFETZ PRESENTS HANDEL VIOLIN SONATA
His Second Recital of Season is Given as Benefit

Jascha Heifetz gave his second recital of the season at Carnegie Hall yesterday in a benefit evening under auspices of the Walden School. The program, after a classic beginning with Handel's violin sonata in D major and the chaconne from Bach's fourth partita, continued with Glazounoff's concerto and Erich Korngold's "Much Ado About Nothing" suite, and a group of transcriptions at the close.

The violinist exhibited the consummate technical mastery, tonal delectability and unerring taste and musicianship which are constant characteristics of his playing and require no extensive recapitulation here. But the program gave a good opportunity to note one of the important factors which distinguish an artist such as Mr. Heifetz from the many well equipped but unexceptional practitioners in his field. This was his essential sense of style and stylistic differences; his interpretations were notably evocative of the particular style and individuality of each of his major works. The Handel sonata was played with a happy combination of vitality and classic dignity; the architectonic stature of the chaconne (its fifth performance in the seventeen recitals given thus far this season) was fully set forth, while in the Glazounoff concerto Mr. Heifetz expressed its thorough romanticism with a tone of memorable opulence. Emanuel Bay was the accompanist.

FEBRUARY 18, 1938
CARNEGIE HALL

JASCHA HEIFETZ IS SOLOIST WITH PHILHARMONIC
Violinist Plays Sir Edward Elgar's Concerto, Opus 61—
Is Seldom Heard Here

By Francis D. Perkins

Jascha Heifetz was the soloist with the Philharmonic-Symphony Orchestra under John Barbirolli's direction in last night's concert in Carnegie Hall, playing Sir Edward Elgar's violin concerto, Op. 61, in the latter half of a program which began with Weber's overture to "Oberon" and Schubert's second symphony, in B flat, completed not long after the phenomenal Franz's eighteenth birthday.

The Elgar violin concerto, now twenty-seven years old, is probably the foremost British work in this form and also can be ranked as one of the most significant contributions to the literature for violin and orchestra since the turn of the century. Yet it has been heard here very seldom; its only New York performances by a major orchestra in more than a dozen years were those given by the Philharmonic and Mr. Heifetz in December, 1933, with Bruno Walter conducting.

There are many elements in the concerto which gave reason to be grateful to Mr. Heifetz, not only for his willingness to look beyond the limited round of the frequently played concertos, but also for his offering of another opportunity to hear this particular work. Much could be said about its ponderability, its sincerity, its personal and deeply felt eloquence, as well as about its gratefulness for the violin and the richness that often marks its scoring. Something also could be said about its occasional prolixity—an impression which closer acquaintance might confirm or deny—and some measures in which its generous supply of melody becomes a little over sweetened. Its occasional Brahmsianisms and a few recollections of other composers have been commented on before, but at the same time the character and individuality of the work as a whole is unmistakably Elgar's even when he reveals some of his influences.

Mr. Heifetz, displaying his familiar, admirable technical skill and tonal clarity and richness, played the concerto with intent devotion and a convincing realization of its expressive resources, and similar characteristics marked the eloquent and sonorous playing of the notable musicians under Mr. Barbirolli's leadership.

The orchestra was in good form in the Weber overture; the strings singing as they do always when the Philharmonic-Symphony is at its best. The pleasing early symphony of Schubert, with its hints of the composer's developing individuality and others of the influence of Haydn, Mozart and early Beethoven, was played here, possibly for the first time, under Mr. Barbirolli in November, 1936. Its performance last night was commendable, except that its style might have been better suited to a smaller orchestra. There was ardent applause for Mr. Heifetz, the conductor and the orchestra at the close.

FEBRUARY 18, 1938
CARNEGIE HALL

SCHUBERT'S MUSIC AT CARNEGIE HALL
Second Symphony in B-Flat is Played by Philharmonic,
Barbirolli Conducting
HEIFETZ ALSO IS HEARD
The Violinist's Performance of Elgar's Second Concerto Wins Applause
By Olin Downes

The concert given by the New York Philharmonic-Symphony Orchestra, John Barbirolli, conductor, last night in Carnegie Hall had two exceptional features. One was an adorable symphony composed in his youth by a great master, too little known here, and delightfully performed. The other was a great virtuoso's interpretation of a score of insufferable length, pretentiousness and mediocrity, a performance so

314

Erick Friedman had the "k" added to his first name by Heifetz so that it would make 13 letters. . . "the same number as in Jascha Heifetz and Fritz Kreisler." Heifetz is superstitious! Note that Friedman plays the same repertoire as his teacher Heifetz. . . who played the same repertoire as his teacher Auer.

*After his Lewisohn Stadium concert of July 29, 1938,
which drew almost 20,000 people, Heifetz returned to
his family at a vacation home in Balboa, California.
The first Mrs. Heifetz was the former Florence Vidor,
a very popular motion picture star. Daughter Josepha
(age 8) and son Robert (age 6) find their father very
comforting, though a very strict disciplinarian.*

316

brilliant and masterly that it bestowed upon the said composition an importance it never inherently possessed.

The symphony was a work in the key of B flat, designated as No. 2, by one Franz Peter Schubert, who had the idea when he was a lad of 18. The virtuoso interpretation, so great that it had not only interpretive but almost creative power, was that of Jascha Heifetz, when he played Elgar's Second Violin Concerto. The concert opened with the "oberon" overture.

It was Mr. Barbirolli who introduced the early Schubert symphony in New York last season. Very evidently it is a work near his heart, and it deserves all the affection and understanding which he bestows upon it. In its performance he achieves one of the most difficult things, a true simplicity. The symphony sang itself artlessly, and matchlessly, and that is Schubert.

This delicious fancy would have been still more itself with a smaller orchestra, since the scoring is so transparent and in the character of chamber music. As it was, a full-sized modern orchestra played with exemplary finish, feeling and lyrical grace. They were discoursing the most naive and exquisite music. The influence of Mozart is manifest, but this is essentially and inimitably Schubert, a simple, kindly, loving man, who knew little of the great world, and cared less, and sang in seraphic strains, and was shy and gawky in company.

This symphony is not like other early works of Schubert in the form which are often uneven in style and matter. The work played last night is perfect in its continuity and consistency of inspiration. To mention each

separate felicity would be to discuss each movement, almost theme by theme. The trio of the scherzo is one of the most simple and magical manifestation. The second theme of the first movement; the theme and all the variations of the second; the humor and drollery and tenderness of the last—where could one stop?

Schubert showed up the bad, involved style of the pompous beginning in the orchestra of Elgar's concerto. What changed the situation was Mr. Heifetz's solo. The effect lay first of all in his authoritative attack and in the tone which becomes more glowing and sumptuous every season. The first solo passage of the violin is an admirably complete statement, if projected by an interpreter who appreciates tonal design. The entrance of the violin gripped the audience. The whole first movement is the best organized and the best in its material.

When he came to the lyrical theme, Mr. Heifetz gave it haunting beauty, so that the sentimental and obvious character of the phrase was overlooked. The elaborate movement was given exceptional continuity and brought to a brilliant conclusion.

From there on the concerto gets steadily worse. The slow movement is commonplace, bourgeois, Belgravian. The finale is built up pretentiously, where form is concerned, but the structure has neither tension nor cohesion in it. Doubtless the concerto has places that play beautifully, problems that challenge an interpreter and technician. Had it been duller and more infelicitous than it is, the audience would still have listened engrossed, to the magnificent playing. It was Mr. Heifetz, not Elgar, who caused the salvos of appreciation when he had finished.

APRIL 28, 1938
CARNEGIE HALL

HEIFETZ IS SOLOIST IN AUSTRIANS' AID
Artur Rodzinski Directs NBC Orchestra in Carnegie Hall
Concert for Refugees
MOZART CONCERTO HEARD
Bruch Composition is Played Also by Violinist — Music of Strauss Offered
By Olin Downes

A concert brilliantly successful, was given last night in Carnegie Hall for the benefit of Austrian refugees. The NBC Symphony Orchestra, Jascha Heifetz, as soloist, and Artur Rodzinski, conducting, were the performers. The program was unusual, aside from the fact that one of the world's leading virtuosi played two violin concertos, those of Mozart in D major and Bruch in G minor. For the purely orchestral part of the program reached its climax with the tone-poem of Richard Strauss, after Friedrich Nietzsche, "Thus Spake Zarathustra." Nor was it unworthy of the great music which had preceded to end with the overture to "Fledermaus" and the "Vienna Woods" waltzes of Richard Strauss.

This concert could have been, from the critic's point of view, merely an occasion. That is, it could have ranked as a public occasion when great names were used to make money for a great cause. But it was more than that. Mr. Heifetz, for example, played the Mozart as neither he nor any other great violinist has often played it. It was as if the occasion incited him to accomplish one of his greatest duties toward his art. That art, phenomenal when Heifetz was a child, has now ripened, and the maturity of it which Mozart's music proclaimed, is a wonderful development which could not possibly be attained by any quicker method than the passage and the experience of years.

Here was supreme beauty and purity of line with intense feeling. The feeling was not that of some passionate Russian, or, let us say, a romanticism such as inhabits the Bruch concerto. The very intensity of Mozart's spirit lies in the clarity and the loveliness of his design, which may evoke a profounder response than could be aroused by loud-mouthed pretension. With consummate mastery and solicitousness for every particle of the music, Mr. Heifetz reverently but joyously and tenderly revealed Mozart's genius.

This is a task for which his special mastery and native feeling for classic beauty equip him. Some play Mozart with pedantic exactitude, and think they are presenting him in his true simplicity. More artists sentimentalize or distort his perfect phrases. Mr. Heifetz sang them with adorable grace and an exquisite sense of proportion. He made not the slightest concession to concert effect; ending the slow movement with the precise inflection the composer intended; refusing to hurry a note or phrase of the finale, which he sounded, theme by theme, giving each period its special character, its punctuation, as it might be called, its contrast and relation to the whole design.

The Bruch concerto, nobly conceived, is articulate in quite a different way than Mozart, and with far more obvious emotion. It was a little as if Mr. Heifetz's heart, and his most concentrated effort, had gone into the earlier work. He played Bruch with the proper warmth, rhetoric, dramatic accent. He intoned the song of the slow movement with infectious eloquence. But this was pleasing an audience with a familiar masterpiece. The playing of Mozart was an achievement long to be remembered.

Mr. Rodzinski began the concert with a rousing performance of the "oberon" overture. Later he gave a striking reading of Strauss's wildly rhapsodic tone-poem. He dared to take the introduction to "Zarathustra" with the deliveration and solemnity that the sunrise music demands. He made the page as grand as it is and pulled the score closely together, though hastening certain passages in a way that occasionally lost the full measure of their power.

But there was the great dream one could appropriately say, the flaming vision—of Strauss, inspired by Nietzsche, and it was thrilling to hear. The superbly imaginative score stands, even today, as music of the future. It points clearly to a prouder, freer art than any of Strauss's contemporaries had dreamed, and more intrepid in exploring the reaches of the imaginative than any other modern composer has dared.

There is in it a Nietzchean exultancy and scornful laughter, and a superman's vision which vaults the heavens. Sometimes, hitching his wagon to this star, Strauss falls, or measurably descends. But the great line of his flight is to always higher altitudes and nobler fantasy.

Last night's audience broke into applause after one of the blazing climaxes, when some thought the piece had ended. At the conclusion Mr. Rodzinski was called back again and again. This should be noted: The audience, containing, among others, Jewish refugees and their sympathizers, applauded to the very echo the music of German composers, past and present, without thought of religious or racial issues, and only in glad recognition of great art. It is a pity that fanatics and book-burners of Strauss' nation are incapable of similar intelligence.

For this concert Carnegie Hall was packed, and there was a high tide of enthusiasm throughout the evening.

Jascha Heifetz with Emanuel Bay at the piano during rehearsal. January 29, 1938

JULY 2, 1938

HEIFETZ WANTS TO BE HIMSELF
Special to the World-Telegram

HOLLYWOOD, July 2. — Jascha Heifetz is burning while Sam Goldwyn fiddles with the story for the great musician's first picture. The producer had wanted him to be a refugee from Austria who comes to this country and becomes famous. Heifetz wants no fictitious role, though; he insists upon being himself in the same way that Stokowski was Stokowski in the Deanna Durbin film.

Their differences probably will be patched up, though. Heifetz once was signed by Henry Ford for one radio performance at $9,000. The motor mogul suggested that he play "Humoresque," and the violinist refused—said it was a composition suitable only for amateurs.

"I'll give you $3,000 more if you'll play 'Humoresque,'" said Ford. And Heifetz played "Humoresque."

JULY 29, 1938
LEWISSOHN STADIUM

19,000 AT STADIUM LISTEN TO HEIFETZ
Violinist Draws the Largest Crowd of Any That Have Heard Him There
PLAYS BRAHMS CONCERTO
Soloist Offers Bach Air for G String as Encore After Prolonged Applause

Jascha Heifetz was the soloist with the Philharmonic-Symphony Orchestra last night at the Lewissohn Stadium. This was the fourth consecutive year the violinist had appeared at these concerts. He had always attracted huge audiences there, but never before as large a one as that of yesterday evening, which was estimated at almost 19,000 persons.

Mr. Heifetz had decided on the Brahms concerto as his vehicle for this occasion. Few works for the instrument make as great demands on the strength and technical prowess of an artist. Even under ideal weather conditions indoors, the opus is a supreme test of its executant's command and control of tone. The superb performance accorded it by Mr. Heifetz in the open under the handicap of the mugginess that prevailed was all the more remarkable for the consummate ease with which it made light of such adverse circumstances.

The water-saturated atmosphere would have raised havoc with a less greatly endowed violinist's delivery of the concerto. But the sounds Mr. Heifetz produced were as rich, pure and vibrant as though the night were perfect for his purpose. Even more amazing was the absolute fidelity to pitch maintained throughout every measure of the three movements. Lapses might easily have been condoned on such a night. There were none, however, in an interpretation which ranked high among Mr. Heifetz's achievements here.

For application of color, sensitive outlining of phrases and technical address even Mr. Heifetz has not often reached so high a level of attainment. This was his 150th performance of the Brahms concerto during the thirty years of his career before the public, and every bit of it seemed to have become part and parcel of his own inner life. Despite the uncanny facility with which all its mechanical difficulties were conquered, seldom has the masterpiece made so little a showpiece and so much a poem fraught with significance, tenderness and appeal. The play of dynamics

Heifetz in concert, as he appeared in the motion picture "They Shall Have Music." October, 1938

was extraordinary in this reading, the clarity of the passage work above reproach, the adjustment of tone unrivaled in sensitiveness. But all these factors were but the means to an end—that of conveying to the hearer the full message of Brahms' thought and inspiration.

The concerto brought on an ovation which led to an encore. Almost any piece in the repertoire would have proved a let-down after the work. Mr. Heifetz got out of the dilemma ideally by responding with the Bach Air for the G string. And in this number he again made known his mastery of the classic style in a most subtly restrained and soulful encompassment of this favorite melody.

The orchestra, under Willem van Hoogstraten's direction, gave carefully considered and effective support in the concerto and the Bach extra number. Mr. van Hoogstraten and his men also were enthusiastically applauded for their accomplishments in the rest of the program, which consisted of the Brahms "Academic Festival" overture, Ravel's "Le Tombeau de Couperin," Liszt's "Les Preludes" and the Weber "Oberon" overture.

N.S.

JULY 24, 1938

Jascha Heifetz's fourth annual appearance at Lewissohn Stadium this Thursday night will be one of the last engagements of his twentieth concert season in America. His performance of the Brahms concerto that night will be his 150th (in public, of course), and in the thirty years of concert work he has figured out that he has traveled 1,350,000 miles and has played the violin some 65,000 hours. (There seems nothing left for Mr. Heifetz's arithmetical penchant to exercise itself upon except the number of notes he has sounded.)

In the course of those thirty years he has played during the days of the Russian upheaval, the Sinn Fein uprising in Ireland, the 1923 earthquake in Japan and the Gandhi-troubled days in Bombay. Which substantiates Mr. Heifetz's opinion that "the artist requires the nerves of a bullfighter, the vitality of a night-club hostess and the concentration of a Buddhist monk."

AUGUST 7, 1938

HEIFETZ GIVES HIS PLAN FOR A FESTIVAL
Thinks American Southwest Appropriate Site for Musical Purposes on the Salzburg Scale

Jascha Heifetz, who at his present appearance as soloist with the Philharmonic-Symphony Orchestra attracted an audience of about 19,000 persons to the Lewissohn Stadium, rounded out his summer activities with an engagement at the Hollywood Bowl last Friday at which he performed the Mendelssohn and Bruch G minor concertos.

Work on the picture in which he will make his film debut is supposed to begin in Hollywood toward the end of August, he said in an interview shortly before his Stadium appearance. In this he will appear as himself in a musical capacity, but what music he is to play depends upon the plot, "which has not yet been completed. I can't interfere with the music. I can't guarantee that the recording will be good," Asked about a recent film in which a musician plays a prominent part, Paderewski's "Moonlight Sonata," he said that he liked it so far as Paderewski's participation was concerned, thinking that this gave a good idea of the great pianist's playing and personality, while he also praised Marie Tempest's work as the Baroness Lindenberg. The title of the film, in which Mr. Heifetz will appear, according to an announcement from Samuel Goldwyn's office, is "The Daring Ae" with a scenario by I.A.R. Wylie.

Place For a Music Festival

Mr. Heifetz is interested in the idea of a large-scale American national music festival, which, he thought, should be considered very seriously and taken up quickly, as it is much in the mind of the musical public now, and would, he believed, soon be welcomed. But he did not favor an Eastern site for such a festival, what with the element of uncertainty caused at least in the case of outdoor events, by the vagaries of the weather and the handicaps thus imposed upon the necessary planning well in advance.

As to the element of romance, its publication would be up to the local chambers of commerce or publicity staffs. There is much romance to be found in Arizona or New Mexico, with their historic Spanish, Mexican and Indian associations. In the case of Salzburg, it is true that the Austrian city had its associations with Mozart but the responsibility for good performances there did not depend upon Mozart.

The Question of Repertoire

Asked if he thought that the available repertoire for the violin is too limited—an impression which reviewers are likely to form after hearing a season's crop of New York recitals—Mr. Heifetz said that he did not think that it was necessarily too limited, although it will seem so if artists play only the works that are most frequently played. He pointed to the ten sonatas of Bach, ten of Beethoven and eight of Mozart, and also to music which he considers unnecessarily neglected, including works of Spohr, Ernst, Vieuxtemps, Viotti and Vivaldi. Respect and performance, he thought, is merited by much music such as that of Vieuxtemps or Wieniawski; not great music, indeed, not Brahms, but good and sincere music. He would be in favor more of playing music such as this than music "which is supposed to be something, and isn't."

While the practice of playing concertos with piano accompaniment is often deprecated, he thought that its advisability depended upon the individual work. Music such as Chausson's "Poeme" (a favorite in last season's recitals), impressionistic in character, does, he thought, suffer some loss when played without an orchestra, but the case is different in the matter of straightforward music such as the Mendelssohn concerto. But to exclude all works originally scored for orchestra from recitals would, he thought, tend unduly to limit the repertoire.

AUGUST 15, 1938
LEWISSOHN STADIUM

HEAVY MUSIC IN NEW YORK

When summer music first became popular, conductors seldom dared venture anything weightier than a Strauss waltz. To their surprise, mur-

324

murs of "We want Beethoven" and "We want Bach" were heard. Given Beethoven and Bach, audiences rapidly grew larger. Today, outdoor music is as heavily classical as anything played indoors. On July 28, 19,000 music-lovers crowded New York's Lewissohn Stadium to hear Jascha Heifetz play a Brahms concerto. At rehearsal that morning, *Life's* photographer took the unique photographs below. The great Heifetz, absorbed in his playing, suddenly becomes disturbed at the conductor's interpretation, stops the whole orchestra to get the point cleared up.

By 1938 Heifetz published under his own signature more than 40 transcriptions and arrangements for violin and piano, 13 compositions edited by him, as well as a folio of 15 of his favorite encores, edited and fingered by the eminent violinist. Circa 1938.

ELGAR'S VIOLIN CONCERTO IS PLAYED BY HEIFETZ
AT THE PHILHARMONIC

CONCERT BY THE PHILHARMONIC-SYMPHONY SOCIETY, BRUNO WALTER, CONDUCTOR; ASSISTING ARTIST, JASCHA HEIFETZ, VIOLINIST; AT CARNEGIE HALL.

PROGRAM

1. Beethoven . . . . Symphony No. 3 ("Eroica")

Intermission

2. Elgar . . . . Concerto for Violin and Orchestra
Jascha Heifetz, Violinist

3. Weber . . . . Overture to "Oberon"

There must be a considerable number of music lovers who are grateful to Mr. Heifetz for having played at last night's Philharmonic-Symphony concert the violin concerto of Elgar—and not merely because it is always a cause for gratitude to hear Mr. Heifetz touch bow to strings, whatever he may elect to play. He performed last evening as consummately as one expected him to. But he did more than that. He deepened and enriched our experience of his extraordinary art by playing one of the relatively few violin concertos that an adult musical intelligence can find rewarding—one that is so little dreamt of in the philosophy of the average fiddler that it had never before appeared on a Philharmonic-Symphony program, though it was composed twenty-three years ago.

One would have cause to thank Mr. Heifetz if only for his enterprise in varying the hard-worn violinistic round of Beethoven-Brahms-Mendelssohn-Tchaikovsky by the exhibition of this concerto that hardly any fiddler seems to have remembered.

The score of Elgar's violin concerto is superscribed with a Spanish motto, "Aqui esta encerrada el alma de. . .," which, being interpreted, means: "Here is enshrined the soul of. . . ." Sir Edward has always delighted in being cryptic; and he has never identified the soul in question. Perhaps it is the soul of Mr. Colles—who, in his edition of "Grove's Dictionary," handsomely allots fifteen columns to Sir Edward, though he devotes only seven to Debussy and four and one-half to Hugo Wolf. One of Elgar's biographers suggests that it is the soul of the violin and is thus enshrined. Perhaps—and this seems most likely—it is the soul of Elgar himself.

Certainly it is difficult to listen to the slow movement, and to the most remarkable passage in the work, the cadenza accompagnata in the Finale (in which themes from the earlier movements are recalled) without feeling that the composer is speaking to us with singular intimacy and expressiveness. For at its best this music is deeply personal in style and feeling.

There are reminders of other men in the score to be sure—of Wagner and Brahms and Strauss; but Elgar has managed to transmute them, to cause them to speak with his voice, utter his idiom, convey that peculiar quality of blended thoughtfulness and passion which makes his music, when it is most truly characteristic, so touching and noble and sincere.

A British admirer of Elgar has placed on record his conviction that Sir Edward's concerto makes a fourth in "that noble company which com-

prises the violin concertos of Beethoven, Mendelssohn (sic!) and Brahms."

Perhaps one would not put the matter in quite that way. Elgar cannot always refrain from drawing the sentimental stop; and there are measures in this work that one would wish out of it. We are, on the whole, quite a distance from Beethoven. Yet, by and large, this is a masterly and often moving work; one of the two or three violin concertos written since the death of Brahms which are worthy to be named with his.

Mr. Heifetz played the work with evident affection, bestowing upon his interpretation a continuity of beauty and sensibility and technical address which provoked, at the close of the performance, a spontaneous outburst of applause from the large audience.

Mr. Bruno Walter and his orchestra were as fully in the vein as he, and gave us an account of the concerto which left no part of it undisclosed.

It was an engrossing concert, with Mr. Walter's large-molded and full-stored "Eroica" pitching high the key of the evening's achievements.

OCTOBER 1, 1938

THAT HEIFETZ FILM

Mayor LaGuardia did a bit of impromptu technical advising for the Jascha Heifetz film, "The Restless Age," on his recent visit to Los Angeles, if a tale that followed him home is true. He visited the Samuel Goldwyn lot while a scene in which Heifetz was supposedly playing at Lewissohn Stadium concert was being filmed. The Mayor, a regular patron of the concerts, promptly called it to the attention of his hosts. The Stadium was pretty accurately reproduced save in one important particular. The designers had completely forgotten the reserved, table-seat section directly in front of the orchestra-shell. Mr. Heifetz and the others concerned who are familiar with the Stadium, apparently hadn't noticed. The set was corrected, and the scene was retaken.

The music which Mr. Heifetz will play in the picture already has been recorded, and it is expected that the filming of all scenes in which he appears will be completed by the end of next week. He will be heard in his own arrangement of the Prelude from the Bach E Major Partita; Saint-Saen's Rondo Capriccioso; Tchaikovsky's Andante Cantabile; the slow movement of the Mendelssohn Concerto; the slow movement of the Brahms Sonata in D Minor; the Wieniawski D Major Polonaise; Dinicu's scintillating "Hora Staccato," one of Heifetz's favorite encore-pieces; Rimsky-Korsakoff's "Flight of the Bumble Bee," and the Ponce-Heifetz "Estrellita." A symphony orchestra of 125, conducted by Alfred Newman, musical director of Goldwyn films, supported the soloist.

Mayor Fiorello LaGuardia visiting Heifetz on the set at United Artists Studio. The violin he is using is his 1742 Guarnerius del Gesu. Circa 1938.

HEIFETZ IS SOLOIST IN ELGAR CONCERTO
Philharmonic Gives Its First Performance of
1910 Work By British Composer
WALTER GETS AN OVATION
Conductor Begins Final Week of Stay with
Beethoven "Eroica" Symphony

Bruno Walter met his Thursday night audience for the last time this season at Carnegie Hall last night as he began his eleventh week with the Philharmonic-Symphony Orchestra. The orchestra rose for him as he entered and the applause was warm and prolonged throughout the evening. The program consisted of Beethoven's third symphony, Elgar's violin concerto, with Jascha Heifetz as the soloist, in its first performance by the orchestra, and Weber's "Oberon" overture.

It was inevitable, since Mr. Walter chose to start with the "Eroica," that Beethoven's tremendous masterpiece would tend to dwarf the Elgar concerto. And it did. The surprising thing was the refusal of the contemporary composition to be entirely belittled. It has a life and resistance of its own. It is fashioned by the hand of an artist; it is forthright and comely in structure and solid in substance.

Mr. Heifetz joined Mr. Walter and the orchestra in giving it a persuasive performance. They captured the substantial quality of the mature Elgar, without ignoring the anonymous "soul enshrined," to which the composer alludes in the laconic motto on the fly-leaf of the score. Having begun as a violinist himself, Elgar knew what to expect from the virtuoso, and Mr. Heifetz rendered the concerto its due. He played the gentle opening theme with an opulent cantilena, and he had an easy command of the contrasting flashing passages where Elgar demands both brilliance and daring. The orchestra was responsive to the needs of the composer. The interpretation was thoroughly integrated.

The concerto was written in 1910 and was performed for the first time that year with the composer conducting and Fritz Kreisler as soloist. In its first movement at least its inspiration certainly is not dated, and the second movement has a quiet charm that is still appealing. But the closing section is hardly more than a pendant; its chief usefulness is to give the soloist a chance for pyrotechnics, for as a summing up it is redundant in part.

Every conductor seeks for something striking for his farewell. The "Eroica" would be welcome whatever the occasion. Mr. Walter and the orchestra played the symphony with painstaking devotion and fidelity almost too painstaking. The first movement did not quite have its essential ecstatic magnificence, and there were moments in the last two movements that were wanting in propulsion and passion. But Mr. Walter has been through a strenuous season and he may have been tired. The essence of the symphony, moreover, was not missing. Its epic splendor, compassion and affirmation were there, once more to stir and purge and exalt the hearts of men.

H.T.

*Heifetz the apple farmer hands fruit to his children,
Josepha and Robert circa 1938.*

JASCHA HEIFETZ DEAD PAN-ICS MR. SAM GOLDWYN
They Can't Make the Violinist Over Into a Movie Actor, Even When He Plays the Part of Himself

By Henry Beckett

Jascha Heifetz is back in town, boasting that neither Sam Goldwyn nor any of his minions could make an actor out of Heifetz, even if Heifetz did go to Hollywood and play the role of Heifetz for a picture.

"Before going to Hollywood I told them that I wouldn't act," said Heifetz, proudly, "and I didn't."

So far as this interview is concerned Mr. Heifetz did his bragging at the Hotel Madison, where he was caught in the act of playing the piano. He was fixing up an accompaniment to the Negro spiritual, "Deep River," which he will play, with five other compositions by as many American composers, in his concert at Carnegie Hall November 9.

Goldwyn, the movie mogul, had been on the trail of Heifetz for a long time. When Heifetz wanted four times as much money as Goldwyn first offered, Goldwyn tried to make the violinist ashamed by appealing to his nobler self.

"Listen, there are other things to consider besides money," said Goldwyn in a fatherly way. "This picture will make you famous."

After that, Heifetz thought it would serve Goldwyn right if he, Heifetz, did agree to appear in a movie as a great concert violinist.

Because Heifetz knew that he was not the type for a violinist. He has, to use the expression which Goldwyn used in speaking of his find Anna Sten of Poland, "the face of a Spink." For years people have been likening Heifetz to Buddha, because of his calm detachment, his heavy-lidded eyes, his moonlike impassivity.

So Sam Goldwyn thought he could make a movie violinist out of him!

How did they go about it? Did they try to make Heifetz toss his head, look soulful, roll his eyes, lean ecstatically on his $40,000 Guarnerius?

"No, I suppose they thought it would not be a good policy to ask me to change my facial expression," the violinist replied. His facial expression did not change as he said it.

Heifetz said that he merely walked across the stage, stood still, and played the fiddle. He made no attempt to act like a violinist.

"I didn't even make up," he added, his forehead in disciplined waves, as it always is when he plays in concert.

. . . His philosophy, as contained this admonition to a fellow artist— "You are too amiable to the audience. Why do you have anything to do with them?"

Whether it's because he hasn't been paid yet, or because, to quote Goldwyn again, he "doesn't believe in biting the hand that lays the golden egg," Heifetz pretended that he has no funny Goldwyn lines to pass on to New York. He told only this:

"Goldwyn's office was close to where I was playing the violin. The sound, coming through a loudspeaker, was loud. Goldwyn called a boy and said, 'Go and tell them to turn off that radio; it's driving me nuts.' "

Heifetz, in his light, ironic way, spoke of this as "my fourth movie." Originally Goldwyn signed him to play in a picture to be called "The Great Music Festival." That didn't pan out. Next he was to portray a Viennese expatriate in "The Exiles." That didn't pan out. "Golden Boy"

Jascha Heifetz as he appeared in the motion picture "They Shall Have Music." October, 1938.

was another idea. And it's still uncertain whether this picture will be "The Restless Age," "The Daring Age," or some other kind of age.

In fact, the picture hasn't been made yet. In the month that Heifetz passed on the lot they shot 50,000 feet of film involving him, the orchestra and the audience from all angles and in two story-book concerts, one in a grand concert hall and the other outside. Heifetz believes they may use 1,500 feet of that.

He played a Bach prelude, with a piano accompaniment of his own arrangement, and the slow movement of a Brahms sonata and the slow movement of the Mendelssohn concerto, and some lighter pieces as encores. His voice will be heard announcing the encores, as is the case when he gives real concerts.

Heifetz played so many times, in the making of the film, that "movie people were singing and whistling Bach all over the place." Each scene in which he appears was shot at least three times. The music itself is pre-recorded, to be synchronized with the picture of him playing. Special pains were taken on that. A girl held a score and checked the notes and his playing of them. There were close-ups, meaning even shots of the agile Heifetz fingers on the finger board of the instrument.

For years other violinists have been saying that Heifetz is the complete master, that his technique is flawless and that his playing has so matured and improved that surely he can go no farther. But he is not of that opinion.

"Yes, I should like to be a conductor," he said, when the question was raised, "but I know that I am not good enough. I still have a lot to learn about the violin. Why should I drop that? I have a feeling that as a conductor I would do so many things as they should be done. Therefore I must not conduct, because I know better. I know it is not so. It is only a feeling."

OCTOBER 29, 1938

JASCHA HEIFETZ ON AMERICAN MUSIC—
'ACCOMPANYING' ORCHESTRA—GAMBLING SYSTEM
By William G. King

"I just feel that music by American composers ought to get a little better break," said Jascha Heifetz. "I'm in somewhat the same mood as the fellow in 'You Can't Take It With You,' who says 'How about trying a little Americanism for a change?' "

We were talking about the program for his first New York recital of the season, which takes place in Carnegie Hall on November 9. Its final half is made up entirely of works by contemporary or near-contemporary Americans.

"But," said Mr. Heifetz, "let's not call it an 'all-American' group—that makes it sound like a football team. And, understand, I'm not playing these pieces simply because they are by Americans, but because I think they are good music. America is my adopted country, and as an American, I think I ought to have an opportunity to hear, whatever really good music is being created by our countrymen."

The works on his November 9 program are all short, but he intends to add "several major American compositions" to his repertory in the near future. There is, for instance, something called "Swing Boy," by Frederick Jacobi.

Heifetz, circa 1939.

The six compositions scheduled for the Carnegie Hall recital are his own transcription of "Deep River," Clarence Cameron-White's "Levee-Dance," Cecil Burleigh's "Giant Hills," "A la Valse," by Victor Herbert, "From the Canebrake," by Samuel Gardner, and Louis Kroll's "Perpetual Motion."

He has just finished a violin arrangement of the first of George Gershwin's "Three Preludes for Piano," but it probably will not be heard on November 9 because "I haven't had time to get it in my fingers yet." However, there is a chance that he'll get it ready and give it as an encore. Having transcribed Prelude No. 1 for the violin, he is now engaged on No. 2, which he hopes to play later in the season.

About That Film

The non-American part of the November 9 program includes his transcription of the Prelude from the Bach E Major Partita, which he made for the motion picture in which Samuel Goldwyn intends to star him. (Mr. Heifetz's part of that opus, by the way, is done, although, as far as he has been informed, it still has neither name, plot nor characters other than the violinist himself.)

He had to make the transcription because he was told at the last hour that under the copyright laws, he couldn't use the Kreisler version which he had been playing in concert for years, in the movies. Between takes of the other compositions he was recording for the film, he worked on the transcription, and twenty minutes after he finished the last five bars, he played it for the sound-cameras.

His contract with the Goldwyn studio has been entirely fulfilled with the recording, by camera and microphone, of his playing of nine compositions. If, when the studio finally decides upon a scenario, it wants Mr. Heifetz for additional scenes, new arrangements with him will have to be made.

I asked him if he would be willing to appear in another picture.

"I don't know," he said slowly. "Next time, if there is a next time, I'll sit and wait until they have a suitable story before I enter into any agreement. That will be fairer both to me and to the motion picture people." He expressed himself as "very pleased" with the sound-track recordings of his playing.

Last Thursday, by the way, marked Mr. Heifetz's "coming of age" as an American recitalist. It was on October 27, 1917, twenty-one years ago, that he made his debut in this country with a sensational recital in Carnegie Hall. He was then some three months short of his seventeenth birthday.

OCTOBER 30, 1938

A VIOLINIST'S HOLLYWOOD ADVENTURES

Hollywood has reached the fiddle. Singers were employed first and in abundance; the record includes names such as Lawrence Tibbett, Grace Moore, Lily Pons, Gladys Swarthout, Nino Martini and Kirsten Flagstad. Then a conductor, Leopold Stokowski, had his licks. A London company recruited Paderewski to represent the great pianists. And now Samuel Goldwyn has chosen Jascha Heifetz for the accolade.

Mr. Heifetz, as a matter of fact, has completed his share of the work for his cinema debut. He was back in New York several days ago, recounting his Hollywood experiences and impressions. He did not return to belittle Hollywood. In the first place, it is too late to asperse the movies; in the second place, there is much to commend them.

What of the picture he made? Mr. Heifetz did not know what it would be like. He did not know if Mr. Goldwyn knew. All he could discuss with assurance was his own share in the movie. The rest of it, you must understand, has not been made. The rest, for all Mr. Heifetz knew, had not yet been determined upon.

Mr. Heifetz worked on the lot for about a month. During this period about 50,000 feet of film were shot. They included every conceivable view of a violinist in action. If several thousand feet of this film were assembled and edited properly, they could probably be made into an eloquent dissertation of the anatomy of fiddling. In any event, what the moviegoer will see will be a remarkable series of close-ups of the hands, fingers and face of a great violinist as well as hear him in music of his own selection.

Heifetz in the film "They Shall Have Music."
Circa 1938.

337

The shots of Mr. Heifetz and the recording of his playing should show him at his best, or at least what he considers to be his best. For he chose his own music and had the final say as to the cutting and editing of the sequences that deal with him. That was stipulated in the contract. Mr. Heifetz, it need scarcely be observed here, takes an uncompromising stand where his art is concerned, Hollywood or no Hollywood.

For this reason the violinist declined to be turned into a matinee idol or into an actor of any kind. He insisted that he must be what he is—Jascha Heifetz, the violinist. In the film he will be seen and heard as just that. He will appear in concert, with a pianist or with an orchestra, in Carnegie Hall or the Lewissohn Stadium. But always he will remain what he is in life.

What will go with the pictures and playing of Mr. Heifetz is not divulged, and may not even be known to the producers of the film. Various stories have been considered and rejected. The proposed titles have ranged from "The Great Music Festival" through "The Exiles" to "The Restless Age." Whatever the story, it will revolve around Heifetz the artist.

The film technique posed new problems for the violinist. First, of course, Mr. Heifetz recorded for the sound track all the music to be heard in the film. He tried to be catholic in his selection, remembering that several light and brilliant things had to be included. Among the works he chose were to slow movement of the Brahms D minor sonata, the slow movement of the Mendelssohn concerto, Saint-Saens's "Rondo Capriccioso" and the prelude of a Bach partita.

Once the sound track was made, the job of filming the scenes was undertaken. While the music was played back through an enormous loudspeaker, Mr. Heifetz had to synchronize his playing for the camera with the tones of his previous performance. It should be explained that no musician can play the same work exactly the same way twice. There are always delicate nuances that differ between interpretations; tempi are not always identical. But for the camera Mr. Heifetz had to follow the earlier interpretation. He could not merely bow casually. He had to play for the lens as he had for the sound track. Otherwise the audience would see that he was faking. And he did not know how to fake convincingly. He thinks, in fact, that no musician could get away with faking.

After a time Mr. Heifetz found himself so at one with the music emerging from the loudspeaker that it had an uncanny effect on him. There were occasions, he recalls, when he was not quite sure whence the tone came—from the loudspeaker or the violin in his hands. The two merged so completely in his own ear that he could scarcely tell them apart.

It was illuminating to him, Mr. Heifetz reports, to see the rushes each night of what had been shot during the day. And when the job of cutting and editing was done he sat in the studio and watched and heard himself dispassionately. He declares that it cast new light for him on his appearance and playing. He saw that certain things could be developed and improved.

Mr. Heifetz made his sequences without make-up, save for a little powder. He could not afford to use make-up under his chin, where it made contact with the violin, for fear that his Guarnerius—or Stradivarius—would be harmed. Moreover, the screen tests show that make-up was not necessary.

The shots of the violin, by the way, were exciting. The lights and shadows of the grain and varnish are brought out brilliantly by the camera. Mr. Heifetz also observed that the film would give the public a clearer view of a violinist than any person in a concert hall, no matter how fortunately situated, could have. For the camera came close to the musician. There are detailed shots of the intricate maneuvers of the left hand. How a Heifetz plays harmonics or a difficult interval like a tenth are clearly etched.

These things, however, may not interest the casual movie-goer. For him the story is the thing. Perhaps, in this case, also the music. Mr. Heifetz hopes so. He believes that the movies reach the largest audience of all, larger than radio, records or concerts. And if a taste for fine music can be cultivated in millions of people through the movies he is strongly in favor of having outstanding musicians appear in them.

He found that the workers on the set were interested in his music. Some stopped to hear him play. He was told that two burly stage hands paused for a moment while he played Saint-Saen's "Rondo Capriccioso."

One of them nodded wisely and said, "That's a rondo! Tchaikovsky!"

The other looked at him scornfully.

"Tchaikovsky, ya dumb lug?" he roared. "That's Heifetz!"

As for the eventual product, Mr. Heifetz professed no alarm. After all, he had been given carte blanche to choose the music. He felt he had no right to interfere with the choice of a story.

What if no story is ever found? Mr. Heifetz would not consider the possibility. But a friend of his observed:

"If that happened Sam Goldwyn might, with satisfaction, write off the cost to musical education."

H.T.

NOVEMBER 8, 1938

HEIFETZ PERFORMS IN PADDED CUBICLE
He Tests Tonal Values of a Stradivarius and $5 Violin
for Harvard Physicist

CAMBRIDGE, Mass., Nov. 7 — Jascha Heifetz, violinist, played one of the strangest concerts of his career today when he sat alone for two hours in a tiny cubicle, faintly resembling a padded cell, and demonstrated his artistry on the violin in the interest of science.

The occasion was one of a series of tests being made in the Cruft Laboratory at Harvard by Frederick E. Saunders, Professor of Physics, to determine if the tonal qualities of violins made by the Italian masters might eventually be matched by instruments brought out on a mass-production basis.

Two of the violins used in the experiment were Mr. Heifetz's $75,000 Guarnerius, with which he charmed a capacity audience at Symphony Hall here last night and his $30,000 Stradivarius. Another was a $5 fiddle, described as a "standard of badness."

From the cubicle, heavily padded for acoustical purposes, the notes produced by Mr. Heifetz were "piped" through a microphone into a device which made moving pictures of the sound waves and an ink graph of the tonal quality as well as actually recording the sound.

The cubicle measured 15 by 15 feet and was 6 feet high. At one end was a small platform, in the center of which Mr. Heifetz sat upon a stool and faced only blank walls.

Heifetz looks over apparatus in the sound-proof studio of Dr. Frederick A. Saunders (right). Heifetz valued his Strad and Guarnerius at $100,000 when this photograph was taken on November 7, 1938. They were probably worth $750,000 in 1976.

On each of his famous violins he played the range of sixty-four notes twice, holding each note until a signal light informed him that it had been sufficiently recorded. The light was operated by Robert Watson of Urbana, Illinois, a graduate student who was in charge of the recording machine.

Afterward, the violinist said that holding each note the required length of time was the most difficult phase of the experiment. He said that in concert work a violinist seldom had to hold the note more than an instant, but today he held most of the notes two and three seconds.

Mr. Heifetz, who believes that the art of the old masters of violin making died with them, arranged to have detailed results of the test, including the graph of tonal qualities and the moving picture of sound wave, sent to him. After he finished playing he studied the machine, which was developed by Professor Frederick V. Hunt and Dr. Harry R. Hall of the Harvard faculty.

NOVEMBER 10, 1938
CARNEGIE HALL

HEIFETZ IS HEARD AT CARNEGIE HALL
**Violinist Opens Concert With Transcription of Prelude to E Major
Partita of Bach**
OFFERS BRAHM'S SONATA
Paganini D Major Concerto is Played—Emanuel Bay Appears at Piano
By Olin Downes

From Mendelssohn and Schumann down to Kreisler and others of greater and of lesser stature, musicians have monkeyed with the Prelude to the originally unaccompanied E major Partita of Bach, and other of the Bach compositions that belong to this genre. Jascha Heifetz opened his recital last night in Carnegie Hall with his own transcription of the work.

Mr. Heifetz has been playing for a film in Hollywood, and this his transcription of the Prelude is a part of the music he arranged and performed for that show. Probably in Hollywood they would not believe that the producers were getting their money's worth if Mr. Heifetz had only played the piece without a piano accompaniment, as it was written. But that is Hollywood. Why the accompaniment in Carnegie Hall? The audiences there are fairly well inured to the Bach unaccompanied sonatas and partitas in the original.

The Prelude of the E major Partita has yet, in this writer's experience, to gain by the addition of any piano part. With flooding inspiration and the most cunning workmanship Bach by means of his melodic traceries of the solo violin gives the clear impression of harmony, so that accompanying chords on the keyed instrument are superfluous. When the arrangement gives sundry motives derived from the violin part to the pianist as a species of development of the composer's thought they are simply superfluous.

The Prelude loses, definitely by this treatment, loses its lightness and its sculpturesque detail. Last night it also lost by the tempo Mr. Heifetz took in the performance. He turned the passage into a kind of "Moto Perpetuo," showing clearly that he could play the thing as fast as he choose without the batting of an eye. But that has long been known to Mr. Heifetz's audiences, who are also accustomed to looking to him for substantial music. And there is melodic interest in the violin figurations. The Prelude is more than a technical and rhythmical exercise.

A much finer reading was that of Brahms's piano and violin sonata in D minor, though there have been finer-grained performances of this intimate music. There was perhaps in the mind of both players, but especially, one would say, in that of Emanuel Bay, the pianist, the thought of the wide open spaces of Carnegie Hall. But the mood could have been more intimate; more subtle shades of beauty could have been expounded in the course of the interpretation, which was simply, straight-forward, fulltoned, with an admirable absence of sentimentality and true eloquence in the slow movement.

In the Paganini D major concerto, Mr. Heifetz did the most impressive feats of derring-do. Every violinist who plays this piece is expected to accomplish technical feats, but they do not do this as Mr. Heifetz does it. He performed the curuscating bravura passages of every nature with almost contemptuous mastery.

He could have held his prowess up to display more than he did, and have followed a perfectly legitimate path in so doing. For the pyrotechnics are put in the piece a-purpose, and then have a part in its structural scheme. When the violinist embarks upon a special flight of tight-rope dexterity he is supposed to be free in his tempi and to improvise in an impromptu manner. Mr. Heifetz hardly hinted at this, which he could have done so easily. He took the most breath-taking chances in strict tempo. They were incidental to the melodic scheme and form of the concerto. Since they offered him no impediment whatever he simply swung them off as if he did not want to be interrupted in the real matter of his musical discourse.

Also he played the Paganini melodies in a genuinely lyrical and Italian way. Once in a while there was tonal roughness, but this, too, was incidental and not of account, for the attention of the listener was fixed, not upon the playing but upon the music. Few attempt to do these things with a Paganini concerto, and Mr. Heifetz showed that it is worthwhile to treat Paganini music not as a P.T. Barnum of the violin, but as the remarkable musician, as well as virtuoso, that we know him to have been.

The concert proceeded with short pieces by various composers, of the type which always delight an audience, and which did not fail to do so on this occasion. Mr. Heifetz added to the program. He plays here season after season. He has his moods, his great nights and his less great ones, but he is never less than amazing, this Heifetz.

NOVEMBER 10, 1938
CARNEGIE HALL

HEIFETZ GIVES HIS FIRST RECITAL OF THE SEASON
AT CARNEGIE HALL

VIOLIN RECITAL BY JASCHA HEIFETZ; ACCOMPANIST, EMANUEL BAY; AT CARNEGIE HALL.

PROGRAM

1. Prelude ....Bach
2. Sonata (D minor)...Brahms
   Allegro
   Adagio
   Un poco presto e con sentimento
   Presto agitato
3. Concerto...Paganini
4. Deep River ....Traditional Negro
5. Levee Dance ....Clarence Cameron White
6. Giant Hills...Cecil Burleigh
7. A la Valse ....Victor Herbert
8. From the Canebrake ....Samuel Gardner
9. Perpetual Motion...Louis Kroll
11. Valse...(from orchestral suite)
12. Scherzo...Tchaikovsky

Mr. Heifetz's first recital of a season is always heartening to those who realize the kind of artist that he is and the nature of his contribution to our music-making.

It is twenty-one years since he made his debut here. He has changed since that day, naturally. He was a genius then, a startling prodigy. He is something rarer than that now; he is a great artist, poised, contained, deeply touched with that high seriousness, that alembicated feeling, that

Heifetz tutors his children, Josepha and Robert, on the piano. He never shared the stage with any of his children; what a great disappointment that must have been for him. September 16, 1938.

insight and gravity and self-effacement, which mark the exceptional master.

Violinists come and go, their brilliance flares for a while upon the platforms of our concert-halls, sinks and dies and is forgotten. Or their art grows stale or perfunctory; or becomes obese, acquires a paunch and double chin; or shrinks and fades and withers. Or the virtuoso loses his control and skill, and begs us to remember that he was once a master, and we forgive and indulge him for old time's sake.

Mr. Heifetz's art remains curiously fit and spare and strong, fine-grained and muscular, vital and delicate and secure. Perhaps because he does not strain in the race, does not press and overdo, is not anxious, he contrives to seem unworn and dust-free and unwearied. His playing speaks more largely with the years, touches deeper springs, is effortless increasingly. Hearing him today, one remembers what Leopardi said of those artists "who are modest, because they continually compare themselves, not with other men, but with that idea of the perfect which they have before their mind."

Mr. Heifetz's playing, like his aspect and deportment, has today that unvanquishable dignity, that "high and excellent seriousness," which an Attic philosopher long ago described as one of the major virtues of poetic speech, and which, for the classic mind, was inseparable from great poetic diction and excelling beauty. With Mr. Heifetz, this command of a pure and beautiful musical speech is held with the utmost simplicity and unpretentiousness. It is impossible to think of him as resorting to the use of those counterfeit expedients that are the bane of musical virtuosity. No merchant traffics in his art—and his integrity of purpose defies impeachment.

It might be said that he is sometimes over-generous in the music that he admits to his programs; he, above all other artists in his field, can afford to be challengingly choice. But even when his hospitality is ill-rewarded, the rarity of the artist and his art remain as compensation. The violinist who can deal with Brahms's Sonata in D minor as Mr. Heifetz did at his recital may be forgiven if he leaves his door too casually unlatched.

It is nearly half a century since this sonata was first heard in public when Hubay and Brahms himself played it from manuscript at Budapest on a December day in 1889. It cannot have been, in all the years since then, more beautifully played than Mr. Heifetz plays it—with more poetical and deep an insight, with a shapeliness and eloquence of phrasing and a luminous purity of tone more fitting and expressive. This was a master's utterance, worthy of the rare matter it discoursed.

NOVEMBER 10, 1938
CARNEGIE HALL

AMERICAN GROUP GIVEN BY HEIFETZ
Violinist Also Performs the Paganini Concerto

By Oscar Thompson

Time was when otherwise reasonable devotees of the violin expected perfection of Jascha Heifetz. He has been carrying the burden imposed upon him by that expectation through a good many years and he is still living down, by an occasional slip, the reputation of being some sort of godlike automaton. There were slips or semblances of slips in his playing in Carnegie Hall last night. But it approached, as it never fails to approach, that impossible standard which he or his audiences set for his playing in his first years of concertizing in America, more than two decades ago.

The technical showpiece of the evening was the truncated Paganini Concerto in D major, with the Wilhelmj cadenza. The performance was one to explore its musical values, which are neither the greatest nor the poorest, as violin showpieces go. On the side of bravura, it was poised and easy, rather than spectacular. The fastidious listener could take pleasure in difficult passages played smoothly and securely. But it was not very exciting. Paganini never could have built his own somewhat macabre fame on performances of the same solemnity of spirit. But perhaps Paganini, who, after all, has been dead a long time, was too much of a showman ever to have played properly his own concerto.

Mr. and Mrs. Jascha Heifetz and their son, Jay. January 11, 1949. Jay is in music administration in California.

In its quite different world, the other large-scale composition of last night's program was the D minor Sonata of Brahms. With the able if sometimes over-weighty collaboration of Emanuel Bay at the piano, the violinist gave the sonata the full benefit of his opulent tone—a tone rather more sensuous than an old-school Brahmsian might have considered best for it. The performance was one reflective of much care, the slow movement in particular having an excess of deliberation, with ritards that were a little open to question.

After the intermission—and American composers are used to that—Mr. Heifetz played what the program described as an "American Group." It might as readily have been listed as "encore group," since no one of the six works included was of a character to lift it out of the genre of encore pieces. Cecil Burleigh's "Giant Hills," if anything but gigantic in its own stature, was almost ascetic in contrast with the music which preceded and followed it. The repetition it well merited was given instead to Victor Herbert's airily popular "A la Valse."

Mr. Heifetz was represented in the music played by two of his own transcriptions: One of "Deep River," the other of the Bach E major prelude. The spiritual retained its simplicity. The Bach arrangement was to be distinguished from its fellows chiefly by its ingenious treatment of the piano part. Performances of the smaller pieces were sensitive and adroit and a large audience was moved to the enthusiastic demonstrations of applause expected at a Heifetz recital.

MACKAY MEMORIAL FEATURES CONCERT
Philharmonic Plays Wagner's 'Liebestod' in Honor of
Head of Society's Board
BAX WORK HAS PREMIERE
Heifetz Serves as Soloist in Tchaikovsky Concerto and Barbirolli Conducts

By Olin Downes

The most impressive moment of the concert given last night in Carnegie Hall by the Philharmonic-Symphony Orchestra, John Barbirolli conducting, and the finest interpretation of the evening, was that of the "Liebestod" from Wagner's "Tristan," performed at the beginning of the concert in memory of Clarence Mackay, chairman of the Philharmonic board of directors from 1921 until his death. The "Liebestod" was a favorite composition with Mr. Mackay. Mr. Barbirolli played the soaring music with a solemnity and feeling which befitted the score and the thought of one of the most generous and high-minded patrons of music that this city has known. The applause that would have swept the house after this music was stilled because of the occasion.

The sequence of the program was then changed. Mendelssohn's overture to "A Midsummer Night's Dream" was transferred from the position originally given it to the latter part of the Tchaikovsky concerto, and Mr. Barbirolli and his men proceeded to the first performance in New York of Arnold Bax's Fourth symphony.

Ordinarily a commentator refrains from a conclusive estimate of a new work by a contemporaneous composer of importance on a first hearing. This writer is constrained to remark that he has not in some time heard a score which impressed as being so futile, forced and long-winded as this symphony. It is conventional and repetitious; the ideas at best are mediocre; essentially the music is without invention or vitality. It is much ado about nothing.

Mendelssohn Overture

Mendelssohn, though no Aryan, provided with his matchless overture a refreshment from a long and dreary waste. For the overture to "A Midsummer Night's Dream," inspired in every note and rest, exhaling a sylvan magic, is imperishable and miraculous. The orchestration in itself would constitute the creation of a master; it is the more wonderful because it is inconceivable separate from the ideas. One is certain that the youthful composer heard the music in his mind, just as it is, precisely as it is distributed among the instruments.

One marvels again at the complete unity of the musical conception with the fancy and poetry of Shakespeare, who inspired many composers, among them Berlioz, Verdi, Tchaikovsky, Sibelius. None of these has penetrated to this essence of Shakespeare as Mendelssohn in the music heard last night.

In some respects Mr. Barbirolli's performance was excellent, more especially in the mercurial passages for the strings that follow the chords for wind instruments and constitute the principal motive of the overture. These passages were played with a nimbleness and finesse that perfectly became them. But the climaxes of the full orchestra and the festive brilliancy of later places were somewhat out of scale, sonorously speaking, and involved some poor balances and some coarse tone. The pianissimo

*Mr. and Mrs. Jascha Heifetz shown upon their arrival
from Israel after a four week engagement with the Israel
Philharmonic Orchestra. June 28, 1950.*

347

may be as delicate as you please, but a forte or fortissimo must be proportionate to the spirit and nature of a piece of music.

Orchestral Tone Suffers

The enthusiasm of Mr. Barbirolli in some places got the best of him and the orchestral tone and style suffered—to say nothing of some pretty bad intonation on the part of the woodwinds in the chords to which reference has been made.

Then Mr. Heifetz played the Tchaikovsky concerto. He played this concerto for the first time, as the program stated, when he was a boy of 10, in Berlin. His technical mastery of the music—or, let us say, his technical capacity to play it upside down, in spite of unnecessary technical flaws last night—is uncontestable. But it is to the point to discuss Mr. Heifetz's surprising and disappointing interpretation.

The high point of this interpretation was not in any portion of the violin part proper. It came with the cadenza, which Mr. Heifetz took very earnestly, and of which he made not only an exhibition of astonishing skill but also of brilliant coloring and dramatic commentary on the concerto's motives. In other places he appeared to perform with indifference at one moment and impatient speed and exaggeration at others.

Faults of Interpretation

It is not for a reviewer, even were he able to do so, to read a distinguished musician's mind, but the impression could easily have been gained that Mr. Heifetz was tired of the Tchaikovsky concerto, and either unmoved by its Slavic sensuousness and impetuosity or out of all patience with it. The first movement, in the main, was unimpressive and the principal theme had not its lordly swing and splendor until Mr. Barbirolli proclaimed it in the orchestral tutti that comes later in the movement. The slow movement was finer in every way. The last movement for the greater part was taken at such a breathless speed that often the violinist could not give the necessary weight and fullness of tone to brilliant passages, and the orchestra was put to it to scramble after him. When the lyric themes appeared there had to be sudden and excessive ritards. The tempo of the theme that is sounded over the fifths in the accompaniment was so slow that it almost dropped apart, until every one scurried again, suddenly, back to the headlong tempo.

By these excessive means the effect of the concerto was distorted and cheapened—one would say, to make a virtuoso's holiday. And if the diagnosis be correct, that Mr. Heifetz is bored with the concerto, then why not play some other work upon which he is willing to expend his musical knowledge, taste and superb equipment?

Mr. and Mrs. Jascha Heifetz, at the rail of the steamship Mauretania when the ship docked in New York.
November 24, 1947.

348

DECEMBER 8, 1938
CARNEGIE HALL

BIG CROWD HEARS HEIFETZ RECITAL
Violinist Opens His Program With a Schumann Sonata at Carnegie Hall
BRUCH CONCERTO IS GIVEN
Stravinsky's 'Pergolesi' Suite, Bloch's 'Nigun' and Hebrew Melodies Are Offered

By Noel Straus

Jascha Heifetz was in top form at the recital which he gave last night in Carnegie Hall, under the auspices of the Society for the Advancement of Judaism. With supreme mastery the violinist went his way through a program which was rather off the beaten track both in its arrangement and content. None of its offerings were of the highest rank in the violin literature, yet nearly all of them possessed superior virtues and were worthy of the loving care expended on them by the soloist.

Mr. Heifetz had not progressed far in his performance of the opening Schumann sonata in A minor before it was evident that the large audience was destined to hear an evening of exceptional playing in every regard.

Although this sonata derives from Schumann's last period when his invention was not what it had been in his prime, it rejoices in much of the composer's earlier clarity and freshness of statement. With remarkable reserve power Mr. Heifetz kept the whole work within a dynamic frame that exactly suited its prevailing atmosphere of tender lyricism, adding just enough extra emotional stress in the last movement to carry out the composer's intentions to the letter.

Mr. Heifetz's interpretation of the sonata was notably successful in capturing the tender but impassioned mood of the initial division and voicing its melodies and their development with all the necessary lyricism, sublety and romantic spirit. The silky smoothness of tone, charm of accent and phrasing, and deft application of a most carefully chosen scheme of tints combined to give this part of the work unusual effectiveness and appeal. In the following allegretto Mr. Heifetz moved with a certain command of that section's simple, unaffected poetry, while the finale was a tour-de-force of feathery-light bowing and maintenance of absolute clarity in passages of a rather unviolinistic type.

After holding himself in leash in the sonata, the artist employed the full warmth and richness of his noble tone when he arrived at the following Bruch concerto in D minor. This second and last work in the form by the German composer is a weaker, more loosely constructed and less inspired affair than its all-too-familiar sister opus, but it afforded Mr. Heifetz plenty of opportunity for highly imaginative and dramatic treatment, of which he took utmost advantage. His was a reading memorable alike for its tonal intensity, gusto and technical adroitness.

The second half of the program was given over to Stravinsky's "Pergolesi" suite and a group containing Bloch's "Nigun" and three Hebrew melodies by Achron. Stravinsky's questionable tamperings with Pergolesi's naive but fascinating little melodies were played for all they were worth in a rendition which established a happy medium between real classic simplicity and latter-day sophistication. Emanuel Bay gave finished support at the piano throughout a schedule all of which was warmly received.

350

JASCHA, THAT'S MY BABY
Mr. Heifetz is Genially Appraised by One of His Ardent Admirers
By Deems Taylor

Years ago, when portable typewriters were more of a novelty than they are now, I carried one with me to France. On the way over I showed it one day to the ship's purser, who had never before seen one. He examined it admiringly, exclaimed over its lightness and compactness and finally relinquished it with a sigh, remarking regretfully, "But, of course, Monsieur, such a machine would be of little use to me. I never go anywhere!"

I thought of that incident when Heifetz and I were discussing this sketch.

"What about the biographical part of it?" I asked.

"I wish you'd keep it short," he answered. "Just make it: 'Born in Russia, first lessons at 3, debut in Russia at 7, debut in America in 1917.' That's all there is to say, really. About two lines."

And so, obediently, I give you Jascha Heifetz's autobiography, exactly as dictated. In a way, he is right. That is about all there is to say. A man can run away to sea at an early age, work as a cook in a lumber camp, serve with the Foreign Legion, boss a railroad construction gang, and finally emerge as a first-rate novelist. Most assuredly he will never end up as a great violinist. No concert artist can afford the sort of personal life that makes melodramatic reading for the layman.

Heifetz, who, like so many musicians, is fond of figuring, will tell you that up to now he has spend upward of 66,000 hours—about two-fifths of his waking life—in playing the violin. In the course of spending them he has been around the world four times and has played in almost every country on the face of the globe; at 38, he has already traveled a distance equivalent to two round trips to the moon and is well on the first leg of a third. Nevertheless, his career, stripped to its essentials, has inevitably been one of practice, travel, rehearse, play, sleep, and repeated, with slight variations, year after year, for thirty-one years.

Heifetz has played the fiddle—played it in a manner that few men, living or dead, have ever equaled. Ranking artists is a silly business, and "the greatest in the world" is nothing more, in the last analysis, than the expression of somebody's opinion. But as far back as that fabulous twenty-seventh of October in 1917 when a slender 17-year old Russian boy first stepped on the stage of New York's Carnegie Hall, we all knew that the ranks of the living masters of the violin had received another recruit.

The most obvious aspect of his playing was, and still is, his incredible technical mastery, a mastery so complete that the lay listener becomes unconscious of it. It takes another violinist, I think, fully to appreciate Heifetz's technique, just as it takes an engineer to appreciate the silent perfection of a smoothly running piece of machinery. You may differ with his interpretation of a given piece of music, but so far as concerns his ability to play it, you can settle back in your seat without misgivings. You can count on the crystal purity of his intonation, the perfection of his harmonics, the evenness of his tone and the dazzling surety of his bowing. He will never let you down.

There is a famous story connected with his New York debut. Since it is a true story, I shall suppress the names of the principals, relating merely that sitting in a box at that debut recital were a world-famous pianist and an equally famous violinist. As the program progressed the violinist began to show signs of distress. The longer Heifetz played the more uncomfortable his listener became. Finally, running his handkerchief around his collar, he turned and whispered, "It's awfully hot in here, isn't it?" Upon which his companion remarked, simply, "Not for pianists."

I thought of that story as I sat in the projection room on the Goldwyn lot in Hollywood one afternoon last May, watching—and hearing— a sequence from his picture, "They Shall Have Music." It shows Heifetz, on the platform of a concert hall, playing Saint-Saen's "Introduction and Rondo Capriccioso" (a magnificent job of sound-recording, by the way), and, in accordance with motion picture technique, shows the player not merely as one would see him from a seat in the auditorium, but from many angles and at varying distances—long shots, medium long shots, close-ups and what one might call close-close-ups, views of the bow and the wonderfully controlled arm that propels it, glimpses of the flashing fingers of that miraculous left hand. I thought then, with what despairing admiration a violinist must watch those fingers. But I thought, too, how I would haunt this picture, if I were a violinist, if only for the sake of seeing, as no one has ever seen before, how Heifetz does it.

But sheer mechanical perfection would never have brought Heifetz to the place he occupies in the world of music. There are other great technicians. It is the use to which he puts his technique that entitles him to the adjective "great." The versatility of his style, the breadth and nobility of his interpretations, are traditional. The only serious criticism that I have ever heard leveled against his playing (generally by people who had heard him very little) is that it lacks warmth. He is too Olympian, too detached, they say; he touches your head too much, and your heart not enough.

I am pretty sure that, in part at least, that opinion has a subconscious physical basis. People are childishly dependent upon visual impressions, and, watching Heifetz, they might easily confuse the sound of the playing with the appearance of the player. And Heifetz is the least demonstrative of any concert artist I know. Even among his friends, although he laughs readily, curiously enough he seldom smiles. On the platform, almost never. His attitude to his listeners is one of perfect, unsmiling courtesy, and when he plays he does so with such complete absorption in the music that, looking at his remote, almost mask-like face, one might make the mistake of thinking "here is a cold man."

To give an idea of the man himself is not so easy, chiefly because he has so few eccentricities that would make picturesque reading. Two trivial memories of him may give you a vague picture of him. One is of a late party at Neysa McMein's studio, back in 1923, I think it was, when Jascha, about four in the morning, played as I have seldom heard him or any one else play in concert. I told him so, and he explained. "I was using the Strad tonight, and she's never played so well as since I bought the Guarnerius. You know, she's jealous!"—and half believed it.

The other is a recollection of Jascha, backstage at an absurd revue a crowd of us were putting on for charity—Jascha, with his music stand propped up in the wings, jostled by stage hands, tripped up by electric cables, nervous but determined, playing unaccompanied offstage music for a burlesque melodrama with the devotion and earnestness that he would have given to a command performance before royalty.

There, exemplified, are what to me are his two most striking charac-

Heifetz bought this walking stick violin in Europe. The cane is hollow and holds a bow inside. He is shown here on deck of the steamship Leviathan.

teristics: a simplicity and directness that are almost childlike, and a complete seriousness about his art. He gets along wonderfully with children. Not that he is a head-patter. For all I know, he may not even care much about them. But he meets them on an equal footing, and they accept him as an equal.

A children's orchestra figures prominently in the story of "They Shall Have Music" (an amazing aggregation, by the way, recruited and trained in Hollywood by a devoted Russian musician named Peter Meremblum). When Heifetz first saw and heard them on the screen he refused to believe that they were doing the actual playing and had to be taken to hear them in person before he could be convinced. The studio heads had hoped to induce him to appear with them on the screen, and spent anxious hours debating the most diplomatic way of asking him to do so. When he had heard the youngsters, he asked to be allowed to play with them.

I was on the Goldwyn lot the morning that he finished his part of the picture. Just before he left he asked to have the orchestra assembled so that he could say good-bye. He made no speech, spoke no words of praise. Instead, he called every child over and gave him or her a picture of himself, autographed to that child—a gift from one artist to another.

Just now I mentioned the seriousness of his approach to music. I have never known a musician with more complete artistic integrity. He will rehearse for hours to prepare for a benefit concert whose audience would be satisfied if he came out and played "Pop Goes the Weasel." During the shooting of "They Shall Have Music" he wore out even the fatigue-proof studio crews with his patient and tireless "Let's shoot that again."

Nor have I ever known a musician with less of the show-off element in his make-up, or less conceit. He knows he is good—why shouldn't he? But he has reached the point, I think, that every great artist, creative or interpretative, must reach—the point where he has achieved such mastery of his craft that he knows he will never completely master it. He plays the violin well as he knows what a lesser artist will never know: How good violin playing might be. And so, as he nears his forties, he is still learning to play. He has only one rival, one violinist whom he is trying to beat: Jascha Heifetz.

JULY 18, 1939

HEIFETZ AND THE FILM THAT GOLDWYN BUILT
"They Shall Have Music" as it Has Progressed
From a Few Recordings to a Picture

By Frank Daugherty

HOLLYWOOD, Calif. — Quick thinking and innate showmanship have given Sam Goldwyn a presumably profitable picture in *"They Shall Have Music"* where a less astute producer might have found himself with nothing but a few more or less valueless phonograph records.

It all began in June, 1938, when Goldwyn signed Jascha Heifetz for a picture. Not any picture in particular, just a picture. Stokowski, you will remember, had just aided in a film for Universal with Deanna Durbin. The period was one when just about any good musician who could be found available was a possibility. Heifetz agreed to make several recordings, and allowed himself to be photographed making them. That was all. He wasn't to act. And the contract he made said that he was to be finished with the whole thing by October, 1938.

By September, no story had been found. But the Los Angeles Philharmonic Orchestra was engaged, and with them Heifetz made several recordings, including the Prelude from Partita E Major, Bach-Heifetz; Saint Saens' Rondo Capriccioso; the slow movement from Mendelssohn's violin concerto in E minor; Wieniawski's D Major Polonaise; slow movement from Brahms' D Minor Sonata; Tchaikovsky's Melodie; and the Dinicu-Heifetz "Hora Staccato."

Heifetz checked off the lot, and Goldwyn again set about trying to find a picture into which to dump the music, so to speak. Warner Brothers were making "The Confessions of a Nazi Spy," which seemed like a great idea at the time (though it is said here to have owned a piece of writing known as "The Exiles" dealing with a similar anti-German subject). It was decided to put the Heifetz music into this.

It is here that Goldwyn's knowledge of the business of making pictures entered. In spite of all the publicity surrounding the making of the Warner film, he decided that in the end an American audience would turn from any sort of propaganda in motion pictures. He shelved "The Exiles."

The fortunate appearance of Irmgard von Cube on the scene (she had written the successful "Mayerling") with a story about a music school for poor children was the next stage in the development of the Heifetz picture. The story was purchased, and Goldwyn's casting director was sent out to discover if Los Angeles held a school corresponding in any way to the New York Chatham Music School, upon which Miss von Cube had based her theme. The Neighborhood Music School was discovered in Los Angeles' Boyle Heights district—and, what proved more significant, it was found that the headmistress of the school was trying to raise rent money to keep it going for another month. No movie-maker would miss an opportunity of that sort, and the incident was at once written into the Goldwyn script.

From that point things moved rapidly. The Neighborhood School said that most of its "graduates" went into the Peter Meremblum California Junior Symphony Orchestra; so 40 students from this orchestra were hired for the picture to do the playing, both of the music and of the scenes depicting the music school. It is said that Heifetz, visiting the studio in April 1939, and hearing the recordings of the junior orchestra, would not believe at first that it was not an aggregation of professionals. When they were called in and played for him, he agreed to do more recordings for the picture with them, and he accepted a role in the picture as well. I know it reads like Cinderella; but in its essentials I believe the story of *"They Shall Have Music"* shows one of the reasons Sam Goldwyn makes successful pictures one after another year in and year out.

JULY 26, 1939

ON THE SCREEN

By Howard Barnes

"They Shall Have Music" — Rivoli

"THEY SHALL HAVE MUSIC," a screen drama by John Howard Lawson, based on an original story by Irmgard von Cube, directed by Archie Mayo and presented by Samuel Goldwyn at the Rivoli Theater with the following cast:

355

Himself	Jascha Heifetz
Ann Lawson	Andrea Leeds
Peter	Joel McCrea
Frankie	Gene Reynolds
Professor Lawson	Walter Brennan
Flower	Porter Hall
Limey	Terry Kilburn
Rocks	Walter Tetley
Fever	Chuck Stubbs
Willie	Tommy Kelly
Betty	Jacqueline Nash
Musical director	Alfred Newman
Suzie	Mary Ruth
Davis	John St. Polis
Menken	Alexander Schonberg
Mrs. Miller	Marjorie Main
Miller	Arthur Hohl
Heifet's manager	Paul Harvey
"Sucker"	"Zero"

and the Peter Meremblum California Junior Symphony Orchestra

What is almost certain to be known as "the Jascha Heifetz picture" opened at the Rivoli last night and proved to be just that. With the great violinist filmed from every possible camera angle as he plays solos and concertos, "They Shall Have Music" is a notable event in the screen's wooing of a rival muse. His playing is as consummate as it ever was in the concert hall, while one is permitted to study the perfection of his technique at close range. Moreover, this new Samuel Goldwyn production does an intriguing job of examining musical education in this country, as it traces the ups and downs of a school for poor prodigies.

No matter how fine the offering may be musically, though, it is still a motion picture. As such, it is open to considerable criticism. Fully admitting that it was a tough task to build a dramatic fabric around the playing of a famous violinist, I think that a better plot could have been devised than that which you will find in "They Shall Have Music." The scenarists have fallen back on melodramatic cliches to keep the action going between musical numbers. Employing a somewhat similar theme to that which distinguished "100 Men and a Girl," they have failed to make it properly engrossing or convincing. Even with Archie Mayo's excellent direction, the Heifetz film leaves a good deal to be desired as straight entertainment.

As it stands, the story tells how a gamin, about to be sent to the reformatory, stumbles into a sort of settlement musical institution and with the help of some dead-end pals keeps the school from being closed. By hook or crook, and mostly the latter, he gets Mr. Heifetz to cancel another concert and play with the aspiring youngsters. Unfortunately, the situations get so tangled in melodramatic before the final orchestral rendition that they let the continuity down, where they should have sustained vitality and suspense between the big moments of music.

It behooves a music critic, rather than a cinema reviewer to tell you how well Mr. Heifetz plays in the film, but I will settle for his performance without a quibble. In addition to several arrangements of his own, including "Hora Staccato" and "Estrellita," he plays Tchaikovsky's "Melodie," Saint-Saens's Rondo Capriccioso and the last movement from Mendelssohn's Concerto in E minor. It seems to me that there is something important missing in the reproduction of any great musical performance, but on the screen there is the compensation of watching the violinist's consummate creations at his elbow, as it were. Certainly "They Shall Have Music" deserves to be called the Heifetz picture.

At the same time, the child musicians who play with him and separately, as members of the school, are extremely winning. They perform as talented children should, with a rapt concentration that stands up well in screen terms. I only wish that there had been more scenes of their ensemble work and fewer familiar melodramatics. The latter are well enough enacted by Joel McCrea, Andrea Leeds, Gene Reynolds, Porter Hall, Terry Kilburn and the others. It is only that a conventional motion picture plot seems like pretty silly support for what would have been an extraordinary musical document without it. While "They Shall Have Music" is outstanding musically, it is no more than passable as a screen drama.

● ● ● ●

The evening of October 27, 1917 is gloriously memorable in the annals of American music, for it was on that evening that Jascha Heifetz, a 17-year-old violinist from Russia, made his American debut at Carnegie Hall. No such breathless excitement as marked that historic occasion may have been perceptible last evening in the Rivoli Theatre, where Mr. Heifetz made his screen debut, by courtesy of Samuel Goldwyn, in "They Shall Have Music." It was a hot night (for everybody), and Mr. Heifetz is past being "discovered." But the occasion had its historic aspects and was the source of considerable delight.

When Mr. Goldwyn announced two years ago that he had obtained the consent of the great violinist to appear in a motion picture, the obvious question asked by everyone was "What will Heifetz do?" That problem was likewise of some apparent annoyance to Mr. Goldwyn, too, for he was more than a year finding a story to suit the talents of his renowned artist. The question was answered last evening: Mr. Heifetz plays the violin, that's all. He plays it rapturously, and with surpassing brilliance—such a quality and abundance of magnificent fiddling as has never before been heard from a screen.

Perhaps a critic of music might better remark upon its excellence. Suffice it for a journeyman of the films to comment enthusiastically that the crystal purity of Mr. Heifetz's playing, the eloquent flow of melody from his violin and the dramatic presentation of the artist commanding his instrument—close-ups of his graceful fingers upon the strings, of the majestic sweeps of his bowing arm and brilliant angle-shots of the man before an orchestra—create an effect of transcendent beauty which is close to unique in this medium.

The story? It is sufficient to support the ethereal grace of the music and little more. It is a sentimental tale of an underprivileged boy who falls in love with music, is driven from his squalid home because of it, lands in a modest musical foundation where a lovable old maestro enkindles the souls of youngsters with the magic of melody and eventually saves the school from evil creditors by persuading Heifetz to come there and give a concert. It is the sort of story which is known as a "tear-jerker"—a direct assault upon the soft spots in all doting parents and elder folk. It is made more so by music, and will probably be very popular.

A good cast of actors supports Mr. Heifetz, who is woefully deficient in the few brief excursions he makes in that department. (Just enough to keep the story together). Gene Reynolds, as the boy who makes good, carries the heaviest role commendably, if one excuses the tearful moments. And especial mention must be made of the Peter Meremblum California Junior Symphony Orchestra, which accompanies Mr. Heifetz in one number. It is the grandest appeal for musical education in the picture. It—and, of course, Mr. Heifetz.

JULY 30, 1939

"THEY SHALL HAVE MUSIC"

By Olin Downes

We fancy that no one will dispute the unanimous verdict of the moving-picture critics of this city that the story of Jascha Heifetz's film "They Shall Have Music" is a poor one. It is unnecessarily poor. In fact, it misses patent opportunities for a significant story which would have given Mr. Heifetz's glorious performance its proper setting and not left it almost entirely to his reputation and genius to carry the show.

This is in line with too much that the films have done when they undertook to deal with serious music or the personalities of great musicians. In most cases the producers have bungled their opportunities. A glaring example was the Paderewski film, "Moonlight Sonata," made on the other side of the water. Think what could have been done with the drama of Paderewski the man and the artist and the grand and spectacular part he has played on the world's stage! Instead we perceived one of the great figures of the age, acting as accompanist of children's parties and various sentimental scenes of a trivial narrative.

Leopold Stokowski has experimented boldly and with farther-reaching results, although, where subject-matter was concerned, he too had to stoop to conquer. Walter Damrosch has more recently participated at Hollywood in a part which the famous veteran has characteristically described as that of the "glamour boy" of a production in which he figures as conductor and distinguished protagonist. Operatic films have been made carrying many a famous musical name, including those of Lawrence Tibbett and Grace Moore, but presenting altered or truncated versions of masterpieces.

Mr. Heifetz's film has more than one sovereign virtue. The first of these if the fact that the musician is no longer the accessory but the mainspring of the plot, and that music itself, principally in the person of Mr. Heifetz, but also present in various other human manifestations, is the hero of the drama.

The title is the motive of the story, and the story has not only a musical but a social moral, of the "Dead End" sort. It is testimony to the need of music as a constructive social force. The setting, as Mr. Goldwyn has informed us, was suggested by one of the number of music settlement schools which do their great work for the under-privileged in the arts in this city. In this instance it is the Chatham Square School, down on Clinton Street, which served as model. The orchestra is not local. It is the Peter Meremblum California Junior Symphony Orchestra, which plays astonishingly well. A pity that its regular conductor, probably owing to the necessity of finished acting, could not function in the picture! For Walter Brennan, excellent, on the whole, as his impersonation proves to be, reminds one rather forcibly of the leader who stopped in the midst of the rehearsal, rapped sharply with the stick for attention and addressed the players: "Gentlemen, you are good musicians, and know your business. I know I am a good conductor, and know my business. Now don't make me nervous by watching me!"

As for Mr. Heifetz, histrionically speaking, he never attempts to act. This is wise, and fortunate. He is Heifetz, exactly as known to friends and observers these many years—there for the purpose of making music, outwardly reserved to the point of taciturnity, wearing even the customary mask when he plays. Thus under-acting is natural to the man who, supersensitive, abhors ostentation. Heifetz never raises his voice or gesticulates. There is only one place in which he is disappointing and surely less expressive than he could be. That is when he examines and verifies the identity of his stolen violin. We do not believe that any virtuoso on the eve of a concert—even he—with his stolen violin miraculously restored to him, would show quite such equanimity, or give quite such an impression of "Yes, that's the violin," and nothing whatever more. But on the whole, by the complete absence of acting, Mr. Heifetz is the more himself, the while that he pours forth, without stint or limit, his emotion and his genius in his musical performance. His playing is not masked, and it must be ranked among his greatest achievements.

His playing in this film is the result of the care which we know that he lavished upon his task and his unyielding seriousness in it. We are informed that he totally refused to go through with some parts of the script which asked improbable or trivial things. He stands here uncompromisingly upon his ideals as an artist, and he has put everything he has into the achievement, which, indeed, is a summing up of his ripe mastery and greatest moments.

It is a wonderful performance—exciting, fascinating, even to those who have the privilege of listening frequently to Mr. Heifetz in the concert hall. As a matter of fact, he has never in our recollection played with more completely released passion and virtuoso fire. This is coupled with Heifetz's impeccable technic, which must be impressive for the musically illiterate as well as the sophisticates to watch. For the photography, from the musician's standpoint, is a revelation. Those who want to know how the violin can sound, and the ultimate way in which it should be played, can simply go and listen and gaze. One would like to see the film, if technical matters were the sole concern, in slow motion, because it is the clearest of illustrations of a perfection and felicity of technical approach which in themselves amount almost to an art.

But this is all subordinate to the interpretation. Mr. Heifetz may well have said in his heart of hearts, as certainly he did, "They shall have music." He has seen to it. He has seen to it with a conscience and persistence in the pursuit of perfection which are past praise.

How he did that, under the blaze and heat of the Klieg lights and the grueling repetitions in the environment of the studios, is to be told only by himself, if by any one. If he had less than those nerves of iron, which fortunately are a Heifetz possession, less than a technique as pure and precise as his, and so firmly based on a solid rock of achievement, he simply could not have gone through with it. This is to be noted; where most musicians are hampered by the conditions of sound pictures and appear in them at less than their customary advantage, Heifetz, if anything, conveys himself more completely through this medium than he does on the public platform.

It would be interesting to have enough of the data, practical and psychological, to trace all the processes within him which went to this performance. The great majority of artists can very easily push a rehearsal or repetitions of a particular work too far and become stale, unsteady or perfunctory in the task. It is evident that the harder Heifetz worked the better became his accomplishment.

He plays here as though fully aware of his responsibility to his art, himself and the future. The compositions he interprets have been very wisely selected. They are prevailingly of the brilliant and melodious sort, not representing any remote peak of the literature of the violin, but in each case music admirably written for the instrument and revealing every aspect of the tone, technic and breath-taking virtuosity of a master—the Saint-Saens "Rondo Capriccioso" and the finale of the Mendelssohn concerto, with orchestra, and solo violin pieces by Dinicu-Heifetz ("Hora-Staccato"), Ponce-Heifetz ("Estrellita") and Tchaikovsky ("Melodie").

We know the Paganini story, no doubt apocryphal, of the Englishman who hired an adjoining room, then peered through the keyhole that he might witness the genius at practice. Here is the complete picture in every detail and thrill of a Heifetz performance. The film would remain—if it had no other value—as a record of the actual playing of one who will surely endure in history as a pre-eminent artist of this period upon his instrument. And the picture will doubtless have the same communicative power after Heifetz has disappeared. For time to come audiences, as they do today at the Rivoli, will crash into applause after he finishes on the film, much as they do when he is present in the flesh at Carnegie Hall.

AUGUST 6, 1939

IMPRESSION OF THE HEIFETZ FILM

"They Shall Have Music," the film now running at the Rivoli Theater in which Jascha Heifetz appears as himself, provides a liberal opportunity to see and hear this eminent violinist playing as soloist with orchestra and with piano accompaniment. Among his contributions are the Saint-Saens "Introduction and Rondo Capriccioso" in the Carnegie Hall concert depicted early in the film; his arrangements of Dinicu's "Hora Staccato" and Ponce's "Estrellita" in the motion picture—a film within a film— which he presents for exhibition at the remarkable struggling music school which finally obtains his services for its concert, and, at that event, a "Melodie" by Tchaikovsky and, with the aid of the school orchestra, the finale of the Mendelssohn concerto. There also is a generous supply of other music provided by the children of the school, most of whom are members of the California Junior Symphony Association, organized and directed by Peter Meremblum.

The reproduction of Mr. Heifetz's playing is admirable, giving a convincing idea of his technical mastery and musicianship and of the delectable quality of his tone, and the presentation of the music by the youthful orchestral players and soloists also gives an impression of remarkable faithfulness. In this respect the film gives virtually no grounds for cavil.

One might question, indeed, a few points of detail. The outside of the hall where Mr. Heifetz gives his concert early in the film is undoubtedly that of Carnegie Hall, but the interior does not particularly resemble that of the noted auditorium on West Fifty-seventh Street. The concert itself is not of the type of the usual Heifetz recital, which would be with piano accompaniment, or of the usual orchestral concert with him as soloist, in which his appearance would not be so early in the program. Even if this were a special program of violin solos with orchestra, it would probably open with eighteenth century music rather than with the Saint-Saens work. The costumes of the conductor and the soloist, and the white trousers of the orchestra players, suggest an outdoor concert, such as a Stadium program, rather than a performance at Carnegie Hall.

At times the work of the children at the school, especially the singing of the two coloratura airs "Caro Nome" and "Casta Diva" by a girl of apparently few years, seems almost too good to be true, but yet our settlement schools have produced solo instrumentalists and soloists of remarkable ability. But, while they are fully as altruistic as the appealing institution depicted in the film, this department's impression is that their heads have considerably more business ability than is shown by this school's lovable director.

Nor, according to the answer to a query addressed to Mr. Heifetz's management, is the violinist so closely shepherded by his managers as some of the scenes might be taken to indicate.

Dwelling at this length on such points is, indeed, hardly fair to the film and the musical pleasure which it affords; there is no particular reason why they should be noticed at all by the great majority of those who witness the picture, and they are, on the whole, of minor importance. But, in view of the notable attempts made by motion picture producers for entire accuracy in surroundings and details, they may be worth mentioning from the standpoint of complete convincingness in a picture on a musical subject.

AUGUST 8, 1939
LEWISSOHN STADIUM

STADIUM TO END CONCERT SERIES NEXT TUESDAY
Season Curtailed a Week; Heifetz Plays Concerto of Beethoven for 21,000

The season of concerts by the Philharmonic-Symphony Orchestra at the Lewissohn Stadium of City College will close next Tuesday night, August 15, at the end of its ninth week, according to an announcement yesterday by Mrs. Charles S. Guggenheimer, chairman of the Stadium Concerts Committee. The series was originally planned to extend through a tenth week, until Tuesday, Aug. 22, but even with this earlier close it will be longer than any previous season in its history of these concerts. Eight weeks was the standard length from 1925, the eighth season of the series, through last summer.

One reason for this decision to close the series next week instead of the week following was said to be the unavailability of any noted soloists for Stadium appearances after Aug. 15, and the difficulty in arranging special features at short notice. The engagement of Fritz Reiner during the final fortnight of the season and the Beethoven cycle which is its principal feature were both advanced a week when Erich Leinsdorf, Metropolitan Opera conductor, canceled his Stadium engagement.

Heifetz Plays to 21,000

Jascha Heifetz, filling his fifth annual engagement in this series, played Beethoven's violin concerto at the Stadium last night with the Philharmonic-Symphony under Fritz Reiner's direction. The program, the third of the Beethoven cycle, began with the overture to "Coriolanus" and the fourth symphony. The audience, estimated at 21,000, was probably the largest gathering that has attended a single performance by Mr. Heifetz here thus far. Those reaching the field entrances within the quarter hour before the concert were told that only standing room was left. The consensus of surmises was that yesterday's crowd was not quite so large as the record-breaking audience which had heard Lily Pons at the Stadium on July 17, but that the difference was probably not more than a few hundred.

Although Mr. Heifetz's 1939 Stadium appearance coincided with the run of his film, "They Shall Have Music," at the Rivoli Theater, he drew a crowd nearly as large to the neighborhood of City College last summer, so that the size of yesterday's attendance can be interpreted as a tribute to his thoroughly deserved reputation as a consummate artist. The reasons for this reputation were illustrated on this occasion by a performance of a standard corresponding to that of the great music which he performed. His playing, as before, was characterized by a tone of delectable quality, unerring technical mastery and brilliance and impeccable taste, and the combination of dignity and persuasive expressiveness which marked his interpretation were particularly well suited to this concerto. But the merits of the violinist and of the music are too well known to need extensive encomiums here. The audience showed corresponding enthusiasm, and Mr. Heifetz, for an encore, played Beethoven's Romance in F.

Jascha Heifetz, always interested in sports, takes on Isidor Achron in a fencing match atop a New York skyscraper. Circa 1939.

Fourth Symphony Played

The Fourth Symphony, one of the least often heard of the unparalleled nine, has endearing qualities of its own, and these were well set forth by the musicians under Mr. Reiner, who also gave the violinist laudable co-operation in the concerto.

Mr. Reiner will conduct a program including Berlioz's "Roman Carnival" overture, Glinka's "Kamarinskaya," Sibelius's "Swan of Tuonelo" and "Karelia" march, "Navarra," by Albeniz and Strauss's "Don Juan" and "Till Eulenspiegel" at the Stadium tonight. The fourth concert of the Beethoven cycle will take place tomorrow night and the fifth on Thursday, with Harold Bauer as soloist in the "Emperor" concerto. Mr. Reiner will also conduct on Friday. A Czech program will be presented Saturday under Josef Blant, a conductor new to this series, with Zlatko Balokovic, violinist, as soloist. The Beethoven cycle closes with the Ninth Symphony under Mr. Reiner next Monday.

F.D.P.

AUGUST 8, 1939
LEWISOHN STADIUM

20,000 AT STADIUM HEAR HEIFETZ PLAY
Violinist Gives the Beethoven Concerto in D Major —
Soloist Also Delivers Romance in F at Cycle Concert of the Philharmonic
By Gama Gilbert

A fair report of last night's concert at Lewisohn Stadium must point out that—in alphabetical order—Beethoven, Jascha Heifetz, Hollywood and Fritz Reiner attracted some 20,000 persons for the third part of the Beethoven cycle. But if a music reviewer may for once be permitted an avowed partiality for music's side, it is worth noting that in past seasons at the Stadium Mr. Heifetz has drawn similar houses, and that this season Beethoven and Mr. Reiner have not been neglected by the public. From which may be deduced the fact that Beethoven, Heifetz and Reiner are a sufficient trio for the box-office.

Mr. Heifetz flew from the West Coast to play Beethoven's concerto in D major, the master's only work in that form; Mr. Reiner opened the evening with the "Coriolanus" Overture and the Fourth Symphony. There is no need now to enlarge on Mr. Reiner's way with the latter works; and, at any rate, late-comers tramping through the maze of field tables made it impossible to consider critically the overture and symphony or indeed to hear them at times. The management would do well to study the traffic problem within the Stadium walls when the attendance runs into five figures.

However, by the time the concerto was about to begin, the audience had found its places and was properly attentive. Mr. Heifetz rewarded it with a performance that commanded its concentration. In its larger outlines and in its details it was like countless others that have come from his hands—but from his hands alone. One marvelled again at the gem-like clarity of the fingerwork, the chaste delicacy of the phrasing, the warmth and beauty of the tone. These constituted the vessel that conveyed a noble conception, without which, howsoever beautiful the externals, no such applause would have followed the performance as did last night. It was the natural demonstration of a sincerely moved audience. It listened gratefully to Beethoven's Romance in F, which Mr. Heifetz played after the concerto.

AUGUST 8, 1939
LEWISOHN STADIUM

22,000 HEAR HEIFETZ ON BEETHOVEN PROGRAM
Stadium Filled to Capacity for Fifth Reiner Program—Season Curtailed
By Edward O'Gorman

Jascha Heifetz, Fritz Reiner and an all-Beethoven program drew a capacity crowd of 22,000 to the Stadium last night, and it was probably the first time in his career that the violinist has had serious competition, the formidable counter-attraction being himself at the Rivoli in "They Shall Have Music."

Of Beethoven's three works for violin and orchestra, Heifetz played two: the Concerto in D major, which was programmed, and the F major Romance which was offered as the lone encore.

One can generally find a particular design or purpose behind a Reiner program, and such was the case last night. The Fourth Symphony, the Violin Concerto and the "Coriolanus" Overture, the three compositions on the printed bill, bear the opus numbers 60, 61 and 62, respectively.

For every listener that Heifetz thrilled last night must have been another, a student, who was made miserably unhappy, who, having been shown the goal toward which he must strive, must have despaired of ever reaching it.

This is the sort of music-making that drives to distraction those who must compete against it, and sends frantic reviewers to the nearest thesaurus in search of the most exalted superlatives.

Only those who have heard Heifetz play the Beethoven Concerto time and again can fully appreciate the quality of his performance, a technically flawless performance, which allows the composer full scope to speak for himself and yet which bears indelibly the imprint of the soloist's personality.

DECEMBER 2, 1939

HEIFETZ TALKS OF MODERN MUSIC AND VIRTUOSITY— HOLLYWOOD TO TOWN HALL
By William G. King

Jascha Heifetz has recently commissioned major works from three of the most important present-day composers, and inevitably, talk across the luncheon table the other day turned to modern music.

Not having the scores of the three new works before us (two of them are still in the embryo stage, anyway) we perforce ignored the particular for the general. We agreed that much, if not most, of the music written in our time suffers from too much cold intelligence, too much technical proficiency and too little "genuine" emotion; that "clever," "brilliant" or "interesting" are the adjectives best suited to praise it.

And for this, Mr. Heifetz believes, the learned critics and their concert-patron followers are at least partially responsible. They have over-emphasized the value of "originality" in the efforts of those seeking to establish themselves as composers. Consequently many young writers of music, in their natural desire to obtain recognition, have attempted to be "original" at any cost.

Jascha Heifetz was made an officer of the French Legion to help in the war effort. He is shown here accepting the decoration from Charles de Fontnouvelle, the American consul general. February 14, 1939.

"I'm convinced a lot of composers have literally been frightened into the kind of music they write by the knowledge that critics and listeners delight in pointing out phrases that 'sound like Tchaikovsky,' or 'obviously are derived from such and such a passage of Beethoven,' " he said. "If they weren't so certain they'd be dismissed as 'unoriginal' if their work reminded some one of that of other composers, perhaps they'd write more from hearts and less from heads deliberately striving to avoid imitation."

Although it is true that every composer has a "flavor" distinctly and unmistakably his own, it is equally true that not one of them achieved it without first imitating, consciously or unconsciously, some other composer or composers. And the flavor, even at its strongest, is seldom made up entirely of "original" elements.

"Also," said Mr. Heifetz, "I think composers have hampered their talents by allowing themselves to be influenced by the rather general attitude that sentiment is a little shameful. I'm sick of that attitude. How can you create music if you're afraid of expressing your own emotions or of stirring those of others?"

Some time in the future, when he feels he can afford a year or so of retirement from the concert-platform, Mr. Heifetz will make a trial of himself as a composer. It is something he has always wanted to do, and something he definitely intends to do.

"I'll probably write pages and pages and throw them away," he said. "And even feeling as I do, I know I'll be a bit scared of the things I may consider good, because they may not seem 'original' to the critics, no matter how well they express what I want to express."

No Virtuoso

Although Heifetz is one of the greatest masters of the violin who ever drew bow, with a technic that is perhaps as nearly flawless as it is given to a human being to achieve, you'll have an argument on your hands if you call him a "virtuoso." He doesn't like the emphasis upon the purely mechanical that loosely used term implies, and he is justifiably resentful of the further implication that he is concerned with displaying his technic, which, like every other true musician, he acquired, and keeps by unending arduous practice, only in order to re-create music as perfectly as possible. The "show pieces" of the violin literature, written solely for the purpose of permitting a performer to dazzle his hearers with his virtuosity, have never interested him.

He's needed every resource of technic, however, to master some of the modern works he has added to his repertory.

"Sometimes I think all the modern composers must have got together and agreed to make it just as tough as possible for us fiddlers," he said. "For instance, passages in the Prokofiev." Prokofiev is one of the outstanding composers who have been given specific commissions by Heifetz recently. The violinist has asked him to write a new concerto for him, and hopes that Prokofiev will have at least an outline completed when he returns to this country. Mario Castelnuovo-Tedesco is also at work on a concerto for him, and on December 7, Heifetz will give the world premiere performance of William Walton's First Violin Concerto with the Cleveland Symphony Orchestra. Walton had intended to come here in time to make any last minute revisions that actual rehearsals with orchestra indicated were desirable, but he has been called into the British Army. A short time ago he wrote Heifetz a lengthy letter, listing certain corrections he wished made, and giving his permission for the violinist to make any others he desired. He added that he hoped the censors would not take the musical notations for code, and ink them out. They didn't.

At his Carnegie Hall recital next Wednesday, Mr. Heifetz will introduce another of his commissioned works—Cyril Scott's "Fantasie Orientale'"—to New York. He expects to continue giving commissions to composers "as long as I can do so financially," he said.

"I want to stimulate the creation of new music," he explained, "and in doing so, to help composers earn a living through their work. How can you expect a composer to go on writing music when he gets no return from it? That's as unfair as it would be to expect me to go on playing the violin if no one was willing to hear me."

• • • •

Musically, the first week of December will be one of "firsts" for Jascha Heifetz. In two successive appearances, one at his annual New York recital in Carnegie Hall on Wednesday evening, December 6, and the following evening in Cleveland, as soloist with the Cleveland Orchestra, the distinguished artist will play two new musical compositions for the first time.

Because it is a world premiere, more importance may be attached to his performance in Cleveland of William Walton's Concerto for violin and orchestra. However, Mr. Heifetz's first New York performance of Cyril Scott's "Fantasie Orientale" is additional evidence of the fact that he has not confined to mere words his desire to enrich the repertoire for the violin.

Both compositions, coincidentally, are by Englishmen. Mr. Walton's concerto was commissioned by Mr. Heifetz in 1936, and the young composer, who dedicated it to the violinist, completed it in April of this year. Coming to the United States in May, Mr. Walton spent three weeks with Mr. Heifetz, while they revised and reworked it together. A tragic sidelight of the war in Europe was revealed in a recent communication from Walton to Mr. Heifetz. "For the first time," Walton wrote, "I will not be present at a world premiere of my own work. I have been called to the service, and am now driving an ambulance. You have my blessings, and permission to make any necessary changes at your first orchestral rehearsal."

Scott, a prolific composer, has written often for violin and piano as well. Mr. Heifetz performed the "Fantasie Orientale" for the first time publicly on November 9, at a concert in South Hadley, Massachusetts.

Included on the program too will be Castelnuovo-Tedesco's "The Lark," edited by Mr. Heifetz, which he has performed frequently in the past few years.

The gifted Italian composer, who is now in this country, recently made reference to Mr. Heifetz's interest in new works and lesser known composers. In a recent article in the *New York Times* Castelnuovo-Tedesco wrote:

"I owe to the 'Concerto Italiano' the precious friendship of Jascha Heifetz. I met and heard him for the first time in Florence in 1926 (the year I composed this work). He was very kind, told me that he knew my music from another eminent violinist. . . and asked me to send him my concerto. Naturally, I did so at once, but I must confess that I was a bit skeptical. I couldn't hope that such a great violinist of world reputation might be interested in the work of a young, yet unknown composer. Well, I was mistaken. A year later I received a program from New York in which he had played my concerto at the Metropolitan Opera House with the Philharmonic-Symphony Orchestra."

Aside from Beethoven's Sonata No. 1, his program will be devoted to compositions by Conus and Pierne, worthy but rarely heard composers. Also Tchaikovsky, Godowsky, Scott and Castelnuovo-Tedesco. Mr. Heifetz feels that in the interests of enlarging the repertoire for the violin, it is extremely important that other works of repute should be heard. For he sincerely believes that this kind of encouragement will stimulate creative effort among contemporary composers, and will ensure the healthy growth of the library of violin literature.

Mr. Heifetz's own contribution is not insignificant. Available in published form under his signature are more than 40 transcriptions and arrangements for violin and piano, 13 compositions edited by him, as well as a folio of 15 of his favorite encores, edited and fingered by the eminent violinist.

Mischa Elman at age 50, shown below, lost his supreme career when Heifetz arrived on the scene. Fodor, one of Heifetz's star students, is shown (facing page) in Russia where he visited the home of Tchaikovsky after winning the Tchaikovsky Competition for violin in 1974. Fodor credited Heifetz for setting an almost unattainable standard in violin technique.

500 TURNED AWAY AT HEIFETZ RECITAL
Violinist's Only Appearance Here This Season
Draws Throng to Carnegie Hall
CONUS CONCERTO HEARD
It Holds Place of Honor on the Program —
Beethoven's D Major Sonata Played

So great was the demand to hear Jascha Heifetz at his sole New York recital of the season, given last night in Carnegie Hall, that more than 500 persons were turned away at the box-office. The vast gathering of the fortunate who were present during the violinist's program, found him in the peak of form throughout a list of offerings, which, though it contained a dearth of music of the highest rank, nevertheless provided the artist with ample opportunities to display his supreme attainments as technician and interpreter.

The place of honor on the schedule was held by the Conus Concerto, a work that Mr. Heifetz glorified by some of the most amazing playing in the entire series of masterly performances that the evening brought forth. For this climactic number, Mr. Heifetz had reserved a tone of the greatest intensity, vibrant with life and feeling, which was applied from the opening bit of recitative to the brilliant coda of the one-movement composition with seemingly inexhaustible imagination for effects of color and light and shade.

In the chief theme of the initial Andante division the broad melody was begun with an ardor that gradually gained impetus until it reached wildly impassioned utterance during the "largamente" measures. The following section in rapid triplet figuration was delivered with an outstanding display of extraordinary deftness of bowing in spiccato playing of which there were so many notable examples in the course of the recital. As for the ensuing second theme, it was read with a lyricism held just enough in leash to give the desired sense of contrast, in the scheme of the work as a whole.

But it was in the concerto's central Adagio division that Mr. Heifetz reached the apex of his achievement on this occasion. In an interpretation of almost unbelievable beauty, the violinist transfigured this music by way of richness of tone and sensitiveness of feeling that worked with shattering effect.

Before the concerto Mr. Heifetz performed the first of Beethoven's violin sonatas, the D major of Op. 12. Here an entirely different type of tone was adopted from that employed in the concerto, a silken tone of the utmost refinement of sound, invariably held within a restrained frame of dynamics ideally suited to this composition. The entire work was given with exquisite treatment of detail, as was the sonata, Op. 36, by Gabriel Pierne presented later. The Pierne opus is far too long for what it has to say, but the first movement with its peculiar decuple rhythm poses interesting problems for both the violinist and the supporting pianist, which were superbly solved by Mr. Heifetz and his adroit accompanist, Emanuel Bay.

The program began with Castelnuovo-Tedesco's "The Lark." This item, like Cyril Scott's "Fantasie Orientale," a novelty used as the closing selection, proved less important from the musical angle than as a vehicle for the display of technical prowess in difficult feats of bowing, harmonics, pizzicati and flying ornamental passage work, all of which were superbly envisaged by the soloist. Tchaikovsky's "Melodia" and Godowsky's "Valse" completed the program. At the end of the recital many crowded down to the footlights for the encores required to satisfy the enthusiastic gathering.

N.S.

DECEMBER 6, 1939
CARNEGIE HALL

CAPACITY AUDIENCE HEARS HEIFETZ IN CARNEGIE HALL
Violinist Gives Only Concert He Plans Here This Season

Every seat was taken in Carnegie Hall last night and the standing room was packed to the last inch of space for the only New York recital in which Jascha Heifetz is scheduled to appear this season. The eminent violinist was in good form, playing with customary smoothness of tone and technique. And yet, owing to a poorly constructed program, the evening was unrewarding from a musical standpoint.

Only the Beethoven sonata in D, played impeccably by Mr. Heifetz, emerged with any degree of profile from the mass of indifferent music assembled by the artist. Here, the variations of the second movement were treated with an aristocracy of taste and a beauty of line that represented Mr. Heifetz at his best. The other movements, too, were splendidly treated.

"The Lark," a composition of the contemporary Italian composer Castelnuovo-Tedesco, now resident in America, served to open the program. Although an effective vehicle for Mr. Heifetz and his accompanist, Mr. Bay, the work closely resembled salon music in its melodic outline. Not far above "The Lark" in point of merit was Cyril Scott's "Fantasie Orientale," which closed the program. In its first New York performance, it turned out to be a series of variations of the same composer's debatable "Lotus Land."

Midway in the evening came the gaudy concerto of Jules Conus, which Mr. Heifetz delivered with such nobility as to disguise its essential poverty of ideas. Then followed the Pierne sonata, music that is charmingly Gallic and ingratiating in everything save content. The "Melodie" of Tchaikovsky and waltz of Godowsky completed a program which, in musical value, did scant justice to Mr. Heifetz's artistry or to his audience. At the end of the printed list there was the usual rush of eager students to the footlights.

R.L.

DECEMBER 6, 1939
CARNEGIE HALL

HEIFETZ HEARD IN RECITAL AT CARNEGIE HALL

Jascha Heifetz, undisputed king of fiddledom, played at Carnegie Hall last night. Taking into account the violinist's recent venture in the movies, it should be stated that he made a personal appearance. With him was Emanuel Bay who accompanied him in a program that included three works in the larger forms; Beethoven's Sonata No. 1, in D major; the Conus Concerto and the Pierne Sonata. Two novelties, serving as prelude and postlude, were a "poem in the form of a rond," entitled "The Lark," by Castelnuovo-Tedesco, and the "Fantasie Orientale," by Cyril Scott, Tchaikovsky's "Melodie" and a "Valse" by Godowsky completed the printed bill.

Mr. Heifetz, displaying that seemingly reckless daring which is an earmark of his playing, began with a scintillating novelty that his more cautious colleagues would tuck away in the center of his programs, safe from whatever ills opening numbers, whether they be larks or nightingales, are apt to suffer. Mr. Castelnuovo-Tedesco's lark sings a lengthy song, and there are trills, filigree scale-work, delicate arpeggios and no want for lyric essay, in short, everything to delight the adept fiddler's heart. The original bird may be stuffed, but last night's version had wings.

It seems that Mr. Heifetz alone knows the formula for distilling the illusive Oriental perfume from the Conus Concerto, that intangible Eastern flavor that one often encounters in Finnish works. Mr. Heifetz's performance, despite some sleepy accompanying by Mr. Bay, realized to the point of perfection the work's lyric character. Usually a violinist's holiday, the concerto pleased all concerned last night.

O.G.

DECEMBER 8, 1939
SEVERANCE HALL

PRAISES HEIFETZ, RODZINSKI IN PIONEER CONCERTO
Loesser Lauds Performances in Work of English Composer

By Arthur Loesser

Jascha Heifetz, peerless violinist, was the soloist with the Cleveland Orchestra at Severance Hall last night.

374

Disdaining the easy success that he could have had by playing one of the well-worn, old concertos, he chose this time to put his enormous technical and musical resources at the disposal of a new work.

It was the Concerto by William Walton, distinguished English composer, that he presented to us, its last night's performance being its first on any public platform.

The concerto is a serious work but without any rigors. The harmonic scheme is modern, but does not wallow in any uncompromising atonality; the thematic developments are logical, but there is no overloading of devices; the idiom personal, yet reveals no unmannerly pursuit of eccentricity; it does not disdain lyrical expression, yet attains no emotional ecstasies.

True Violin Concerto

It is a true violin concerto, with the solo instrument taking the lead almost everywhere. The somewhat elegiac first movement and the playfully sprinting second movement were easily enjoyable, save perhaps to the rather large section of the audience that is still trying to live musically in the year 1890.

It was the concerto's last movement that fell short, at first hearing, of completely convincing this reviewer. It seems to suffer from a kind of climactic failure. Though the movement is admirably clear in pattern, it seems to dispense with any compelling drive toward an irresistible conclusion.

The orchestral portion of the concerto was most skillfully and discreetly handled by Dr. Artur Rodzinski. To say that the solo part was played with superlative brilliance and understanding, and with unapproachable mastery of bow and fingers, is merely a long-winded way of saying that it was played by Jascha Heifetz. The audience indulged in protracted applause.

Tribute to Finland

The program continued with Dr. Rodzinski conducting a stirring performance of Strauss' lengthy, magniloquent tone-poem, "A Hero's Life." An important feature of this was the extraordinarily beautiful playing of Joseph Fuchs, the orchestra's concertmaster, in the long and varied violin solo part.

The concert seemed to be over, the audience rose to leave, but Dr. Rodzinski held up his hand for attention; he said:

"As a tribute to a country which is now the victim of brutal aggression, we will now play Finlandia, by Sibelius."

The conductor and orchestra played it; the audience had a chance to applaud and cheer both the music, the gesture and Finland.

375

HEIFETZ WINS OVATION FOR CONCERTO

By Elmore Bacon

Jascha Heifetz, Dr. Artur Rodzinski and the Cleveland Orchestra were given a stirring ovation after the world premiere of William Walton's new concerto at Severance Hall last night.

An overflow audience was clamorous in its reception of this new addition to the violin repertoire. The demonstration was further heightened by Heifetz insisting upon the orchestra standing with him to share in the acclaim.

And there was another thrill at the close of the program. Dr. Rodzinski turned to the audience, quieted the applause and announced:

"As a tribute to a great people now the victims of brutal aggression, we will play Sibelius' 'Finlandia.' "

Severance Hall patrons found that Walton paints tone colors with a master stroke. And heard Heifetz at the top of his artistry, as the Walton work is dazzlingly difficult. The orchestra, under Dr. Rodzinski's inspired direction, matched the Heifetz virtuosity.

The new concerto has modern pungency without disturbing dissonance. There are splashes of great lyric beauty running through its ever-shifting pattern. Ingenious orchestral coloring abounds. And yet despite the freshness of its vision, the beauty of its intriguing ebb and flow of color, it lacks depth at times.

Walton, an Englishman now serving with the British army in France, wrote the work especially for Heifetz. The latter collaborated with him in some parts of it. That was back last fall while Walton was in this country on a visit.

The solo part is a marvel of intricacy and yet in the opening slow movement and elsewhere there is a golden flow of melody that is highly emotional.

Much of the time the solo instrument is peeping out from the orchestral drapery. And in this warm enfoldment there is a glow of color, an animation and a piquancy that are delightful. Especially fetching is the lovely melody played by the violin with a waltz-like accompaniment in the orchestra.

Occasionally one hears slight reference to the pastel and pastoral fluttings of Debussy, the woodwind creakings of Dukas, a sort of Rossini lilt, cave-man thumpings in bass and brasses—and more than a suggestion of syncopation—the rhythm that put the B in Benny Goodman.

The orchestra was quite as enthusiastic over the concerto as the audience. Heifetz, too, seemed to enjoy every minute of its performance. How soon it will be played again is a question. Its intricacies are not insurmountable, of course, yet they are such that few violinists could offer a virtuosic performance of them. If you want to hear it, the program is repeated tomorrow night at 8:30.

Dr. Rodzinski opened the program with an inspired reading of the Overture to von Weber's "Die Frieschultz." It apparently is one of the director's favorites. Under his baton it assumed a dignity and an air of mysticism that were highly effective.

A performance of the Richard Strauss "Ein Heldenleben," a musical picture of a hero's life—a work that Dr. Rodzinski always gives with fine artistry—closed the program.

DECEMBER 8, 1939
SEVERANCE HALL

HEIFETZ TRIUMPHS IN NEW CONCERTO

CLEVELAND, Dec. 8—Jascha Heifetz and the Cleveland Orchestra won a fine ovation last night at their world premiere of a concerto by William Walton, thirty-seven year-old English composer.

Artur Rodzinski termed it one of the finest violin concertos ever written. It was written at Heifetz's suggestion and dedicated to him.

FEBRUARY 18, 1940
CARNEGIE HALL

BOSTON SYMPHONY IS DIRECTED BY FINN
Hannikainen Gets Ovation for Interpretation of the Sibelius Work at Carnegie Hall
HEIFETZ VIOLIN SOLOIST
Plays Prokofiev 2nd Concerto—
Bach Organ Passacaglia Heard Under Koussevitzky

By Olin Downes

A wholly exceptional feature of the memorable concert given by the Boston Symphony Orchestra, Dr. Sergei Koussevitzky conductor, yesterday afternoon in Carnegie Hall was the appearance as guest leader for the first time in this city of Tauno Hannikainen, who directed in that capacity the performance of the First Symphony of his countryman, Jean Sibelius.

Following performances by Dr. Koussevitzky of the Bach-Respighi organ Passacaglia and Fugue, and the New York premiere of Prokofiev's Second Violin Concerto, with Jascha Heifetz as soloist, the director appeared with Mr. Hannikainen on the stage. Dr. Koussevitzky remarked that while every one wished to aid Finland, his procedure was not based upon that consideration alone but the fact that Finland had great conductors as well as composers. Then Dr. Koussevitzky presented Mr. Hanninkainen to the audience.

With the opening measures—the molding of the clarinet solo to the acme of expressiveness—Mr. Hanninkainen showed his quality as a musician and impressed his audience by his heroic spirit and poise and control of the situation.

Knew Every Note of Score

Mr. Hannikainen knew every note of his score and put all his young heart and his good musician's brain into it. He was not there to prove his prowess as a virtuoso; only to drive home the music. No detail of it was neglected by him, whether it were one of instrumental color or wildly dramatic utterance. The consuming emotion of the composer when he created the music was also the conductor's. The sense of heroic tragedy and the vibrations of the natural world were fused in his wholly comprehending conception, which had the sweep of the tempest.

At the same time there was the quality which is that of a thorough musician and a thoughtful artist, and, also apparently, of the Finnish nature; that of balance, reserve power, and synthesis. No climax was so intense that it was disproportionate, or that the orchestra ran away with the leader. There was complete and unspoken control. When a headlong development reached its peak it was after long ascent and the irresistible accumulation of energy.

To Return to Finland Soon

Mr. Hannikainen soon returns to Finland, where heroics are not confined to music, and musicians and even perfectly common men value principles and liberties and know how to die. This could be felt in the symphony he interpreted, and the spirit of his presentation. He was applauded and cheered for long moments when he finished.

These were dramatic moments of the afternoon, but not the only impressive ones. For Dr. Koussevitzky opened the concert with a masterly and mightily climaxed reading of the Bach Passacaglia, and he and Mr. Heifetz, the two masters that they are, for the benefit of Prokofiev's concerto.

That composer could hardly have hoped for a better showing. The concerto is undeniably a clever and ingenious composition, very adroitly scored both for orchestra and solo instrument. Whether it is more than that is to be determined by later hearings or by those more confident than this commentator is of the composition's intrinsic merits. Performer and concerto were well received by the audience.

MUSIC

By Francis D. Perkins

BOSTON SYMPHONY ORCHESTRA, Serge Koussevitzky, conductor; Tauno Hannikainen, guest conductor, yesterday afternoon in Carnegie Hall with Jascha Heifetz, violinist, as soloist in the following program:

Bach-Respighi....................Passacaglia and Fugue in C Minor
Prokofiev................Violin Concerto No. 2, in G Minor, Op. 63
Serge Koussevitzky conducting
Sibelius......................Symphony No. 1, in E minor, Op. 89
Mr. Hannikainen conducting

During the fifteen years which have elapsed since Serge Koussevitzky made his American debut and for two decades before that, the Boston Symphony Orchestra has always played under the leadership of its regular conductor in its concerts in Carnegie Hall. But Serge Koussevitzky did not cite the current ardent sympathy for Finland as the principal reason for turning over the podium to Tauno Hannikainen, conductor of the Orchestra of Turku (Abo), in the latter half of yesterday afternoon's program. "You will see," he told the capacity audience, "that this heroic little country had not only great composers, but brilliant conductors."

Mr. Hannikainen, who will celebrate his forty-fifth birthday a week from tomorrow, is one of four brothers who hold important positions with Finnish musical organizations. Several years of activity as a cellist preceded his first major conductorial engagement with the State Opera in Helsinki from 1922 to 1927, when he was appointed to his present position. On the outbreak of the Russian war, he was assigned to civil guard duty, but was released by the Finnish authorities in order to fill his engagement with the Boston Symphony. Both in Boston on Feb. 2 and 3, and in Brooklyn Thursday evening, his programs included the first symphony of his great compatriot which was the vehicle for his Manhattan debut.

It takes, of course, more than a single work to give comprehensive evidence for an estimate of a conductor's interpretative powers, but the impression gathered from the performance of the symphony was one of notable talent and authority. His direction, often marked by vigorous and forceful gestures, suggested the mastery of the technical aspect of his art, clearly set forth expressive ideas and the ability to have them reproduced in the playing of his musicians. It seemed undeniably apparent that his acquaintance with Sibelius's symphony in E minor has been of long standing, that his understanding of the score is thorough from an emotional as well as a technical point of view. The wide and contrasted expressive resources of the music, its vivid and generous colors; its poignant outbursts and broad, ingratiating lyric measures were disclosed in a manner which won the conductor an ovation of unusual length at the close.

Sibelius's later symphonic style had not been fully integrated when he wrote this work before the turn of the century, but, in this rehearing, its individual characteristics and atmosphere made an impression far outweighing occasional and frequently noticed hints of the influence of the composer's seniors. The stamp of the composer's creative musical personality seemed unusually pronounced in a composition which is still vivid and eloquent after more than forty years.

Prokofiev's second violin concerto postdates his first work in this form by twenty-two years. It has been heard here in the recording made by Mr. Heifetz with this orchestra, who introduced it to Boston in December, 1937, and twice in recital with piano accompaniment. This concert, however, provided the first opportunity to hear it in a New York concert hall.

Mr. Prokofiev, in the music which has been performed here by himself and others, has revealed himself as a composer of various styles. His command of clashing, plangent harmonic and instrumental color had an especially convincing revelation in the early Scythian Suite; his suggestion of brooding horror in "Sept, ils sont sept" is still memorable after fifteen years or more. We have frequently heard him in a neo-classic vein in his Classical Symphony, or as an expert musical wit in his relatively recent "Peter and the Wolf."

None of these characteristics, however, is exhibited in the second violin concerto. This can be taken as bearing out a remark made by the composer in *The New York Times* ten years ago, when he expressed his hope that he had become simpler and more melodic. "Of course," he observed, "I have used dissonance in my time, but there has been too much dissonance." Lyricism, indeed, characterizes most of the thematic material of the concerto. Another characteristic is its prevailingly meditative and unproclamative mood. The orchestration is notable both for its skill and its delicacy and subtlety of color, but the color is seldom pronounced; even in the relatively sprightly finale, there are few, if any, full-throated instrumental outbursts. The violin solo, as in several other recently wrought concertos, is often conceived as a part, while the principal part, of the orchestral fabric. Both the solo instrument and the ensemble fill and exchange the roles of proponent of the main musical idea and of commentator and embroiderer upon it. It is grateful to the soloist, while exacting; there are demands for swift-paced deftness as well as the disclosure of a long lyric line, but it offers no apparent cadenzas or primarily bravura passages.

Some of the long-breathed themes lack a pronounced and memorable profile, and a certain lack of thematic contrast can be noticed in the first two movements; interest is not always evenly sustained. But the work as a whole appeals as sincere music of considerable imaginativeness, and the slow movement has a persuasive poetic appeal. Mr. Heifetz, in his familiar and admirable interpretative form, and the orchestra under Dr.

Koussevitsky gave the concerto a thoroughly integrated and expressively devoted performance which reflected their thorough understanding of the notes and atmosphere of the music, and was fervently applauded.

MARCH 31, 1940

HEIFETZ BEGINS TOUR TO LAST THREE MONTHS
VIOLINIST VISITS WEST INDIES AND SOUTH AMERICA

Jascha Heifetz, the noted violinist, departed by air last Thursday on one of the most extensive tours of Latin America ever undertaken by a concert artist. With him were his wife and his accompanist, Emanuel Bay.

The first recital of the tour took place last night at Ciudad Trujillo, the Dominican Republic. Thereafter, Mr. Heifetz will be heard in Puerto Rico, where he is listed for San Juan, Ponce and Mayaguez. The British and Dutch West Indies comprise the next stage of his trip, with Port au Spain, Trinidad, and Curacao on his schedule. Appearances in Venezuela, Caracas, Maracaibo, and La Guaira precede the violinist's arrival in Brazil, where he has been announced for concerts in Belem, Bello Horizonte, Sao Paulo, Pernambuco, Santos and Rio de Janeiro. He will spend one week in Rio, giving four recitals during that period. Following a concert in Montevideo, Mr. Heifetz will fly to Argentina, giving nine recitals in Buenos Aires, as well as concerts in Bahia Blanca, Cordoba, La Plata, Mendoza, Rosario and Santa Fe.

In June Mr. Heifetz's tour will be extended to Chile, with appearances in Santiago, Valparaiso, and Vina del Mar. After concerts in Ecuador and Peru, the violinist will fly north to Colombia, returning to Puerto Rico, and playing in Panama City. He is announced as concluding the first portion of his tour with a concert in San Jose, Costa Rica, on June 18, after which he will return to California for a brief midsummer vacation. The Latin-American journey will be resumed in late summer with recitals in Mexico.

Heifetz, circa 1939.

HEIFETZ BEGINS ANOTHER SEASON—

By William G. King

Jascha Heifetz took the menu the waiter handed him and sighed.

"I haven't had to look at one of these things since last July," he said. "When I find myself picking my meals off of cards again, I know the season has started."

His menu-less vacation—an unusually long one this year—was spent at his home in California, to which he went immediately after completing a tour of South and Central America, which he began almost six months ago. He, Mrs. Heifetz and their two children came East to their Connecticut farm only last week, and Mr. Heifetz plays his first New York recital of the year in Carnegie Hall next Wednesday night.

He's prepared an extraordinarily interesting program for that occasion, which includes two works by modern Americans. One of them is Robert Russell Bennett's "Hexapoda, Five Studies in Jitteroptera." Thus, the man whom many consider the greatest violinist of the day will treat his admirers to performances of "Gut-Bucket Gus," "Jane Shakes Her Hair," "Betty Closes Her Eyes," "Jim Jives" and "Till Dawn Sunday." That doesn't mean, however, that the Heifetz standards have been suddenly lowered in an effort to capture the swing-tavern trade. He considers Mr. Bennett's new work exceptionally good music, despite the somewhat alarming sub-titles affixed to its five sections.

"I hope Mr. Bennett will write many other things for the violin," he said. "I think he's one of the most interesting of our composers."

The other new work on Wednesday's program is his own violin arrangement of the first and second of George Gershwin's Three Preludes for Piano.

Mr. Heifetz, by the way, was considerably amused by a certain embattled union official's recent statement that as far as the union was concerned, there is no difference between Heifetz and a fiddler in a tavern.

"That gentleman," he said, "paid me one of the highest concert fees I ever received."

Heifetz, in recent years, has become more and more interested in contemporary composers, and has brought a number of new works of major importance to public attention. (He's playing the Concerto composed for him by the very gifted William Walton five times this season, and next year he expects to introduce another work in that form which he has commissioned from Mario Castelnuovo-Tedesco). But even a Heifetz can't always play just what he chooses to play.

"We artists are hired to perform," he explained, "and those who hire us frequently engage us to play specific works. That sometimes makes it difficult to present new things. Take the radio, for example. Sponsors of

commercial programs, who naturally want to attract as many listeners as possible, aren't eager to experiment. And they're still afraid to let an artist play a 'big' work over the air. They'll pay you a large fee, and then insist that you play only short numbers. Even to persuade them to let you perform a single movement from a concerto, which might take nine or ten minutes, is difficult. You understand, of course, that I'm talking only of commercial programs, which are, I have discovered, ruled by the gentlemen who spend their time studying charts and statistics which supposedly tell them exactly what the public wants. I'm convinced that these gentlemen are wrong. The people who listen to the radio for good music want more than the bits and pieces they usually get on the big commercial broadcasts."

In Buenos Aires this summer Heifetz was engaged to play on a radio program sponsored by a business firm for advertising purposes. He was permitted to treat his listeners to an entire concerto and a number of shorter works.

"I felt that I was really giving those people what they wanted to hear from me," he said. "I wish that sort of program could be presented here— if only as an experiment. I think it might change the sponsors' ideas of what the radio public prefers to hear from a musical artist."

Although Mr. Heifetz probably never saw a "listener-response" chart in his life, he nevertheless, on his record, is entitled to rank as an authority on what interests and attracts music patrons. He's been going around the world for a good many years now, playing before crowds who pay cash to hear him. They wouldn't continue to do so if he didn't know what they want and give it to them.

OCTOBER 31, 1940
CARNEGIE HALL

JASCHA HEIFETZ HEARD IN RECITAL
Mozart's Sonata Achieves the High Point of Program at Carnegie Hall
EMANUEL BAY IS AT PIANO
Richard Strauss's Violin and Piano Sonata is Presented
With Splendor of Tone

By Olin Downes

One could not with impunity state that Jascha Heifetz had never made a greater display of his sovereign qualities as virtuoso and interpreter than he made at his recital last night in Carnegie Hall. The statement would have to be proved by a record of attendance at all his concerts of recent seasons, including those of the good-will tour of South America which he recently made. But the present reviewer looks back over many a season and does not find in his own experience such a fascinating demonstration of a great art as Mr. Heifetz gave on this occasion.

As usual, he arranged his program, comported himself, interpreted the music without the slightest concession to the conventions of the concert platform. He has no stock pose or gesture, nor are there any such meretricious elements in his playing. A disdain of appeal to gallery, an almost disdainful mastery, are suggested, perhaps, by his reserve on the platform, but his playing is the antithesis of that. It pulses with feeling and sensibility, last night fully communicated to an immense audience which listened absorbed to every tone that came from the strings. This tone, of exquisite texture, and full of subtle gradations of color, was employed with consummate perception and the most aristocratic taste.

Extremely difficult passages, thrown off, on occasion, with exhilarating virtuosity, were never exhibitions of skill, but always pertained to the interpretive end. There were also certain legitimate places where this bravura became in itself intoxication.

With all this, the Mozart sonata, which came second on the program, was one of the most beautiful moments of the evening. It seemed for the moment that such music should never be played save by an artist of Mr. Heifetz's consummate mastery, which involved subtlest proportion, and a releasing of instrumental song that seemed to free the art from all earthly bondage. Yet here, too, was the utmost precision, the most carefully conceived nuance. The simplicity was not artificial; neither was it unconscious, or less than supreme art. And it must be admitted, with due acknowledgment of the musicianly and responsive piano playing of Emanuel Bay, that by the side of the violin, or that violin, the piano appeared somewhat pedestrian.

Strauss Work Follows

The contrast between this music and that of Richard Strauss's violin and piano sonata which followed was very striking, and a good stroke of program making. The Strauss sonata is certainly music of coarser fiber than that of Mozart. It is music, nevertheless, of a noble line, and a symphonic manner. It could well be called "sonata eroica," and it is elaborate and dramatic in development. Of this sonata Mr. Heifetz has long been a champion, and here he played less with delicacy than splendor of tone and a grand stride, with an opulent style and a dramatic accent.

His program was very substantial, but sustained its fascination to the very end. After Strauss came a welcome revival in the form of the Spohr "Gesangscen," and this was interpretation of another sort; the classic periods sustained with such dignity and manner, the intrepid playing of the bravura passages of double stops, octaves, and other devices, delivered with an aplomb which brought down the house, was perfectly in accordance with the nature of the music.

The final groups comprised two Heifetz transcriptions of Piano Preludes of George Gershwin, the last of these a most felicitous and original treatment, and five short violin and piano pieces by Robert Russell Bennett called "Hexapoda," or "Studies in Jitteroptera." The composer explains: " 'Hexapoda' is merely one of the accepted names of insects or bugs. The subtitle narrows it down to that comparatively recent hybrid, 'Jitterbug.' " The pieces, highly modern in texture and resourceful in device, are very amusing and make an uncommonly piquant effect. Two of these and the second of the Gershwin transcriptions had to be repeated. But not all violinists should attempt all of them!

OCTOBER 31, 1940

SILK-UNDERWEAR MUSIC

By Virgil Thomson

JASCHA HEIFETZ, violinist; recital last night at Carnegie Hall, with Emmanuel Bay as accompanist.

Sonatensatz . . . . .Brahms
Sonata No. 10 (K. 378) . . . . .Mozart
Sonata . . . . .Strauss
Concerto No. 8 (Gesangscene) . . . . .Spohr
Two Preludes . . . . .Gershwin
Hexapoda (*Five Studies in Jitteroptera*) . . . . .Bennett
    1. "Gut-Bucket Gus"
    2. "Jane Shakes Her Hair"
    3. "Betty and Harold Close Their Eyes"
    4. "Jim Jives"
    5. ". . . Till Dawn Sunday"

ROBERT RUSSELL BENNETT'S musical sketches of the jitterbug world are pretty music. Also they are evocative of swing music without being themselves swing music or any imitation of swing music. They manage with skill and integrity to use swing formulas as a decor for the musical depiction of those nerve reflexes and soul states that swing-lovers commonly manifest when exposed to swing music. They are, in addition, expertly written for the violin. They come off, as the phrase has it, like a million dollars.

Mr. Heifetz's whole concert rather reminded one of large sums of money like that. If ever I heard luxury expressed in music it was there. His famous silken tone, his equally famous double-stops, his well-known way of hitting the true pitch squarely in the middle, his justly remunerated mastery of the musical marshmallow, were like so many cushions of damask and down to the musical ear.

He is like Sarah Bernhardt, with her famous "small voice of purest gold" and her mastery of the wow-technique. First-class plays got in her way; she seldom appeared in one after thirty. Heifetz is at his best in short encore pieces (the Bennetts are beautifully that) and in lengthy chestnuts like Spohr's *Gesangscene* (an old-time war-horse for violinists), where every device of recitative style, of melodic phrase turning, and of brilliant passage work is laid out, like the best evening clothes and the best jewelry, for Monsieur to put his elegant person into. No destination, no musical or emotional significance, is implied.

The Strauss Sonata, a work of the author's early manhood, lacks none of that composer's characteristic style. The themes could only be his (albeit one was practically straight out of *Carmen*), bombastic, second-rate (I except the one that starts the last movement, which is bombastic and first-rate), inflated, expressing nothing but the composer's fantastic facility, his jubilant gusto at writing music. Mr. Heifetz's execution of this was almost embarrassingly refined.

Of his Mozart, the less said the better. It is of the school that makes a diminuendo on every feminine phrase-ending, that never plays any phrase through with the same weight, that thinks Mozart's whole aim was to charm, that tries so hard to make out of the greatest musician the world has ever known (those are Joseph Haydn's words) something between a sentimental Pierot and a Dresden china clock that his music ends by sounding affected, frivolous, and picayune. If that is Mozart, I'll buy a hat and eat it.

I realize that my liking or not liking what Mr. Heifetz plays and how he plays it is a matter of no import to the stellar spaces in which he moves. But it happens that I did go to the concert last night and that I did observe pretty carefully his virtuosity. It was admirable and occasionally very, very beautiful. The fellow can fiddle. But he sacrifices everything to polish. He does it knowingly. He is justly admired and handsomely paid for it. To ask anything else of him is like asking tenderness of the ocelot.

Four-starred super-luxury hotels are a legitimate commerce. The fact remains, however, that there is about their machine-tooled finish and empty elegance something more than just a trifle vulgar.

FEBRUARY 6, 1941
CARNEGIE HALL

RODZINSKI DIRECTS CLEVELAND GROUP
Symphony Orchestra Opens Concert in Carnegie Hall With Piston Work
HEIFETZ IS THE SOLOIST
Violinist Presents Concerto by William Walton
Before Enthusiastic Audience

By Olin Downes

The Cleveland Symphony Orchestra, Artur Rodzinski, conductor, was the second symphonic visitor in the space of two consecutive days to this city, performing last night in Carnegie Hall. The program for the major part offered material of fresh interest; the familiar item was the Strauss "Heldenleben."

The concert opened with a composition by an American, one of the most accomplished of our native composers of today. He was Walter Piston of the music department of Harvard University, who has some time since proved his right to be heard upon symphonic programs, and who was called to the platform to acknowledge long and sincere applause of a work novel to audiences of this city.

Arranged From Ballet

This is a suite arranged for concert purposes from Mr. Piston's ballet, "The Incredible Flutist," which, composed in collaboration with the American dancer, Hans Wiener, has been performed in several cities since its premiere at the Boston "Pop" concert in Symphony Hall of May 30, 1939. It is music in the lighter vein, done with a sure hand. It has not the structural or technical substance of other scores of Mr. Piston, and it obviously requires the stage spectacle for its complete effect. But instrumentation is colorful and unerring, as also is the employment of various rhythmical devices, accentuations and figure developments required by the dance. There is a sensuousness of phrase in which Mr. Piston has not indulged in any other score heard by this writer, and certainly not in his concerti and other orchestral movements written in modern counterpoint after classic models. The score heard last night is unblushingly and directly for the stage, and it is astonishing to see how immediately and successfully the composer adapts himself to its requirements.

The other novelty came with the first New York hearing of William Walton's violin concerto, written for Jascha Heifetz and performed magnificently by him on this occasion. This writer does not propose to utter an ex-cathedra verdict upon a work by one of the most skillful and accomplished of the younger English composers of this period. But, at a first hearing, it is clear that the form is supplely handed and craftily integrated. The idiom, naturally, is contemporaneous; the harmonic would have been startling twenty-five years ago, but is now an accepted procedure, and one that fits well with the glittering instrumentation.

Treatment is Symphonic

There is a virtuoso part for the violinist, but the treatment is unfailingly symphonic. The first movement is richest and broadest. The scherzo utilizes and develops irregular rhythms. It has well defined divisions with a simple and pleasing melodic phrase for the horn in the trio. The finale is at least titillating and a dramatic and somewhat military conclusion goes slap over the footlights.

To what extent Mr. Heifetz's playing, aside from the value of the composition, was responsible for the undisguised pleasure of the audience need not to be opined here. One would like, not only to hear the concerto again, but to estimate it in the hands of a violinist of less than Mr. Heifetz's mastery, which, long phenomenal, seems to grow with the years, and by no means to be confined to exciting virtuosity. He grows as an interpreter, in the warmth of his sentiment, his scrupulousness in the treatment of detail and indeed in every aspect of his art. A lesser concerto would have flourished if presented as this one was by him last night.

"Heldenleben" Played

The big orchestral work was the "Heldenleben." It is disgustingly well-made music. When it is all over, and even while it is sounding, the listener is aware of its hopeless banality, and stuffy elaborateness, and strutting self-satisfaction. But it has yet to miss fire with an audience, even though Mr. Rodzinski has played it better than he did on this occasion, with a nobler line and finer balance and without the precipitate tempi and the nervous exaggerations that were apparent last night.

The orchestra, which made a very good impression in the previous season here, sounded even better than before. Possibly due to some slight reinforcements, a dryness of string quality, previously noticed, was gratefully conspicuous by absence.

The players responded instantaneously to the conductor's slightest wish, and, regardless of personal estimates of his interpretations, and the manner in which they seem to vary from time to time, Mr. Rodzinski continues to develop as one of the most authoritative and gifted leaders of his generation. He is constantly more posed, more economical of effort and certain of result. He does what he pleases with an orchestra, and he has the instinct and temperament of a born leader. He, as well as the composer and soloist of the evening, was vociferously applauded.

FEBRUARY 6, 1941
CARNEGIE HALL

CLEVELAND ORCHESTRA IN CONCERT
By Louis Biancolli

With a pageant of national orchestras passing through New York, it was the Cleveland Orchestra's turn for a rendezvous in Carnegie Hall last night. The out-of-towners were rousingly greeted.

Artur Rodzinski conducted, and one of the visiting body's tokens of respect was a local premiere of the British William Walton's violin concerto, Jascha Heifetz playing the solo portions. Another was Walter Piston's ballet suite, "The Incredible Flutist," also new to this city.

Mr. Heifetz was soloist last year when Mr. Rodzinski and his men offered the Walton concerto as a world premiere on one of their home programs. The work was a marked success then, and last night's audience also took to it avidly.

391

Of course Mr. Heifetz was just the man to present its credentials. He had worked with Walton on solo passages and the Heifetz fingerprints are identifiable without close scrutiny. Besides, Mr. Heifetz's suave facility can make anything sound tops.

The Walton concerto stands solidly on its own feet, however. The appeal is strong, whether as melody, dramatic sequence, or sheer force of ideas. The violin has wide scope to sing out in warm cantilena.

Novel episodes crop up steadily in the accompaniment. The orchestration is crisp, pungent, kinetic, pulsing with life of its own—never mere padding for solo acrobatics. The whole makes a tautly woven fabric of close threading.

Mr. Heifetz soared breathtakingly through tricky finger-work. Muted passages were hushed dreams. It might have surprised Walton himself to find legato stretches taking on such angelic luster. Not that Mr. Heifetz made gold of dross, as already pointed out.

Mr. Rodzinski led the work con amore, and the orchestra caught the spirit and gave every tiny detail its place in the symphonic sun.

Mr. Piston's suite was born and belongs in a ballet milier, though it offers 14 minutes of frank orchestral fun on a concert program. Tangos, waltzes, sicilianos, and polkas unwind in haphazard sequence.

FEBRUARY 6, 1941
CARNEGIE HALL

BLENDED CORN

By Virgil Thomson

CLEVELAND ORCHESTRA, Artur Rodzinski, conductor, concert last night at Carnegie Hall, with Jascha Heifetz, violinist, as soloist, in the following program:

Suite from ballet, "The Incredible Flutist" . . . . Walter Piston
First time in New York
Tone Poem, "Ein Heldenleben," . . . . Richard Strauss
Concerto for violin and orchestra . . . . William Walton
First time in New York

Mr. Rodzinski is a fine musician and a fine conductor. His Cleveland Orchestra is a fine bunch of musicians that play beautifully together. They also play beautifully as soloists. Mr. Josef Fuchs's violin work in Strauss's "Ein Heldenleben" was something more than merely concert-masterish; it was virtuoso-beautiful in tone, in pitch and in phrasing. Mr. Maurice Sharp's flute was lovely indeed in both the Piston and the Walton works. And Mr. Rudolf Puletz, Jr., the first horn, merited in every way the applause he shared with Mr. Fuchs for their work in the Strauss tone-poem.

Joseph Fuchs, a magnificent musician, became a very good teacher. He received rave notices for his solo work while concertmaster of the Cleveland Orchestra. Circa 1941.

393

It is a pleasant thing to hear new pieces, any kind of new pieces. One is grateful to Mr. Rodzinski for bringing to us Walter Piston's "Incredible Flutist" and William Walton's Violin Concerto, both of them works that have been heard repeatedly in the provincial centers but never before here. This reviewer, although extremely interested to make auditory acquaintance of these works (I have known the Piston score for some time), did not share the audience's enthusiasm about them. Perhaps the audience was not so enthusiastic about the compositions as its applause seemed to indicate. Because an audience will applaud any composer who takes his bow as willingly as Mr. Piston does. And the Walton applause may well have been intended for Mr. Heifetz, who has a devoted following here and who performed the concerto with his usual technical brilliance and rather special elegance of style.

To this listener all three of the pieces last night sounded like corn. The Strauss "Heldenleben" (a musician I know insists on calling it "Mein Kampf") is neither news to music lovers nor meat for critics. It is a rip-snorting hubbub number not without a certain humanity. For all its second rateness as music, it is the livest and the liveliest of the works heard last night. It is honest bathos and friendly fun. One cannot really dislike it. It is pretty corny music, all the same.

Mr. Piston's "Flutist" suite is Harvard corn, synthetic, eclectic, violent. Its libretto (as that was recounted in the program notes) is episodic and trifling. Its circus march, sentimental tango and pseudo-Spanish waltz are virtually indistinguishable from the real second-rate thing they are supposed to evoke. The work has melodic and orchestral facility; but it has the low intellectual tone of work that is "written down," as the phrase goes, to an audience presumably insensitive to style in music and only out for an easy good time.

The Walton Violin Concerto is better than that, but it is not in any sense precise or original music. It is elegant enough and very smooth. Its material is inoffensive but extremely vague. Its violin writing is glittery. Its texture is continuous. The whole surface of it is dainty and luxurious. There is very little substance beneath. If Elgar's music could be described, as it once was, as "holy water in a German beer barrel," Walton's might well be summed up as Strauss and soda. There is more than that in it; there is a lump or two of Sibelius and a slight zest of Stravinski, but mostly it is Straussian "effect" music watered down and sparkled up with French Perrier.

There is every reason, as I said before, to thank Mr. Rodzinski for letting us hear these works. There is, I am afraid, only too good a reason why we haven't heard them before. There is reason to regret, however, that none of them gave this whole string body a chance to show the quality of its playing as that is only brought out by first rate music. There is reason also to wonder if that is the kind of music Mr. Rodzinski likes. If so, we regret it. If that is the kind of music he thinks we like, we regret even more his underestimation of our metropolitan taste.

394

Heifetz is completely unpredictable. While he is certainly the most serious of violinists and often tries to exaggerate his seriousness with poses like the one above, the photo on the following page is anything but serious. . . though Heifetz deadpans it! September 19, 1941.

HIGH-POWERED MUSIC

By Virgil Thomson

PHILHARMONIC-SYMPHONY ORCHESTRA, Dimitri Mitropoulos, guest conductor, 3,696th concert last night at Carnegie Hall with Jascha Heifetz, violinist, as soloist in the following program:

Overture to "The Merchant of Venice" . . . . Castelnuovo-Tedesco
Sinfonia Biblica . . . . Nicholas Nabokoff
First Performance
Violin Concerto in D Major . . . . Beethoven
Jascha Heifetz, Violinist

Mr. Mitropoulos continues to give fine concerts and to please. The rejuvenated Philharmonic sounds every inch an orchestra, smooth-driving, responsive and powerful. The programs are a change too. One has the feeling that the Philharmonic is going places these days and that it is a pleasure to be along.

Last night we went to Venice under Florentine chaperonage. Signor Castelnuovo-Tedesco's "Merchant" has intentions of picturesqueness and of power, in reality very little of either. It was nice hearing it, though.

We also visited the Holy Land under Russian guidance. Mr. Nabokoff's Sinfonia Biblica is a serious work of more than common competence. Its intentions are a trifle more eloquent, however, than its effect. It has dignity and a sound academic tone, and its orchestration is definitely more than skin deep. Short passages were even expressive, such as the opening of the "Fear" movement; and the end of the "Hosannah" was stylish. The work is worthy enough. Orchestrally, it is interesting without being especially difficult either to understand or to play. I should not be surprised if it became for a season or two a useful repertory piece for the provincial orchestras.

The evening closed with a triumphal trio consisting of Mr. Mitropoulos, Mr. Heifetz and Beethoven. All were at their best. There is no finer, sweeter Beethoven than the Beethoven of the Violin Concerto. There are few finer renditions of this lovely work than Mr. Heifetz's, though personally I prefer Kreisler's broader conception. And Mr. Mitropoulos led the accompanying orchestra with such solid rhythm and such well equilibrated mass effects that the accompaniment sounded like something as important as the solo. The solo was suave and thin and brilliant; the orchestra weighty and fearless. They set each other off, therefore, in the most effective way imaginable. At the same time the blending of the violin sonorities with those of the wind instruments in quiet passages was accomplished with mutual courtesy and considerable refinement.

Mr. Mitropoulos, in spite of his orchestral mastery and of his highly intelligent analysis of musical works, does not produce a result that is deeply satisfying musically to this listener. But he does expose a score with rare clarity, and he does keep the music moving along. Everything is in place and everything functions as it should. The chief lack in his performances is of spontaneous song. His case is not unlike that of Mr. Heifetz, in fact. Nothing is wrong; all is of the highest excellence; there is finish and everywhere the soundest workmanship. But I cannot imagine what would happen if the Holy Ghost should whisper something unforeseen into the ear of either of them right there on the platform in front of all those people. I fancy the Philharmonic boys themselves, used as they are to every sort of guest conductor, would be the least surprised and the readiest to play ball with inspiration in such an emergency.

Heifetz gave freely of his services and time to help the war effort. In 1943 Heifetz visited Navy hospitals to play for the wounded sailors.

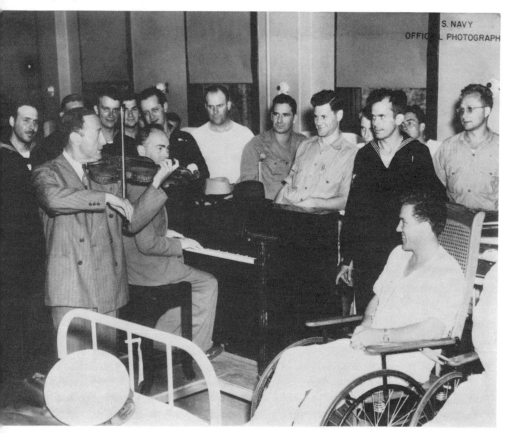

FEBRUARY 8, 1942

VIOLINIST VISITS AN ARMY CAMP

By PFC M.H. Williams
Camp Roberts, Calif.

The musical diet of the men in the Army camps has begun to include some real music. Jascha Heifetz is one of the artists who provide it. He began at this Pacific Coast station, and he will visit many posts before the year ends, playing a seventy-five minute concert sponsored by the U.S.O.

Mr. Heifetz and the soldiers were revelations to each other. An audience of men who come from Western ranges and mines, from small town offices and schools, is likely to be disconcerting to a serious violinist. Mr. Heifetz, by his own admission, was "scared stiff" before the concert.

When it ended, only after the wildly cheering men had consented to let him depart with four encores, he was beaming with delight. It is doubtful that Heifetz has ever been accorded a reception of such tremendous whistles and cheers as these soldiers gave him.

Possibly in the belief that they were more popular, the entertainments here in the past have been of a pretty-chorus plus wisecracking-comedian nature.

Some one evidently guessed wrong. For when Mr. Heifetz walked out on the stage the post theatre was jammed. One thousand men sat. Many others were standing. Some had been waiting on line outside for two hours. And many men were turned away by the military police at the door.

Mr. Heifetz began with a mild joke that set the mood. "The first number will be a prelude by Bach," he said. "Don't be scared. Besides, I've made up my mind to play it whether you like it or not."

They liked it tremendously. Mr. Heifetz announced his selections, since there were no printed programs. It turned out to be an admirable oversight, for he amused the audience many times with his quiet humor. Wieniawski's concerto, he said, would be in three parts, "the second followed by the third."

"The Star-Spangled Banner," a melody by Tchaikovsky, de Falla's "Spanish Dance," Mendelssohn's "On Wings of Song" and "The Gypsy Air" of Sarasate made up the program.

The encores belonged to the audience, Mr. Heifetz declared. He asked for requests, and was deluged. The greatest amount of noise was in behalf of "Hora Staccata," "Ave Maria," "The Flight of the Bumble Bee" and Godowsky's "Old Vienna."

The experiment—for experiment it was—turned out successfully. Mr. Heifetz was well pleased with his soldier audience, and the soldiers hungered for his music. There may be bigger audiences in this huge camp when other artists appear, as the U.S.O. has promised they will. Mr. Heifetz made a deep impression and the word will get around.

'FIDELIO' FEATURED BY PHILHARMONIC
Eugene Goossens Conducts Overture by Beethoven
at Carnegie Hall Concert
JASCHA HEIFETZ SOLOIST
'Lincoln Symphony' by Jaromir Weinberger is Presented
For First Time Here

By Olin Downes

The star performance of the concert given by Eugene Goossens, guest conductor, and the New York Philharmonic-Symphony Orchestra last night in Carnegie Hall was Mr. Goossens's opening interpretation of the Beethoven "Fidelio" Overture, which he directed with admirable spirit and understanding and finely adjusted orchestral tone.

But this was to the credit of the remaining part of the program, which included the recently completed "Lincoln Symphony" of Jaromir Weinberger, heard for the first time in New York on a Lincoln anniversary, and the appearance of Jascha Heifetz as the soloist in the Brahms violin concerto.

Mr. Heifetz did not seem to be in the vein. He is a great violinist and human. Mr. Weinberger was more deliberate when, in the name of Lincoln, he organized a poor and meretricious symphony.

Were we a composer, intent upon writing a symphony on such a theme, we would be inclined to wait rather apprehensively, to be sure that we had produced some great music, before giving an indicative title to the act of homage. Perhaps Mr. Weinberger did so believe, but it is difficult to think so. For the symphony is a collection of unblushing platitudes and old tricks of orchestration, and a junk pile of thematic ideas that other composers, from Beethoven to Bruckner and Mahler, from Brahms to Dvorak and Richard Strauss, had left carelessly lying about when Mr. Weinberger came along with his hopper.

For good measure, the Negro spiritual "Deep River" is worked into the symphony, with connotations intended to be obvious while a short phrase, posted as a Lincoln theme, is in one form or another frequently present. It could be said that the most plausibly mellifluous part of the composition is its final movement, in which principal themes are newly developed and combined. But this section rings no truer than the rest of it. The reputation of the gifted composer of "Schwanda" will not gain by this officious symphony.

There was long current a legend that Mr. Heifetz was a kind of diabolically perfect and self-contained player whose emotional temperature changed no more than the well-nigh infallible correctness of his intonation. As a matter of fact, we have heard few performers in late years of such variability, where interpretation, if not technique, was concerned.

From personal experience, we had not heard Mr. Heifetz play the Brahms concerto as badly as he did last night. Even technically, the performance was far from smooth, and there were moments when intonation was more than suspect. But this was not the principal matter. His performance was not poised. The tempo in the first movement particularly, but also in other places, were hurried, and tone forced. We preferred Mr. Goossens followed suit as Mr. Heifetz went along. Conceding that Mr. Heifetz was not completely himself in this performance, we submit that Brahms is not himself when he is treated that way.

Heifetz presents Mayor Fiorello LaGuardia with his aluminum violin to be turned into scrap for the war effort. The Mayor said he would auction off the fiddle and buy aluminum with the money! July 28, 1941.

GOOSSENS LEADS AS HEIFETZ PLAYS
Weinberger Symphony Introduced

It seemed in prospect that Eugene Goossens was either courting Providence or tempting fate with the program he arranged for his first appearance with the Philharmonic-Symphony Orchestra in Carnegie Hall last night. For he exposed his reappearance, after many seasons' absence, to the challenge of a new work by Jaromir Weinberger and Jascha Heifetz's playing of the Brahms violin concerto. The evening disclosed, however, that Weinberger's "Lincoln" symphony was incapable of overshadowing anything higher than a molehill, and that Mr. Heifetz was not nearly at his best.

In true Weinbergeresque manner, the composer turned loose a whole assembly line of musical mechanics, Biblical and poetic quotations, recurring themes, and even "spirituals" in his effort to convey the stature, the humor, the tragedy of Lincoln. But if ever a composer could be taken to account for lacking "inspiration," Weinberger was in this instance culpable. That the piece sounded well, no one can deny; that it was ingeniously supplied with a fugal scherzo, a "Marcia Funebre," designed as a passacaglia, and a final rondo employing "Deep River" was equally plain. But any real contact with the great and simple man in whose honor it was set down simply did not emerge from the score.

The Heifetz performance of Brahms was a curious and interesting affair, if only from a standpoint of the violinist and his traditionally unassailable art. To write off the unsettled tempi, the roughness of much of the tone, the intonational vagaries of the first and last movements as simply the products of an off-night would be easy and charitable. But that could scarcely be balanced with the transcendent beauty of every note in the adagio. To these ears (and eyes) it seemed that elsewhere Mr. Heifetz applied himself to his instrument with more physical force than at any time in the past; and with a heavier, tighter bow, perhaps in the desire to prove himself capable of massive tonal effects. But it is elementary that quality of sound is a more affecting thing than quantity. Frequently last night Mr. Heifetz had neither, when main strength yielded only harsh sound.

The impression that Mr. Goossens made was not much more than nebulous, for his application to the symphony was not fruitful, his part of the concerto unquestionably affected by the facts listed above. The performance of Beethoven's "Fidelio" overture which opened the evening was admirably spirited and thoroughly musical, but hardly matter for superlatives. The big audience received him warmly.

Primrose (on the right) and Heifetz in the middle, after a rehearsal in 1941.

SCHMALTZ FOR ART'S SAKE
Mr. Heifetz and a Hoary Legend

By John Briggs

It would seem that the "poker-face" legend is pursuing Mr. Heifetz as hard as ever. At his Carnegie Hall concert last week your reviewer, ever a vigilant eavesdropper, heard the same old cliches, "all head and no heart," "beautiful but cold," etc., etc. I am sorry to have to add that a couple of the reviews were only lukewarm, though conceding that Mr. Heifetz has no equal for beauty of tone, brilliant technical virtuosity and elegance of style. I confess I do not see what more you could wish, except possibly a juggling act.

I cannot believe that anyone who plays as Mr. Heifetz does is a cold, precise musical automaton. Isn't it possible that the exact opposite is true, and that Mr. Heifetz is such a fine and sincere artist that he scorns the cheap theatrics of so-called "showmanship"? Maybe what some people miss in his playing is a dose of schmaltz. We are all familiar with the swaying gypsy-fiddler violinist, the pianist whose hands linger interminably on the keys in absurd "verklingend" effects, the vocalist who interprets a song chiefly by facial expression. Generally we spot such stuff for the desperate banality it is, but sometimes even the watchdogs of the press are taken in and write about "eloquent and moving performance," "sweep and grandeur of the interpretation," and so on. We are confusing a visual and an aural impression. What we are mistaking for great art is, in such a case, only malarkey.

Our concert halls spawn amazing mannerisms and affectations. Their possessors are great not because of, but in spite of, such harlequinades, which must be offensive to all persons of refined taste. I often wonder what a layman thinks when he is exposed to a conductor of the epileptic school. His first impulse must be to laugh, but as he sees the musicians playing away without cracking a smile, and the audience looking on with expressions of solemn interest, no doubt he controls himself and soon takes it as much for granted as everyone else does.

An otherwise excellent pianist has a habit of phrasing by leaping partly off the piano bench. One night I kept a record of his "Emperor" concerto (I deemed it no more than fair to ignore his Luftpausen, tallying only when light showed between the chair and the seat of his pants). He was clocked as follows: opening, 11; slow movement, 5; finale, 17. I wish someone would tip him off that indulging this habit is digging a finger in the ribs of the unrighteous, for there is the spoiling of a superb artist in him.

A cellist once kept me spellbound throughout his recital by lifting the heel of his right foot for every crescendo, swerving body and instrument to the left and subsiding again at the decrescendo. One famous viola

Heifetz with 18 year old Seymour Lipkin, his accompanist, returning from Europe aboard an Army plane after completing his third overseas tour for USO Campshows. June 29, 1945.

player always used to stand with his right foot pointing offstage, his left advanced and bent at the knee, exactly like an old-time pugilist. Any number of string virtuosi find it helpful to bend forward at the waist when they come to an especially difficult passage.

In the way of mannerisms singers are the worst offenders of all. In the studio many of them acquire obscure but helpful gestures which provide a sort of kinaesthetic stimulus. One soprano was repeatedly told by her master to "draw out the tone," and has not yet conquered the habit of doing just that, with a literal gesture like disgorging yards of spaghetti.

Anyone who has dabbled in public performance knows that a mannerism is the easiest thing in the world to acquire, and the hardest to get rid of. Only the most relentless self-criticism and the partisan vigilance of friends can insure you a clean bill of health in this department. I shudder to think of the many hours of grinding, back-breaking drudgery that must have gone to make the polished perfection of Mr. Heifetz's playing; but I should think an equal effort of will must have been required to arrive at the elegance of his platform bearing, which every young artist, fiddler or otherwise, ought to take as a model of decorum. Yet for all his pains Mr. Heifetz is criticized as being "cold" and "devoid of feeling." It really is too bad.

MARCH 2, 1944
CARNEGIE HALL

HEIFETZ IN RECITAL
Violinist Plays Bruch Concerto at Carnegie Hall

By Paul Bowles

Jascha Heifetz played last night at Carnegie Hall on a platform crowded with members of the armed forces, male and female.

For some reason which it was not possible to determine, in the first half of his program, comprising the classical works, his tone was small to the point of being occasionally inaudible. The piano was partially open. During the latter portion of the evening one would have said he was using a different instrument, which may indeed have been the case. At the playing of the first phrase of the Bruch Concerto it was immediately obvious that a change had been effected; the tone was full and rich and the performance had little in common sonorously with what had gone on before. To help matters, the piano's lid had been lowered, so that a balance was found more easily.

There is a remarkable quality in Mr. Heifetz's treatment of practically all lengthy or slow legato passages. These mark his most expressive playing, but one feels that the artist means them to be expressive of unhappiness, as if intensity of feeling could be interpreted on the violin only by means of sobs and wails. This conception is not peculiar to Mr. Hei-

406

fetz, but it is a bit surprising to find it in a man who can give such a fine reading of a work like the Bach Sonata, whose fugue and final movement were played with a rare combination of fire and technical smoothness. Perhaps the reluctance with which one accepts his quasi-lachrymose style of rendering the more emotional sections of the works he plays is a part of one's distaste for the idea of a great artist's playing down, even a little, to the public.

From left to right: Heifetz, Rubinstein, Primrose, unidentified gentleman, and Feuermann. Circa 1941.

HEIFETZ IS HEARD AT CARNEGIE HALL
Plays Beethoven Concerto—Philharmonic Also Offers Rachmaninoff Symphony

By Olin Downes

There were great performances of familiar music at the concert of the Philharmonic-Symphony Orchestra under Dr. Rodzinski's direction last night in Carnegie Hall, and there was one short work which constituted a novelty for these programs. This was Douglas Moore's "In Memoriam," a brief composition inspired by the war, and originally commissioned, we believe, by the League of Composers. It is in greater part a dirge for the young and "the middle section is a soliloquy in which youth is imagined as speaking with longing for familiar things now lost." The form of the work is ABA.

The symphony of the evening was the one in E minor of Sergei Rachmaninoff, music of which Dr. Rodzinski gave a superlative performance. The Second Symphony is harmonically old-fashioned. It is highly emotional, often sentimental and in many places reminiscent of Tchaikovsky. At the same time it is one of the most sincere and personal of the symphonies of the modern repertory. Its workmanship is distinguished by the composer's wonderful capacity for the organic development of a few simple and central ideas. The music has the Slavic warmth, lyricism and species of fatalistic pomp which is so characteristic of Rachmaninoff's middle period.

Then there is the spaciousness as well as the superbly integrated form of this Russian symphony. It is a work in which a greatly gifted composer speaks, with contagious sincerity and inspiration that is unquestionable. And it is noteworthy that while a whole generation of music criticism which has come and gone apprises us years ago of the plausible superficiality of Rachmaninoff, his symphony remains secure in the repertory and never fails to impress the public. In this there is perhaps matter for consideration.

Mr. Rodzinski made the most of the color and drama of the score. He may or may not admire it. We do not know. One would have thought from the reading that the work was his favorite masterpiece, which is the effect that a composition may have when it is greatly interpreted.

For many the climax of the concert was Jascha Heifetz playing the Beethoven concerto. This was, in fact, one of Mr. Heifetz' memorable performances, and this despite some curious incidental features which are not like him, and could well condition praise of his achievement. We mean his tendency to a tempo slightly too fast, and a further disposition, not easily explainable, to rush ahead, faster than the established tempo, in certain places.

408

It would not be easy to explain this disposition on the part of such a poised master of his instrument and a musician of the aristocratic style which is the antithesis of disproportion or exaggeration. Let us say then, that Mr. Heifetz, a human being as well as an epochal virtuoso, played with an excitement which, if it resulted in an occasional unsatisfactory detail, had the compensatory qualities that matched in quality of tone and nobility of feeling, Beethoven's music. He was apparently in rare form, and his playing of Auer's imposing cadenza in the first movement was almost orchestral in itself, and sounded as a part of the symphonic conception. The audience applauded Mr. Heifetz rapturously. Even from him, one does not often hear such playing.

JANUARY 23, 1947
CARNEGIE HALL

HEIFETZ RECITAL
Violinist Plays Concerto by Conus at Carnegie Hall

Jascha Heifetz's violin playing was gratifying in his recital last night at Carnegie Hall. What he played provided rather less gratification; the program had its pleasing elements and, except for the group designated as "old favorites" at the close, avoided particularly familiar compositions, but, with Julius Conus's concerto and George Lvovitch Catoire's "Poeme," or second sonata, as its most extensive items, it lacked major works of the first order. The Conus concerto, which is played here from time to time, but not often, gave an impression of diluted tunefulness; it served its purpose as a vehicle for delectable tones and technical brilliance, but its romanticism is faded and significance of ideas and contrasts of mood are lacking.

The "Poeme" by the Russian composer Catoire (1861-1926) suggested the influence of Cesar Franck; it seemed to be well made music with a pervasive melodiousness, but it did not give a sense of independent individuality. The violin parts are of equal importance; the latter was played spiritedly and, at times, too vigorously by Emanuel Bay. Mario Castelnuovo-Tedesco's likeable "The Lark," which opened the program, was composed for Mr. Heifetz sixteen years ago. Fritz Kreisler was represented by his Recitativo and Scherzo for violin alone.

With a few exceptions, Mr. Heifetz's playing observed the high tonal and technical standards which are associated with this notable artist; its characteristics have been mentioned too often to need recapitulation. The tone, in its texture and color, delighted the ear; and his technique gave its customary sense of complete mastery, ease and brilliance. What was missing was music that could give an artist a full opportunity to exhibit his powers of expressive interpretation. A capacity audience, including a large contingent on the stage, applauded enthusiastically.

Heifetz continues to edit and write music. His music was not popular because he recorded it himself and few violinists wanted to be compared to Heifetz on a direct basis! Circa 1946.

JANUARY 23, 1947
CARNEGIE HALL

HEIFETZ IN TOP FORM AT CARNEGIE

By Louis Biancolli

The man who can play rings around any other wielder of the bow packed Carnegie Hall to the doors last night. The name given on the program was Heifetz—Jascha Heifetz to you.

The prince of fiddlers no sooner touched his magic bow to the strings than the crowd, including the few hundred huddled behind him, knew the master of masters was in top form.

Actually, it mattered very little what Mr. Heifetz played. The names listed were Castelnuovo-Tedesco, Conus, Catoire, Dvorak, Kreisler, Beethoven and one or two others.

The big name last night was Heifetz, and it spelled out in slick glistening letters on every phrase of the music. In fact, there wasn't a note in the whole batch that wasn't duly signed.

Just what it was that set Jascha Heifetz apart from the season's colleagues would be hard to note down exactly. The only safe analysis would be a recording of the whole program.

For say what you want about this man's tone and technic, any worded appraisal still leaves the essence out. The same terms would as easily apply to a dozen other fiddlers of our time.

A whole school of recent violinists can reel off tone like silk or velvet, or anything suggesting superfine tone quality. And in technic they measure up pretty closely too.

One feature of Mr. Heifetz's playing was the high-flying ease—what might be called a seraphic nonchalance. Strain is utterly alien to this man's musical outlook.

In fact, at times you wonder if anything so coarse as fiber and wood ever went into the makeup of his bow and fiddle. You can't help feeling the bow and strings only touch in a figurative way.

And he has a way of making ordinary stuff sound like a top-flight masterpiece. Though it all glittered last night, a lot of it was gold only by sheer grace of his playing.

Sometimes it was hard to tell which music was better, because it all sounded equally good and equally the work of a genius. Mr. Heifetz is a great leveler—but the leveling is always upward.

Then, he was strictly the violinist, and you had the feeling he was always the violinist even offstage—that when he thought about anything else it was with a fiddler's mind.

And the thinking was always clean and orderly, as if the merest ruffle would be a faux pas and a lapse from intonation a cardinal sin.

For picking flaws in last night's playing was an idle game. Mr. Heifetz rarely gives the sour-note-spotters a run for their money. Each tone sounded like a criterion to go by.

Anybody else playing last night's program would have invited a few critical brickbats for stressing the surface appeal of most of the numbers listed.

But Jascha Heifetz is his own law—a law of high refinement—and so long as he abides by it, nobody ought to care, really, what he plays. How he plays is what counts.

Emanuel Bay was again the first-rate accompanist.

JANUARY 27, 1949
CARNEGIE HALL

JASCHA HEIFETZ
Violinist in First Appearance Here in 22 Months

By Francis D. Perkins

JASCHA HEIFETZ, violinist, recital last night in Carnegie Hall, assisting pianist, Emanuel Bay. The program:

Sonata in B minor . . . . Respighi
Sonata No. 3, in C major (Violin-alone) . . . . Bach
Il pleure dans mon coeur . . . . Debussy-Hartmann
Valses nobles et sentimentales, Nos. 6, 7 . . . . Ravel-Heifetz
Fairy Tale . . . . Medtner-Heifetz
Etude-Tableau . . . . Rachmaninoff-Heifetz
Concerto No. 5 . . . . Vieuxtemps

Jascha Heifetz, whose current tour marks the end of a year's absence from the concert stage, made his first New York public appearance in twenty-two months last night at Carnegie Hall. In an unfamiliar sonata by the late Ottorino Respighi, more familiar works of Bach and Vieuxtemps and transcriptions of shorter pieces made by Arthur Hartmann and by himself, the eminent violinist gave a performance which, as in previous seasons, was noteworthy for its technical mastery and for its ingratiating quality of tone.

The recital also told of interpretative persuasiveness in a program which included one standard masterpiece in the repertory for violin alone, a concerto whose effectiveness is greater than its intrinsic musical value and the Respighi sonata which has its eloquent measures, but is of uneven cogency. In parts of this work, at the beginning and in the finale, there seemed to be almost too much delicacy of volume and texture, but the appealing characteristics of the violinist's tone were fully in evidence

412

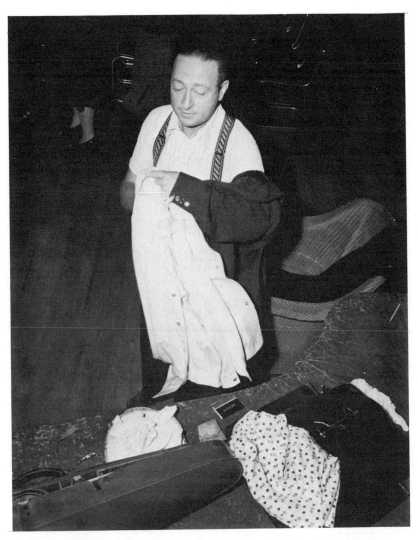

Heifetz has always been meticulous in his music, his art, his books and his clothes. If you look closely, you can even see his name is engraved on his matches!! Circa 1949.

in the sonata at large, especially in the latter half of the first movement and the andante, where the interpretation was admirable for its poetic meditativeness.

The Bach sonata in C major for violin alone received a masterly performance, apart from a touch of unwonted dryness in the chords in the fugue; the adagio and largo were presented as dignified and spacious music, and the performance of the presto was memorable for its clarity as well as for its speed. This aspect of Mr. Heifetz's technical prowess was also imposingly illustrated in the swift measures of the Vieuxtemps concerto. Its interpretation as a whole was expressive, revealing a touch of romantic sentiment, but not bordering upon sentimentality.

The transcriptions, well wrought from an instrumental point of view, revealed the silken and lucid quality of Mr. Heifetz's tone to its full extent; with fineness and nuance of shading as a characteristic rather than emphasis upon largeness of volume

Emanuel Bay furnished admirable accompaniments.

HEIFETZ GOES TRADITIONAL IN CONCERT

By Robert Bagar

Like the girl Muriel in an oldtime cigar advertisement, Jascha Heifetz is "constantly gaining new admirers," or words to that effect. The celebrated violinist played in Carnegie Hall last evening, accompanied by Emanuel Bay, as usual.

The program was traditional. No startling new works, in fact, no new ones at all. But then a recital is a recital, and custom calls for the straight familiar stuff, nothing adventurous or even, let's say, different.

Mr. Heifetz's new admirer was little Toby who, hunched between her parents, Mr. and Mrs. Harold Friedlander, sat in front of me last night. She is 7½ years old. She has been studying violin ever since last September, and, as she said, she is "about ready for Vivaldi." Toby really carried on—she applauded, shouted bravo, danced in the aisle and all with great joy and enthusiasm.

The joy and enthusiasm, incidentally, were hardly hers alone, for the large audience went totally pro-Heifetz, overlooking no chance to make noises of appreciation.

And, in a general sense, the violinist deserved all that. He is still incomparable in certain aspects of violin playing, the flawless technique, the poise, the ridiculous ease of his performing.

With all that, Mr. Heifetz fell short of communicating everything there is in the Glazounoff Concerto, for instance. Its clean surface, polished contours, wonderfully fluid line regardless, one got little of the mood of abandon, the sensuousness in the music.

The parts of the Beethoven Sonata No. 10 that we were permitted to hear fairly glistened. The rest of it might as well have been performed in a sealed vault, like some secret, prohibited music. Possibly the fact that Mr. Heifetz was using his newly acquired Strad had something to do with that and also with the occasional fuzziness of tone.

Handel, via the Sonata in E major, came through with flying colors, particularly the two slow movements. Other works included a Heifetz transcription of an Allegro from the Mozart Divertimento No. 17, in D major and pieces by Dvorak, Alan Shulmen, Rachmaninoff and Ravel.

Fritz Reiner with Heifetz in Carnegie Hall. Circa 1947.

415

JASCHA HEIFETZ

By Jerome D. Bohm

Jascha Heifetz gave his only violin recital of the season in Carnegie Hall last night. His program listed his own arrangement of the Allegro from Mozart's Divertimento No. 17 in D, Handel's E major Sonata, Glazounoff's A minor Concerto, Beethoven's Sonata No. 10 and compositions by Dvorak-Kreisler, Alan Schumann, Rachmaninoff and Ravel.

As always Mr. Heifetz's extraordinary technical attainments warranted the highest admiration. The wonderful flexibility of his bow arm, which permits him to play with the subtlest of nuances, the astounding ease with which he tosses off the most intricate passages, the perfection of his intonation under all circumstances, are attributes which have long lent his playing distinction. These qualities found their most congenial material for exploitation in the Glazounoff Concerto in which the sentimental tunes were invested with silvery sounds and performed with such patrician taste that they momentarily assumed a not innate dignity. The final movement has been accounted for more incandescently, but it too bore the imprint of Mr. Heifetz's impeccable taste.

The opening Mozart number served more in the nature of a finger-warmer than as a work to be vitally interpreted, but there was again much that was impressive in Mr. Heifetz's discourse of the Handel Sonata, especially in the Largo movement which was imbued with serenity of mood and tonal loveliness.

Whether because of the fact that he was using a Stradivarius violin which he had never before played on in public, or because his conception was planned on too small a scale to be effective in the huge spaces of Carnegie Hall, his conception of Beethoven's Tenth Sonata failed to carry conviction. This listener, who sat in the middle of the auditorium, often found himself unable to hear any sounds emanating from Mr. Heifetz's instrument, and had he not seen his bow in action would have thought that he had ceased performing. Emanuel Bay was the discreet accompanist.

Jascha Heifetz and his wife, the former Mrs. Frances Spiegelberg, after a flight to New York from San Francisco. Heifetz announced he was taking a long vacation from April, 1947 until January 1949.

ESSENTIALLY FRIVOLOUS

By Virgil Thomson

Jascha Heifetz, Carnegie Hall, Violin recital last night, assisting pianist, Emanuel Bay.

PROGRAM

Sonata . . . . Strauss
Concerto in G minor . . . . Bruch
Sonatina (No. 3) . . . . Schubert
Nocturne . . . . Sibelius
Valses nobles et sentimentales Nos. 6 & 7 . . . . Ravel-Heifetz
Nocturne . . . . Lili Boulanger
"Alt Wien" . . . . Castelnuovo-Tedesco
Notturno . . . . Szymanowski
Polonaise Brillante (D) . . . . Wieniawski

Jascha Heifetz, playing a violin recital last night in Carnegie Hall, proved himself still to be a king among the violin operators. In the opinion of many this king can do no wrong. Certainly the dictum holds if you define "right" whatever it is that a king does. But if you admit in advance that he might, just might be guilty of something, then you do not have to look very far to find something for him to be guilty of.

What Heifetz is guilty of (always supposing, just supposing that he might be less than perfect) has always been the same thing, a certain lightness of mind commonly known as bad taste. Technically, he plays the violin better than anybody else living. He makes unusually pretty sounds, too. It was the appropriateness of the kind of sounds he used last night to the pieces he used them on that could be called in question as taste. So was the choice of pieces that he played, since the Strauss Sonata and the Bruch G-minor Concerto, entertaining as they are for demonstrating instrumental mastery, are not really serious repertory for a serious artist of his fame to play in a New York recital. The Schubert Sonatina No. 3 might have been, had he played it more graciously, made one feel less than one had somehow got on the Queen Mary to go to Brooklyn.

The faults of taste that occur within an interpretation by Heifetz, almost any interpretation, have to do with irregularities in the application of right arm weight. His bow-stroke is likely to be so emphatic that it produces, even on an up-bow in a soft passage, accents that are not proper part of the music's line. He makes crescendos, too, in the middle of a note that has no rhetorical importance, simply, one imagines, because he finds it interesting to vary the tonal weight. As a result, his melodic line, for all its perfection of pitch and sweetness of sound, has no continuing emo-

418

tional tension and makes no sustained musical sense. Not, at any rate, in the way that I understand emotional tension and musical sense.

It is this teasing way of treating musical sounds and musical structures that led me long ago to consider Mr. Heifetz as essentially a frivolous artist, in spite of his incomparable mastery of violinistic operations. There is no weakness in him; he can do anything he wants to do with the instrument. There is merely, for this listener, a vast banality about what he seems to want, or at any rate to be satisfied with as musical communication. I am not inclined, even, to grant him the word "communication." "Effects," rather, are what he produces for me.

These were more in keeping last night with the Bruch Concerto than with the sonata literature that he also essayed. The Bruch piece is broadly conceived, rhetorical, has more gesture than substance. The soloist's reading, worked out no doubt for orchestral performances in great halls, was just what the piece would have needed had this been an orchestral performance. As a half image (for the piano is incapable of matching the violin at this kind of dramatics) of a non-existent orchestral performance it had evocative power. Nothing else, all evening long, evoked anything at all to this listener. There was some perfectly wonderful disembodied violin playing, all of it carefully, cagily, completely disengaged from any semblance of a personal responsibility to the music it was draped over.

MARCH 2, 1952

LIBRARY OF CONGRESS ADDS HEIFETZ'S MUSIC COLLECTION

The Library of Congress is richer by a large collection of musical scores, manuscripts, letters and early editions. They were presented to the Library by the celebrated violinist, Jascha Heifetz.

Mr. Heifetz has expressed the wish that the material be made available for use by scholars and placed on exhibition as often as possible. The collection, now on display, will be exhibited until March 16.

Among the modern composers represented by manuscripts are Elgar, Walton, Godowsky, Castelnuovo-Tedesco, Weiner and Gruenberg. The letters in the collection were written to Mr. Heifetz by Shaw, Chaliapin, Melba, Garden, Boulanger, Glazunoff and others.

NOVEMBER 5, 1952

SAYS JASCHA HEIFETZ, perfectionist: "It was a critic who taught me it is not enough to play a piece—you must think it."

At a time when audiences and critics alike were mixing applause and superlatives to describe Heifetz, one stubborn reviewer on *The New York Sun* turned in a minority report:

419

"His name was Henderson. In 1921, he gave me a scathing review. He said that I was content to stand still. He said I owed it to myself and to music never to be content. I read that review and it frightened me, woke me up. I knew the man wished me well—he hit home, because he wrote the truth. He died some years ago, and I will always regret I did not meet him. He did me a great service."

Born in Russia on Fritz Kreisler's birthday, Feb. 2, 1901, Heifetz has been a great success since he was six years old. Groucho Marx summed up his prodigy period best with one classic crack:

"A genius at six! What were you before that—just a bum?"

One more laugh-line marks another point in his career—his debut at Carnegie Hall, at sixteen. Many famous musicians were in the audience, among them Mischa Elman, the then already famous violinist, and Leopold Godowsky, the pianist, were among the great who had come to hear the debut of this young genius who was challenging the fame of his elders. It was a very warm afternoon in October. . . said violinist Elman to pianist Godowsky:

"Terribly hot, isn't it?"

Reply: "Not for pianists."

And before that debut was over, every great violinist knew that a new great violinist had arrived.

Skeptically, we wondered if that story ever happened, or was it invented by some shrewd press agent?

"It happened. I remember the date—Oct. 27, 1917. Godowsky came to me during the intermission and told me the story. And it has been dogging my footsteps ever since. What amuses me is the sequel to that story, and a pianist is the target this time:

"At a concert in London one warm summer night, a famous pianist was listening to Josef Hoffmann play the piano. He started to take his handkerchief out of his pocket and mop his forehead—but he noticed that several of us, violinists, were looking at him, with the obvious remark of Godowsky on our lips, and he placed his handkerchief sheepishly back into his pocket and sweated it out!"

On stage, Heifetz does all his "sweating-out" inside; a mask seems to creep across his face: "Most of the time, my emotions are . . . turbulent. . . underneath."

Once, out of curiosity, he weighed himself before and after a concert —net loss: three pounds. Almost eagerly, he asked us: "Tell me frankly, haven't you noticed, in the last few years, a certain relaxation on my part ". . .

Offstage, there is a sense of humor, even a sense of fun in Heifetz— under the name of Jim Hoyt, keeping his own initials, he wrote a popular song called, "When You Make Love to Me." He kept the dark secret until the tune wound up on the Hit Parade, and then he confessed. You can bring the flush of anger to his face by using words like "highbrow" or "longhair" to describe good music:

420

During a rehearsal for the new Korngold Concerto, the composer, Eric Korngold (left), discusses the world premier performance with Vladimir Goldschmann and Heifetz as they get ready for the St. Louis Symphony to join them. Circa 1947.

"I will be most happy to see the day when those words are no longer used. You hear that serious music is on its way out in radio and television —yet more good music is being understood by more people now than ever before. At first, you have to make an effort to enjoy it, but the reward is always great. That is why I say to people who claim it is 'over their head' —come and get it!"

There is no lofty conceit in Heifetz, as this story indicates: At a concert in Tel Aviv, 9,000 seats were sold for a 1,000-seat theater, which meant Heifetz had to play the concert nine times:

"After the first playing, the cab driver who brought me to the concert, and stayed to listen while he waited for me, said in the wings: 'I have never heard that cadenza before.'

"I replied: It's my own. The pity is, I will have to play it eight more times!"

"And then the cab driver put me in my place: 'You don't have it so bad—I'll have to sit through it eight more times!' "

MARCH 4, 1953
CARNEGIE HALL

HEIFETZ DISPLAYS TOP VIRTUOSO FORM
Playing of Kreisler Scherzo, With the Composer Taking a Bow, Thrills Audience

By Olin Downes

JASCHA HEIFETZ, violinist, Emanuel Bay, pianist, at Carnegie Hall.

PROGRAM

Prelude . . . . Bach-Heifetz
Concerto in E Minor . . . . Nardini
Sonata No. 8 in G . . . . Beethoven
Sonata . . . . Bloch
Recitativo and Scherzo . . . . Kreisler
Daisies . . . . Rachmaninoff-Heifetz
Figaro, from "The Barber of Seville . . . . Rossini-Castelnuovo-Tedesco

Jascha Heifetz, who opened his recital last night in Carnegie Hall by playing the prelude of a Bach partita at a far livelier clip than the music demanded, continued with an evening of superlative violin playing, of which perhaps only he, of all living virtuosos, is capable.

Heifetz announcing his refusal to play at a Hollywood Bowl concert because of a difference in opinion with management. Circa 1946.

422

The Bach excerpt was followed by the Nardini concerto in E minor, and its performance was to this writer's mind an impeccable example of the classic style. By "classic style" is not meant a precision, coldness and emotionless presentation—quite the contrary.

Mr. Heifetz sang the slow movement as warmly, as humanly and with as expressive a tone as that of the fabulous prima donnas of history; yet his interpretation made every melodic line, every smallest or most elaborate ornamentation distinguished and a triumph of proportion and taste.

The Beethoven sonata selected was the eighth one, in G. In this sonata, Beethoven writes with a delicacy and fancy that have no duplication—unusual as it was to choose such a work for the spaces of Carnegie Hall. Here, too, there could be questions of preference of tempos and minor matters of interpretation. The effect, as a whole, was that of sovereign art, in which Emanuel Bay, the pianist, took a distinguished part.

Bloch Sonata Performed

Mr. Heifetz opened the second part of the program with Ernest Bloch's early sonata for violin and piano. He had not played this work, if we are reliably informed, for seventeen years.

How the earlier interpretation matched with that of last night, this writer does not know. But it is difficult to believe that on returning to the sonata Mr. Heifetz did not bring to it a ripened wisdom and a matured insight in communicating its passionate and richly colored music.

His style here was, of course, a complete contrast to everything done earlier in the evening. He was as rhapsodic, dramatic, subjective in as great a degree as he had been the classicist in the communication of Nardini's music. The music mourned and denounced and was deep in reverie by turns. The barbaric triumph of the finale ended in a mood of serenity and poetic meditation.

Regarding the physical difficulties of a score that is orchestral rather than violinistic in its nature, it need only be said that Mr. Heifetz was, as ever, in easy command of all the immense technical equipment that Bloch requires, not for purposes of soloist display, but for the communication of overwhelming emotion.

Kreisler Gets Ovation

There followed a dramatic moment; the performance by one master violinist—Heifetz—of the work of another master of the instrument and of the composer's art—Fritz Kreisler—of Kreisler's Recitative and Scherzo for the violin alone. From the violinist's standpoint, and the composer's as well, the piece is superbly written. Playing it, Mr. Heifetz gave us as consummate an example of violin mastery and interpretive eloquence as this writer feels he ever can expect to hear.

Having done so, Mr. Heifetz followed his act of homage by quietly indicating with his bow Mr. Kreisler's presence in the auditorium. The applause compelled the older master to rise and be seen, to the thunderous demonstration of the audience.

Mr. Heifetz' simple and excellent arrangement of Rachmaninoff's song, "Daisies," and his electrical playing of the very amusing and extremely difficult and dazzling transcription by Castelnuovo-Tedesco of the "Largo al factotum" from "Barber of Seville" brought the end of the printed program. And that, too, was the occasion for demonstrations of delight by the gathering that packed the hall.

MARCH 4, 1953
CARNEGIE HALL

JASCHA HEIFETZ

By Arthur Berger

Jascha Heifetz, appearing in Carnegie Hall last night, delivered a concert that was, for him, characterized by unusual seriousness and understatement. He had the good taste to leave the fireworks and fun for the final group and he showed the highest degree of self-effacement in sending his audience out at the intermission with the quiet, unruffled memory of his playing of one of Beethoven's most gossamer sonatas, the G major, Op. 30, No. 3.

For Heifetz, the choice of Bloch's violin sonata as the core of his program was a decided departure from routine, even though this somewhat impressionistic work has been around a long time and would scarcely seem unusual on the program of almost any other violinist. The freshness of the impulse, at least in Heifetz' mind, seemed to me to give rise to the finest results of the evening. I am not too fond of the work itself. It is long and discursive, and the movements, while varying somewhat in pace, each assumes the same general rhapsodic form. For my taste, the viola suite achieves the same thing more successfully. But I have never enjoyed the violin sonata quite so well as I did last night.

Bloch has, of course, long been known as one of the composers who cater to string virtuosity, and this work is no exception, however grand its aim may be. The lyricism gave full scope for Heifetz to demonstrate his suave tone, legato and capacity for nuance. It was not without its more obvious moments for display through such means as ponticello and tremolo.

It may be that last night's concert is a symptom of Heifetz' aspirations now to achieve greater depth to add to his well known fabulous grasp of violin resources. One wonders, however, whether it was a coincidence that much the least satisfying of his playing last night occurred in the music with the most solid musical properties. His arrangement of the Prelude from Bach's Partita in E major made its source almost unrecognizable for me. It was played almost for velocity alone, and not for its fine shapes. In the Beethoven, he played so quietly at times that several of the figures were inaudible, and there was a general air of being disinterested in the music and unexcited by its forceful accents.

But Heifetz purveys a highly tangible product, and this is what his overflow audiences pay for. The intangibles of interpretation and transporting musicianship are too debatable to be so easily marketable. Violinists recognize the exceptional qualities in Heifetz, and there is no arguing with them as to their being exceptional. For when he rattles off something like the Kreisler Recitative and Scherzo, that thoroughly exploits the instrument, they know he has accomplished a feat, and they probably can even prove it. Kreisler was in the second row last night, and after much urging on the part of Heifetz, rose to acknowledge the reception of his unaccompanied piece.

In general, the intonation last night, even for Heifetz, was quite remarkable. By the time he finished the Rossini arrangement that closed the printed list, the audience was bubbling over with enthusiasm. By this time, too, one had forgotten a certain paleness both in musical quality and sound that had pervaded the first half, even in Nardini's Concerto in E minor, which had made beautiful things. The audience finally had its reward. I cannot help expressing some surprise, however, that a violinist from whom we expect such mechanical efficiency should have miscalculated his dynamics in the Beethoven to the extent of making some of the notes either inaudible or vague.

APRIL 19, 1953

HEIFETZ, ON TOUR, ARRIVES IN ROME

ROME, April 20 (UP) — Jascha Heifetz arrived here today from Israel with his hand bandaged as a result of the attack on him in Jerusalem. The violin virtuoso said his injury was slight, and would not interfere with his concert tour of Europe, which starts tomorrow night with a concert in Naples and continues to mid-June, when he returns to the United States. In Israel an unidentified assailant hit him with an iron bar, presumably because he had defied a twenty-year ban on German music.

Heifetz, circa 1947.

JASCHA HEIFETZ

Like a lot of big and small fry, Jascha Heifetz believes in luck. Luck believes in him, too—but Heifetz takes it not at all for granted. In spite of more than thirty years on the concert stage, he still worries about that string which is always about to break. The lights in the concert hall—they are just about to go out, in his imagination. Of course, the lights never have gone out in Heifetz's musical world. He says that is only luck, and meanwhile he lives in unhappy anticipation.

Perhaps it can all be traced back to some infant trauma, a horrible fall from his highchair. It may have been those early violin lessons he suffered at the age of three. He simply did not like the violin. He did not want to play it. He kept on not wanting to play for more years than he cares to remember. With such a resistance to music, he almost succeeded in not becoming a great violinist.

His father, Rubin, was a violinist himself, and so luck was against the child. The father ordered and Jascha suffered. He suffered at first under the hands of his father; then he suffered in the Imperial Conservatory in Petrograd under the hands of Leopold Auer. He had the misfortune to have his first great success at the unwilling age of ten, as soloist with the Berlin Philharmonic Orchestra under Arthur Nickisch. After that, there was no escaping his fate. Some six years later, on October 27, 1917, he painfully heard the tumultuous applause of New Yorkers, after a performance that at once enrolled him among the really great virtuosi. Since then, he has been suffering success after success, travelling more than a million miles as world violinist. He still believes, however, that everybody needs luck, lots of it. He is certain that "music is a most unrewarding profession," believing that only genius can suffer so much. He is glad that his children, Robert and Josepha, have no sparks of genius. He merely wants them to be happy, ordinary, blithe.

He himself feels much better since he abandoned New York, a few years ago. The Heifetzes began getting that peculiar homesickness which so many New Yorkers feel in the spring, summer and autumn. Suddenly they realized that what they wanted was a real home, with trees, a fireplace, a piece of woodland and fresh air. They found their home in Saugatuck Valley, Connecticut. There, Heifetz uses his famous Heifetz hands doing all the things he wants to do. He clears the underbush and grinds scissors, picks apples and builds sheds. In blue denims he feels himself—a simple farmer whose work is never done.

He looks back on his New York years with little regret. Life, for him, is in the country, and New Yorkers are not even aware of what they are missing. He thinks they are all sissies because they refuse to walk in the rain, unless they cannot help it. Says Heifetz, "When it rains everybody takes a taxicab. Then everybody can't get anywhere."

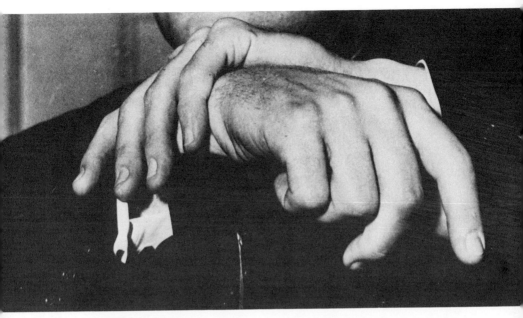

The most capable hands in the violin "business" belong to Jascha Heifetz. Note the way the fingers of the left hand curl up at the tips. Many violinists who practice hours a day for many years have this same characteristic. Szeryng told Fodor that Fodor's fingers would curl when he was about 40 years old. Szeryng has the same curled fingertips as Heifetz.

But Heifetz is not only a great virtuoso, a lover of rain, the countryside, the simple life. He is a good pal to composers. Heifetz says, "Why should composers do anything for the violin when they don't get anything out of it." Therefore he has formed a one-man-society for the encouragement of modern music. Right now, Castelnuovo-Tedesco and Serge Prokofiev are humming away at new concertos which he has commissioned. In December, 1939, Heifetz performed for the first time anywhere, William Walton's violin concerto, which he had paid for in hard cash. His performance with the Cleveland Orchestra was a notable event of the season. As for his own writings, Heifetz has added not a little to the repertory of the violin. His transcriptions for violin and piano are known to all musicians.

Not so long ago, an enthusiastic reporter asked Heifetz how he liked himself. Heifetz refused to answer. The truth is that he has lived with himself for a good many years. He can now take himself not too seriously; with the right luck, he knows what he can do and what he cannot. In either case, he sees nothing to feel too happy or too sad about.

Deems Taylor, who knows Heifetz as well as anybody else, says: "I have never known a musician with more artistic integrity. He has reached the point, I think, that every great artist, creative or interpretative, must reach; the point where he has achieved such mastery of his craft that he knows he will never completely master it. He plays the violin so well that he knows what a lesser artist will never know; how good violin playing might be. . . He is still learning to play. He has only one rival, one violinist whom he is trying to beat: Jascha Heifetz."

FEBRUARY 16, 1955
CARNEGIE HALL

HEIFETZ, AT CARNEGIE HALL, PLAYS BRAHMS, VIEUXTEMPS
By Jay S. Harrison

JASCHA HEIFETZ, violinist, in recital last night at Carnegie Hall. Accompanist: Brooks Smith. The program:

Sonata No. 10. . . . . Mozart
Sonata in D minor. . . . . Brahms
Prelude, Loure, Gavotte and Rondeau
    (from the Partita No. 3) . . . . J.S. Bach
Theme and Variations from Sonata No. 2. Medtner
Belligerent; Slow and Lonely, Madly Dancing . . . . Robert Russell Bennett
Concerto No. 5 . . . . Vieuxtemps

Although it might appear somewhat anomalous, Jascha Heifetz' violin recital last night in Carnegie Hall was an essentially intellectual affair. At any rate, it made its appeal to the mind rather than the heart, for the demon virtuoso, wrapped up in his own pyrotechnics, seemed devoted to no higher calling than getting to his notes in time and in tune. As such, it was a pleasant chore to sit and contemplate his miracles of fingers and bow without for a moment experiencing that elevation of spirit which music is known to induce.

In terms of technical wizardry however, Heifetz retains his almost superhuman faculty of making the most elaborate and horrifying difficulties seem like mere child's play. He is shaken by no complexity, harassed by no digital requirements, whatever their vicious demands. With supreme and imperturbable calm he wends his way through labyrinthine frills and figures that would send many another musician back to his conservatory a broken man. He has, in addition, virtually hundreds of

430

Heifetz poses in front of his famous book collection. Circa 1940.

tone colors which are by turns mellow or biting, bland or brilliant. His wrists are of steel, his bow pressure firm. In him the whole mechanism of fiddling spins and churns with uncanny precision. But there, last night, his performance stopped.

The Mozart, though properly held within a small frame, served as nothing more than a demonstration of Heifetz' power to project sonority even at an almost inaudible level. And the Brahms emerged a web of thin silver lines utterly lacking in warmth and expressivity. By the time he had arrived at the Bach and gilded chestnut department, it is true, his readings took on a certain Gypsy fire and passion, but by then it was too late. For what is the use of making Medtner sound like Brahms if Brahms is not made to sound like himself?

In sum, last night's event permitted the watchful observer's mind to amaze at the legion wonders of which man's fingers are capable. But the heart went untouched, went unmoved.

431

FEBRUARY 16, 1955
CARNEGIE HALL

HEIFETZ RECITAL
Violinist in Program at Carnegie Hall

By Howard Taubman

PROGRAM

Sonata No. 10	Mozart
Sonata in D minor	Brahms
Prelude, Loure, Gavotte en rondeau, from Partita No. 3	Bach
Theme and Variations, from Sonata No. 2	Medtner
Belligerent; Slow and Lonely; Madly Dancing	Bennett
Concerto No. 2	Vieuxtemps

The disciplined mastery of Jascha Heifetz' violin playing remains undimmed. In his only New York appearance of the season at Carnegie Hall last night, he played with the precision and commanding authority that are the hallmarks of his art. Everything had the purity of simplicity. Nothing to it, in fact, if you are Heifetz.

There was a moment when the violinist seemed to be compounding the feat of being Heifetz. He took the Prelude of Bach's Partita No. 3 at the tempo that would have meant disaster for most other virtuosos, and he kept it going firmly and securely as though it were a simple thing to do. Possibly this was not the tempo that everyone would have agreed with, but there was no resisting the brilliance of the achievement. The audience responded with a brief flurry of applause, even though it was clear that Mr. Heifetz was poised for the next movement.

The evening began with a Mozart sonata, which Mr. Heifetz carefully kept within its classic, eighteenth-century proportions. The piano part, played expertly by Brooks Smith, the accomplished accompanist, is often the predominant one in this sonata. Mr. Heifetz did not do anything to disturb the composer's balance. He was content often to let the violin remain in the background. When it had an opportunity to sing, Mr. Heifetz caused it to do so with delicacy of style.

The Brahms sonata moved the program into the glowing, rhapsodic nineteenth century. Here Mr. Heifetz could let his rich tone pour out in all its colors. But at no time did he tear a passion to tatters. The work had added emotional impact because its basic approach had great dignity.

He played the three sections of the Bach partita so appealingly that one regretted he did not see fit to perform the entire work. One regretted it the more because the Medtner music that followed was thin stuff, even if it was played impeccably.

The excerpts from Robert Russell Bennett's "A Song Sonata" were full of rhythmic vitality and sensuous colors. This is music made to order idiomatically for the violin, especially for a virtuoso like Heifetz, but it does not contain material that clings to the ribs. The Vieuxtemps concerto offered by Mr. Heifetz an opportunity for a tour de force.

JANUARY 10, 1956
CARNEGIE HALL

HEIFETZ STILL TOPS AMONG FIDDLERS

By Louis Biancolli

After what seemed much too long an absence, Jascha Heifetz fiddled his way right back into the hearts of Philharmonic patrons last night.

Appearing in Carnegie Hall as soloist in the Beethoven Concerto, the celebrated master of the bow reminded us all once more that when it comes to elegance and finesse there is only one Heifetz.

The refinement and poise were incredible. It wasn't just the tone, which was sweet and pure and infinitely shaded, and it wasn't just the technique, which was fabulous.

These things one has come to hail again and again in a season of superlative fiddling. Mr. Heifetz moved far beyond both. They were the means by which he achieved an aristocracy of art no distinction of skill could counterfeit.

Frankly, I had almost forgotten how beautifully this man could play. A kind of legend had already attached to the name. It was good to have the legend and the name materialize once more in a miracle of reality.

The slow movement was a dream last night. Dimitri Mitropoulos and the orchestra paved the way with a poetic hush and Mr. Heifetz went on from there in a whispered wonder of tone.

If anybody was getting the idea that some of the luster was rubbing off the Heifetz bow, last night's performance banished said idea. The Auer and Joachim cadenzas alone showed it in astonishing trim.

Mr. Mitropoulos was also in high form last night—in the Concerto and in Haydn's "Drum Roll" Symphony and Bizet's sprightly "Jeux d'Enfants" suite. All combined that inner and outer flow that is his strength.

HEIFETZ, THE MASTER, PLAYS

By Howard Taubman

After all the violinists who have appeared with the New York Philharmonic this season, it was fitting to have Jascha Heifetz as the soloist at Carnegie Hall last night. He is still an unsurpassed master, and his appearance was like a climactic chapter in a running story of violin virtuosos.

433

In the Beethoven concerto Mr. Heifetz had a work worthy of his gifts, and he gave it a memorable performance. His playing had all the virtues of understanding and simplicity that a mature artist could bring to this noble composition. Seldom has Mr. Heifetz played with greater penetration.

The style was aristocratic without being aloof. The tone was pure and responsive to the subtlest requirements of light and shade. The phrasing was full of nuance, but there was no fussiness for the sake of effect. Everything in the way of virtuosity and control was ordered for the greatest good of the music.

The tremendous first movement had power and drama, and there was unstinted bravura in the Auer cadenza here, which Mr. Heifetz almost persuaded one was integral to the work. The last movement danced and sang with high spirits. But what one will remember longest is the song of the slow movement, played with breadth of feeling and a serene comprehension.

Dimitri Mitropoulos and the Philharmonic gave Mr. Heifetz well-balanced support. The orchestra was in good form.

It began the program with Haydn's E flat Symphony, No. 103, which was played with considerable sympathy for the classic style. In the slow movement particularly there was the kind of contrast and proportion that Mr. Mitropoulos has not always established in eighteenth-century music.

Instead of a new American work, Ralph Shapey's "Challenge—The Family of Man," which was originally announced, the orchestra offered Bizet's "Jeux d'Enfants" Suite. The Shapey score was evidently too difficult to prepare. There was nothing troublesome about the Bizet suite. It is made up of five charming trifles, which were tossed off cheerfully by the Philharmonic. There is no reason why a symphonic concert should not have its good-humored moments.

It was Mr. Heifetz, however, that most came to hear. He is planning to take a sabbatical next season, and he will be missed. The Philharmonic, which has not had many sellouts this year, had one last night. Heifetz is still Heifetz.

OCTOBER 2, 1959

PROFESSOR'S PROPHECY COMES TRUE
Heifetz Will Teach Violin to Outstanding Students

BEVERLY HILLS, Calif., Oct. 1 (AP) — In his white-carpeted aerie, a temporarily nestbound eagle of the music world watches a prophecy being fulfilled—and just smiles.

"My old professor put a finger on me," says violinist Jascha Heifetz. "He said that some day I would be good enough to teach."

Famous musicians gather to hear music at the Hollywood Bowl. Gregor Piatigorsky with Mr. and Mrs. Heifetz, circa 1958.

Mr. Heifetz, one of the great figures of the concert stage for nearly half a century, has been named a regents professor of music at the University of California at Los Angeles.

In a rare interview at his hilltop home, Mr. Heifetz explained why he plans to spend a year auditioning and instructing outstanding students.

"Violin playing is a perishable art," he said. "It must be passed on as a personal skill—otherwise it is lost."

Mr. Heifetz today is on crutches—he hurt his left leg in July in a fall—but insists this had nothing to do with his decision to teach at the university.

"I had already decided to accept," he said. "Actually this is a continuation on a larger scale of an experiment we tried at U.C.L.A. last fall."

Mr. Heifetz, who hopes to graduate soon to a cane, will spend the next few months seeking out promising violin students across the country. In February he will start teaching his master class of eight students and ten auditors.

"There will be no credits, no medals, no gold and silver stars," he said, "and no microphones and no tape-recording machines. There will be just us, teacher and students, and what we can learn to do with our hands."

The music master, an impeccably dressed youngish fifty-eight, studied as a child prodigy under Prof. Leopold Auer at the St. Petersburg Conservatory in Czarist Russia.

Jascha Heifetz, Leonard Pennario and Gregor Piatigorsky take a break during an informal afternoon concert at the University of Southern California. Circa 1955.

436

DECEMBER 10, 1959
UNITED NATIONS

MASTER OF HIS ART HEIFETZ RETURNS AFTER FOUR YEARS IN U.N. CONCERT

By Howard Taubman

UNITED NATIONS HUMAN RIGHTS DAY CONCERT. Detroit Symphony Orchestra, conducted by Paul Paray. Jascha Heifetz, violinist. At General Assembly Hall.

PROGRAM

Introduction and Procession From Coq d'Or .... Rimsky-Korsakoff
Symphony No. 4 .... Schumann
Violin Concerto .... Beethoven

Jascha Heifetz reminded us last night how much he has been missed. In an appearance at the United Nations, his first in New York in almost four years, the violinist made it clear that he was still the unsurpassed master of his art.

The occasion was a concert celebrating the eleventh anniversary of the proclamation of the Universal Declaration of Human Rights. A distinguished gathering filled the General Assembly Hall for the program, which was prefaced by a brief address by Dr. Victor A. Belaunde, president of the fourteenth session of the General Assembly. The orchestra was the Detroit Symphony conducted by Paul Paray.

But the story was Mr. Heifetz. He has absented himself not only from the New York concert stage but also from nearly all others in the last few years. When pressed, he calls the long interlude of relative silence a "sabbatical." But the truth is that it is something more.

For most of his life, he has been a traveling virtuoso. Though no musician has been more admired in our time, he has had to endure, like other performers, all the discomforts that go with a peripatetic career. Mr. Heifetz, in short, evidently does not want to be a barnstormer any longer. But let us hope that he can find some happy compromise that enables him to play as much as he chooses so that we may hear him more often than once a quadrennium.

Mr. Heifetz played under a handicap, but one would hardly have known it unless one looked sharply. One would never have known if one just listened. Because he broke his hip in an accident several months ago, he used a cane when he walked to his place before the orchestra. Behind him was a small gold railing if he were to need support.

He made no concession, however, to the difficulty. Once he set the violin under his chin and brought his bow across the strings, he was the sovereign performer. The concerto was the Beethoven, which he probably had played hundreds of times, but there was not a hint that he was taking it for granted.

438

On December 9, 1950 Jascha Heifetz played the Beethoven Violin Concerto with Paul Paray and the Detroit Symphony Orchestra at the United Nations, New York.

Mindful of the fact that the hall's unpredictable acoustics tend to brilliance, Mr. Heifetz chose to establish his interpretation on modest proportions. There was nothing small-scale or subdued in this approach. For Mr. Heifetz commands an incredible wealth of nuance. In the course of one bow he can summon up a breath-taking variety of shadings. Within this controlled compass, he provided a reading of the familiar concerto that made it as fresh as the new morning.

One could expatiate on countless felicities of detail. It is enough to recall the traversal of the slow movement. Mr. Heifetz' tone was a thing of pellucid and yet fluid purity. It never raised its voice above a mezza-forte, if it rose that loud. But how subtle was the phrasing, how sustained Beethoven's seraphic vision!

Mr. Paray modulated the orchestral tone to match the distinction of Mr. Heifetz' style. In the concerto, as in the Schumann Symphony and the curtain-raising pieces by Rimsky-Korsakoff and Durufle, the visitors played with homogeneity and spirited ensemble. Mr. Paray has been building firmly and well in Detroit. This is another to add to America's growing list of fine orchestras.

Scene at the reception which followed the concert by the Detroit Symphony Orchestra when they played for the United Nations. The reception was held at the delegate's lounge. Left to right: Heifetz, Mrs. Paul Paray, Victor Belaunde, President of the General Assembly of the United Nations, Paul Paray, and Mrs. Belaunde. December 9, 1959.

The Detroit players, like orchestral musicians everywhere, are no doubt case-hardened, but in the slow movement they listened to the soloist with as much rapt admiration as the audience. His absence has not affected the aristocracy of his musicianship. May we expect you back soon, Mr. H.?

DECEMBER 10, 1959

A VIOLINIST AT REST—JASCHA HEIFETZ

One of the classic musical stories concerns the Carnegie Hall debut, on October 27, 1917, of a 17-year-old violinist named Jascha Heifetz.

Mischa Elman, the violinist, sitting in a box with a pianist, Leopold Godowsky, mopped his brow and remarked: "Whew, it's hot in here." "Not for pianists," Godowsky replied. Last night, forty-two years and innumerable world tours later, the onetime prodigy played at the United Nations as soloist for the United Nations Human Rights Day concert.

The concert was Mr. Heifetz's first appearance here since his Hunter College recital on Feb. 19, 1956, which began his "sabbatical" from the concert stage. Once before, during a twenty-month stretch of 1947 and 1948, the violinist had taken time off to put away his instrument and meditate about himself and his music.

Having performed in public more or less continually since 1906, Mr. Heifetz may be excused for desiring to take time off now and then. He might even be casual about practice now, because he acquired solid technical training in his youth.

His father, Ruvin Heifetz, a violinist and teacher who until his death could be seen on the back row at Town Hall at every violin recital, scrutinizing the performer through opera glasses, gave the boy his first lessons and remained his severest critic. Often, after a brilliant performance with the Philharmonic, the violinist could be seen at an after-concert party, replying apologetically to his father's merciless rundown of the evening's flaws.

Made Debut at 10

So thorough was Mr. Heifetz' early training that when he entered Leopold Auer's violin class in Petrograd, after having graduated at the age of 8 from the Royal College of Music in his native Vilna, Professor Auer was perplexed to know what to teach him. The gifted boy made his debut at 10 with the Berlin Philharmonic, and later appeared in other European countries.

In 1917, the Heifetz family, consisting of Mr. Heifetz, his father, mother and two sisters, left Russia one step ahead of the revolution, reaching this country by way of San Francisco. Mr. Heifetz' Carnegie Hall recital immediately established him as one of the top names of the concert field.

His colleague Mr. Elman once told of riding with a taxi driver who recognized him and showed himself knowledgeable about violins and violinists. He was rewarded with a generous tip.

"Gee, thanks, Mr. Elman." said the driver. "Now I can go to hear Heifetz!"

In 1929 Mr. Heifetz married Florence Vidor, a star of silent films. The marriage ended in divorce in 1945. Their children are Josepha and Robert. In 1947 the violinist married Mrs. Frances Spiegelberg. They have a son, Joseph (Jay).

For years Mr. Heifetz has spent much of his time in California, where, among other things, he has sailed his yawl, Serenade, in the race to Honolulu. Last season, his ties with California were strengthened when he conducted a master class for five advanced pupils at the University of California at Los Angeles. Students toiled in three-hour sessions, with Mr. Heifetz accompanying at the piano or taking up his violin to illustrate a point.

Mr. Heifetz disclosed talent for mimicry, caricaturing physical or musical mannerisms so deftly and humorously that students were certain never to make that particular mistake again.

Permanent at U.C.L.A.

Last September, U.C.L.A. announced that Mr. Heifetz had been appointed Regents' Professor of Music and Artist in Residence at the university. He is continuing his master class and also will conduct seminars and musically illustrated lectures.

During World War II, Mr. Heifetz made a number of overseas tours for the United Services Organizations. He recalled that on one occasion in Italy, while he was playing from the tailgate of an Army truck, an air-raid siren interrupted the performance. His audience disappeared in a flash, his violin was snatched out of his hands and in a matter of seconds he was alone. After a moment's reflection Mr. Heifetz crawled under the truck for shelter.

When the all-clear sounded, a soldier appeared with the missing violin.

"I'm sorry," he explained, "but I didn't want anything to happen to that wonderful fiddle."

Heifetz was guest of honor at the Hollywood Bowl Patrons Committee buffet supper. Left to right: Mrs. Heifetz, Hector Escobosa, William Pereira and Heifetz. June, 1958.

442

POLISHED AND ARTISTOCRATIC

THE HEIFETZ/PIATIGORSKY CONCERTS. Jascha Heifetz, violinist, and Gregor Piatigorsky, cellist, with Jacob Lateiner, pianist; Israel Baker, William De Pasquale and Isidore Cohen, violinists; Joseph De Pasquale and Harold Coletta, violists, and Laurence Lesser, cellist. At Carnegie Hall.

PROGRAM

Double Quartet in D minor (Op. 65) . . . . .Spohr
Sextet (Souvenir de Florence, Op. 70) . . . . .Tchaikovsky
Piano Trio in E minor (Dumky, Op. 90) . . . . .Dvorak

Jascha Heifetz, Gregor Piatigorsky & Co. returned to Carnegie Hall last night for the first of three concerts. As last time, they chose the unusual hour of 7 and selected a program of chamber music. It was a program of unusual interest, containing three seldom-heard pieces, one of

Heifetz, Rubinstein and Piatigorsky playing chamber music at Ravinia Park, Chicago. August, 1949.

which—the Double Quartet by Ludwig Spohr—must have been a novelty to almost everybody in the audience. Apparently the work has not even been recorded, ever.

Those who were attracted by the magic name of Heifetz and came expecting fireworks must have been disappointed. The great violinist sat as one of his equals and merely made music. And the emphasis of the evening was on music, not on any individual display.

It was a kind of music that is not often encountered in today's concert halls. The Spohr work represented an absolute novelty. Tchaikovsky's Sextet, named "Souvenir de Florence," is very seldom heard; when it is, it generally turns up in an expanded version for string orchestra. Even the Dvorak E minor Trio, his most popular (though not his best; the F minor is a far superior work), is a rarity these days.

History books have a good deal to say about Spohr, but his music is seldom played and only the Eighth Concerto lingers in the repertory. Spohr, early in the 19th century, was considered the leading classical violinist of the period. Later he became a conductor. He was a prolific composer, immensely popular in his day, especially for his operas. The history books tell us that he anticipated the romantic movement, and that his music contains chromatic harmonics unusual for his period.

His Double Quartet lives up to its history-book reputation. It turned out to be a lovely, lyric piece, with anticipations of Mendelssohn here, Schumann there. The writing is graceful throughout, the melodic content is individual, the string writing highly idiomatic. In a way this is a baby double concerto, with the first violin and the first cello doing the lion's share. With such lions as Messrs. Heifetz and Piatigorsky, the score was lifted right off the ground.

Probably it takes a special kind of mind to relish the longueurs of the Tchaikovsky Sextet. In a way it is a long salon piece, with awkward developments and a good deal of repetition. But it is always Tchaikovsky who speaks; and those long tunes, that strange combination of Italian brightness and Russian melancholy, those typical codas that spurt like a suddenly released arrow—nobody but Tchaikovsky could have been responsible.

The Dvorak is a bundle of Czechoslovak moods; brightly tied packages within packages within packages. It is a pretty score, nowhere near the level of the great Dvorak chamber works but thoroughly agreeable for all that. The performance was prefaced by a brief announcement by Mr. Heifetz, who said that the work was being played in memory of Mrs. Chaim Weitzmann, who died Saturday.

Mr. Heifetz and Mr. Piatigorsky assembled a top group of instrumentalists for this concert. The playing was polished and aristocratic. It was not the kind of program that was going to plumb the depths, and all anybody could ask for was the kind of elegance and technical glitter displayed by all hands. The evening progressed inversely from octet to sextet to trio. In the Dvorak the superbly efficient pianist was Jacob Lateiner.

Harold C. Schonberg

OCTOBER 3, 1966
CARNEGIE HALL

HEIFETZ RETURNS TO RECITAL STAGE
Electrifies Audience in First Bill with Piatigorsky

By Theodore Strongin

Last night's concert at Carnegie Hall had been billed merely as one of three in this fall's Heifetz-Piatigorsky series, mostly of chamber music.

But the audience knew better. It knew that it was really attending Jascha Heifetz's first solo recital in New York in more than 10 years—since Feb. 18, 1956, at Hunter College, to be exact.

The audience proceeded accordingly, that is to say, with thunderous applause the moment Mr. Heifetz walked out on stage with his violin. The atmosphere was electrifying.

Mr. Heifetz walked onstage in his usual cool, almost disdainful, way and proceeded to play as though he hadn't been gone a day. It was Heifetz at his best and most characteristic, the last word in impeccable virtuosity.

Like a Computer Circuit

The tone glowed, the bow arm was as fast and accurate as a computer circuit and the musical effect was of perfect, aristocratic purity. There was not a chink in the design of his playing. Behind the smooth facade were the usual almost unbelievable complexities of color, accent, speed up, slow down—all applied in lightning succession. Heifetz is still Heifetz.

The evening opened with Beethoven's "Kreutzer" Sonata, for which Jacob Lateiner was pianist. It was a broad "Kreutzer," lyrical, free and impetuous. Mr. Heifetz's Beethoven was not brainy and craggy, but it was all homogeneous. He took the final movement at ultra-high speed. Passages exploded and took flight like rockets.

Sometimes there seemed a lack of personal involvement, particularly at moments where the piano overwhelmed the violin. There were quite a few of these.

The balance of the recital had no such discrepancy. In Kreisler's unaccompanied Recitative and Scherzo, in Milhaud's "Sumare," Prokofiev's "March" (from the Classical Symphony), in Richard Strauss's "An einsamer Quelle," and in Falla's "Spanish Dance," Mr. Heifetz was consistently on top. (Brooks Smith was the accompanist here. Mr. Lateiner played only for the Beethoven).

And in the Saint-Saens Sonata No. 1, he reached peaks difficult to remember even for Mr. Heifetz. He played with absolute patience. He left exactly the right amount of time for every twinge of feeling to sink in. Naturally, he was never maudlin or even earthy—he rarely is. But if you accept the Heifetz milieu, the Saint-Saens was an incredible triumph.

Mr. Heifetz played three encores, the last Gershwin's "It Ain't Necessarily So," which he transformed into the most elegant confection imaginable, a far cry from "Porgy and Bess."

No one wanted to leave. The recital officially ended at 8:49 P.M. At 9:09, after the stage lights had been turned off twice, the curtain closed, finally convincing the audience that it had had all it was going to get.

Jascha Heifetz abandons the rigors of a full concert career for the campus at UCLA where he is a regent's professor. February, 1960.

447

HEIFETZ'S ART ALONE
Beautiful Sounds With Violin

By Alan Rich

TIME AND CUSTOM have worked no ravages on Jascha Heifetz. His art stands alone, and it concerns only one thing; how to make beautiful sounds with the violin. He has mastered this art, to the delectation of the multitude, and to the consternation of his colleagues. Most of the unhappy people at Carnegie Hall last night were violinists.

There were a few others, however. They are those unreconstructed souls who choose to look upon the violin, or any other instrument for that matter, merely as means to an end. That end is not merely playing, but making music somewhat along lines conceived by music's various composers. They, too, have every reason to be unhappy at what Mr. Heifetz did at this, his first solo recital in these parts in 10 years.

Mr. Heifetz does not play music. He uses it. Last night he used one genuine masterpiece, and a few works of far lesser quality, to show off his way with the swooning phrase. From the way he played Beethoven's "Kreutzer" Sonata, it was clear that not very much else interested him in this piece.

He walked through its wondrous patterns stiff and uninvolved, pausing only when some passing idea seemed to whisper "try me." There weren't many such ideas to his liking, however, and the end result was a half-hour or so of pure passagework. Jacob Lateiner tried hard at the keyboard to establish some kind of musical sense, and he is an excellent man for that job. But Mr. Heifetz uses pianists the way he uses music.

The remainder of the program was more entertaining, only in that the discrepancy between the kind of music and the kind of performance wasn't as vast. It consisted in the main of a long (the Saint-Saens D minor Sonata) and some short.

The group was carefully chosen for its avowed purpose, and it was a setup. There were fast pieces and slow ones, soul and sentiment and dash and zip, a kind of textbook-collection of fancy effects. Mr. Heifetz gave each of them—or should I say, each of them gave Mr. Heifetz—its proper due.

It was all very silken, very much the cat's pajamas. "Silken" is one of the press' favorite adjectives for Mr. Heifetz, and there is no need to question it at this date. Another pet term is "aristocratic," which also very much applies. Aristocrats, by tradition, walk straight ahead at a fast pace, and seldom risk becoming involved in anything around them. Mr. Heifetz is a master of non-involvement and therefore, if you insist, he is an aristocrat. I'm sorry to say, however, that I did not have a very good time at his concert.

Heifetz and Mrs. Myron T. Chapro at a party honoring
Zubin Mehta and John Browning, Jr. August, 1965.

Heifetz listens to one of his students at his master class at the University of Southern California. Heifetz feels his classes have been successful, but limited. That's why he he is constantly on the search for really outstanding talent, he says. "I am a teacher; I need students." April 26, 1965.

DECEMBER 13, 1968

HEIFETZ URGES RITARD IN TEMPO OF MUSICIAN'S LIFE
By Howard Taubman

BEVERLY HILLS, Calif. — Although Jascha Heifetz rarely performs in public these days, he has not wearied of music, the violin or the world, and his views are as crisp as his scales and his double-stopping. Despite his matchless public career, he has always been a private man, but at the urging of an old friend he agrees to an infrequent interview.

Why does he play so little?

"Who says I play little?" he demands. "I play often. I practice. We have evenings of chamber music regularly, taking turns in different homes and going through all kinds of repertory. And from time to time we appear together in concert."

But he has not played in New York for more than two years, and then it was chamber music with Gregor Piatigorsky, the cellist, who has also reduced his public performances drastically, and others. As for a solo recital in New York, he hadn't played one in almost 13 years. How come?

"They Don't Pause"

"I've done my share of touring," he replies. "I have no further interest in that kind of career. And I can't say I admire the pace at which today's musicians travel. They move too fast; they play too often; they don't pause to reflect."

Mr. Heifetz, who will be 68 in February, and who has been playing in public for more than 60 years, warms up to a subject close to his thoughts—the haste and superficiality of many young musicians.

Because his demeanor on the concert stage has always been virtually expressionless, he has been called impersonal, detached and even stone-faced, but anyone with ears to hear has always been aware of his flashing artistic temperament and his profound involvement in the music he played. Sitting with him in his home high on a hilltop here, a tete, his face is vividly mobile and his eyes sparkle with expression.

"I don't see how a young musican can find the time to grow at today's tempo," he continues. "Of course, I played a great deal when I was younger, but there was always time for reflection. We didn't travel in jets. We used trains and ships, and we had time between engagements no matter how many we filled, to think, to study music, to read books. In the summer we might appear at the Lewisohn Stadium in New York or at the Hollywood Bowl out here, but that was all."

"Everywhere you look today there are festivals," he observes disdainfully, "in Europe, Asia, all over the United States. Everywhere they want the leading musician, and most of them go everywhere. Hardly anyone takes off a few weeks to rest, study and think, let alone a whole summer as we used to do."

Heifetz, circa 1970.

Is there too much music in the world today?

"Too much of the wrong kind, too much that is glib and superficial. And even though you have music constantly on the radio, on records, in concert halls and at festivals, there is too little of the highest quality."

What about the new generation of violinists, some of whom he teaches?

"There aren't many ready for this kind of postgraduate work. At the moment I have two students twice a week. I go down to the Los Angeles Music Center, which is developing a performing arts academy. I used to teach at the University of Southern California, where they insisted on giving me the title of Distinguished Professor of Music. Why distinguished? Professor is bad enough, and "Extinguished" Professor would be better.

"Two students are enough for my purposes. We have a lot to do. We work on everything from scales to interpretation. I won't take anyone who isn't ready for uncompromising work. But I might as well admit that I can't get all those I would like to work with."

You would think that a chance to study with Heifetz would be a highly sought privilege?

"Put it anyway you like," he says wryly. "But the teachers and schools—won't send me their best talents, even for a short period. Why not? I don't understand. When I traveled a lot, I listened often to young violinists, and when I heard talented ones, I sent them to the very teachers and schools that are reluctant to cooperate with me. Do they think I want to deprive them of credit for developing talent? What nonsense!

"And speaking of talent, I look for that, but Heaven keep me away from young 'geniuses.' You know, the kind whose parents, especially mothers, think are beyond compare. Some do have talent, but when mother gets in the way, I send the 'genius' away."

Does Mr. Heifetz play for his students to illustrate what he is after?

"I play but not to illustrate so much as to concentrate on error. I sometimes imitate what a student is doing and"—here his smile becomes a shade wicked—"I exaggerate the error. But the way to learn is to laugh at one's self. A touch of humor in music is good for maturing an artist.

"I learn from the lessons, too. My students ask me things and I don't always know the answer. I go home and do research."

Mr. Heifetz travels nowadays more for pleasure than for performance. Nevertheless, he usually takes his violin along.

"I have to practice, don't I?" he says. "Oh I always practice privately. I even make sure that no one notices that the violin is traveling with me."

Where does he keep it?

He smiles enigmatically. "I won't tell you."

We don't really need to know. What we want is to hear him. If he won't give many concerts, at least he continues to record, and his latest disks reveal that he retains his mastery as virtuoso and musician.

Heifetz lives in Beverly Hills, part of the smog-filled Los Angeles area. He was one of the first to use an all-electric car in an effort to keep Los Angeles alive. He thinks the smog will eventually kill everything growing on the Los Angeles plains. He has a Bentley in the same garage! June 1, 1967.

SEPTEMBER 22, 1970
JASCHA HEIFETZ PLAYS AND CONDUCTS FOR FRENCH TV

By Henry Raymont

PARIS, Sept. 20—A single figure under the white glare of three batteries of spotlights on the naked stage slowly raises a violin to begin an impeccable performance of Bach Chaconne. Jascha Heifetz plays for television.

The performance was filmed last week by the French television system together with smaller works by Debussy and Falla, which Mr. Heifetz played with the piano accompaniment of Brooks Smith. Last night, the 69 year-old violinist rounded out the program with Max Bruch's "Scottish Fantasy," one of his favorites.

The stage was that of the Theatre des Champs-Elysees. An invited audience of 700 broke into a storm of applause as Mr. Heifetz took his place before the French National Orchestra to appear both as soloist and as conductor.

A Concerned Director

For the past 15 years Mr. Heifetz has made only occasional public appearances, mainly in chamber works with his long-time friend and Los Angeles neighbor, the cellist Gregor Piatigorsky. Last May the two made a concert tour of Israel.

Backstage last night, Pierre Vozlinsky, musical director of the Office de Radiodiffusion et Television Francaise, checked last-minute technical arrangements with the program's American director, Kirk Browning. "Nothing must go wrong now," Mr. Vozlinsky said. "We worked one year for this moment."

The music director's face brightened and his concern seemed to vanish as he watched Mr. Heifetz, appearing relaxed with a trace of a smile on his pursed lips, raise his bow.

The violinist stood in the center of the stage, his back to the orchestra. A vigorous downbeat started the musicians in the orchestral opening.

Mr. Heifetz conducted and played the romantic, folk-style music with an almost casual elegance that was belied only by the frequent arching of his bushy eyebrows, lending his face an expression of intense concentration. At the end of the 22-minute work, the audience rose to give him a long ovation and call for encores.

After returning to the stage for the fifth time, Mr. Heifetz raised a hand imperiously and said in English:

"For those of you who liked it, thanks; for those who didn't, perhaps we'll catch you the next time."

No date has been set for the showing here of the hour-long television program, which opens with a brief interview with Mr. Heifetz at his home in Beverly Hills. In the United States it will be shown early next year over the National Broadcasting Company network.

456

Heifetz, circa 1965.

Musical Program

His musical program will start with the Rondo from the Haffner Serenade of Mozart. The transcription is by Fritz Kreisler. This will be followed by the March from "The Love for Three Oranges," by Prokofieff, arranged by Heifetz; Debussy's "Girl With the Flaxen Hair," and "It Ain't Necessarily So."

As Robinson points out in a bylined article written about the program, Bach comes in the middle and the Chaconne from the Partita in D Minor may set a record of sorts. It will probably be the first time a TV network will have presented 12 minutes and 40 seconds of unaccompanied violin.

Prefers No Conductor

The French National Orchestra, without a maestro, accompanies Heifetz in the Bruch Scottish Fantasy. It is, according to Robinson, a preference of the violinist to work with an unconducted orchestra. Heifetz himself said it is the reason he returned to Paris, "so the musicians and I could work together without interruption." Robinson says he likes "an atmosphere where each musician is a responsible collaborator to one musical concept."

Aware of much about the great musician, Robinson relates that Heifetz fled Russia to the United States in 1917 at age 16. Robinson said the violin he'll be playing is his favorite. It's a Guarnerius dated 1742. It belonged to Ferdinand David, who helped Mendelssohn with his violin Concerto and gave the first performance of the work on the instrument.

"He has several fine violins, but this is his favorite," said Robinson. "It was a gift from his father."

Robinson, who stands in awe of Heifetz, said, "You'd take a liberty with a king before you would him. I don't ever think of him as a person. I think of him as a god. There's nothing ordinary about him. He has the uncanny gift of perception and selection. To me he will always be Mr. Heifetz."

During a late supper with Lester Shure, the program's American producer, his manager, William Judd, and a group of friends at the nearby Plaza Athenee Hotel, Mr. Heifetz recounted his feelings after the plunge into television.

"I went into it with anxiety, interest and dread—all at the same time," he said. "Now I'm immensely relieved."

Heifetz. April,
1971.

458

Prof. Auer with his class in St. Petersburg. This is the photograph which led many people to think that Heifetz was older than he proclaimed. The date of this

picture is given as 1914, which would make Heifetz 13 years old in this picture. He does look a bit older, but his sister and several of his close relatives proclaim he truly was born in 1901.

No 'Interference'

Why did he choose France for his concert?

"They have the best color, I am told, and they offered me an orchestra without a conductor so that we could work together without interference," he said with the mischievous grin soloists often assume when speaking about conductors.

Speaking of the orchestra, he said, "We worked together extremely well. They understand that I rather make contact than conduct."

SEPTEMBER 29, 1970

HEIFETZ'S 25-MINUTES AND NO ENCORE: DRIVES PARISIANS UP WALLS

Jascha Heifetz gave a concert (if that is the word) at the Theatre des Champs-Elysees. Full House, naturally, with the television cameras grinding and celebrities fluttering. It was his first appearance in Paris since 1962. He played one item, Bruch's "The Scottish Concerto," 25 minutes long, took his bows to a standing ovation, refused all encores, and called it a night.

Naturally, the audience was not happy. They applauded, yelled, whistled and stamped their feet. But Heifetz would not budge. He had played his piece and he was through.

Later, in his dressing room he explained to his friends. "I have played in public 62 years. My first concert was at the age of seven. Enough already. This year I gave one other concert, in Israel, and I have no intention of playing any more. Maybe next year somewhere, once or twice."

A young man exclaimed, "But maestro, you played so beautifully!"

Heifetz nodded his head. "That's your problem," he explained. "Not mine."

Heifetz on television. No violinist, before or since, has captured so large an audience as when Heifetz played on television. Circa 1970.

April 18, 1971
ROBINSON SAYS THAT HEIFETZ HAS NO PEERS
Violinist Jascha Heifetz rehearses for his concert appearance on NBC-TV's special, "Heifetz," set for Friday night at 10.
By Kay Gardella

When Jascha Heifetz makes his concert debut on television Friday night on NBC for the Bell System Family Theater (10 p.m.), Francis Robinson, a man steeped in Heifetz lore but admittedly not a close friend of the famed violinist, will narrate the musical special.

"Heifetz, in my opinion, is an absolute," said Robinson, assistant manager of the Metropolitan Opera. "He's in a class with Caesar, Napoleon, Babe Ruth, or any champion who has no peers. I agree totally with violinist David Oistrakh, who once said: "There are violinists. Then there's Heifetz."

Robinson, who has authored several articles and books on music, including "Caruso: His Life in Pictures," met Heifetz when he was an usher in a Nashville, Tenn. theater. "I went backstage to get his autograph," recalled Robinson, who said the event took place more than 35 years ago. "I responded to his music then and I still do."

Concert Debut

Heifetz, according to Robinson, considers his Friday night television appearance his "concert debut," because he will reach more people in one evening than the total of all the audiences who have heard him in his more than 60 years before the public. His manager, William M. Judd, estimates that in the 40 years he was on tour he gave 100 concerts a year. Fifteen years ago he gave up the rough schedule.

"I know of no man who has the property to go right to the heart of the matter like Heifetz," said Robinson, as memories of another meeting with the musician came into focus. It involved a tour for the violinist through the new Metropolitan Opera House.

Hates Lateness

As Robinson recalled it:

"It was a fearful day. Rain was coming down in buckets. Drivers still had difficulty finding our stage door and Heifetz was late. It annoyed him. Woe to you if you are not on time with him; he demands the same of himself."

Heifetz, Robinson said, wanted to be conducted through the house as though he were a singer with the Met. Aware of the grubby conditions that existed in the past, he wanted to be sure the artists had a better lot today.

Heifeta, circa 1970.

465

"As the tour proceeded through the house we got to the orchestra pit and he tried one of the new tubular chairs," narrated Robinson. "It squeaked. I was afraid to look at him. I prayed for the floor to swallow me. I knew what I would read in his Tartar eyes: 'A $46 million opera house and your musicians' chairs squeak!'"

Robinson said further that he has never known Heifetz to be out of control. "He's on a plane all his own. He gives as much meticulous care to a three minute selection as he does a Brahms Concerto. "Art... there's no small thing in art,' he says."

The NBC hour, Robinson says, is more than a concert. It will present a more complete picture of the artist, including intimate glimpses of him strolling along the beach at Malibu, the place he loves most on earth. "For the first time, too," according to Robinson, "his speaking voice will be heard. But there will be no shots of inside of his house, since he is particular about his privacy."

April 24, 1971
HEIFETZ ENTHRALLS VIEWERS IN AN IMPECCABLE TV HOUR
By Kay Gardella

Maybe it's presumptuous of television to try to penetrate the mystique of Jascha Heifetz. But under the experienced hand of director Kirk Browning, the famed violinist, who has been enthroned in the hearts of music lovers for more than 50 years, was ideally showcased last night on NBC-TV in a one-hour special simply entitled "Heifetz."

For television it was another musical milestone. For Heifetz admirers an opportunity to see the disciplined, precisely understated violinist as a performer and a person. Combined with his music, programmed specifically for TV, since the short pieces customarily played at the end of a concert were at the beginning, were glimpses of Heifetz on the beach at Malibu, outside his Beverly Hills home and working with his pupils.

The overriding impression from the hour was that nothing or nobody, not even the eminent violinist himself, could upstage the music. If there is a single, lingering memory of Heifetz that is not true of so many other violinists it is his ability to subordinate himself to the soul of the composition he is performing. His effortless style, his impassive face, and his unchallenged skill to make his audience continually attentive to his music, not him, is the testimony to his greatness.

Heifetz, circa 1970.

Demanding Performer

Perhaps it's the reason the violinist chose to tape the musical portions of his program in Paris last fall because he was offered the accompaniment of the French National Orchestra, without conductor. Francis Robinson said, he likes an atmosphere in which "each musician is a responsible collaborator to one musical concept." He acts as a mirror, or transmitter, for the great composers and in his striving for perfection, as in the case of Bruch's stirring "Scottish Fantasy," he is unstinting in the demands he places upon himself and the collaborating musicians.

Handsome and virile at 70, Heifetz, impeccable in performance, provided viewers with a musical program that was profoundly beautiful. For those who might have found Bach's "Chaconne" too demanding there were such entertaining and lighter works as Gershwin's "It Ain't Necessarily So" to delight the ear and Prokofieff's march from "The Love of Three Oranges."

Heifetz performed alone, with his long-time accompanist Brooks Smith and with orchestra. His opening number, Mozart's Rondo from the "Haffner Serenade" as arranged by Fritz Kreisler, immediately romanced viewers. His other selection was Debussy's "The Girl with the Flaxen Hair."

Producers for the hour were Lester Shurr and Paul Louis, audio director John Pfeiffer, writer-narrator Francis Robinson and director the aforementioned Kirk Browning.

APRIL 28, 1971
NBC-TV

HEIFETZ (Bell System Family Theatre]

With Jascha Heifetz, Brooks Smith, ORTF French National Orchestra, Francis Robinson. Exec. Producer: Lester Shurr. Producer: Paul Louis. Director: Kirk Browning. Writer: Francis Robinson. 60 minutes, Friday, 10:00 p.m. AT & T, NBC-TV.

Jascha Heifetz in concert may not be the mass audience's idea of exceptional programming, but for admirers of the 70-year-old violin virtuoso, the Friday (23) "Heifetz" special had to be an unqualified treat. His appearances on the tube (or in public for that matter) have been limited in recent years, but his masterful powers are seemingly in as great a shape as they ever were.

For this concert, the camera sensibly focused on the master while he played, starting with his usual short encore pieces, impeccably played as less strenuous fare for less-classically steeped audiences. Accompanied by Brooks Smith at the piano, he zipped through Mozart's "Haffner Sere-

468

Heifetz, circa 1970.

The Mischa Elman family including his wife, daughter and two granddaughters. Circa 1957. On the facing page, Samuel Applebaum, Henryk Szeryng and Roman Totenberg. They all agree that as a musician Heifetz is supreme and that his ability has never been duplicated. Circa 1974.

nade" Rondo, Prokofiev's "Love for Three Oranges" march, Debussy's "The Girl With the Flaxen Hair" and Gershwin's "It Ain't Necessarily So" —all winningly played.

For his showpiece, Heifetz performed the difficult "Chaconne" by J.S. Bach in effortless and compelling style—unaccompanied. For the musical finale, he led (leisurely) the ORTF French National Orchestra as he played Max Bruch's "Scottish Fantasy," a demanding selection which does not provide musical rewards commensurate with effort expended. Throughout the entire musical phase of the show, however, Heifetz' presence, mien and authority were sufficient magnet to occupy the viewer's attention, no matter how sophisticated his musical tastes. There were also some quick glimpses of the virtuoso at play in California, which merely corroborated the image of vitality and enthusiasm which his violin playing reflected.

Production, as noted, was primarily turning the camera loose to study Heifetz at work, the exception being when he fronted the full orchestra which permitted a little diversity of camera angles. This austerity of production technique seemed the proper approach, permitting the viewer to bask in his own reflections as a great master did his thing.

MAY 2, 1971
NBC-TV

POKER-FACED, RESERVED, BUT STILL CHAMP

By Harold C. Schonberg

Watching the Heifetz show on Channel 4 the other week brought back memory after memory. Jascha Heifetz has been around for a long, long time, and his concert appearances always were a highlight of any music season. To the public, he was the violinist. Maybe Kreisler had more charm. Maybe Szigeti was his intellectual superior. Maybe Elman made prettier sounds. Maybe Huberman was a better musician. It made no difference. Heifetz remained the criterion.

He would come out on stage, poker-faced as always. He trailed power and dignity, and that air of authority peculiarly his own. It was for the audience a shivery experience. Heifetz was unique and everybody knew it. Apparently he was that way from the beginning. His teacher, Leopold Auer, would throw up his hands when discussing him. Talents on the order of a young Heifetz or, at the piano, Josef Hoffmann, cannot be rationally explained.

Heifetz made his first public appearance in 1907, when he was 6 years old. (His 70th birthday, earlier this year, went largely unnoticed.) When he was 12 he made a debut in Berlin that confounded every musician around. Heifetz simply made all other violinists think. He had, even at that age, a flawless technique and incredible tonal purity.

472

Rabinoff

The violinist Benno Rabinoff, a close friend of Heifetz, tells a little-known story about Heifetz's Berlin debut. It seems that after the concert, the critic and musicologist Arthur Abell invited the young Russian to his house for a dinner party in his honor. Abell rounded up every important violinist in town. After dinner, Heifetz decided to play the Mendelssohn Concerto. To his embarrassment, he discovered that he had forgotten to bring the piano reduction for the accompanist. Whereupon a distinguished gentleman with a monocle got up. "May I have the honor of accompanying you?" The distinguished gentleman was Fritz Kreisler, almost as good a pianist as he was a violinist. After Heifetz had finished the Mendelssohn, with Kreisler of course playing the piano part from memory, there was an awed silence. Kreisler got up, looked at the guests—among them Bronislaw Huberman, Carl Flesch, Juan Manen, Willy Hess and Jan Kubelik—and said: "Well, gentlemen, now we can all break our violins."

Kreisler was the most beloved violinist of the century. Heifetz is incomparably the most perfect, and is recognized as such by his peers. There are those who denigrate Heifetz the musician. Virgil Thomson once sneered at him as the most perfect player of encore pieces in history. The younger generation laughs at his repertory and his habit of playing fluffy transcriptions. But never has any musician had anything but admiration for Heifetz the violinist. He raised technique to a new standard. Nobody had his kind of easy-going execution, arched tone, accuracy of intonation, ability to get an infinite variety of nuance into one bow. There never was a bow arm like that, just as there never was a left hand like that. Rabinoff believes that Heifetz has a peculiar hand formation, with the first (index) finger of abnormal height and a little finger that "falls exactly in the right place so that he never plays octaves or tenths out of tune."

Heifetz always has been a 19th-century kind of violinist, meaning that his instrumental and intellectual approach are geared more to romantic than to any other kind of music. That is one reason why younger violinists and critics question his interpretations of Bach and Mozart. Heifetz, they say, has always been identified with the instrument rather than with music. His way of playing the Bach Chaconne or a Mozart concerto represents the bad old way of doing things, they say, surface gloss, no real identification with the music, elegance without substance. Their feeling is that he should stick to things like the Chausson "Poeme," or the Tchaikovsky Concerto, or his encore pieces.

It is true that Heifetz's way of playing Bach and Mozart is not today's. How could it be? He was trained in the Russian romantic style, and his musical identification necessarily has to be romantic. But what many of the youngsters fail to realize about Heifetz is that, of all the romantic violinists, he has been the coolest, the most patrician, the most restrained. His vibrato never wandered into adjacent regions, and he never slobbered over music as did so many of his contemporaries.

Benno Rabinoff (he added the other "f" to make the necessary 13 letters after Heifetz so suggested) with Prof. Auer. Benno was Auer's favorite student in America; Benno was the author's favorite violinist; Heifetz was Benno's favorite violinist. December, 1927.

Indeed, if anything, the one criticism heard about Heifetz until the new generation of musicians arrived was that his interpretations were "cold." Perhaps this "coldness" was read into his playing because of his unemotional platform behavior. Heifetz never smiled, never changed facial expression, never teetered, never became physically involved with the music. That gave the impression of aloofness, whereas it really was part of his discipline. Heifetz never really was a cold violinist. He may have been reserved, which is a different thing entirely. Certain it is that when he spun out the melody of the slow movement of the Brahms Concerto, he managed to create something in which descriptions like "aloof," or "cool" were completely beside the point. He played with ultimate authority there, and it was enough that this kind of flawless projection existed. Nobody else ever had it.

Then why should such a flawless instrumentalist sully his image by playing so many trite shorter pieces? Again, it must be realized, this was part of Heifetz's background. Nobody objected much, for instance, when Kreisler played fluff, and I am not referring to Kreisler's own charming vignettes. For Kreisler played, and recorded, some godawful trash. But that was part of the period, and while Heifetz came later than Kreisler, it was just as much his period as it was his elder colleague's.

Pianists, singers, violinists those days had certain repertory items today regarded with disfavor. Even the greatest of singers would entertain audiences with things like "Ma Curley Headed Baby" or the latest Carrie Jacobs Bond. Pianists doted on Moszkowski. Violinists loved to play arrangements of Chopin's E flat Nocturne. They can no more be blamed for this than kittens can be blamed for being cuddly.

Looking at his place historically, it is clear that Heifetz belongs more to the generation of Sarasate than to Stern. In condemning him for certain interpretative traits, his critics are committing the esthetic fallacy of judging a past age by their own standards. And by any standards, past or present, Heifetz is still the world's greatest violinist in certain phases of the repertory. Those who saw the telecast, and watched him in Bruch's "Scottish Fantasy," were in the presence of a transcendent order of violin playing.

It was characteristic of Heifetz that he select this piece. Hardly anybody plays it; it is out of fashion and at best a period piece; it is addressed to the violin rather than to music. As Heifetz played the work, it took on life and character. Heifetz here not only revived an old-fashioned score; he revived an age along with it. It was unmatched violin playing, and one thought of Isaac Stern's remark about Heifetz. Stern represents a different school and a different philosophy, and Heifetz's style is not his. But Stern the other week, talking about Heifetz, summed him up with the statement that Heifetz "represents a standard of polished execution unrivalled in my memory by any violinist either by book or personal knowledge."

Stern fiddles while Heifetz paints! Isaac Stern, with Pierre Montieux conducting the San Francisco Orchestra, had a very difficult time to reach the great success which he attained. Stern's forte was working with people and he discovered and encouraged such great violinists as Pinchas Zukerman and Itzak Perlman. Stern's associates love and admire him. Heifetz has no such following. He never developed personal relationships with his students and with very few of his associates. January 23, 1954.

RECORD REVIEW
Vet Master

By Douglas Watt

One side of "Heifetz on Television" (Victor) consists of excerpts from the sound-track of the recent taped telecast devoted to the violinist Jascha Heifetz. The other side is given over to an older, complete recording of Bruch's "Scottish" Symphony, of which only a portion was heard on the program. Accompanying this record is a smaller one containing some of the soloist's comments on the air and performances of Rachmaninoff's "Daisies" in Heifetz' own transcription and excerpts from Korngold's "Garden Scene," both of which were edited from the show tape.

The nature of some of his choices might appear a bit odd to today's audiences. There are, for examples, Prokofiev's "Love for Three Oranges" March, Debussy's "The Girl With the Flaxen Hair" and even Gershwin's "It Ain't Necessarily So." But Heifetz's skill is such that doubts are quickly stilled. And as for the Gershwin, the violinist's transcription is so deft and charming that Gershwin, if he ever heard it in his lifetime, must have wished he'd thought of some of the devices himself.

OCTOBER 10, 1971

RECORDINGS
Heifetz—Something Old, Something New

By Howard Klein

Heifetz was 70 this year. Heifetz, the ultra-cool dazzler who seemed effortlessly to sweep us through the great violin literature with an elan bordering on the cocky, began his seventh decade last February 2. In his prime, a period which must have lasted almost 60 years, Heifetz was the paragon of violinists. A white hot temperament burned just beneath an icy control. What it was at all possible to do on or with the violin, Jascha Heifetz could do, and do without being vulgar. To see the shortish man with the sad and sombre face plant his feet just so on stage and sail into a concert, never seeming to budge from the spot, never going into show-man-like gyrations and meanwhile stroking magic from the violin with his bow, was a thrill incomparable during his long rule over the concert stage. He kept them coming back, sitting on the edges of their seats, and buying his records almost from the time of his Carnegie Hall debut, in 1917, to today. The concerts have all but stopped, but the recordings go on.

Heifetz, April, 1970.

During his long career as the number one violinist, a career which must now be seen as over, Heifetz has recorded for one company, RCA Victor. I remember the record stores back in the 1940's, when they were company stores. Huge reproductions of what looked like oil paintings of the great Victor artists lined the walls. Heifetz was always there looking terribly superior and soulful. Ten years ago Victor brought out a lavish album commemorating a series of chamber music recitals Heifetz presented with a distinguished group of musicians in Los Angeles, including Gregor Piatigorsky and William Primrose. What an album that was—one of the discontinued line of the Soria Series, specially designed packages that attempted to match the wrapping to the music. Deluxe was the word.

But times change. The economy is bad. Record companies haven't been too happy with their classical divisions, and it shows. RCA Victor has just released a batch of Heifetz performances, most of which have been offered the public before. There is every reason to keep Heifetz performances of most of the repertory he played active, and the reissuing of these items can be called a good thing. But what a falling off there has been in the style of presentation from the dignity of the good old days to the razzmatazz sell of 1971. The works represented in the six albums constitute a legacy of violin playing and it would have been fitting tribute to this artist to have packaged them as a set, with some decent biographical matter and a wide spread of his repertory.

Instead, what we have are six slickly produced albums aimed at the "young" record buyer and designed, one assumes, simply to make money. I suppose the most offensive is the Concerto album (RCA LSC-3234). A serious musician or record collector would shudder at the idea of "Favorite movements from great violin concertos," but that's what the cover proudly announces. The "pretty parts," don't you know. There is the first movement of the Tchaikovsky, the second movements of the Bach D minor (with Erick Friedman, second violin), and Prokofiev G minor, and the third movements from the Mendelssohn, Beethoven, and Brahms. All have been available before complete, which is the only way, in this opinion, to offer them.

Of genuine news value is the album, Showpieces (LSC 3232e), which includes a performance of Brahms' Hungarian Dance No. 7 played by Heifetz and the Los Angeles Philharmonic conducted by Alfred Wallenstein. This was recorded in December of 1953, and never before released. It is familiar Heifetz of this period—incredible technical finesse, dash and daring and imagination. The other works on this disk are fine fun, Sarasate's "Zigeunerweisen," Saint-Saens' "Havanaise" and Introduction and Rondo Capriccioso; Chausson's "Poeme," and Franz Waxman's "Carmen" Fantasy, the one he wrote for the John Garfield film, "Intermezzo."

A kindred album is Heifetz Encores, which presents the crowd-pleaser side of the great virtuoso (LSC 3233e). This disk and the "Showpieces" album just discussed are monophonic recordings which have been re-dubbed to simulate stereo. Much has been written about this practice. Suffice to say they don't sound bad. The encores are brilliant trifles including Heifetz's arrangement of the "Hora Staccato," Godowsky's "Alt Wien," Khachaturian's "Sabre Dance," Schubert's "Ave Maria," Kroll's "Banjo and Fiddle," Mendelssohn's "On Wings of Song," Debussy's "La plus que lente" and Achron's "Hebrew Melody." New to LP are six titles which were recorded for 78's between 1947 and 1953, Wieniawski's "Scherzo Tarantelle," Drigo's "Valse Bluette," Poulenc's "Presto," Sarasate's "Zapateado," Ponce's "Estrellita" and Rachmaninoff's "Vocalise." Heifetz collectors will be delighted with these two disks, for they reach back twenty years to what may have been Heifetz's greatest period.

Heifetz working in Paris on his television program. Circa 1970.

One always thought of Heifetz as being an epicurean player, aloof from commonplace emotion or sentiment. And yet his playing not only dazed the listener by its pyrotechnics, but moved him by its passion. The perfect technician frequently made "ugly" sounds, wild scrapings of the bow as if he flung it in temper against the string. The scratch is always immediately offset by a tone of incredible purity, dead center in tune and vibrant with inner life, whether in the typsy hoarseness of the G string, or the diamond-bright facets of high E string positions. So the listener is aware more of the intense singing tone than of the aural laceration that sometimes preceded. The "Hora Staccato" is a perfect example of the incandescent variety of Heifetz's playing.

The other disks are straightforward re-issues: TWO GREAT DOUBLE CONCERTOS (LSC 3228) combines the Brahms Concerto for Violin and Cello, with Gregor Piatigorsky, and Mozart's Sinfonia concertante in E flat, with William Primrose as violist; Favorite Beethoven Concertos (VCS 7087) combines the Violin Concerto in the great performance with Charles Munch leading the Boston Symphony, and the "Emperor" Piano Concerto with Artur Rubinstein as soloist and Erich Leinsdorf leading the orchestra; and Favorite Brahms Concertos (VCS 7088) with Fritz Reiner conducting the Chicago Symphony in the Violin Concerto and Artur Rubinstein playing the Piano Concerto No. 2 with Josef Krips conducting the RCA Symphony.

The coupling of Heifetz and Rubinstein in these reissues reminds one of the stories going around after the so-called "million dollar trio" stopped making music and money together about 20 years ago. It seems there was disagreement who should get top billing, the pianist or the violinist. (Piatigorsky was the cellist, but unless your name is Casals, you never get top billing.) It was claimed that Heifetz wanted top slot, over Rubinstein although, traditionally, in piano trios, the pianist gets named first. Well, now it's settled. On each album, it's Heifetz-Rubinstein. I hope Artur doesn't mind.

Heifetz has always been a finicky man, to say the least. A perfectionist in music, he carried his creative mania into his daily life. I remember ordering pictures of the great violinist for a story in these record pages about eight years ago. The photographer told me Heifetz was fussy about what shots he allowed to be used. He had once exposed several rolls of the violinist and dutifully took the contact sheets to Heifetz for approval. Face impassive, his eyes blinking calmly, Heifetz asked for the negatives as well. The surprised photographer handed them over and watched as Heifetz produced a paper punch and proceeded to destroy the negatives of any picture he didn't like.

A perfectionist's eccentricity, understandable and forgivable. Too bad Heifetz wasn't able to impart some of those standards to the reissuing of these performances. It could have been a nice documentary of what a great violinist accomplished on the recordings for the company he helped to make what it was. Well, belated Happy Birthday anyway, Jascha.

APRIL 21, 1972
HANCOCK AUDITORIUM

MUSIC IN L.A.: HEIFETZ-PIATIGORSKY

By Karen Monson

Faculty recitals aren't such extraordinary events on most campuses. The University of Southern California, however, happened to be able to summon the now-legendary team of Jascha Heifetz and Gregor Piatigorsky from its faculty for a recent recital to benefit the school's string scholarship fund.

Assisting the two masters were pianist Daniel Pollack (also a USC teacher), and three young members of Heifetz's master class—a faculty-student affair, but one of the highest order.

Heifetz and Piatigorsky, assisted by Daniel Pollack. 1972.

Four years had passed since Heifetz and Piatigorsky gave their last set of concerts here in the Music Center, so this single event drew an almost reverential capacity audience to the university's intimate Hancock Auditorium. Heifetz doesn't believe in starting concerts at the traditional time —this one was set for 7 p.m.—but one suspected that he could play at four in the morning and still fill a giant amphitheater with alert, eager souls.

"Old School"

If one accepts the distinctions between the clearly modern "new school" of playing and the heartfully expressive "old school," it was the latter that was in distinct evidence on this occasion. Both violinist and cellist serve as living reminders that the notes signify merely the beginning of the musical battle. Not the technical, but the interpretive values always took the fore, with Heifetz's sometimes aggressive manner of directing the violin phrases, and Piatigorsky's ever-conscientious way of turning even the shortest cadential cello figure into something both supportive and significant.

The younger participants did much more than fill the necessary chairs. In Tchaikovsky's A-Minor Piano Trio, Pollack's contributions took on an appropriate feeling of grandeur despite some muddiness of sound that was presumably attributable to either the hall's quirky acoustics or an unworthy instrument. The three opted for tempos on the slow side, then made up for time lost by taking a cut in the finale. The performance was, by Heifetz's brief announcement from the stage, dedicated to the memory of John Crown, another distinguished USC faculty member who recently passed on.

Students

The student artists, all obviously suffering from nervousness, joined in for Brahms's Quintet in G Major, Op. 11. Violinist Christiaan Bor and violist Sheila Rheinhold played admirably, while Yukiko Kamei, on the first viola part, performed with remarkable beauty of sound and sensitivity to the demands of the music and the ensemble.

The program began with the "Suite Italienne" of Stravinsky, an arrangement for violin and cello of "Pulcinella" put together by Piatigorsky and the composer. Though the selection offered the chance to hear the two virtuosi alone, the reduction from the orchestral setting is unsatisfying, the performers seemed at odds as to style, and the reading emerged significantly as less memorable than that given either the Brahms or the Tchaikovsky.

Heifetz, circa 1971. The pianist is unidentified.

JUNE 22, 1972
LOS ANGELES MUSIC CENTER

HEIFETZ TUNES HIS BOW FOR RARE COAST RECITAL

Jascha Heifetz, the violinist, will play a solo recital in the Chandler Pavillion of the Los Angeles Music Center on October 23 as a benefit for the University of Southern California School of Music.

The virtuoso, who is 71, has played in public rarely during the last few years. His last recital here was at Carnegie Hall on Oct. 2, 1966, and was part of a Heifetz-Piatigorsky chamber-music series. He has not played a recital in Los Angeles, where he lives, for 17 years.

Mr. Heifetz joined the U.S.C. music faculty in 1963. He conducts master classes there for small groups of violinists.

OCTOBER 25, 1972

HEIFETZ IN RARE RECITAL ON COAST
TO BOLSTER MUSIC SCHOOL FUND

By Alfred Frankenstein
Special to The New York Times

LOS ANGELES, Oct. 24—Some said it was his first recital in 17 years, some his first in only four years; it depends on what you mean by a recital; in any event, Jascha Heifetz gave his first big, formal, full-dress concert in a long time last night in the Dorothy Chandler Pavillion of the Los Angeles Music Center, and everyone was curious to know how he'd sound. The concert, with a $25 top, was given for the benefit of the scholarship funds at the School of Music of the University of Southern California, where Heifetz teaches. It was sold out and a great popular success.

As an old Heifetz fancier I cannot proclaim this as one of the greatest events in the violinist's career, but it was infinitely superior to the efforts as leader of a chamber ensemble tended to be rushed, rigid and cold. In the Sonatas of Franck and Strauss, on the other hand, he was back on home territory; he was even more at home in the movements of the Bach E Major Partita and in the customary entertainment and show pieces at the end.

The flawlessly beautiful Heifetz tone was there throughout. Whether or not it might still soar above an orchestra in the Brahms Concerto was a question—but he was not playing Brahms nor with orchestra. He was playing with Brooks Smith, who is far more adept at accompaniment than at collaboration and whose performance of the piano parts in the sonatas left a great deal to be desired. So the sonatas were flawed, but the

486

Franck was still very moving, as it always is when Heifetz plays it, and the Strauss at least reached a dramatic climax at its end.

In general, though, it was Heifetz's lyrical playing that told; and sometimes in passagework only the first and last notes were firmly in place and those between—well, indeterminate.

I thought the three movements of the Bach were altogether perfect, both technically and musically, and were the soundest proof the evening offered of the fact that Heifetz is still Heifetz

But the exotic atmosphere of Bloch's "Nigun" at the start of the final group was finely achieved; Fritz Kreisler's "La Chasse" delighted everyone with its appearance of technical difficulty, and Ravel's "Tzigane" attained the same result with its numerous actual difficulties.

When it was all over and one short encore had been played, Heifetz addressed the audience, said the preparation of the program had made him work hard, and excused himself, on the grounds of fatigue, from a party that was being given in his honor by the university.

And then, for the first time in the experience of this old Heifetz fancier, he smiled.

JASCHA HEIFETZ IN CONCERT. Jascha Heifetz, violin; Brooks Smith, piano. (John Pfeiffer, prod.) COLUMBIA M2 33444, $13.98 (two discs) (recorded in concert, October 23, 1972.

FRANCK: Sonata for Violin and Piano in A; STRAUSS: Sonata for Violin and Piano, in E flat, Op. 18; BACH: Partita for Solo Violin, No. 3, in E, Prelude, Loure, Gigue; BLOCH: Baal Shem: Nigun; CASTELNUOVO-TEDESCO: Sea Murmurs (arr. Heifetz); DEBUSSY: La plus que lente (arr. Kochanski); KREISLER: La Chasse; RACHMANINOFF: Etude Tableau in E flat, Op. 33, No. 4 (arr. Heifetz); RAVEL: Tzigane.

On October 23, 1972, Jascha Heifetz came out of semi-retirement to play a solo recital at the Dorothy Chandler Pavilion in Los Angeles on behalf of University of Southern California scholarship funds. He had been on the faculty of USC since 1962, and most of his public appearances during that decade had been with the Heifetz/Piatigorsky/Pennario trio. The sense of anticipation in the packed auditorium was well rewarded. The intonation was as secure as ever, the musical thrust as vigorous, the bow arm—with one or two small lapses—as flexible as of yore. The recital was recorded, with a miraculous minimum of audience noise—except for those occasional bursts of applause that Columbia has retained.

Heifetz opened the program with the Franck sonata, and my impression that night was that he had mellowed with the passage of time. There was warmth in the first movement, a good lusty voice on the G string in the opening of the second, a free-flowing fantasia spirit in the third. The fourth-movement canon was trim, precise, straightforward. A comparison, however, of this 1972 performance with the 1937 version recorded with Rubinstein (on Seraphim 60230) reveals that the actual change was less than one might have thought. It is, in fact, uncanny that over a thirty-five-year span Heifetz should have retained an inner metronome that ticks off the same tempos in the first three movements. The fourth movement was slower with Rubinstein and fancier in the violin line—given more to hairpin dynamics then, done more plainly now. Most other violinists take slower tempos throughout this sonata, and the 1972 Heifetz/Smith is faster than Stern/Zakin (Columbia MS 6139) and Perlman/Askenazy (London CS 6628). And, yes, he is still less "warm" than they—a matter not of speed, but of color and phrasing. Stern has a myriad of color variations with which to suggest shifts of emphasis or to make changes of key; Perlman makes more than Heifetz of the long line, giving more breadth and fullness to phrases as they accumulate toward their goal

While Heifetz' use of color within a phrase is more limited than Stern's, there is nevertheless a remarkable capacity for elasticity in dynamics, and the sinuous opening lines of Strauss's arch-Romantic Op. 18 Sonata bring it to the fore. The ebb and flow of the entire first movement is admirably caught; the love song of the second and the heroic, slightly bombastic muscle-flexing of the third are beautifully conveyed. Brooks Smith's lacework arpeggios in the slow movement deserve special note (let me say at this point that in the live recital the pianist seemed far too self-effacing, the balance often one-sided in the Franck and Strauss. Perhaps it was due to the acoustics of the hall; at any rate, it is far better here, and Smith emerges as a first rate partner).

The short pieces on the remainder of the recital offer a bird's-eye view of Heifetz' strengths and weaknesses. The three movements from the Bach E major Partita are somewhat raw-toned and dry—the Gigue in particular quite ascetic (no luxuriant arrival at any point of rest, with a little extra resonance, for Heifetz). But the Bloch "Nigun" and Debussy "La plus que lente," side by side, demonstrate that the old master can shift gears in tone when he chooses to do so. The Bloch is appropriately muscular, dark, and heavy; the Debussy finespun and fluid. Falla's "Nana" in yet another light, is "covered" and melancholy.

This recital documents vividly that one of the century's great instrumentalists is almost as strong a presence at seventy as he was at twenty, and that is cause for celebration.

Shirley Fleming

Jack Pfieffer and Heifetz, with an unidentified gentleman, in the recording booth. Heifetz had to work over a certain passage several times to get it the way he wanted to. After the second failure he exclaimed: "Out damned spot!

June 29, 1975
The New York Times, Sunday

RECORDINGS VIEW

Peter G. Davis
Music/Recordings

A Virtuoso of Frightening Perfection

RCA's "The Heifetz Collection"—it's enough to give one the staggers. Here laid on 30 LP disks is the recorded career of Jascha Heifetz, a controversial musical personality as we shall see, but for most people the supreme violin virtuoso of the 20th century. This retrospective begins with the first single-sided acoustical recordings Heifetz cut shortly after his American debut in Carnegie Hall on October 27, 1917 at the age of 16, and proceeds methodically through nearly 50 years of vintage Heifetz performances to 1963 and the violinist's stereo version of the Glazunov A Minor Concerto. With the possible exception of Leopold Stokowski (and he was already 35 when he first recorded an orchestra just five days before Heifetz's debut recital), no other major classical musician of this generation has received such thorough phonographic documentation, and thanks to RCA's enterprise we can now see the total picture.

Actually, the 25 hours, 50 minutes and 10 seconds of music on these 30 records represent only about a third of Heifetz's total discography. Collectors with a passion for completeness will have to search out the three dozen other single LP's currently in RCA's catalogue and some 16 more on which Heifetz plays as a collaborating chamber musician; Seraphim lists three disks of solos and concertos, while eight RCA LP's are not presently available; finally, there are the long-deleted encore pieces that Heifetz made during his brief association with Decca in 1945 (including violin obligatos for Bing Crosby's renditions of "Where My Caravan has Rested" and the "Berceuse" from "Jocelyn") plus some lone performances taped in 1972 to be released in the near future. All the details are spelled out in the booklets accompanying the six volumes of RCA's chronological survey.

* * * * *

There are numerous intriguing facets to this monumental reissue. First, of course, there is the enigmatic presence of Heifetz himself, the flawless technician and strangely remote interpreter. Perhaps in the year 2001 we will have many such all-encompassing recorded overviews of important musicians, but Heifetz was among the first to take full advantage of the phonograph's potential to reflect every phase of a career from teen-age prodigy to grand old master. In a sense, too, these records present a capsule history of the medium itself as it evolved in the twenties from the electrical process, followed by various technical refinements (and backslidings) that finally brought the long-playing disk and stereophony. Lastly, one can also trace here the changes in musical tastes that invariably occur from one decade to another. It's all quite fascinating, and RCA deserves the warmest congratulations for producing such an important piece of phonographic history, and for doing the job so well.

The four sides in Volume 1 cover the years 1917-1924—all acoustic recordings and all brief encore-type pieces. Vignettes and transcriptions by Sarasate, Wieniawski, Kreisler and their peers were the order of the day, violin potboilers that Heifetz never tired of playing even when they went out of fashion (we have turned full circle evidently, judging from the renewed popularity of these morceaux with audiences and violinists). RCA's 1918 ad-copy sums up the effect. For Schubert's "Ave Maria" we read about "a tone so sweet that it seems as though the heavenly melody had been wafted from earth to remote regions of ethereal infinity, "while Wieniawski's "Scherzo-Tarantelle" does not consist of mere notes but "points of light, sparkling and flashing in obedience to a magic wand." Purple prose perhaps, but it does convey much of the impact of the young Heifetz's incredible technique and ravishing tonal purity.

Volume 2 contains much of the same, but also the violinist's first two concerto recordings, Mozart's No. 5 and the first version of the Glazunov, both dating from 1934. Volumes 3 and 4 remind us of how many glamorous performances appeared on 78's during the period immediately preceding World War II, among them Heifetz's readings of the classic violin sonatas and concertos in collaboration with such conductors as Toscanini, Koussevitzky, Ormandy and Barbirolli.

Volume 5 (1946-49) dips once again into the basket of musical dainties that Heifetz always kept near at hand ("silk underwear music," as Virgil Thomson used to call these confections), while the final album (1950-55) reissues some of the first mono LP's such as the sonatas by Saint-Saens, Brahms (No. 3 with William Kapell at the piano), Beethoven (the "Kreutzer" with Benno Moiseiwitsch) and two by Ernest Bloch, plus concertos by Tchaikovsky and Bruch (No. 1). As a supplement to these six volumes there is a seventh, a six-record set of ten popular concertos that takes us into the sixties and the stereophonic era.

Heifetz and Piatigorsky during a recording session directed by Jack Pfieffer. Heifetz had a page-turner for many years named Sam Epstein. For 12 years all they said to each other was "Hello" and "Goodbye." One day Epstein told Rabinoff how magnificent Heifetz had recorded Saint'Saens' "Introduction and Rondo." Rabinoff encouraged Epstein to tell Heifetz how he felt; he did. Heifetz was startled that his "silent" partner said anything and he stared into Epstein's adoring eyes replying "You mean I finally played something you liked?"

A fascinating collection of notes, facts and figures, but what sort of an artistic portrait emerges from this enormous documentary? It is definitely one of remarkable consistency, for if Heifetz ever made a "bad" record, it has never been released. The story is really told right at the beginning: the silver-toned 1917 "Ave Maria" with the double stops immaculately in tune and the phrases arched with patrician grace, followed a few bands later by the sputtery "Ronde des Lutins" by Bazzini, a breathtaking tour de force of musicianship—Heifetz had it all right from the start, and the standard never varied throughout his career.

Tone and technique—one could discourse endlessly on the marvelous effects that Heifetz achieves with these two qualities and critics have been doing just that for over 50 years. As for the sound musicianship—well, that too remains a constant, but a topic about which there's less to say. His interpretations are a model of graciousness and even-tempered con-

The last professional pose which Heifetz struck before the final concert on October 23, 1972.

trol with every musical requirement fastidiously observed, whether it's Schubert's "Ave Maria" in 1917 or Bach's Unaccompanied Partita No. 1 in 1935, or Beethoven's Violin Concerto in 1955. Heifetz must be unique in that sense: how many other musicians ever reached the peak of their musical perceptions at the age of 16 and never budged an inch thereafter?

Nothing in the two essays in RCA's program notes, classy fan letters from Joseph Wechsberg and Irving Kolodin, help explain this extraordinary phenomenon. The end result is that the Heifetz career unfolds with a sanity and serenity that can be maddening to anyone looking for artistic growth, fresh ideas and stimulating personal insights. The inscrutable Heifetz gives us none—unless there's something to be read into the fact that the more trivial the music becomes the more committed he sounds. One piece follows another, perfectly poised, gorgeously intoned and exquisitely civilized but somehow lacking a real intellectual core or a deeply felt emotional perspective.

A great many people like to hear music played this way, especially by a virtuoso of Heifetz's caliber, in which the performer does not get between the listener and the music—a rather contradictory position when one stops to think of it. Taken in small doses such performances can generate their own brand of excitement merely through the physical act of making the notes sound. In this sense Heifetz is the quintessential performer, unlike such an introspective violinist as, say, Joseph Szigeti who with far less technical equipment managed to uncover different aspects of a work every time he played it.

How, then, and in what spirit is one to listen to 50 years of Heifetz on disk? When the violinist's second version of the Saint Saens D minor Sonata was released not long ago, one critic evidently found what he felt to be the answer: he compared the two recordings by playing each simultaneously at half speed (16 rpm), switching back and forth from one to the other, measuring each subtle gradation in tone and each stroke of technical wizardry.

A heartless and anti-musical approach, you may say, but after listening to the hours of strangely passionless precision fiddling on these 30 disks, I wonder if the idea is as outrageous as it might at first appear. Perhaps this is, in fact, the only way to truly analyze the total effect of a Heifetz performance. Be that as it may, "The Heifetz Collection" remains a staggering achievement in its own special way. It is the document of a brilliant virtuoso who set his own technical and musical standards and, like it or not, realized them to frightening perfection.

INDEX

Beethoven, Ludwig van, 18,
30,39,57,69,70,72,78,79,
82,86,103,118,133,134,
167,219,223,225,233,236,
238,240,256,257,262,263,
264,269,271,272,274,275,
279,286,298,300,314,324,
325,327,329,330,361,362,
366,368,370,372,373,374,
397,400,402,408,409,411,
415,416,422,424,425,433,
434,438,447,448,480,482,
491,493

Behrman, 153
Belaunde, Victor, 440
Belaunde, Mrs. Victor, 440
Belnick, 118
Benjamin, Arthur, 115
Bennett, Robert Russell, 384,
387,388,430,432
Benny, Jack, 133,169
Benoist, Andre, 224,231,235,
236,242,243
Berg, 93
Berger, Arthur, 425
Berlin Philharmonic
Orchestra, 279,428
Berlioz, Hector, 279,346,363
Bernhardt, Louise, 12
Bernhardt, Sarah, 388
Bernstein, Leonard, 216
Bezrodny, 33,98
Biancolli, Louis, 391,411,433
Bizet, 433,434
Blant, Josef, 363
Bloch, Ernest, 91,173,176,
350,422,424,425,487,488,
491
Boccherini, 118

Boffin, Mrs., 290
Bohemians Music Club, 13,
14,15,16,17,18
Bohm, Jerome D., 416
Bond, Carrie Jacobs, 475
Bor, Christian, 484
Boston Symphony Orchestra,
89,169,279,377,380
Boulanger, Lili, 57,418,419
Bowles, Paul, 406
Brahms, Johannes, 37,39,40,
69,70,86,110,112,116,118,
133,134,167,169,231,233,
236,242,243,244,260,262,
264,286,288,292,298,300,
311,321,323,325,327,329,
334,338,341,342,344,345,
355,388,401,402,430,431,
432,466,480,482,484,486,
491
Brazil, 382
Brennan, Walter, 356,358
Bridges, William, 276
Briggs, John, 404
British West Indies, 382
Britten, Benjamin, 176
Brodsky, Adolf, 311
Brooklyn, 233
Browning, John Jr., 449
Browning, Kirk, 456,466,468
Bruch, Max, 63,69,91,100,
133,134,243,244,245,248,
260,262,280,318,319,323,
350,406,418,419,456,459,
472,478,491
Buenos Aires, 382,386
Burleigh Cecil, 135,243,245,
248,265,267,269,335,342,
345

Frankenstein, Alfred, 486
Freeman, Jay C., 147
French National Orchestra, 458,468,472
French TV, 456
Freund, Marya, 280
Friedberg, 271
Friedemann, 248
Friedheim, 305
Friedlander, Harold, 415
Friedman, Erick, 78,130,315, 480
Fry, Louise, 28,29
Fuchs, Joseph, 10,11,375, 392,393
Furtwangler, Wilhelm, 279

G

Gabrilowitsch, Ossip, 45,262
Galileo, 308
Galli-Curci, 240
Gallup, Dr., 151
Gandhi, 323
Gardella, Kay, 464,466
Garden, 419
Gardner, Samuel, 335,342
Garfield, John, 480
Gehr, Herbert, 284
Gershwin, George, 98,335, 384,387,388,447,468,472, 478
Gilbert, Gama, 363
Gilels, Emil, 115
Gilman, Lawrence, 300
Glazounov (Glazounoff), 63, 91,134,265,313,415,416, 419,489,490
Glinka, 238,242,243,363

Gluck, 260
Godowsky, Dagmar, 122
Godowsky, Leopold, 35,98, 243,245,248,253,255,256, 265,370,373,399,419,420, 441,481
Goethe, 277
Goldberg, Szymon, 11,12
Goldmark, Rubin, 13,258, 259
Goldschmann, Vladimir, 421
Goldwyn, Sam, 321,324,329, 332,335,337,354,355,357
Good Housekeeping, 158
Goodman, Benny, 376
Goossens, Eugene, 400,401, 402
Gottschalg, 305
Graf, Uta, 12
Grainger, 290,294
Grasse, 135,235,240,263,264
Graveure, Louis, 262
Great Music Festival, 338
Grieg, Eduard, 236,252,283
Gross, Marvin, 8,9
Grove's *Dictionary of Music*, 286
Gruenberg, Louis, 91,419
Grumiaux, Arthur, 120
Guadagnini, J.B., 147
Guarnerius del Gesu, 85,136, 137,138,141,143,329,338, 339,341,352
Guggenheimer, Mrs. Charles, 361
Gutenberg Bible, 278

H

Halir, 101

Hall, Harry R., 340
Hall, Porter, 356
Hambro, Leonid, 12
Handel, 229,233,287,298, 313,415,416
Hannenfeldt, Miss, 25,27,28, 29
Hannikainen, Tauno, 377, 378,380
Hansen, Cecile, 127,129
Hardy, 277
Harrell, Mack, 11
Harrison, Jay S., 430
Hartman, 271
Hartmann, Arthur, 412
Harvard, 339,340
Harvey, Paul, 356
Hausmann, 101
Hawthorne, 276
Haydn, 250,262,311,314, 389,433,434
Heifetz, Elza, 33
Heifetz, Frances, 85,92,135, 148,154,159,345,347,417, 435,443
Heifetz, Florence, 151,291, 316
Heifetz, Jay, 92,135,154,155, 159,477
Heifetz, Josepha, 151,291, 316,330,343,428,442
Heifetz, Pauline, 33
Heifetz, Robert, 151,291, 316,330,343,428,442
Heifetz, Ruvin, 19,33,152, 428
Heifetz, Mrs. Ruvin, 33
Heine, 221
Hekking, Anton, 10

Henderson, W.J., 65,274, 284,420
Herald Examiner, 173
Herbert, Victor, 63,335,342, 345
Herzog, Sigmund, 13
Hess, Myra, 11,12
Hess, Willy, 473
Hindemith, 93
Hippodrome (New York), 248
Hoffman, Josef, 45,420,472
Hohl, Arthur, 356
Hollywood, 332,341
Hollywood Bowl, 323
Hoogstraten, Willem van, 323
Hope, Constance, 1,4,145
Horowitz, Vladimir, 284,286
Hotel Madison, 332
Hoyt, Jim, 420
Hubay, 56,169,344
Huberman, Bronislav, 472, 473
Hummel, 283,284
Huneker, James, 312
Hunt, Frederick V., 340
Hurok, Sol, 248

I

Ibert, 93
Israel, 427
Istomin, Eugene, 11

J

Jacobi, Frederick, 334
Jacobson, Sascha, 147
Jagel, Frederick, 12

Los Angeles Music Center, 453

Los Angeles Philharmonic, 355

Los Angeles Times, 173

Louis, Paul, 468

Lubka, Kolessa, 11

Ludwig II, King, 246

Lympany, Moura, 12

Lyons, Leonard, 153

M

MacDowell, 169

Mackay, Clarence, 346

Magaloff, Nikita, 12

Main, Marjorie, 356

Majewski, 118

Malibu, 466

Malkin, Davidovitch, 126

Maltese, John, 4,278

Maltese, John Anthony, 1,5, 167

Manen, Juan, 473

Mannes, 267

Mannsfield, 305

Marly, Jonas, 11

Marteau, Henri, 10

Martenot, Ginette, 12

Martini, Ninio, 337

Martinu, 110

Marx, Harpo, 145

Mayo, Archie, 355

McCrea, Joel, 356

McMein, Neysa, 352

Medtner, 412,430,431,432

Mehta, Zubin, 449

Melba, 419

Mendelssohn, Felix, 22,23,

24,25,26,29,57,58,69,89,
114,118,126,133,134,167,
169,233,308,311,312,313,
323,324,327,329,334,338,
341,346,355,356,360,399,
445,458,473,480,481

Menuhin, Yehudi, 10,11,48,
86,104,120,284

Merckel, 93

Meremblum, Peter, 355,358,
360

Merriman, Nan, 11

Mexico, 298,382

Michelangeli, Benedetto, 11

Milhaud, 447

Milstein, Nathan, 10,11,12,
86

Mitropoulos, Dimitri, 23,24,
26,30,397,398,433,434

Moiseiwitsch, Benno, 84,90,
491

Monson, Karen, 173,483

Montieux, Pierre, 476

Moore, Douglas, 408

Moore, George, 277

Moore, Grace, 337

Morini, Erica, 11

Moszkowski, 238,240,475

Mozart, Wolfgang Amadeus,
39,63,69,86,115,118,133,
146,219,223,225,231,233,
238,240,263,264,280,283,
298,314,317,318,319,324,
386,387,388,389,416,430,
431,432,458,468,473,482,
490

Munch, Charles, 82,89,167,
169,171,174,482